DISNEY MASTERS

MICKEY MOUSE:
THE MONSTER OF
SAWTOOTH MOUNTAIN

by Paul Murry

Publisher: GARY GROTH
Editor: DAVID GERSTEIN
Design: KAYLA E. and DAVID GERSTEIN
Production: PAUL BARESH and CHRISTINA HWANG
Associate Publisher: ERIC REYNOLDS

Disney Masters showcases the work of internationally acclaimed Disney artists. Many of the stories presented in the *Disney Masters* series appear in English for the first time. This is *Disney Masters* Volume 21. Permission to quote or reproduce material for reviews must be obtained from the publisher.

Fantagraphics Books, Inc. | 7563 Lake City Way NE | Seattle WA 98115 | (800) 657-1100

Visit us at fantagraphics.com. Follow us on Twitter at @fantagraphics and on Facebook at facebook.com/fantagraphics.

Thanks to Thomas Jensen, Iliana Lopez, Ken Shue, Joe Torcivia, Fernando Ventura, and Germund Von Wowern.

First printing: August 2022 | ISBN 978-1-68396-568-8
Printed in China
Library of Congress Control Number: 2017956971
The stories in this volume were originally published in English in the United States.

"The Fantastic Fog" in *Walt Disney's Comics and Stories* #226-228, July to September 1959 (W WDC 226-05P)
"The Threat of the Stone-Eaters" in *Walt Disney's Comics and Stories* #217-219, October to December 1958 (W WDC 217-07P)
"The Monster of Sawtooth Mountain" in *Walt Disney's Comics and Stories* #220-222, January to March 1959 (W WDC 220-05P)
"Alaskan Adventure" in *Walt Disney's Comics and Stories* #223-225, April to June 1959 (W WDC 223-05P)
"Pineapple Poachers" in *Walt Disney's Comics and Stories* #234-236, March to May 1960 (W WDC 234-05P)
"The Trail to Treasure" in *Walt Disney's Comics and Stories* #242, November 1960 (W WDC 242-05)
"Mickey's Strange Mission" in *Walt Disney's Comics and Stories* #243-245, December 1960 to February 1961 (W WDC 243-05P)
"The Moon-Blot Plot" in *Walt Disney's Comics and Stories* #246-248, March to May 1961 (W WDC 246-07P)

TITLES IN THIS SERIES

Mickey Mouse: The Delta Dimension (Romano Scarpa) (*Disney Masters* Vol. 1)
Donald Duck: Uncle Scrooge's Money Rocket (Luciano Bottaro) (*Disney Masters* Vol. 2)
Mickey Mouse: The Case of the Vanishing Bandit (Paul Murry) (*Disney Masters* Vol. 3)
Donald Duck: The Great Survival Test (Daan Jippes and Freddy Milton) (*Disney Masters* Vol. 4)
Mickey Mouse: The Phantom Blot's Double Mystery (Romano Scarpa) (*Disney Masters* Vol. 5)
Uncle Scrooge: King of the Golden River (Giovan Battista Carpi) (*Disney Masters* Vol. 6)
Mickey Mouse: The Pirates of Tabasco Bay (Paul Murry) (*Disney Masters* Vol. 7)
Donald Duck: Duck Avenger Strikes Again (Romano Scarpa with Carl Barks) (*Disney Masters* Vol. 8)
Mickey Mouse: The Ice Sword Saga Book 1 (Massimo De Vita) (*Disney Masters* Vol. 9)
Donald Duck: Scandal on the Epoch Express (Mau and Bas Heymans) (*Disney Masters* Vol. 10)
Mickey Mouse: The Ice Sword Saga Book 2 (Massimo De Vita) (*Disney Masters* Vol. 11)
Donald Duck: The Forgetful Hero (Giorgio Cavazzano) (*Disney Masters* Vol. 12)
Mickey Mouse: The Sunken City (Paul Murry) (*Disney Masters* Vol. 13)
Donald Duck: Follow the Fearless Leader (Dick Kinney and Al Hubbard) (*Disney Masters* Vol. 14)
Mickey Mouse: New Adventures of the Phantom Blot (Paul Murry) (*Disney Masters* Vol. 15)
Donald Duck: Jumpin' Jupiter! (Luciano Bottaro) (*Disney Masters* Vol. 16)
Mickey Mouse: The Man From Altacraz (Romano Scarpa) (*Disney Masters* Vol. 17)
Uncle Scrooge: Pie in the Sky (William Van Horn) (*Disney Masters* Vol. 18)
Mickey Mouse: Trapped in the Shadow Dimension (Andrea "Casty" Castellan) (*Disney Masters* Vol. 19)
Donald Duck: 20,000 Leaks Under the Sea (Dick Kinney and Al Hubbard) (*Disney Masters* Vol. 20)

COMING SOON

Uncle Scrooge: Operation Galleon Grab (Giorgio Cavazzano) (*Disney Masters* Vol. 22)

ALSO AVAILABLE

Walt Disney's Donald Duck: "Duck Luck" (Carl Barks)
The Complete Life and Times of Scrooge McDuck Deluxe Edition (Don Rosa)
Mickey Mouse: Zombie Coffee (Régis Loisel)
Uncle Scrooge and Donald Duck: Bear Mountain Tales (Various creators, including Carl Barks and Daniel Branca)

Walt Disney

MICKEY MOUSE

the MONSTER of SAWTOOTH MOUNTAIN

CONTENTS

All stories illustrated and lettered by Paul Murry.

The content in this volume was first created in 1958-1961.

This title includes negative depictions and mistreatment of people or cultures. These stereotypes were wrong then and are wrong now. Rather than remove this content, we want to acknowledge its harmful impact, learn from it and spark conversation to create a more inclusive future together. Disney is committed to creating stories with inspirational and aspirational themes that reflect the rich diversity of the human experience around the globe. To learn more about how stories have impacted society, please visit www.disney.com/StoriesMatter.

The Winds (and Fog) of Change

by JOE TORCIVIA

CONSIDERED AS A WHOLE, the adventures collected in this volume herald something of a transition: one that will begin to turn Paul Murry's Mickey Mouse mythos on its (round and circular) ear. By the second half of the 1960s, wild science fiction plot elements will become commonplace occurrences in Mickey's life; we will see renegade robots, wild excursions through time, and even Mickey becoming an honest-to-goodness 1960s-style costumed superhero. The seeds for such wild events are undeniably planted by the adventures found in this collection.

Originally appearing in mid-1959, "The Fantastic Fog" sets the course for Mickey's, Paul Murry's, and writer Carl Fallberg's move toward the more imaginative type of fantasy storytelling that will become emblematic of 1960s pop culture. The unlikely catalyst for this change is the "crossing-over" of the Carl Barks-created inventor Gyro Gearloose into the mix: as the usually obliging source of everyday miracles, here forced to perfect a "fog magnet" to cover the activities of a pair of criminals.

While lacking in fantastic elements, the subsequent "Mickey's Strange Mission" marks a monumental break with the traditional Murry and Fallberg brand of sea, western, detective, and

A juxtaposition of "The Moon-Blot Plot" (1961) with Carl Barks' "The Strange Shipwrecks" (*Uncle Scrooge* #23, 1958) finds a shocked Fallberg Gyro Gearloose describing the Rover Rogue Boys with comically scary adjectives—much as Barks' Scrooge describes the Beagle Boys. One wonders if Fallberg, having introduced Gyro into Mouseton, briefly considered adding the Beagles as well.

BECAUSE WE'RE THE ROVER ROGUES, THAT'S WHY!
NOT TH-THE DREADFUL ROVER ROGUES!
CRASH!
YES! THE DREADFUL, NASTY, MEAN ROVER ROGUES!
HEY! SOMEONE'S COMING! IT MIGHT BE THE POLICE!
THE BEAGLE BOYS! THE *TERRIBLE* BEAGLE BOYS!
176-167
BEAG BOYS INC.

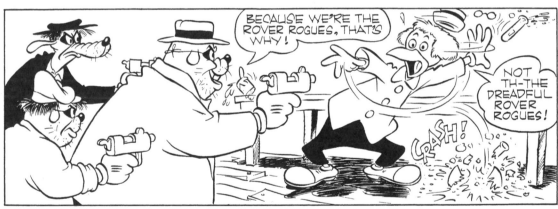

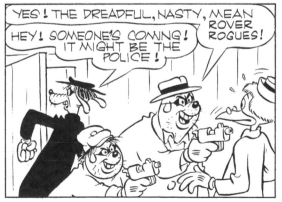

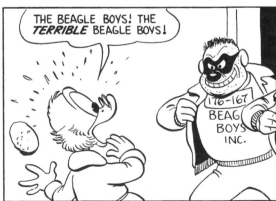

exploration adventures. A decidedly strange turn of events finds Mickey hired to locate his perennial nemesis Pete, so that the rotund rogue can receive a large inheritance... on the condition that he go straight. The audacious genius of the tale is that Mickey, who normally has an uncanny talent for *inadvertently* running across Pete with remarkable regularity, is now in the position of *searching* for him! A setup that might make a fine and dandy "standard adventure"—Mickey stumbling across Pete's plot to waylay an old hermit miner for his gold—becomes much more special with this almost-meta plot twist.

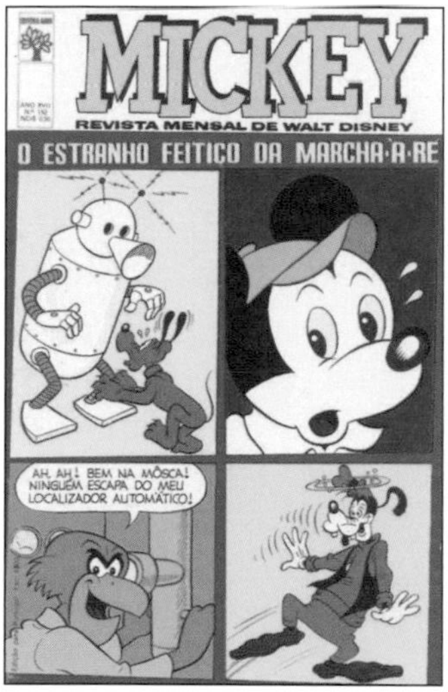
MICKEY
REVISTA MENSAL DE WALT DISNEY
O ESTRANHO FEITIÇO DA MARCHA-A-RÉ
AH, AH! BEM NA MÔSCA! NINGUÉM ESCAPA DO MEU LOCALIZADOR AUTOMÁTICO!
Jorge Kato's cover for Brazilian *Mickey* #392 (1968) illustrates Murry's later "Case of the Dazzling Hoo-Doo" (*Walt Disney's Comics* #330-332, 1968), with elements reflecting the sci-fi mayhem of Mickey's evolving world.

Our closing entry, "The Moon-Blot Plot," has Gyro Gearloose continue his catalyzing for what will be the most outrageous installment of the Murry and Fallberg oeuvre to-date. Again, Gyro must again manufacture a miracle under duress—here, a fantastic black dye to completely darken the very surface of the Moon. Thus commences a merry space-chase with the Rover Rogues (a substitute for the Beagle Boys?), who plan to deploy the concoction across the lunar surface, and Mickey, Goofy, and Gyro, who hope to foil them. Gyro will occasionally appear in Murry's Mickey Mouse serials over the 1960s in similar situations, as will his evil-inventor rival Emil Eagle, bringing more wide-open fantasy with them.

However, readers who prefer the more customary approach to the Mouse's comic book adventures need not fear. As we shall see in future volumes, Murry and his writers will maintain a steady flow of exploration, detective, and historical period tales as an integral part of the mix.

Readers will also find this volume front-loaded with the traditional globe-trotting Mickey and Goofy adventures most associated with Murry and Fallberg. The itinerary includes stopovers in the highest reaches of the Andes and the "new states" of Alaska and Hawaii. Exotic locales aplenty find Paul Murry up to the task of rendering torrential rainstorms, accompanied by blinding blizzards, majestic mountains, and vast valleys. Like Disney comics legends Floyd Gottfredson and Carl Barks, Murry's generation of creators was also inspired by the adventure movies of the 1930s and 1940s, in which characters played by the likes of Humphrey Bogart, Gary Cooper, and Alan Ladd found themselves in any number of exotic locales.

One weakness must also be acknowledged. In twentieth-century pop culture, "exotic locales" often tend to breed unfortunate stereotypes, and so it is with certain stories in this volume. You may notice occasional awkward portrayals of indigenous people—Native Americans and others—as backward, superstitious characters. Such imagery, failing to convey authentic cultural traditions, was common in 1958; but that doesn't excuse the ignorance it reflects, which could come even from the most well-meaning comic book creators.

On the upside, the seeds of today's better cultural understandings can also be found in these stories, particularly when one observes their condemnation of imperialism. Indigenous characters are shown as rightly resentful of outsiders' exploitation; and the outsiders, in the form of villains like Pete and Tiny, are obviously far less intelligent than the locals they would try to rob.

Finally, those with good memories—or largely complete collections of *Walt Disney's Comics and Stories*—may notice the absence of two serialized stories that Murry redrew from original Mickey Mouse newspaper strip continuities by Floyd Gottfredson and Merrill De Maris. Those stories, in their original strip format, can be found in Fantagraphics' *Floyd Gottfredson Library of Walt Disney's Mickey Mouse*. While Murry's redraws might be revisited at a future time, the editors' intent in the present *Disney Masters* volumes is to comprehensively anthologize the classic Paul Murry/Carl Fallberg collaborations that represent story lines created exclusively for comic books.

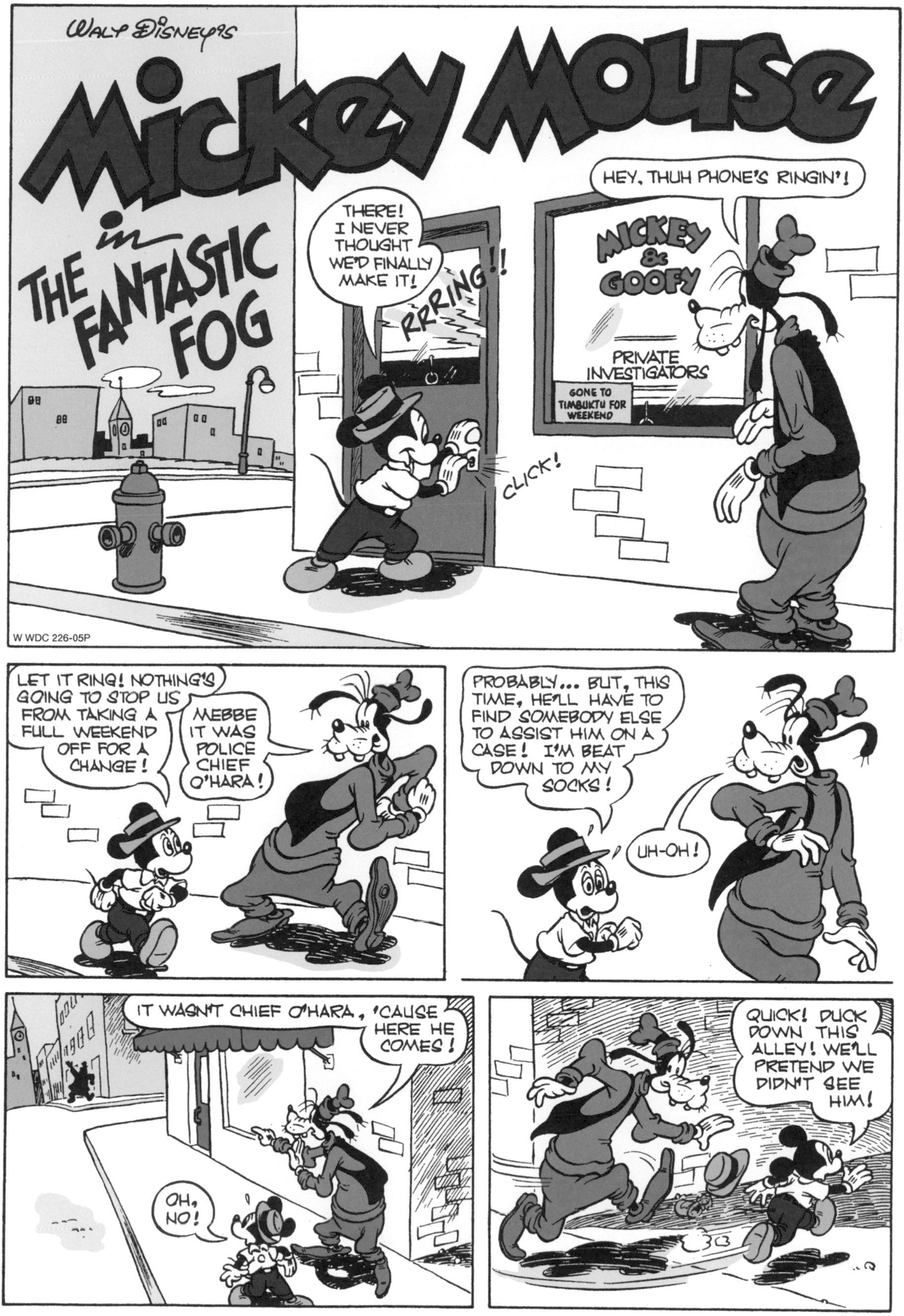
WALT DISNEY'S
MICKEY MOUSE
in THE FANTASTIC FOG
THERE! I NEVER THOUGHT WE'D FINALLY MAKE IT!
RRRING!!
HEY, THUH PHONE'S RINGIN'!
MICKEY & GOOFY
PRIVATE INVESTIGATORS
GONE TO TIMBUKTU FOR WEEKEND
CLICK!
W WDC 226-05P
LET IT RING! NOTHING'S GOING TO STOP US FROM TAKING A FULL WEEKEND OFF FOR A CHANGE!
MEBBE IT WAS POLICE CHIEF O'HARA!
PROBABLY... BUT, THIS TIME, HE'LL HAVE TO FIND SOMEBODY ELSE TO ASSIST HIM ON A CASE! I'M BEAT DOWN TO MY SOCKS!
UH-OH!
IT WASN'T CHIEF O'HARA, 'CAUSE HERE HE COMES!
OH, NO!
QUICK! DUCK DOWN THIS ALLEY! WE'LL PRETEND WE DIDN'T SEE HIM!

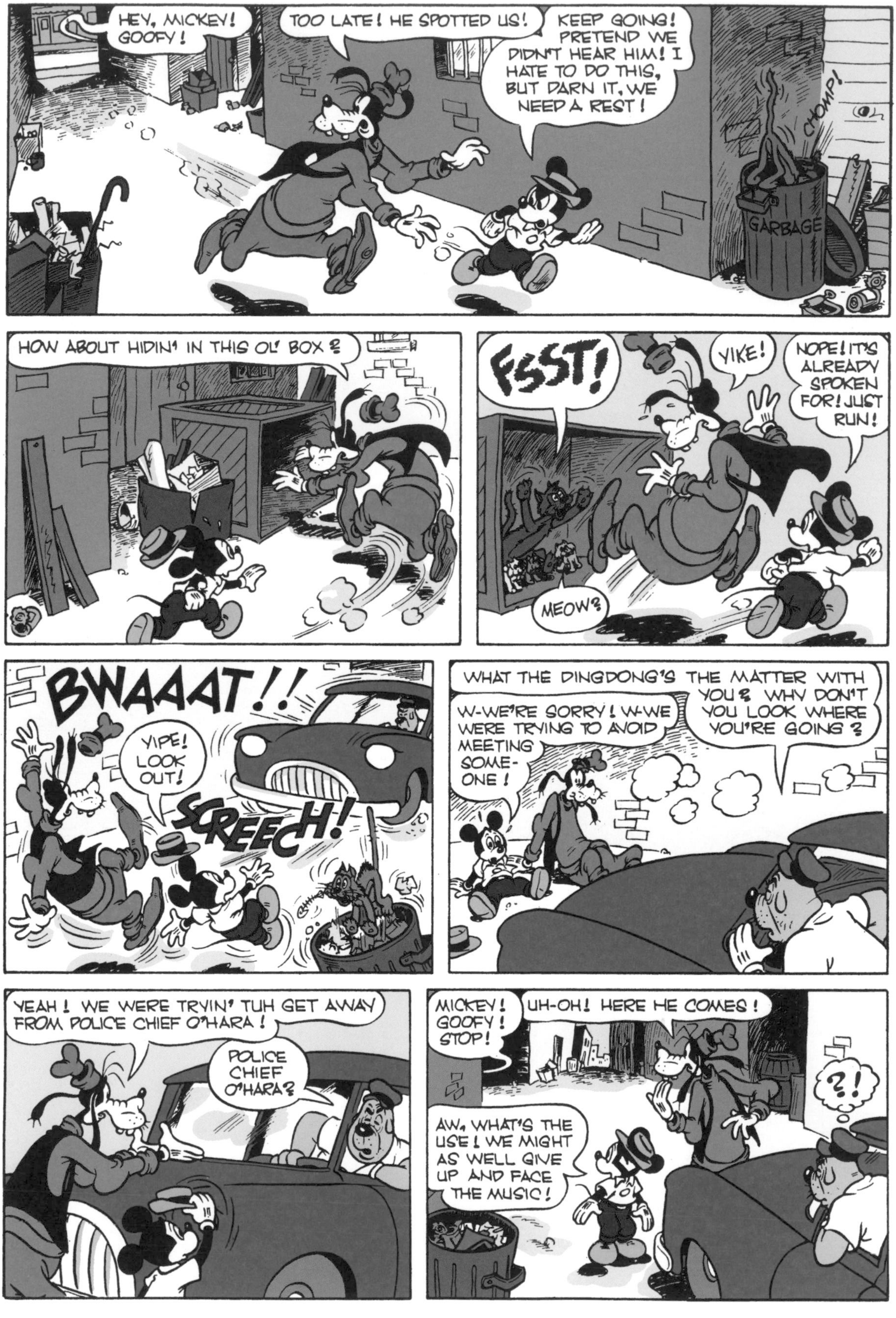
HEY, MICKEY! GOOFY!
TOO LATE! HE SPOTTED US!
KEEP GOING! PRETEND WE DIDN'T HEAR HIM! I HATE TO DO THIS, BUT DARN IT, WE NEED A REST!
CHOMP!
GARBAGE
HOW ABOUT HIDIN' IN THIS OL' BOX?
FSST!
YIKE!
NOPE! IT'S ALREADY SPOKEN FOR! JUST RUN!
MEOW?
BWAAAT!!
YIPE! LOOK OUT!
SCREECH!
WHAT THE DINGDONG'S THE MATTER WITH YOU? WHY DON'T YOU LOOK WHERE YOU'RE GOING?
W-WE'RE SORRY! W-WE WERE TRYING TO AVOID MEETING SOME-ONE!
YEAH! WE WERE TRYIN' TUH GET AWAY FROM POLICE CHIEF O'HARA!
POLICE CHIEF O'HARA?
MICKEY! GOOFY! STOP!
UH-OH! HERE HE COMES!
?!
AW, WHAT'S THE USE! WE MIGHT AS WELL GIVE UP AND FACE THE MUSIC!

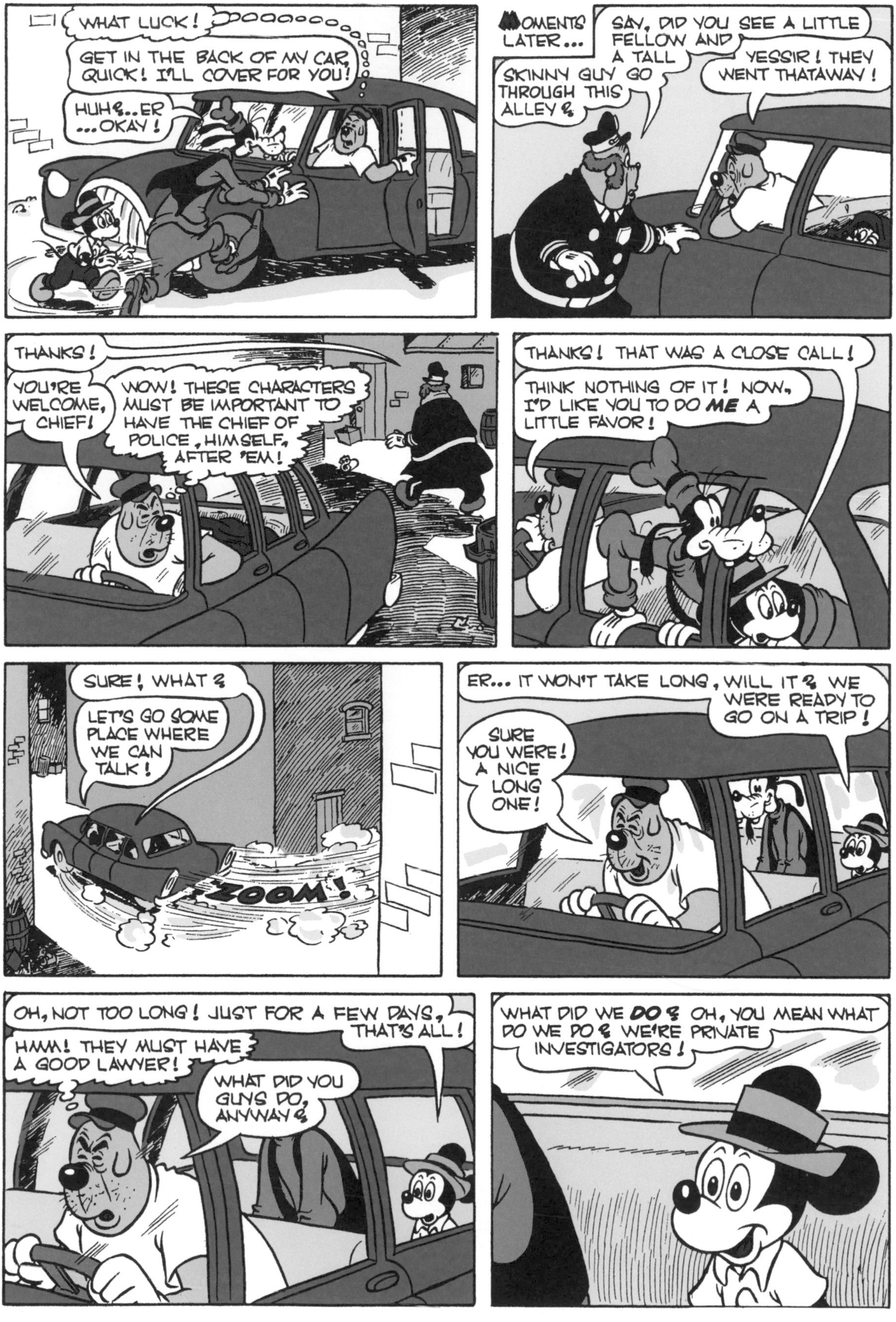
WHAT LUCK!
GET IN THE BACK OF MY CAR, QUICK! I'LL COVER FOR YOU!
HUH?...ER ...OKAY!
MOMENTS LATER...
SAY, DID YOU SEE A LITTLE FELLOW AND A TALL SKINNY GUY GO THROUGH THIS ALLEY?
YESSIR! THEY WENT THATAWAY!
THANKS!
YOU'RE WELCOME, CHIEF!
WOW! THESE CHARACTERS MUST BE IMPORTANT TO HAVE THE CHIEF OF POLICE, HIMSELF, AFTER 'EM!
THANKS! THAT WAS A CLOSE CALL!
THINK NOTHING OF IT! NOW, I'D LIKE YOU TO DO ME A LITTLE FAVOR!
SURE! WHAT?
LET'S GO SOME PLACE WHERE WE CAN TALK!
ZOOM!
ER... IT WON'T TAKE LONG, WILL IT? WE WERE READY TO GO ON A TRIP!
SURE YOU WERE! A NICE LONG ONE!
OH, NOT TOO LONG! JUST FOR A FEW DAYS, THAT'S ALL!
HMM! THEY MUST HAVE A GOOD LAWYER!
WHAT DID YOU GUYS DO, ANYWAY?
WHAT DID WE DO? OH, YOU MEAN WHAT DO WE DO? WE'RE PRIVATE INVESTIGATORS!

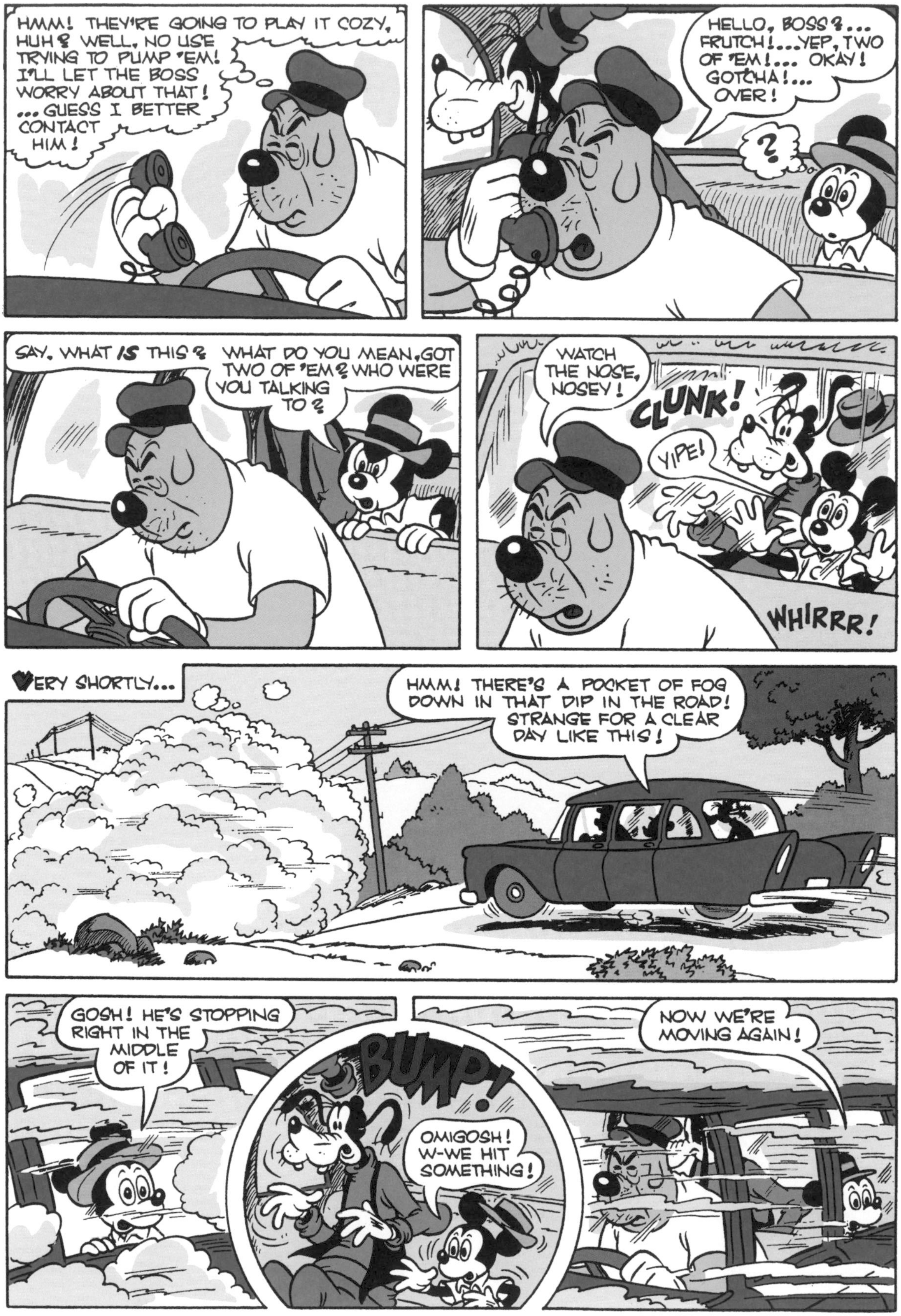
HMM! THEY'RE GOING TO PLAY IT COZY, HUH? WELL, NO USE TRYING TO PUMP 'EM! I'LL LET THE BOSS WORRY ABOUT THAT! ...GUESS I BETTER CONTACT HIM!
HELLO, BOSS?... FRUTCH!...YEP, TWO OF 'EM!... OKAY! GOTCHA!... OVER!
?
SAY, WHAT *IS* THIS?
WHAT DO YOU MEAN, GOT TWO OF 'EM? WHO WERE YOU TALKING TO?
WATCH THE NOSE, NOSEY!
CLUNK!
YIPE!
WHIRRR!
VERY SHORTLY...
HMM! THERE'S A POCKET OF FOG DOWN IN THAT DIP IN THE ROAD! STRANGE FOR A CLEAR DAY LIKE THIS!
GOSH! HE'S STOPPING RIGHT IN THE MIDDLE OF IT!
BUMP!
OMIGOSH! W-WE HIT SOMETHING!
NOW WE'RE MOVING AGAIN!

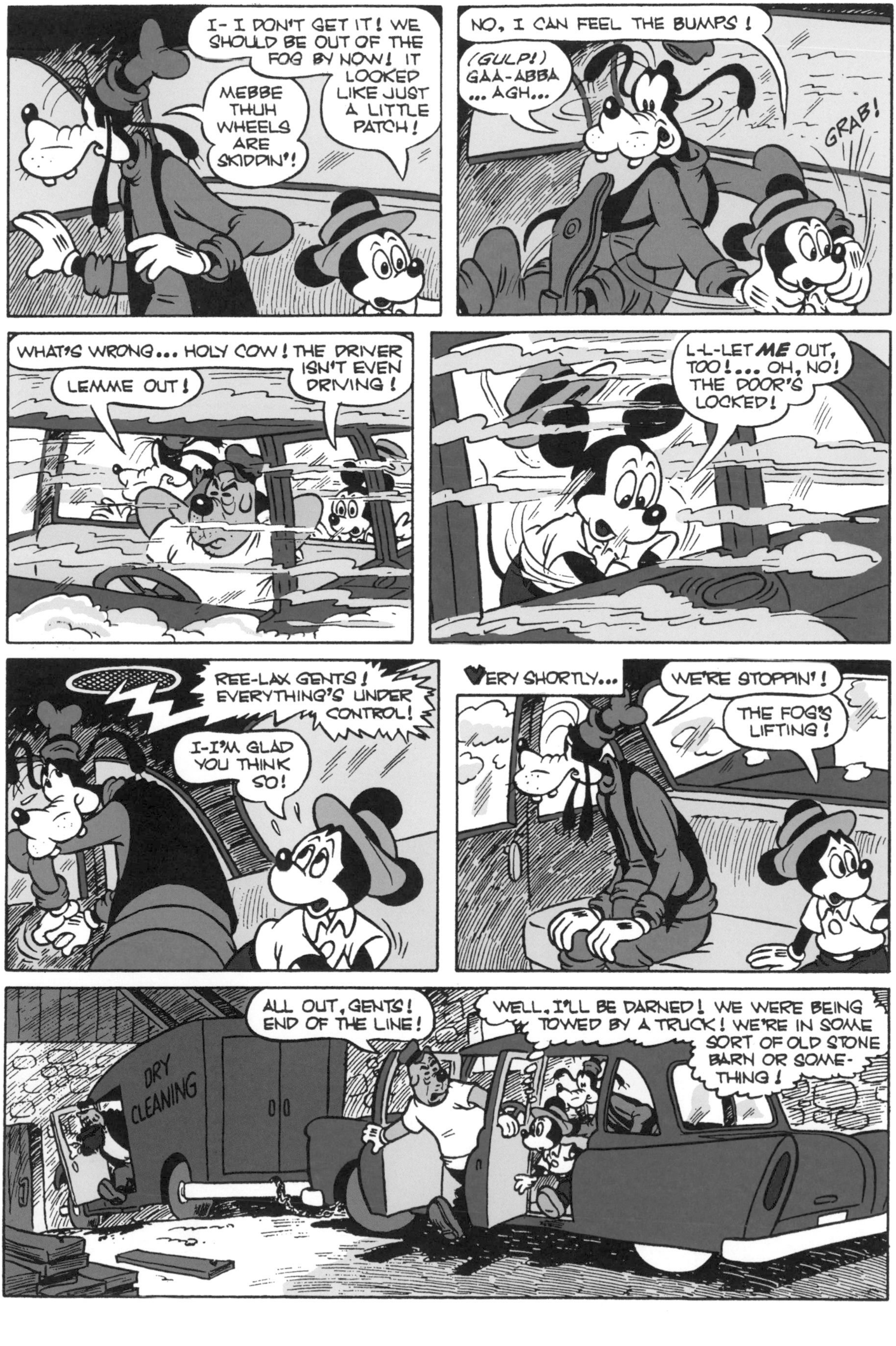

I- I DON'T GET IT! WE SHOULD BE OUT OF THE FOG BY NOW! IT LOOKED LIKE JUST A LITTLE PATCH!
MEBBE THUH WHEELS ARE SKIDDIN'!
NO, I CAN FEEL THE BUMPS!
(GULP!) GAA-ABBA ... AGH...
GRAB!
WHAT'S WRONG... HOLY COW! THE DRIVER ISN'T EVEN DRIVING!
LEMME OUT!
L-L-LET ME OUT, TOO!... OH, NO! THE DOOR'S LOCKED!
REE-LAX GENTS! EVERYTHING'S UNDER CONTROL!
I-I'M GLAD YOU THINK SO!
VERY SHORTLY...
WE'RE STOPPIN'!
THE FOG'S LIFTING!
ALL OUT, GENTS! END OF THE LINE!
WELL, I'LL BE DARNED! WE WERE BEING TOWED BY A TRUCK! WE'RE IN SOME SORT OF OLD STONE BARN OR SOME-THING!
DRY CLEANING

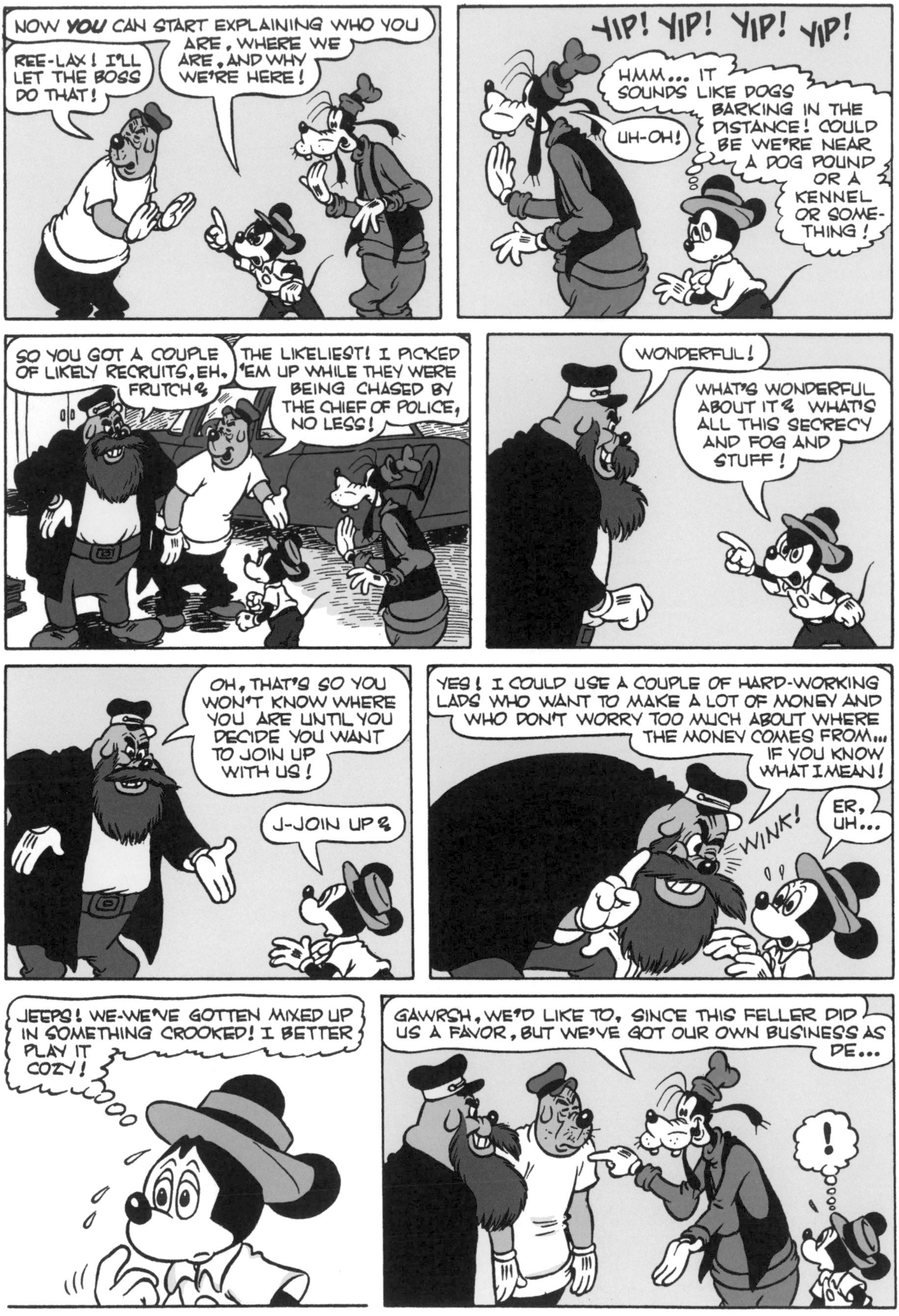
NOW YOU CAN START EXPLAINING WHO YOU ARE, WHERE WE ARE, AND WHY WE'RE HERE!
REE-LAX! I'LL LET THE BOSS DO THAT!
YIP! YIP! YIP! YIP!
HMM... IT SOUNDS LIKE DOGS BARKING IN THE DISTANCE! COULD BE WE'RE NEAR A DOG POUND OR A KENNEL OR SOMETHING!
UH-OH!
SO YOU GOT A COUPLE OF LIKELY RECRUITS, EH, FRUTCH?
THE LIKELIEST! I PICKED 'EM UP WHILE THEY WERE BEING CHASED BY THE CHIEF OF POLICE, NO LESS!
WONDERFUL!
WHAT'S WONDERFUL ABOUT IT? WHAT'S ALL THIS SECRECY AND FOG AND STUFF!
OH, THAT'S SO YOU WON'T KNOW WHERE YOU ARE UNTIL YOU DECIDE YOU WANT TO JOIN UP WITH US!
J-JOIN UP?
YES! I COULD USE A COUPLE OF HARD-WORKING LADS WHO WANT TO MAKE A LOT OF MONEY AND WHO DON'T WORRY TOO MUCH ABOUT WHERE THE MONEY COMES FROM... IF YOU KNOW WHAT I MEAN!
WINK!
ER, UH...
JEEPS! WE-WE'VE GOTTEN MIXED UP IN SOMETHING CROOKED! I BETTER PLAY IT COZY!
GAWRSH, WE'D LIKE TO, SINCE THIS FELLER DID US A FAVOR, BUT WE'VE GOT OUR OWN BUSINESS AS DE...
!

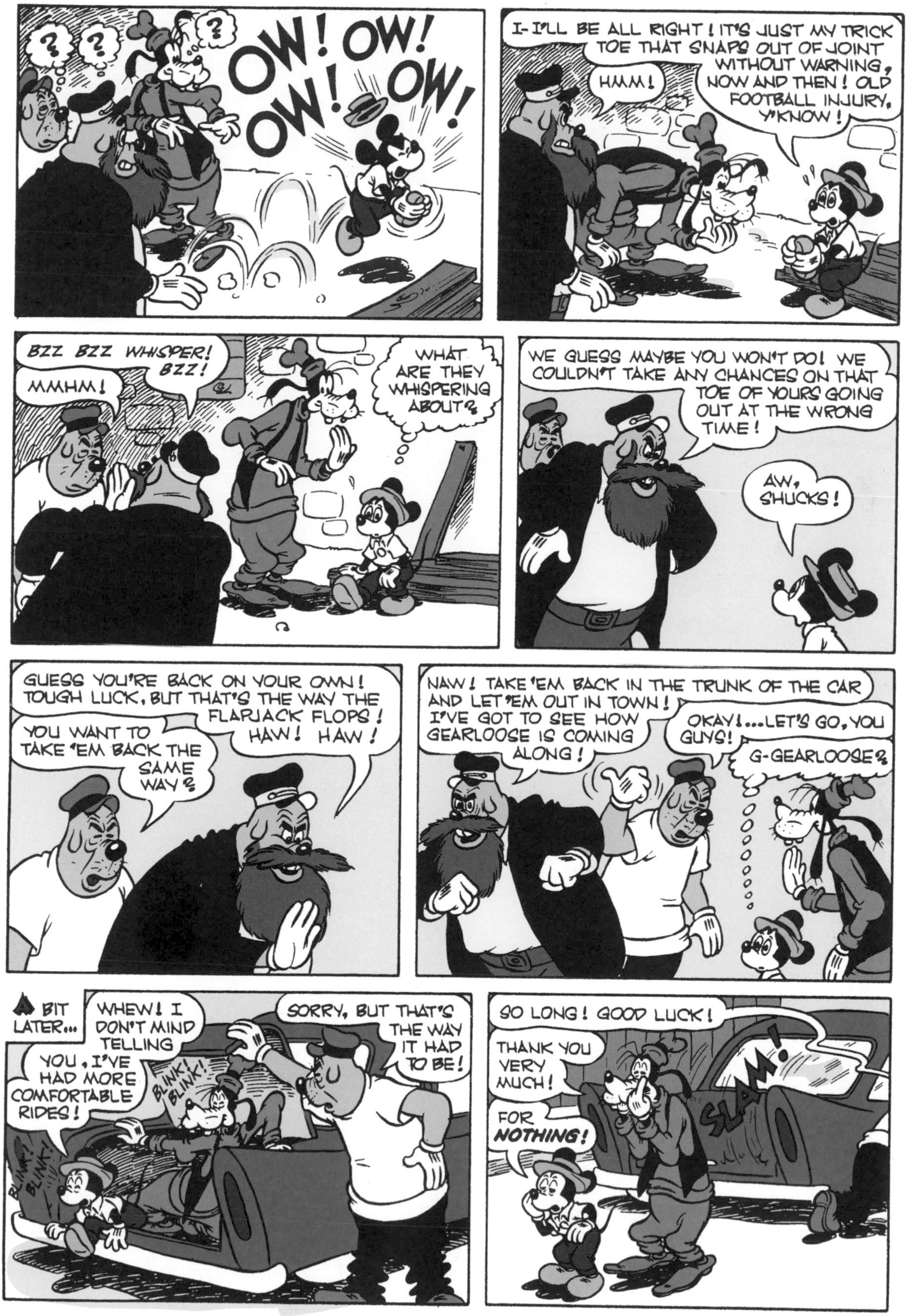
OW! OW! OW! OW!
I-I'LL BE ALL RIGHT! IT'S JUST MY TRICK TOE THAT SNAPS OUT OF JOINT WITHOUT WARNING, NOW AND THEN! OLD FOOTBALL INJURY, Y'KNOW!
HMM!
BZZ BZZ WHISPER! BZZ!
MMHM!
WHAT ARE THEY WHISPERING ABOUT?
WE GUESS MAYBE YOU WON'T DO! WE COULDN'T TAKE ANY CHANCES ON THAT TOE OF YOURS GOING OUT AT THE WRONG TIME!
AW, SHUCKS!
GUESS YOU'RE BACK ON YOUR OWN! TOUGH LUCK, BUT THAT'S THE WAY THE FLAPJACK FLOPS! HAW! HAW!
YOU WANT TO TAKE 'EM BACK THE SAME WAY?
NAW! TAKE 'EM BACK IN THE TRUNK OF THE CAR AND LET 'EM OUT IN TOWN! I'VE GOT TO SEE HOW GEARLOOSE IS COMING ALONG!
OKAY! ...LET'S GO, YOU GUYS!
G-GEARLOOSE?
A BIT LATER...
WHEW! I DON'T MIND TELLING YOU, I'VE HAD MORE COMFORTABLE RIDES!
SORRY, BUT THAT'S THE WAY IT HAD TO BE!
BLINK! BLINK!
BLINK! BLINK!
SO LONG! GOOD LUCK!
THANK YOU VERY MUCH!
FOR NOTHING!
SLAM!

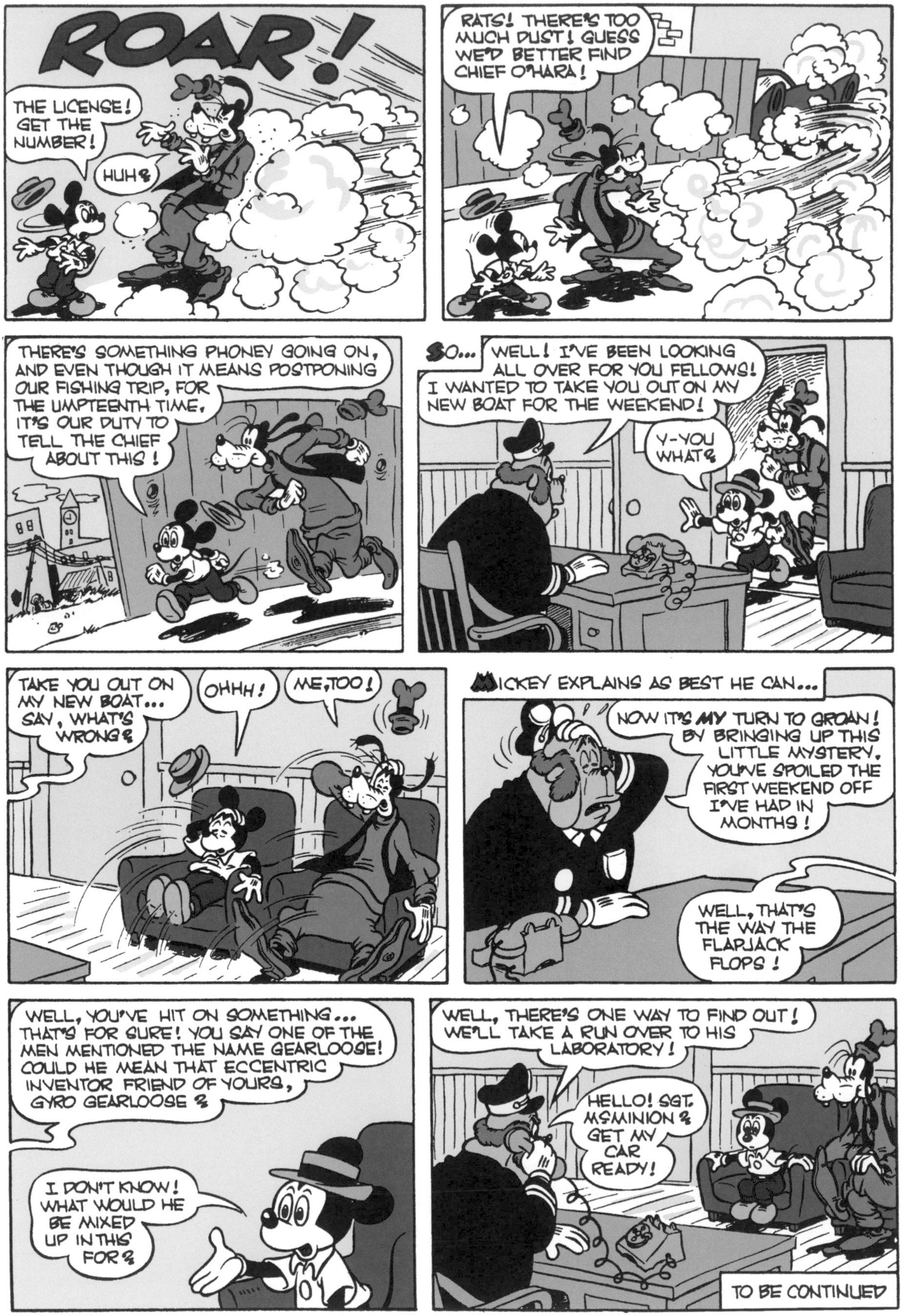

ROAR!
THE LICENSE! GET THE NUMBER!
HUH?
RATS! THERE'S TOO MUCH DUST! GUESS WE'D BETTER FIND CHIEF O'HARA!
THERE'S SOMETHING PHONEY GOING ON, AND EVEN THOUGH IT MEANS POSTPONING OUR FISHING TRIP, FOR THE UMPTEENTH TIME, IT'S OUR DUTY TO TELL THE CHIEF ABOUT THIS!
SO...
WELL! I'VE BEEN LOOKING ALL OVER FOR YOU FELLOWS! I WANTED TO TAKE YOU OUT ON MY NEW BOAT FOR THE WEEKEND!
Y-YOU WHAT?
TAKE YOU OUT ON MY NEW BOAT... SAY, WHAT'S WRONG?
OHHH!
ME, TOO!
MICKEY EXPLAINS AS BEST HE CAN...
NOW IT'S MY TURN TO GROAN! BY BRINGING UP THIS LITTLE MYSTERY, YOU'VE SPOILED THE FIRST WEEKEND OFF I'VE HAD IN MONTHS!
WELL, THAT'S THE WAY THE FLAPJACK FLOPS!
WELL, YOU'VE HIT ON SOMETHING... THAT'S FOR SURE! YOU SAY ONE OF THE MEN MENTIONED THE NAME GEARLOOSE! COULD HE MEAN THAT ECCENTRIC INVENTOR FRIEND OF YOURS, GYRO GEARLOOSE?
I DON'T KNOW! WHAT WOULD HE BE MIXED UP IN THIS FOR?
WELL, THERE'S ONE WAY TO FIND OUT! WE'LL TAKE A RUN OVER TO HIS LABORATORY!
HELLO! SGT. McMINION? GET MY CAR READY!
TO BE CONTINUED

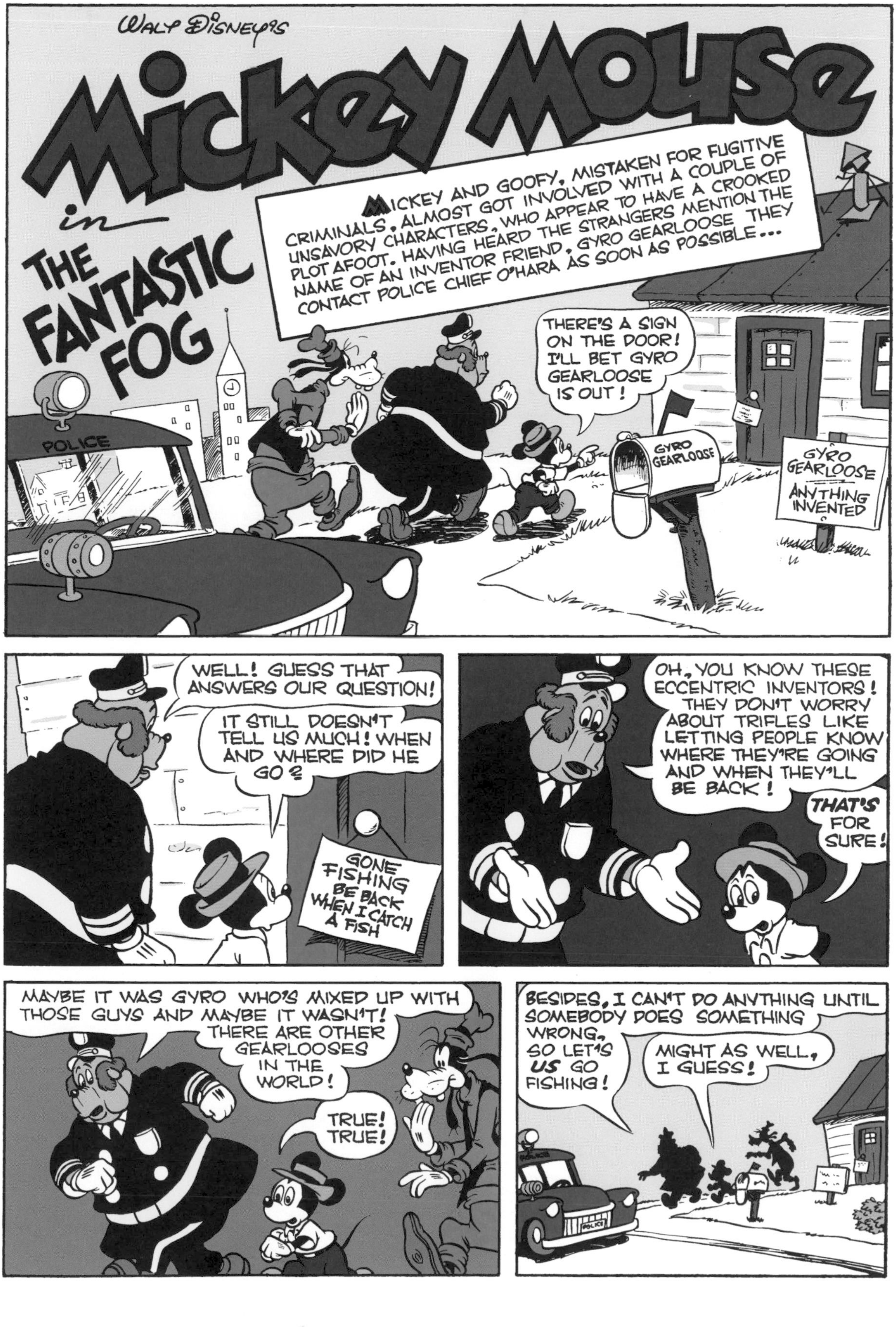
WALT DISNEY'S
MICKEY MOUSE
in
THE FANTASTIC FOG
MICKEY AND GOOFY, MISTAKEN FOR FUGITIVE CRIMINALS, ALMOST GOT INVOLVED WITH A COUPLE OF UNSAVORY CHARACTERS, WHO APPEAR TO HAVE A CROOKED PLOT AFOOT. HAVING HEARD THE STRANGERS MENTION THE NAME OF AN INVENTOR FRIEND, GYRO GEARLOOSE THEY CONTACT POLICE CHIEF O'HARA AS SOON AS POSSIBLE...
THERE'S A SIGN ON THE DOOR! I'LL BET GYRO GEARLOOSE IS OUT!
POLICE
GYRO GEARLOOSE
GYRO GEARLOOSE ANYTHING INVENTED
WELL! GUESS THAT ANSWERS OUR QUESTION!
IT STILL DOESN'T TELL US MUCH! WHEN AND WHERE DID HE GO?
GONE FISHING BE BACK WHEN I CATCH A FISH
OH, YOU KNOW THESE ECCENTRIC INVENTORS! THEY DON'T WORRY ABOUT TRIFLES LIKE LETTING PEOPLE KNOW WHERE THEY'RE GOING AND WHEN THEY'LL BE BACK!
THAT'S FOR SURE!
MAYBE IT WAS GYRO WHO'S MIXED UP WITH THOSE GUYS AND MAYBE IT WASN'T! THERE ARE OTHER GEARLOOSES IN THE WORLD!
TRUE! TRUE!
BESIDES, I CAN'T DO ANYTHING UNTIL SOMEBODY DOES SOMETHING WRONG, SO LET'S US GO FISHING!
MIGHT AS WELL, I GUESS!

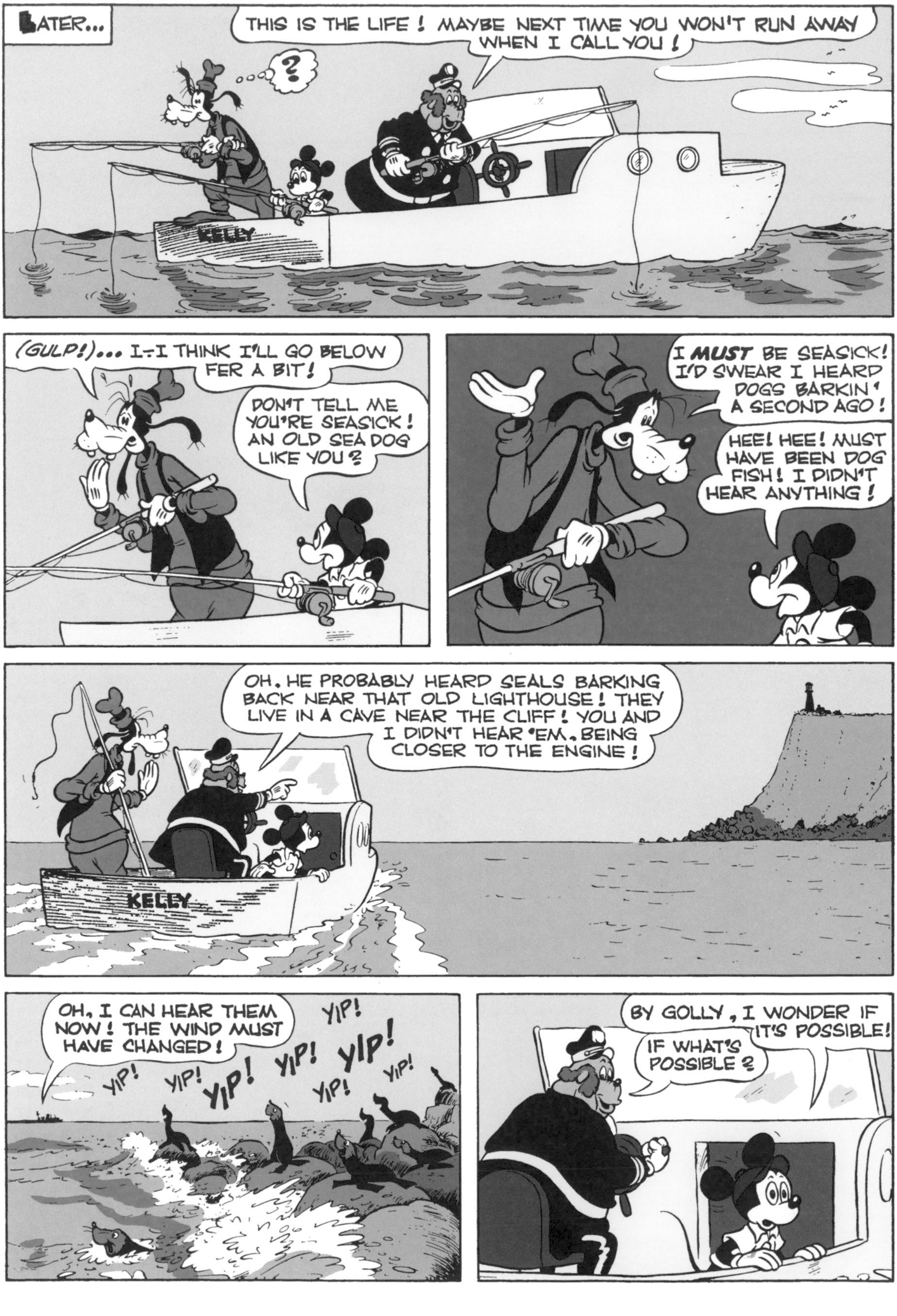
LATER...
THIS IS THE LIFE! MAYBE NEXT TIME YOU WON'T RUN AWAY WHEN I CALL YOU!
?
KELLY
(GULP!)... I-I THINK I'LL GO BELOW FER A BIT!
DON'T TELL ME YOU'RE SEASICK! AN OLD SEA DOG LIKE YOU?
I MUST BE SEASICK! I'D SWEAR I HEARD DOGS BARKIN' A SECOND AGO!
HEE! HEE! MUST HAVE BEEN DOG FISH! I DIDN'T HEAR ANYTHING!
OH, HE PROBABLY HEARD SEALS BARKING BACK NEAR THAT OLD LIGHTHOUSE! THEY LIVE IN A CAVE NEAR THE CLIFF! YOU AND I DIDN'T HEAR 'EM, BEING CLOSER TO THE ENGINE!
KELLY
OH, I CAN HEAR THEM NOW! THE WIND MUST HAVE CHANGED!
YIP! YIP! YIP! YIP! YIP! YIP! YIP! YIP!
BY GOLLY, I WONDER IF IT'S POSSIBLE!
IF WHAT'S POSSIBLE?

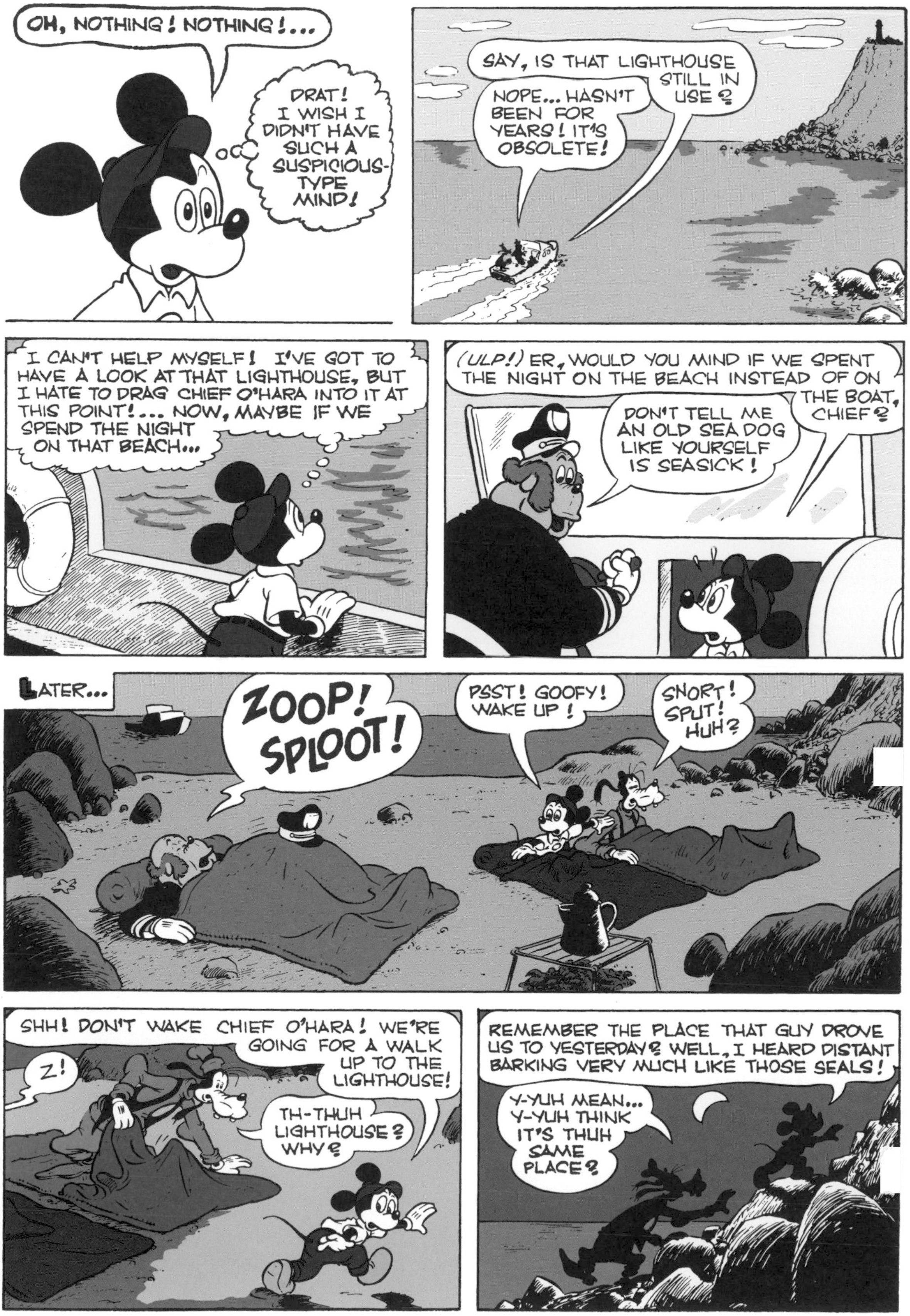
OH, NOTHING! NOTHING!...
DRAT! I WISH I DIDN'T HAVE SUCH A SUSPICIOUS-TYPE MIND!
SAY, IS THAT LIGHTHOUSE STILL IN USE?
NOPE... HASN'T BEEN FOR YEARS! IT'S OBSOLETE!
I CAN'T HELP MYSELF! I'VE GOT TO HAVE A LOOK AT THAT LIGHTHOUSE, BUT I HATE TO DRAG CHIEF O'HARA INTO IT AT THIS POINT!... NOW, MAYBE IF WE SPEND THE NIGHT ON THAT BEACH...
(ULP!) ER, WOULD YOU MIND IF WE SPENT THE NIGHT ON THE BEACH INSTEAD OF ON THE BOAT, CHIEF?
DON'T TELL ME AN OLD SEA DOG LIKE YOURSELF IS SEASICK!
LATER...
ZOOP! SPLOOT!
PSST! GOOFY! WAKE UP!
SNORT! SPUT! HUH?
SHH! DON'T WAKE CHIEF O'HARA! WE'RE GOING FOR A WALK UP TO THE LIGHTHOUSE!
Z!
TH-THUH LIGHTHOUSE? WHY?
REMEMBER THE PLACE THAT GUY DROVE US TO YESTERDAY? WELL, I HEARD DISTANT BARKING VERY MUCH LIKE THOSE SEALS!
Y-YUH MEAN... Y-YUH THINK IT'S THUH SAME PLACE?

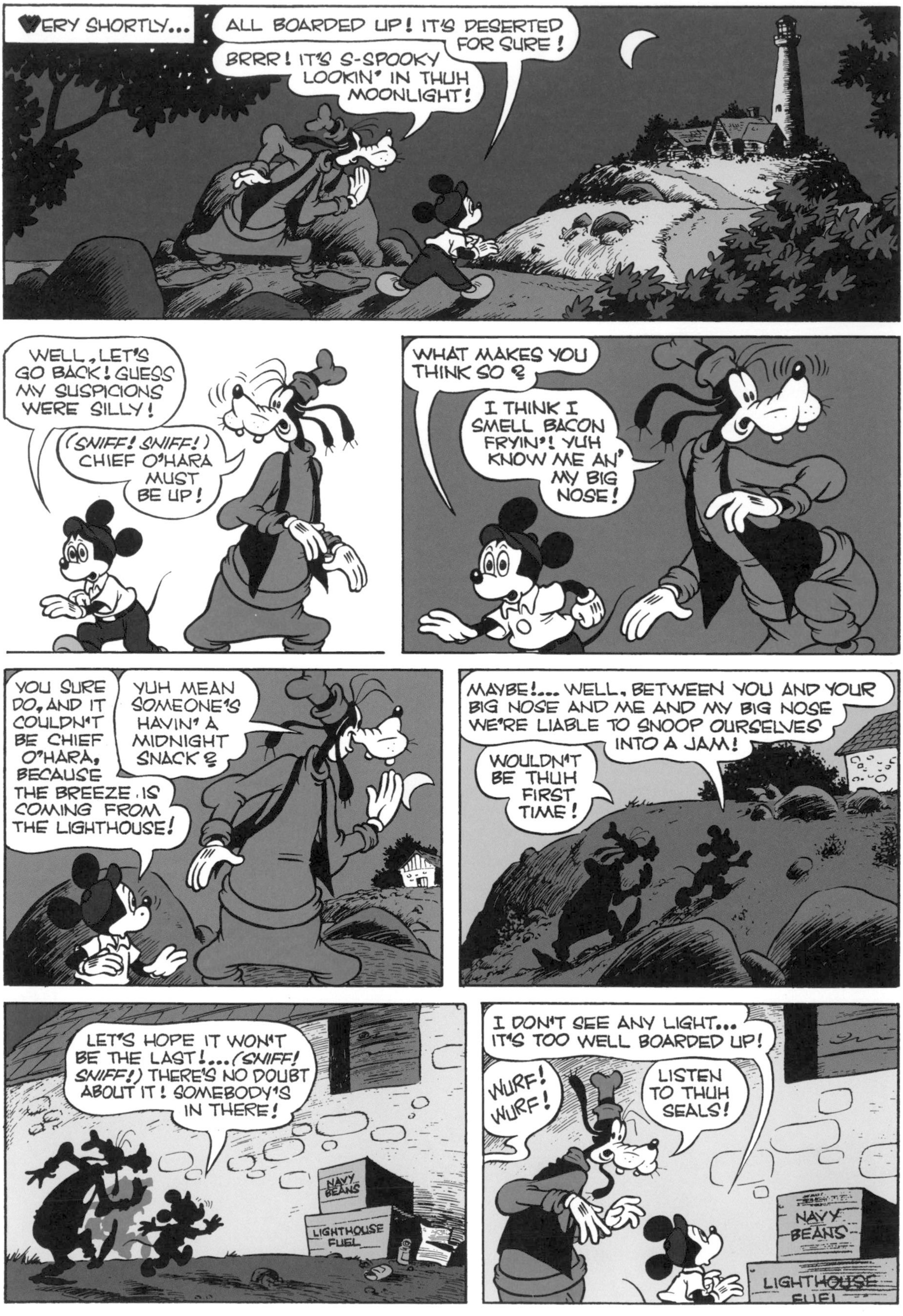

VERY SHORTLY...
ALL BOARDED UP! IT'S DESERTED FOR SURE!
BRRR! IT'S S-SPOOKY LOOKIN' IN THUH MOONLIGHT!
WELL, LET'S GO BACK! GUESS MY SUSPICIONS WERE SILLY!
(SNIFF! SNIFF!) CHIEF O'HARA MUST BE UP!
WHAT MAKES YOU THINK SO?
I THINK I SMELL BACON FRYIN'! YUH KNOW ME AN' MY BIG NOSE!
YUH MEAN SOMEONE'S HAVIN' A MIDNIGHT SNACK?
YOU SURE DO, AND IT COULDN'T BE CHIEF O'HARA, BECAUSE THE BREEZE IS COMING FROM THE LIGHTHOUSE!
MAYBE!... WELL, BETWEEN YOU AND YOUR BIG NOSE AND ME AND MY BIG NOSE WE'RE LIABLE TO SNOOP OURSELVES INTO A JAM!
WOULDN'T BE THUH FIRST TIME!
LET'S HOPE IT WON'T BE THE LAST!... (SNIFF! SNIFF!) THERE'S NO DOUBT ABOUT IT! SOMEBODY'S IN THERE!
NAVY BEANS
LIGHTHOUSE FUEL
I DON'T SEE ANY LIGHT... IT'S TOO WELL BOARDED UP!
WURF! WURF!
LISTEN TO THUH SEALS!
NAVY BEANS
LIGHTHOUSE FUEL

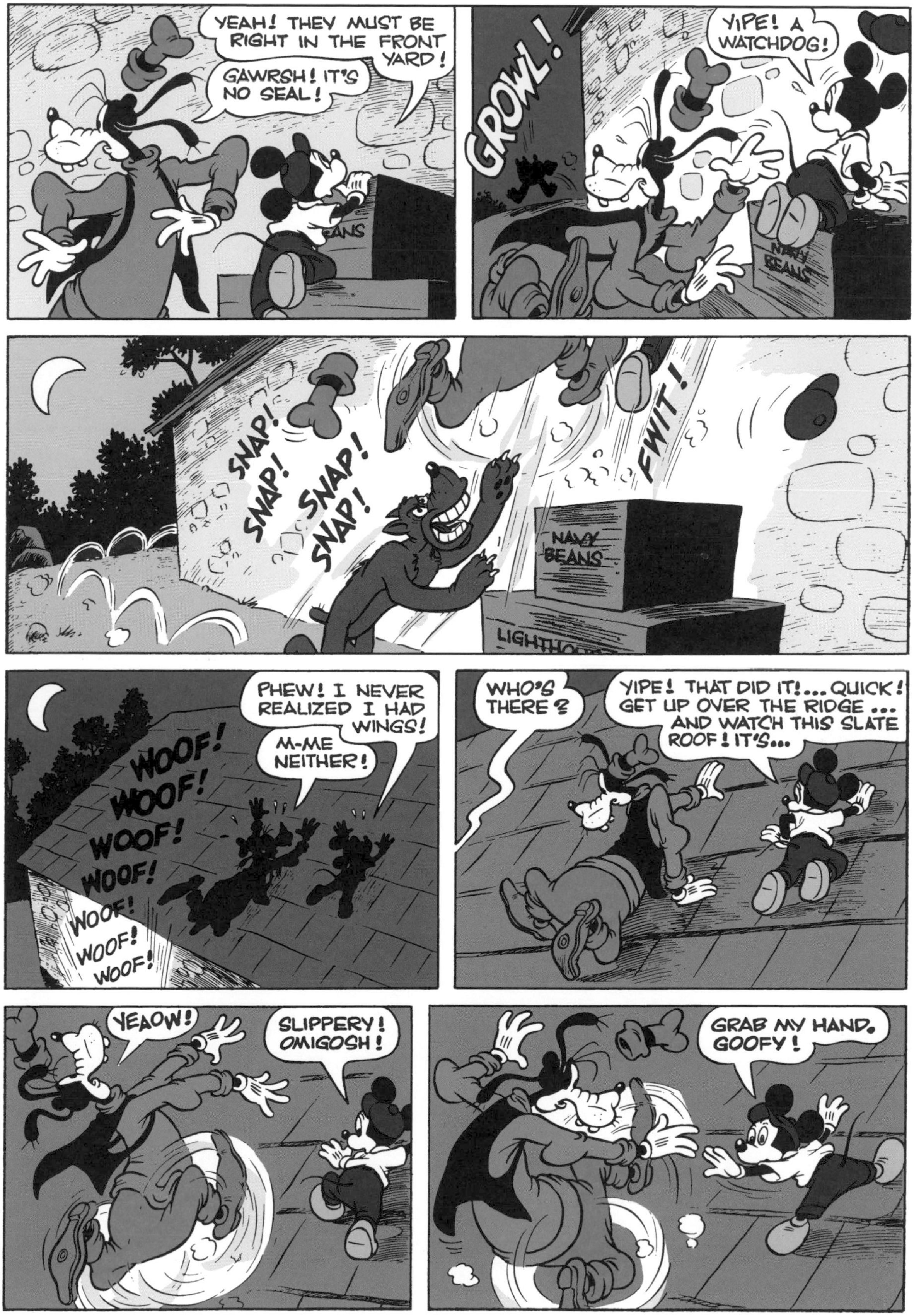
YEAH! THEY MUST BE RIGHT IN THE FRONT YARD!
GAWRSH! IT'S NO SEAL!
BEANS
GROWL!
YIPE! A WATCHDOG!
NAVY BEANS
SNAP! SNAP! SNAP! SNAP!
FWIT!
NAVY BEANS
LIGHTHOU
PHEW! I NEVER REALIZED I HAD WINGS!
M-ME NEITHER!
WOOF! WOOF! WOOF! WOOF! WOOF! WOOF! WOOF!
WHO'S THERE?
YIPE! THAT DID IT!... QUICK! GET UP OVER THE RIDGE ... AND WATCH THIS SLATE ROOF! IT'S...
YEAOW!
SLIPPERY! OMIGOSH!
GRAB MY HAND, GOOFY!

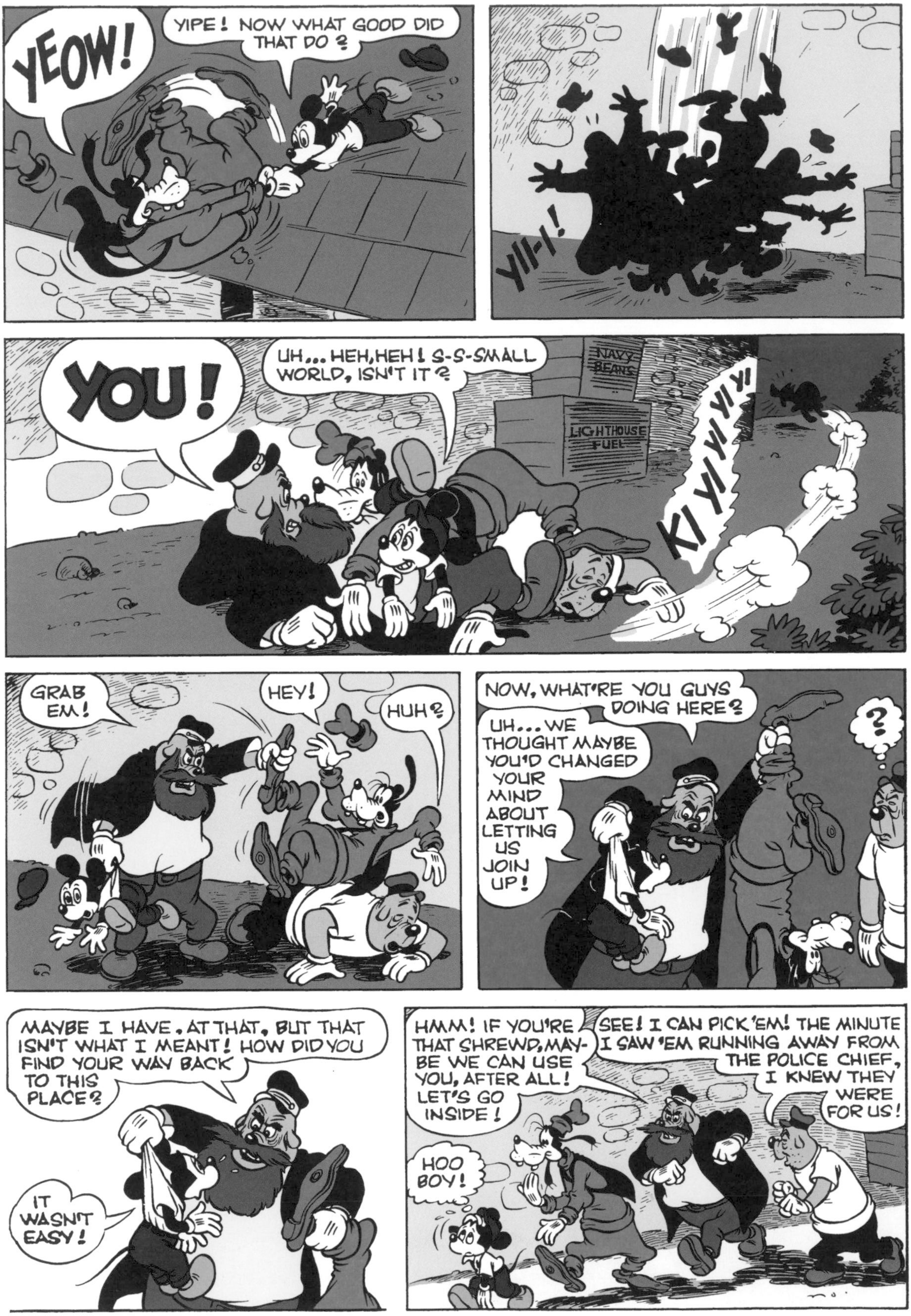
YEOW!
YIPE! NOW WHAT GOOD DID THAT DO?
YIII!
YOU!
UH... HEH, HEH! S-S-SMALL WORLD, ISN'T IT?
NAVY BEANS
LIGHTHOUSE FUEL
KI YI YI YI YI
GRAB EM!
HEY!
HUH?
NOW, WHAT'RE YOU GUYS DOING HERE?
UH... WE THOUGHT MAYBE YOU'D CHANGED YOUR MIND ABOUT LETTING US JOIN UP!
?
MAYBE I HAVE, AT THAT, BUT THAT ISN'T WHAT I MEANT! HOW DID YOU FIND YOUR WAY BACK TO THIS PLACE?
IT WASN'T EASY!
HMM! IF YOU'RE THAT SHREWD, MAY-BE WE CAN USE YOU, AFTER ALL! LET'S GO INSIDE!
SEE! I CAN PICK 'EM! THE MINUTE I SAW 'EM RUNNING AWAY FROM THE POLICE CHIEF, I KNEW THEY WERE FOR US!
HOO BOY!

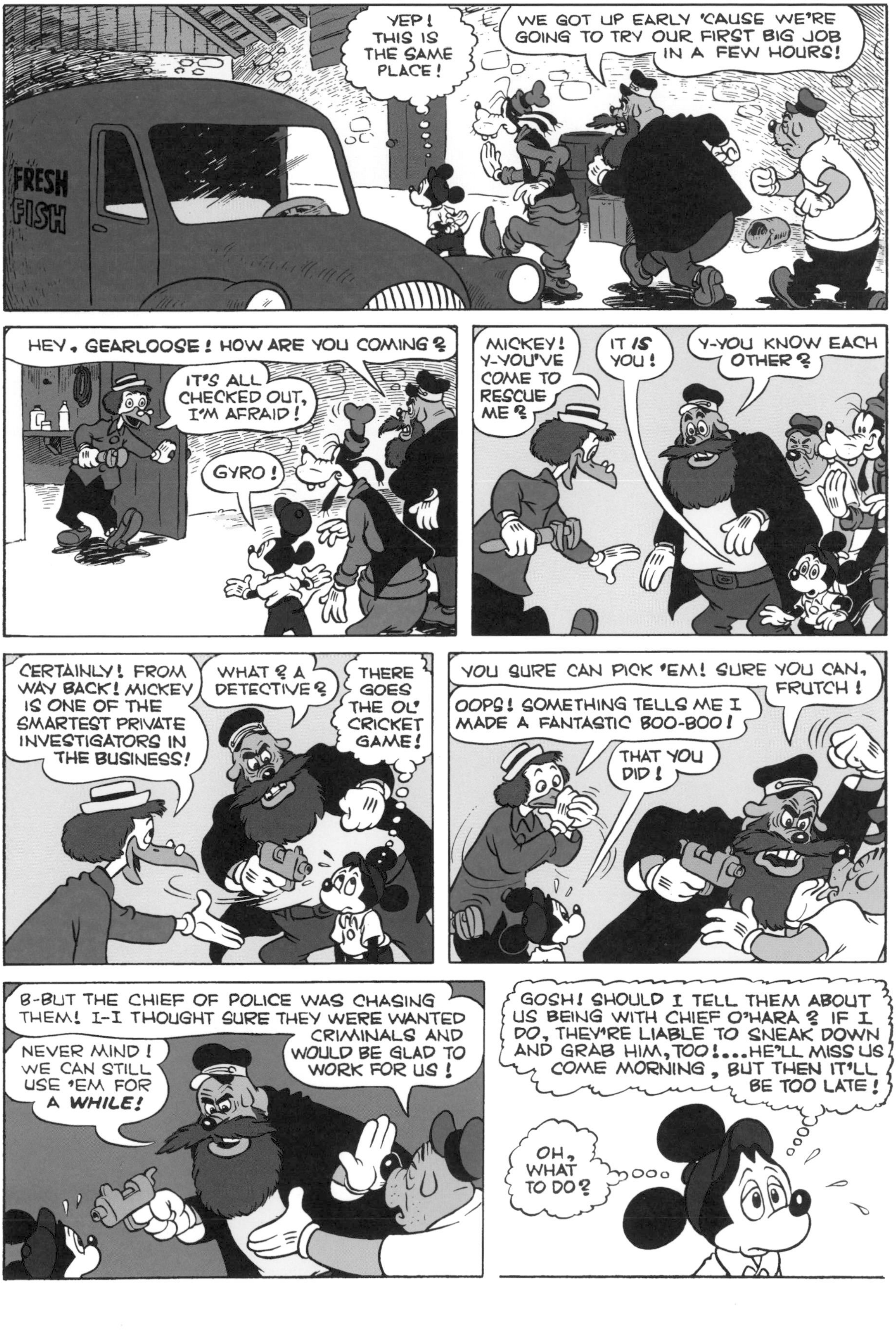
YEP! THIS IS THE SAME PLACE!
WE GOT UP EARLY 'CAUSE WE'RE GOING TO TRY OUR FIRST BIG JOB IN A FEW HOURS!
FRESH FISH
HEY, GEARLOOSE! HOW ARE YOU COMING?
IT'S ALL CHECKED OUT, I'M AFRAID!
GYRO!
MICKEY! Y-YOU'VE COME TO RESCUE ME?
IT IS YOU!
Y-YOU KNOW EACH OTHER?
CERTAINLY! FROM WAY BACK! MICKEY IS ONE OF THE SMARTEST PRIVATE INVESTIGATORS IN THE BUSINESS!
WHAT? A DETECTIVE?
THERE GOES THE OL' CRICKET GAME!
YOU SURE CAN PICK 'EM! SURE YOU CAN, FRUTCH!
OOPS! SOMETHING TELLS ME I MADE A FANTASTIC BOO-BOO!
THAT YOU DID!
B-BUT THE CHIEF OF POLICE WAS CHASING THEM! I-I THOUGHT SURE THEY WERE WANTED CRIMINALS AND WOULD BE GLAD TO WORK FOR US!
NEVER MIND! WE CAN STILL USE 'EM FOR A WHILE!
GOSH! SHOULD I TELL THEM ABOUT US BEING WITH CHIEF O'HARA? IF I DO, THEY'RE LIABLE TO SNEAK DOWN AND GRAB HIM, TOO!...HE'LL MISS US COME MORNING, BUT THEN IT'LL BE TOO LATE!
OH, WHAT TO DO?

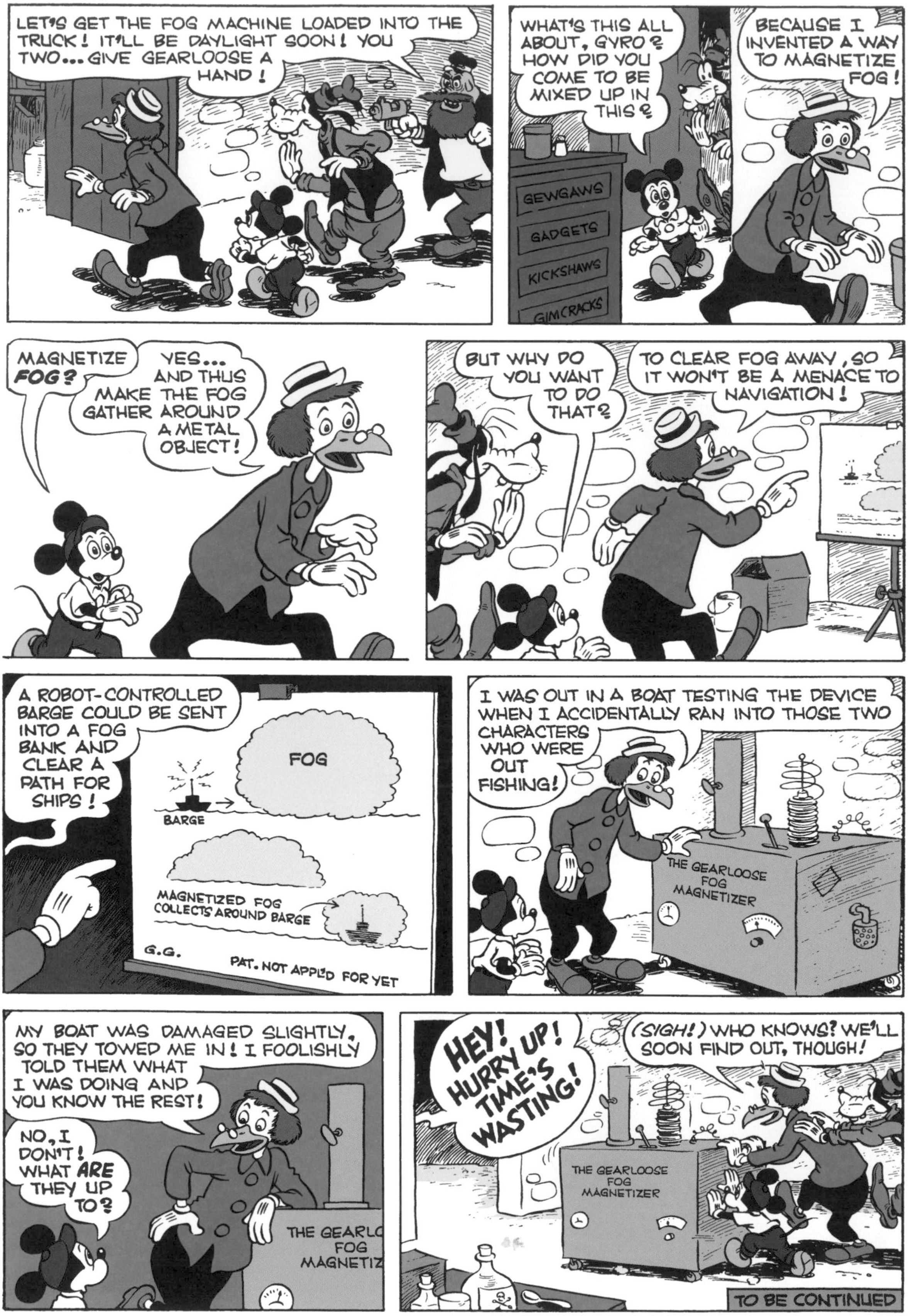

LET'S GET THE FOG MACHINE LOADED INTO THE TRUCK! IT'LL BE DAYLIGHT SOON! YOU TWO... GIVE GEARLOOSE A HAND!
WHAT'S THIS ALL ABOUT, GYRO? HOW DID YOU COME TO BE MIXED UP IN THIS?
BECAUSE I INVENTED A WAY TO MAGNETIZE FOG!
GEWGAWS
GADGETS
KICKSHAWS
GIMCRACKS
MAGNETIZE FOG?
YES... AND THUS MAKE THE FOG GATHER AROUND A METAL OBJECT!
BUT WHY DO YOU WANT TO DO THAT?
TO CLEAR FOG AWAY, SO IT WON'T BE A MENACE TO NAVIGATION!
A ROBOT-CONTROLLED BARGE COULD BE SENT INTO A FOG BANK AND CLEAR A PATH FOR SHIPS!
FOG
BARGE
MAGNETIZED FOG COLLECTS AROUND BARGE
G.G.
PAT. NOT APPL'D FOR YET
I WAS OUT IN A BOAT TESTING THE DEVICE WHEN I ACCIDENTALLY RAN INTO THOSE TWO CHARACTERS WHO WERE OUT FISHING!
THE GEARLOOSE FOG MAGNETIZER
MY BOAT WAS DAMAGED SLIGHTLY, SO THEY TOWED ME IN! I FOOLISHLY TOLD THEM WHAT I WAS DOING AND YOU KNOW THE REST!
NO, I DON'T! WHAT ARE THEY UP TO?
THE GEARLO FOG MAGNETIZ
HEY! HURRY UP! TIME'S WASTING!
(SIGH!) WHO KNOWS? WE'LL SOON FIND OUT, THOUGH!
THE GEARLOOSE FOG MAGNETIZER
TO BE CONTINUED

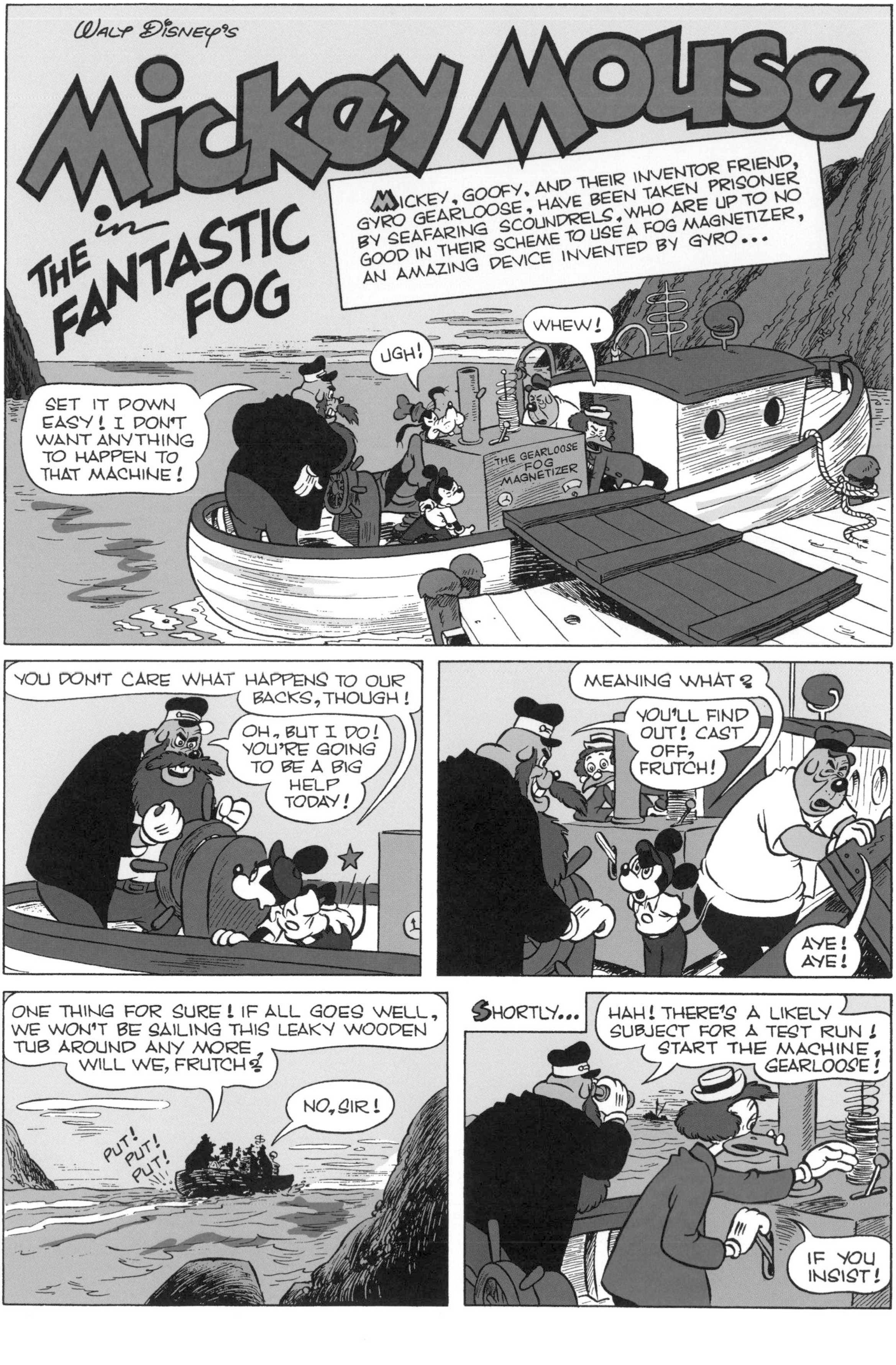

WALT DISNEY'S
MICKEY MOUSE
in
THE FANTASTIC FOG
MICKEY, GOOFY, AND THEIR INVENTOR FRIEND, GYRO GEARLOOSE, HAVE BEEN TAKEN PRISONER BY SEAFARING SCOUNDRELS, WHO ARE UP TO NO GOOD IN THEIR SCHEME TO USE A FOG MAGNETIZER, AN AMAZING DEVICE INVENTED BY GYRO...
SET IT DOWN EASY! I DON'T WANT ANYTHING TO HAPPEN TO THAT MACHINE!
UGH!
WHEW!
THE GEARLOOSE FOG MAGNETIZER
YOU DON'T CARE WHAT HAPPENS TO OUR BACKS, THOUGH!
OH, BUT I DO! YOU'RE GOING TO BE A BIG HELP TODAY!
MEANING WHAT?
YOU'LL FIND OUT! CAST OFF, FRUTCH!
AYE! AYE!
ONE THING FOR SURE! IF ALL GOES WELL, WE WON'T BE SAILING THIS LEAKY WOODEN TUB AROUND ANY MORE, WILL WE, FRUTCH?
NO, SIR!
PUT! PUT! PUT!
SHORTLY...
HAH! THERE'S A LIKELY SUBJECT FOR A TEST RUN! START THE MACHINE, GEARLOOSE!
IF YOU INSIST!

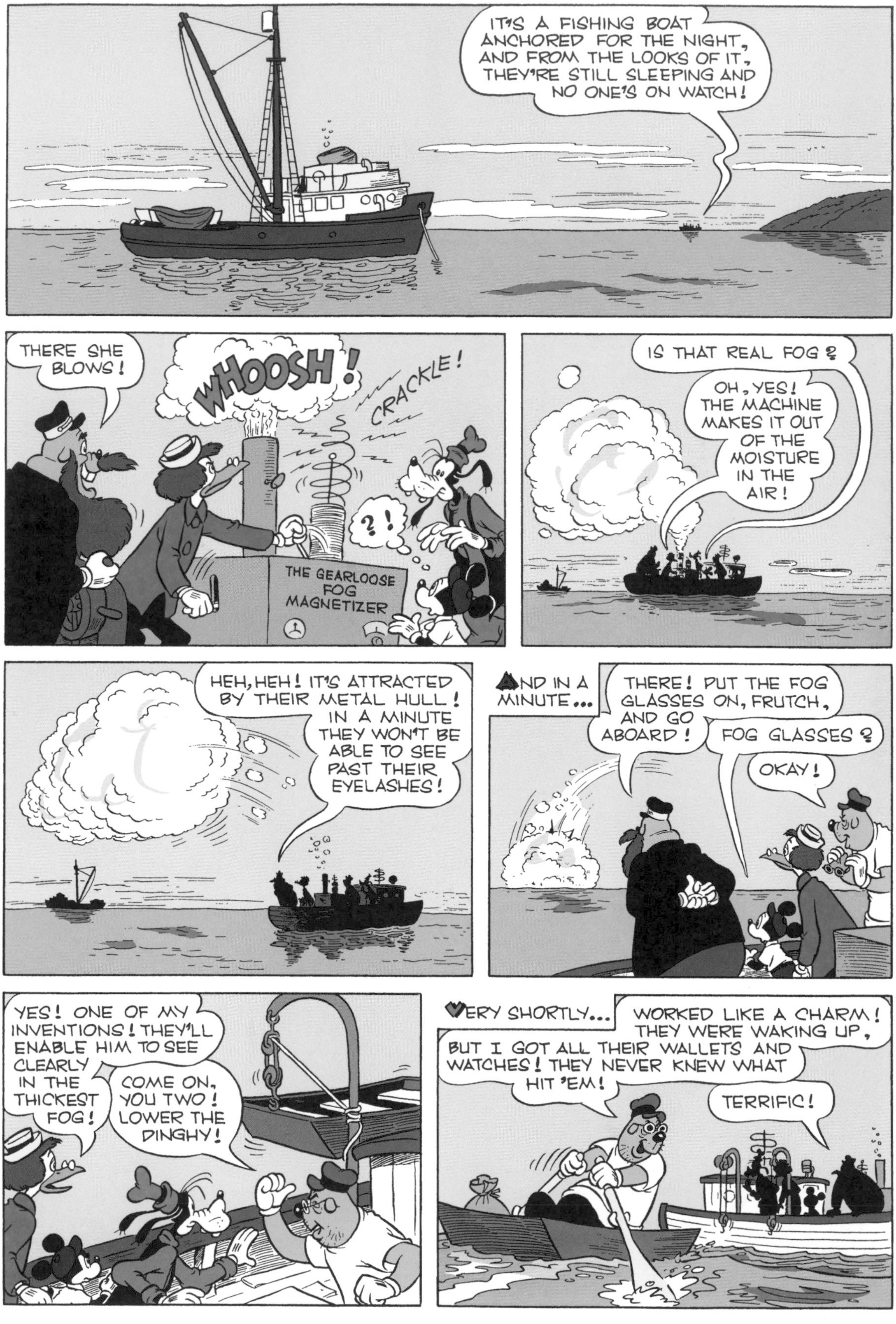
IT'S A FISHING BOAT ANCHORED FOR THE NIGHT, AND FROM THE LOOKS OF IT, THEY'RE STILL SLEEPING AND NO ONE'S ON WATCH!
THERE SHE BLOWS!
WHOOSH!
CRACKLE!
?!
THE GEARLOOSE FOG MAGNETIZER
IS THAT REAL FOG?
OH, YES! THE MACHINE MAKES IT OUT OF THE MOISTURE IN THE AIR!
HEH, HEH! IT'S ATTRACTED BY THEIR METAL HULL! IN A MINUTE THEY WON'T BE ABLE TO SEE PAST THEIR EYELASHES!
AND IN A MINUTE...
THERE! PUT THE FOG GLASSES ON, FRUTCH, AND GO ABOARD!
FOG GLASSES?
OKAY!
YES! ONE OF MY INVENTIONS! THEY'LL ENABLE HIM TO SEE CLEARLY IN THE THICKEST FOG!
COME ON, YOU TWO! LOWER THE DINGHY!
VERY SHORTLY...
WORKED LIKE A CHARM! THEY WERE WAKING UP, BUT I GOT ALL THEIR WALLETS AND WATCHES! THEY NEVER KNEW WHAT HIT 'EM!
TERRIFIC!

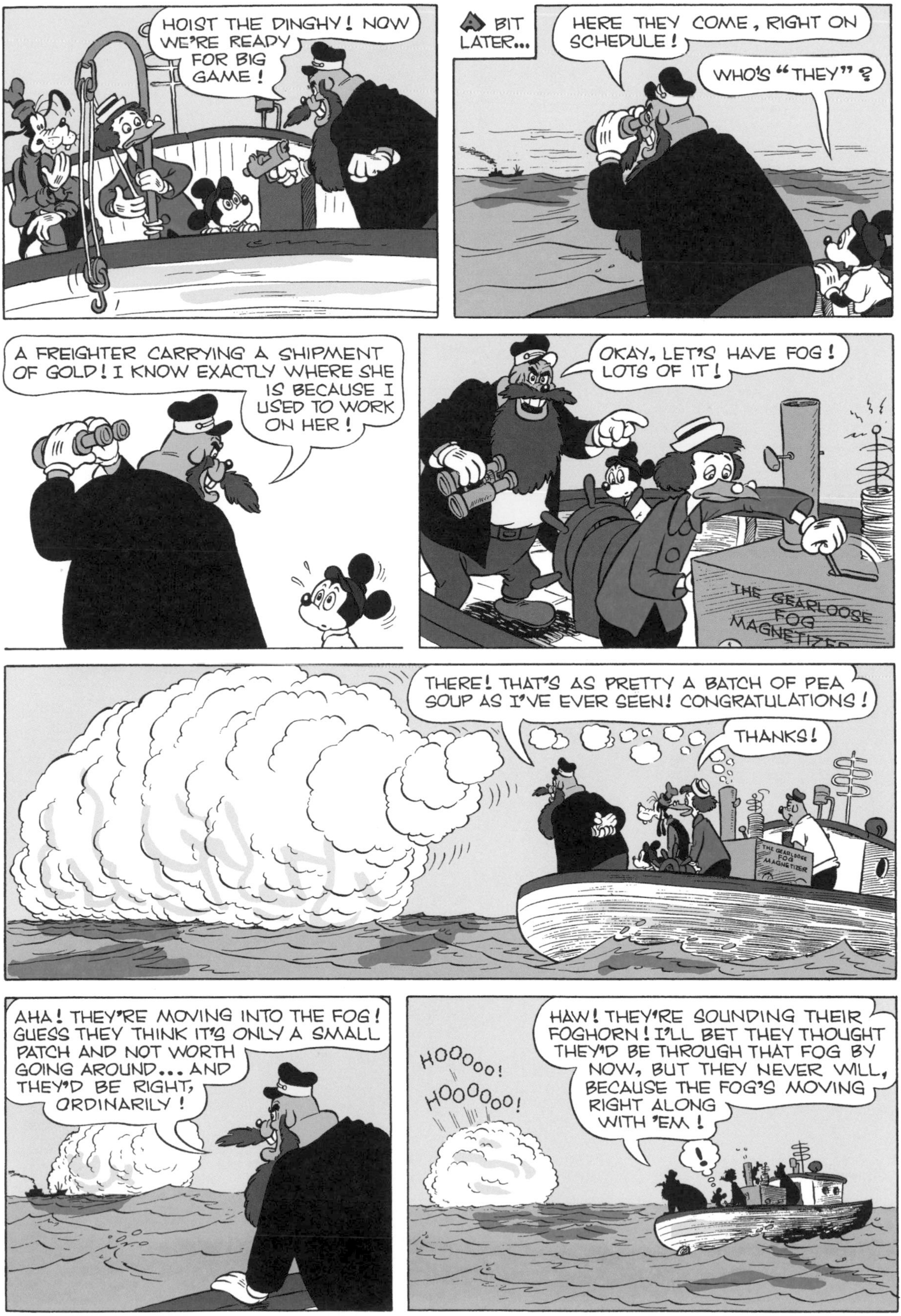
HOIST THE DINGHY! NOW WE'RE READY FOR BIG GAME!
A BIT LATER...
HERE THEY COME, RIGHT ON SCHEDULE!
WHO'S "THEY"?
A FREIGHTER CARRYING A SHIPMENT OF GOLD! I KNOW EXACTLY WHERE SHE IS BECAUSE I USED TO WORK ON HER!
OKAY, LET'S HAVE FOG! LOTS OF IT!
THE GEARLOOSE FOG MAGNETIZER
THERE! THAT'S AS PRETTY A BATCH OF PEA SOUP AS I'VE EVER SEEN! CONGRATULATIONS!
THANKS!
THE GEARLOOSE FOG MAGNETIZER
AHA! THEY'RE MOVING INTO THE FOG! GUESS THEY THINK IT'S ONLY A SMALL PATCH AND NOT WORTH GOING AROUND... AND THEY'D BE RIGHT, ORDINARILY!
HOOOooo!
HOOOOooo!
HAW! THEY'RE SOUNDING THEIR FOGHORN! I'LL BET THEY THOUGHT THEY'D BE THROUGH THAT FOG BY NOW, BUT THEY NEVER WILL, BECAUSE THE FOG'S MOVING RIGHT ALONG WITH 'EM!
!

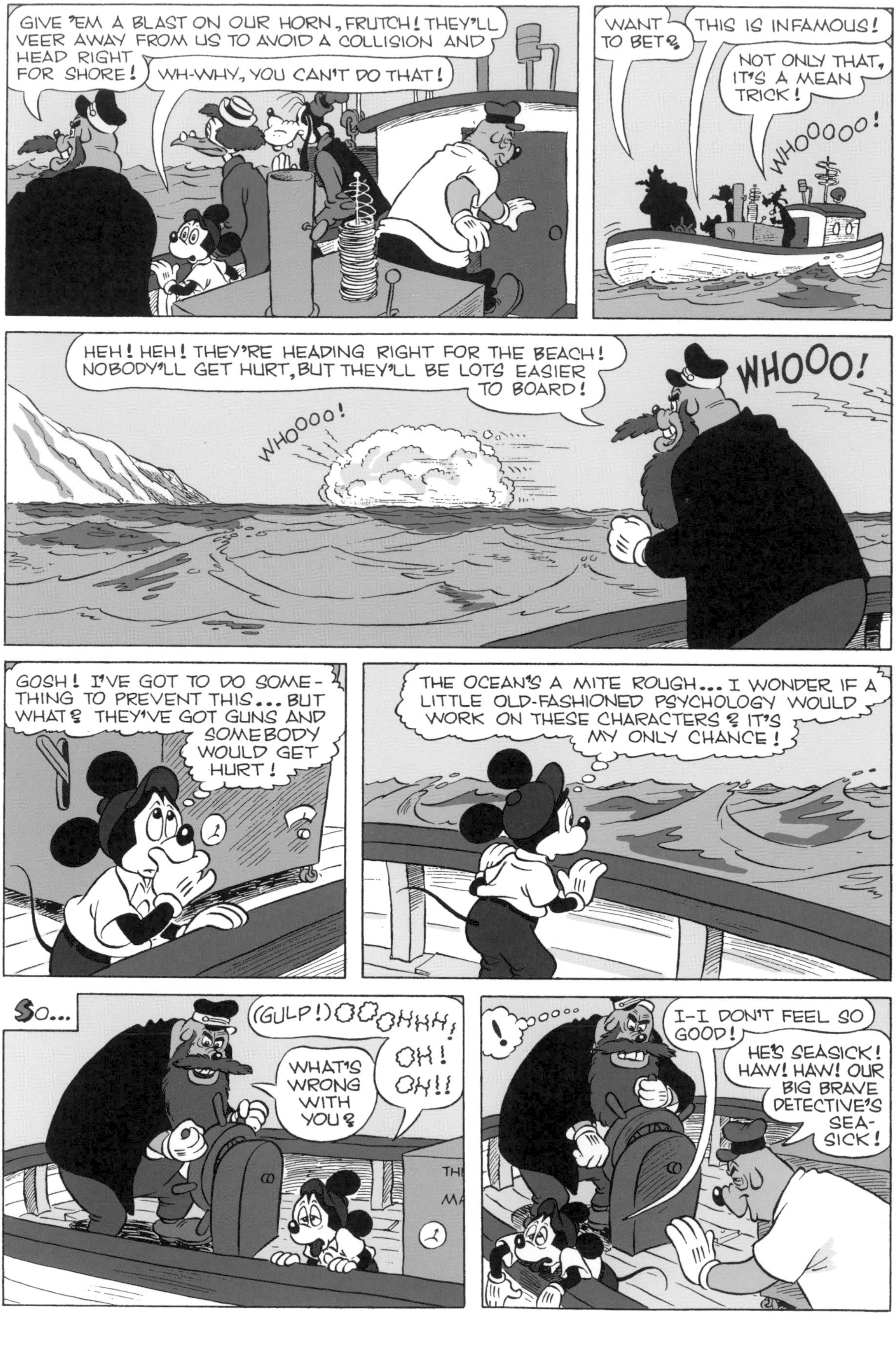
GIVE 'EM A BLAST ON OUR HORN, FRUTCH! THEY'LL VEER AWAY FROM US TO AVOID A COLLISION AND HEAD RIGHT FOR SHORE!
WH-WHY, YOU CAN'T DO THAT!
WANT TO BET?
THIS IS INFAMOUS!
NOT ONLY THAT, IT'S A MEAN TRICK!
WHOOOOO!
HEH! HEH! THEY'RE HEADING RIGHT FOR THE BEACH! NOBODY'LL GET HURT, BUT THEY'LL BE LOTS EASIER TO BOARD!
WHOOO!
WHOOOO!
GOSH! I'VE GOT TO DO SOMETHING TO PREVENT THIS... BUT WHAT? THEY'VE GOT GUNS AND SOMEBODY WOULD GET HURT!
THE OCEAN'S A MITE ROUGH... I WONDER IF A LITTLE OLD-FASHIONED PSYCHOLOGY WOULD WORK ON THESE CHARACTERS? IT'S MY ONLY CHANCE!
SO...
(GULP!) OOOHHH!
OH! OH!!
WHAT'S WRONG WITH YOU?
!
I-I DON'T FEEL SO GOOD!
HE'S SEASICK! HAW! HAW! OUR BIG BRAVE DETECTIVE'S SEA-SICK!

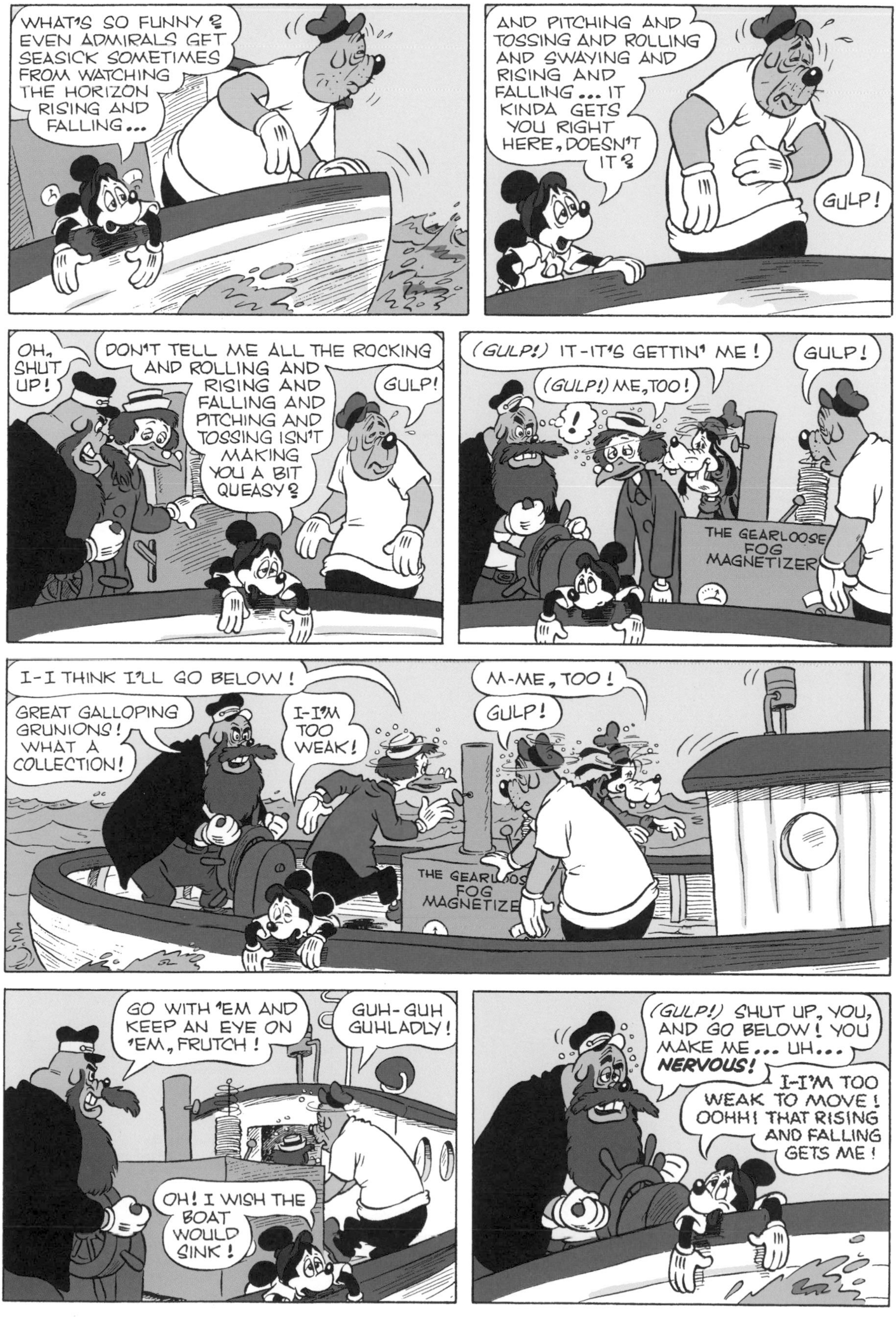
WHAT'S SO FUNNY? EVEN ADMIRALS GET SEASICK SOMETIMES FROM WATCHING THE HORIZON RISING AND FALLING...
AND PITCHING AND TOSSING AND ROLLING AND SWAYING AND RISING AND FALLING... IT KINDA GETS YOU RIGHT HERE, DOESN'T IT?
GULP!
OH, SHUT UP!
DON'T TELL ME ALL THE ROCKING AND ROLLING AND RISING AND FALLING AND PITCHING AND TOSSING ISN'T MAKING YOU A BIT QUEASY?
GULP!
(GULP!) IT-IT'S GETTIN' ME!
(GULP!) ME, TOO!
!
GULP!
THE GEARLOOSE FOG MAGNETIZER
I-I THINK I'LL GO BELOW!
GREAT GALLOPING GRUNIONS! WHAT A COLLECTION!
I-I'M TOO WEAK!
M-ME, TOO!
GULP!
THE GEARLOOS FOG MAGNETIZE
GO WITH 'EM AND KEEP AN EYE ON 'EM, FRUTCH!
GUH-GUH GUHLADLY!
OH! I WISH THE BOAT WOULD SINK!
(GULP!) SHUT UP, YOU, AND GO BELOW! YOU MAKE ME... UH... NERVOUS!
I-I'M TOO WEAK TO MOVE! OOHH! THAT RISING AND FALLING GETS ME!

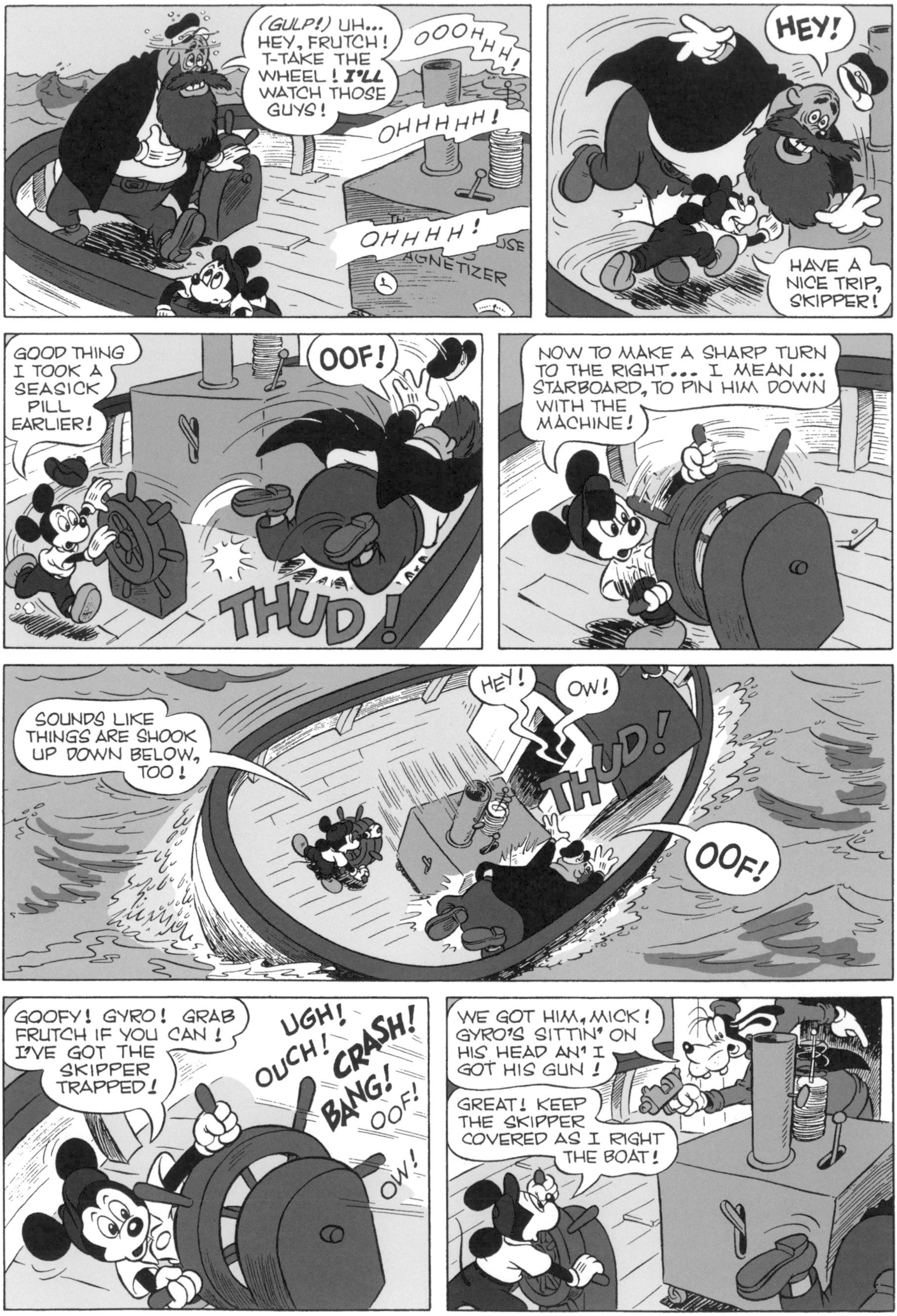
(GULP!) UH... HEY, FRUTCH! T-TAKE THE WHEEL! I'LL WATCH THOSE GUYS!
OOOHHH!
OHHHHH!
OHHHH!
AGNETIZER
HEY!
HAVE A NICE TRIP, SKIPPER!
GOOD THING I TOOK A SEASICK PILL EARLIER!
OOF!
THUD!
NOW TO MAKE A SHARP TURN TO THE RIGHT... I MEAN... STARBOARD, TO PIN HIM DOWN WITH THE MACHINE!
SOUNDS LIKE THINGS ARE SHOOK UP DOWN BELOW, TOO!
HEY!
OW!
THUD!
OOF!
GOOFY! GYRO! GRAB FRUTCH IF YOU CAN! I'VE GOT THE SKIPPER TRAPPED!
UGH!
OUCH!
CRASH!
BANG!
OOF!
OW!
WE GOT HIM, MICK! GYRO'S SITTIN' ON HIS HEAD AN' I GOT HIS GUN!
GREAT! KEEP THE SKIPPER COVERED AS I RIGHT THE BOAT!

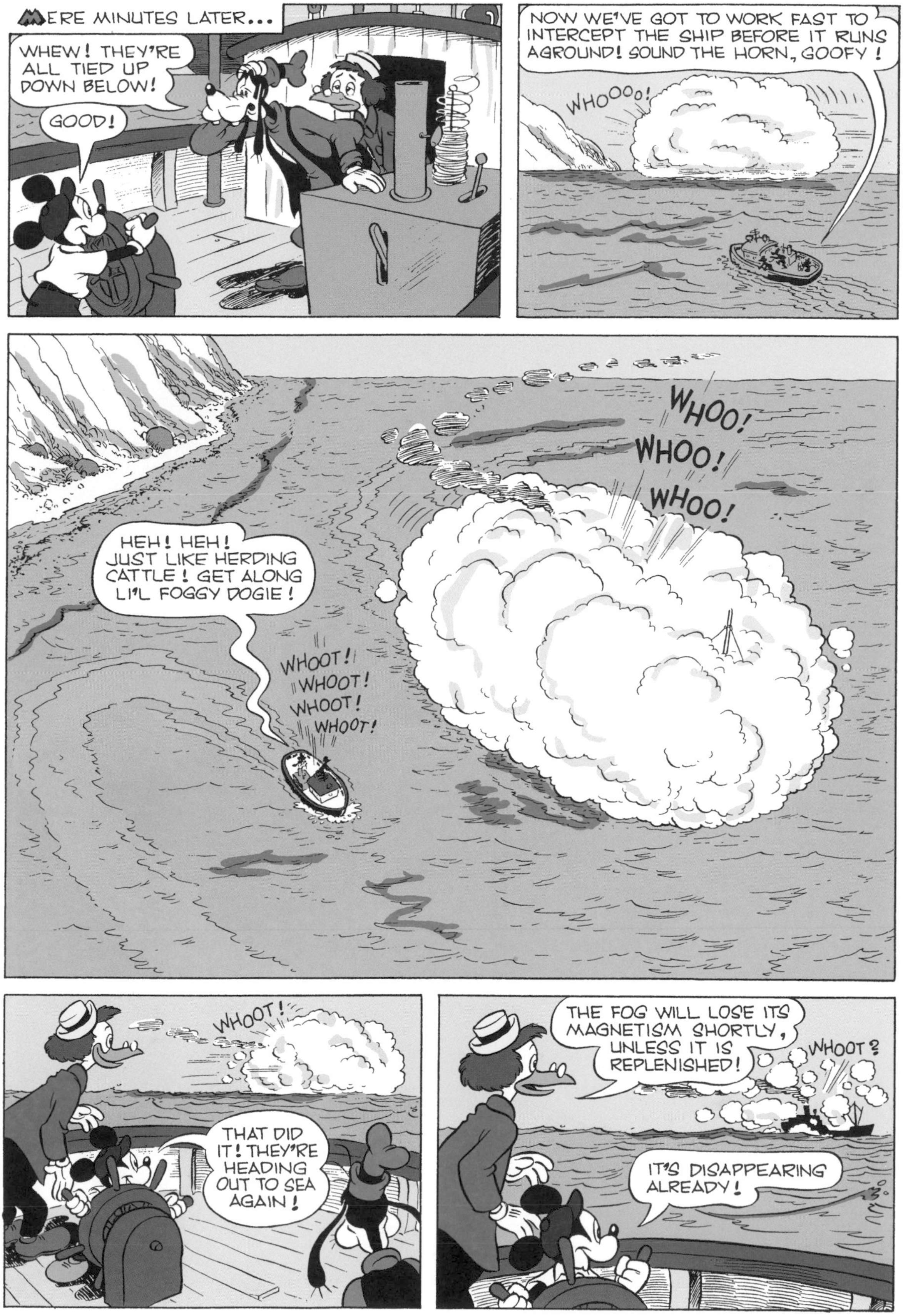
MERE MINUTES LATER...
WHEW! THEY'RE ALL TIED UP DOWN BELOW!
GOOD!
NOW WE'VE GOT TO WORK FAST TO INTERCEPT THE SHIP BEFORE IT RUNS AGROUND! SOUND THE HORN, GOOFY!
WHOOOO!
WHOO!
WHOO!
WHOO!
HEH! HEH! JUST LIKE HERDING CATTLE! GET ALONG LI'L FOGGY DOGIE!
WHOOT!
WHOOT!
WHOOT!
WHOOT!
WHOOT!
THAT DID IT! THEY'RE HEADING OUT TO SEA AGAIN!
THE FOG WILL LOSE ITS MAGNETISM SHORTLY, UNLESS IT IS REPLENISHED!
WHOOT?
IT'S DISAPPEARING ALREADY!

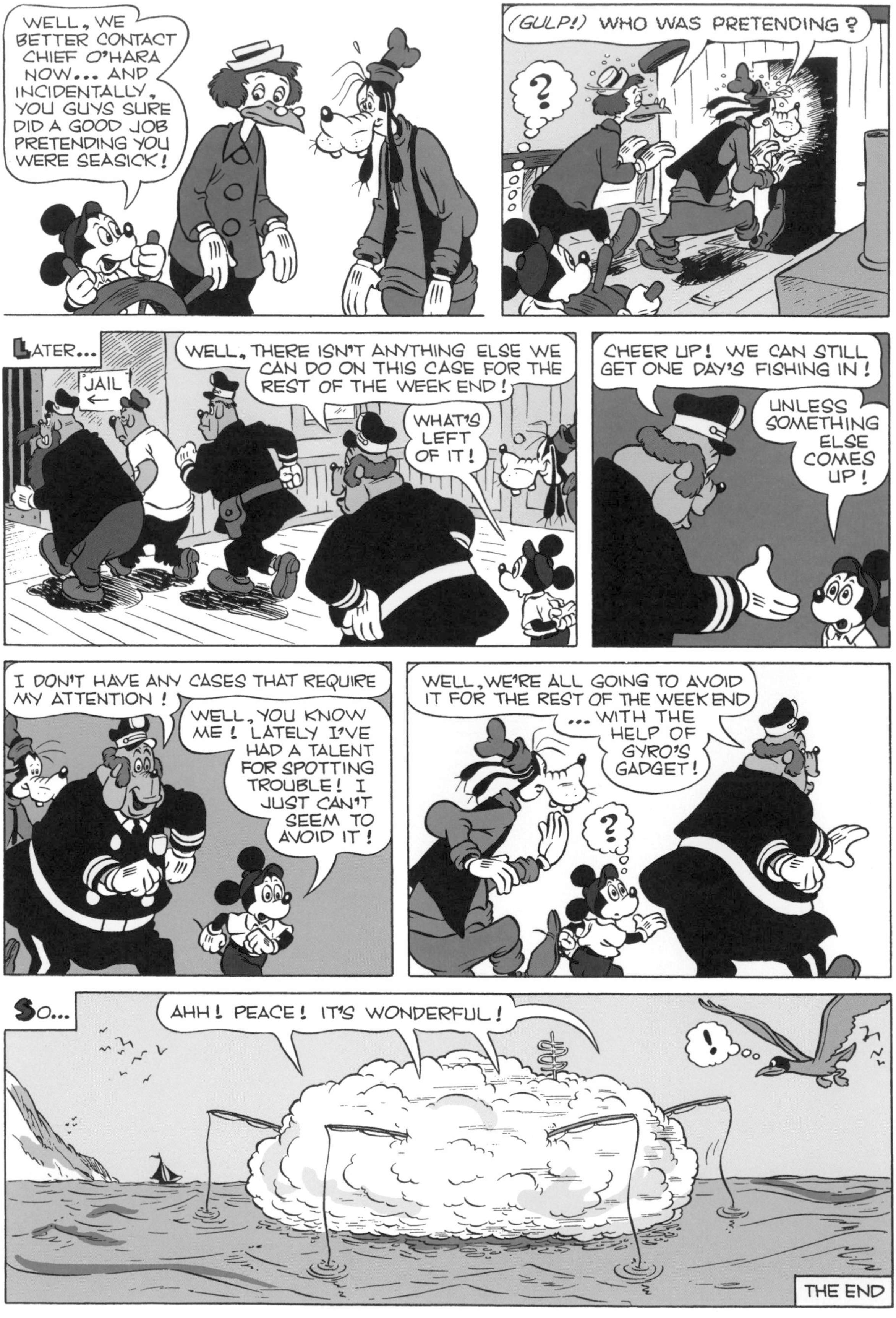

WELL, WE BETTER CONTACT CHIEF O'HARA NOW... AND INCIDENTALLY, YOU GUYS SURE DID A GOOD JOB PRETENDING YOU WERE SEASICK!
(GULP!) WHO WAS PRETENDING?
?
LATER...
JAIL
WELL, THERE ISN'T ANYTHING ELSE WE CAN DO ON THIS CASE FOR THE REST OF THE WEEK END!
WHAT'S LEFT OF IT!
CHEER UP! WE CAN STILL GET ONE DAY'S FISHING IN!
UNLESS SOMETHING ELSE COMES UP!
I DON'T HAVE ANY CASES THAT REQUIRE MY ATTENTION!
WELL, YOU KNOW ME! LATELY I'VE HAD A TALENT FOR SPOTTING TROUBLE! I JUST CAN'T SEEM TO AVOID IT!
WELL, WE'RE ALL GOING TO AVOID IT FOR THE REST OF THE WEEK END ...WITH THE HELP OF GYRO'S GADGET!
?
SO...
AHH! PEACE! IT'S WONDERFUL!
!
THE END

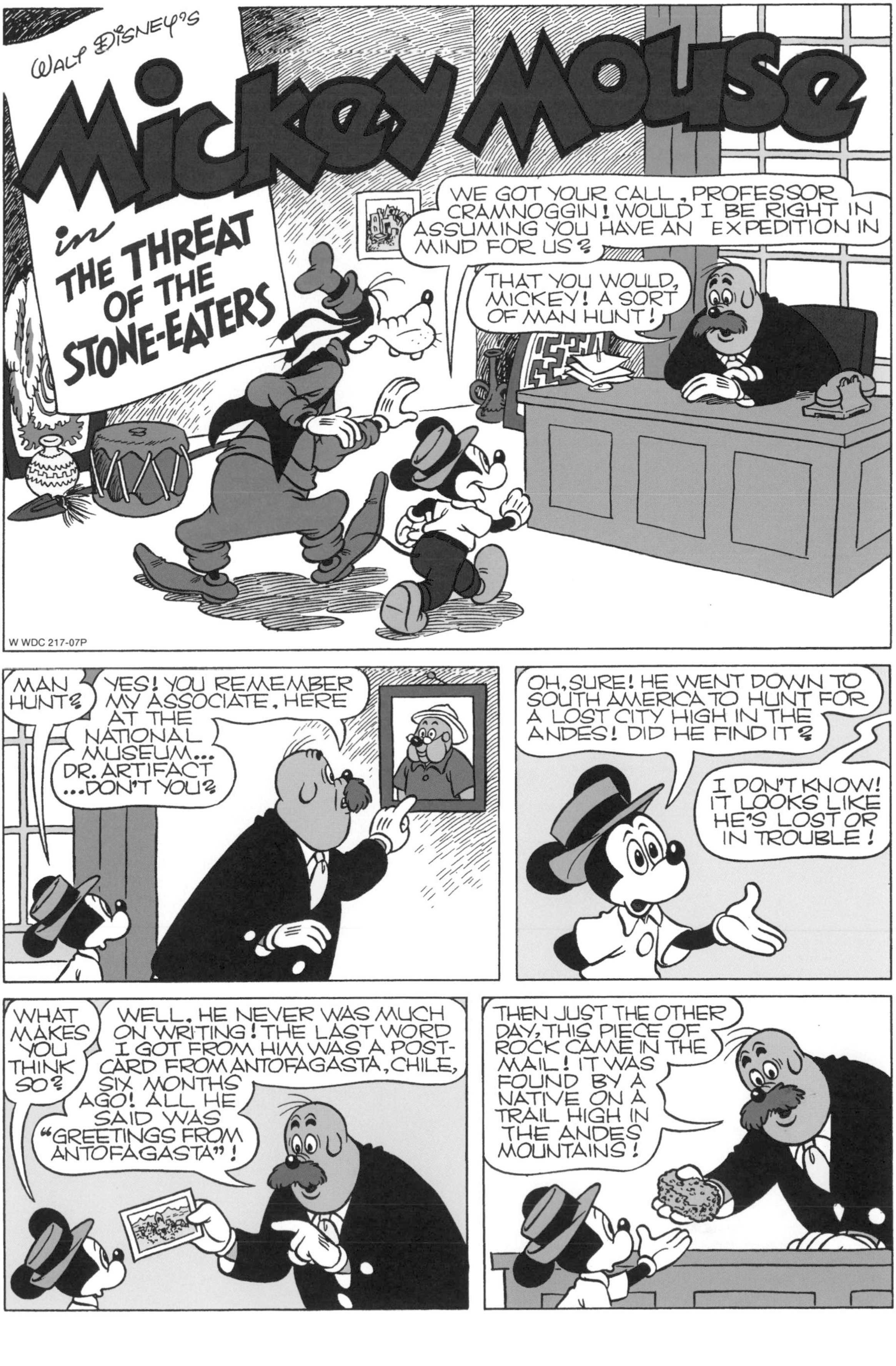
WALT DISNEY'S
MICKEY MOUSE
in
THE THREAT OF THE STONE-EATERS
WE GOT YOUR CALL, PROFESSOR CRAMNOGGIN! WOULD I BE RIGHT IN ASSUMING YOU HAVE AN EXPEDITION IN MIND FOR US?
THAT YOU WOULD, MICKEY! A SORT OF MAN HUNT!
W WDC 217-07P
MAN HUNT?
YES! YOU REMEMBER MY ASSOCIATE, HERE AT THE NATIONAL MUSEUM... DR. ARTIFACT ...DON'T YOU?
OH, SURE! HE WENT DOWN TO SOUTH AMERICA TO HUNT FOR A LOST CITY HIGH IN THE ANDES! DID HE FIND IT?
I DON'T KNOW! IT LOOKS LIKE HE'S LOST OR IN TROUBLE!
WHAT MAKES YOU THINK SO?
WELL, HE NEVER WAS MUCH ON WRITING! THE LAST WORD I GOT FROM HIM WAS A POST-CARD FROM ANTOFAGASTA, CHILE, SIX MONTHS AGO! ALL HE SAID WAS "GREETINGS FROM ANTOFAGASTA"!
THEN JUST THE OTHER DAY, THIS PIECE OF ROCK CAME IN THE MAIL! IT WAS FOUND BY A NATIVE ON A TRAIL HIGH IN THE ANDES MOUNTAINS!

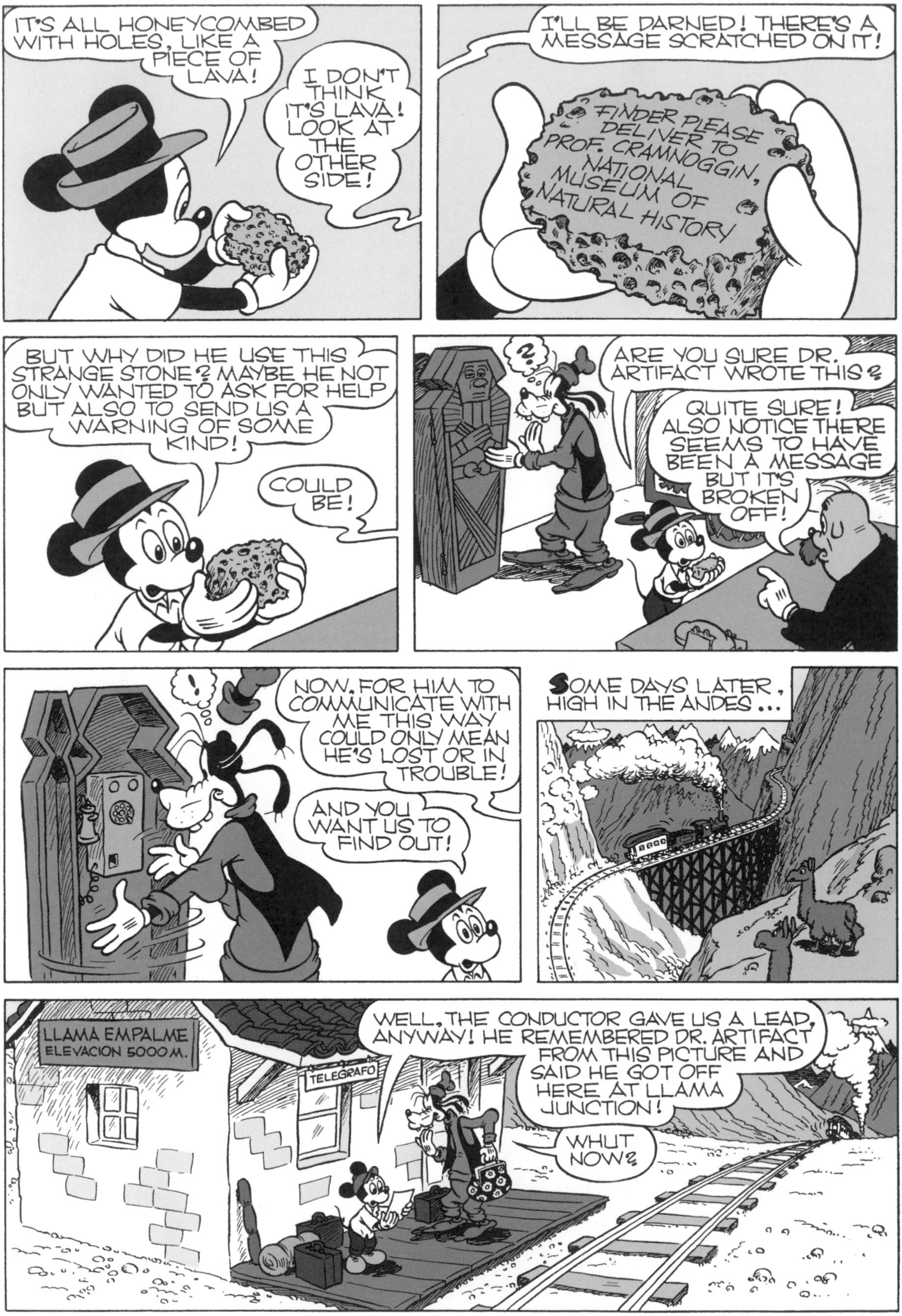
IT'S ALL HONEYCOMBED WITH HOLES, LIKE A PIECE OF LAVA!
I DON'T THINK IT'S LAVA! LOOK AT THE OTHER SIDE!
I'LL BE DARNED! THERE'S A MESSAGE SCRATCHED ON IT!
FINDER PLEASE DELIVER TO PROF. CRAMNOGGIN, NATIONAL MUSEUM OF NATURAL HISTORY
BUT WHY DID HE USE THIS STRANGE STONE? MAYBE HE NOT ONLY WANTED TO ASK FOR HELP BUT ALSO TO SEND US A WARNING OF SOME KIND!
COULD BE!
?
ARE YOU SURE DR. ARTIFACT WROTE THIS?
QUITE SURE! ALSO NOTICE THERE SEEMS TO HAVE BEEN A MESSAGE BUT IT'S BROKEN OFF!
!
NOW, FOR HIM TO COMMUNICATE WITH ME THIS WAY COULD ONLY MEAN HE'S LOST OR IN TROUBLE!
AND YOU WANT US TO FIND OUT!
SOME DAYS LATER, HIGH IN THE ANDES...
LLAMA EMPALME
ELEVACION 5000 M.
TELEGRAFO
WELL, THE CONDUCTOR GAVE US A LEAD, ANYWAY! HE REMEMBERED DR. ARTIFACT FROM THIS PICTURE AND SAID HE GOT OFF HERE AT LLAMA JUNCTION!
WHUT NOW?

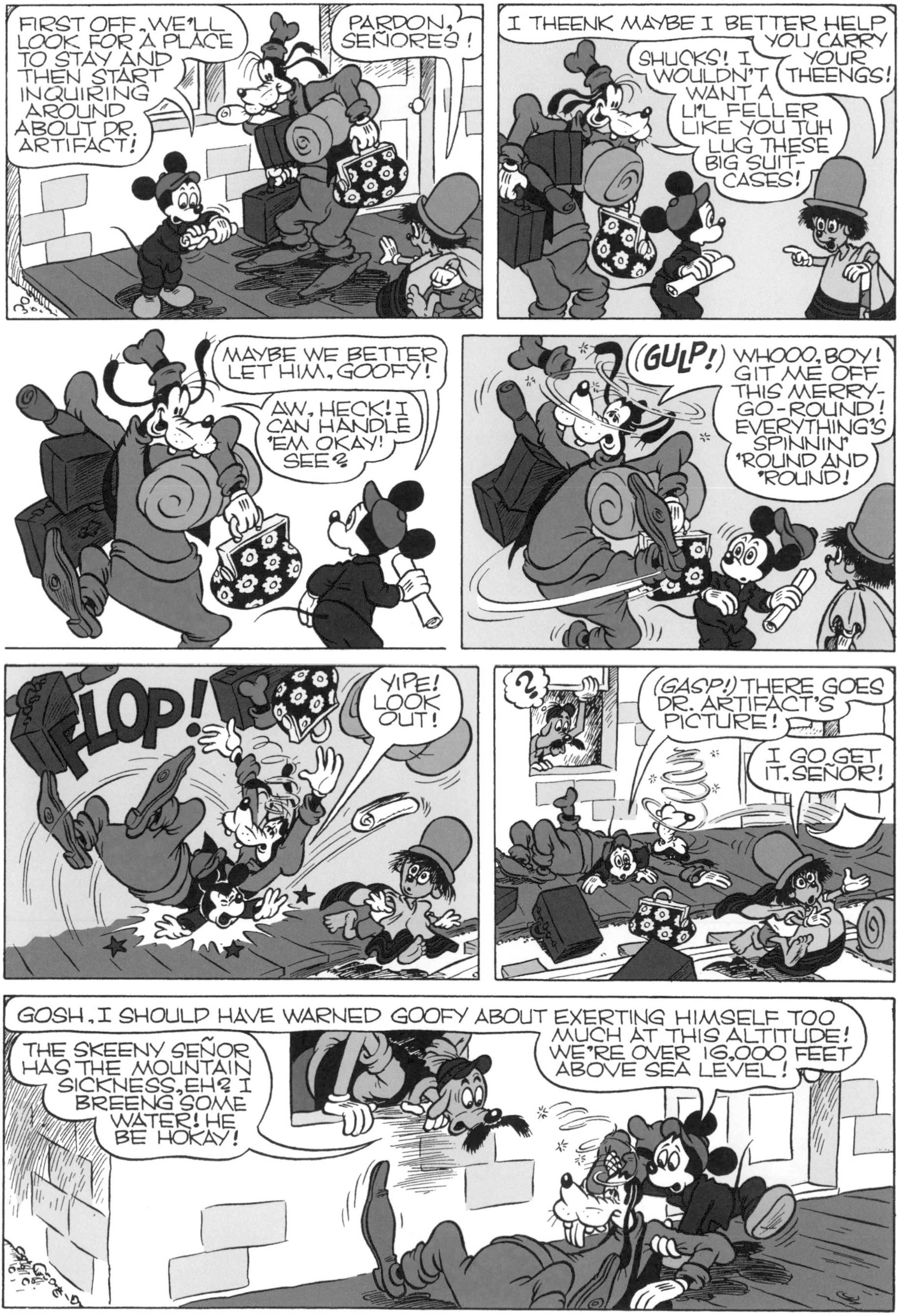
FIRST OFF, WE'LL LOOK FOR A PLACE TO STAY AND THEN START INQUIRING AROUND ABOUT DR. ARTIFACT!
PARDON, SEÑORES!
I THEENK MAYBE I BETTER HELP YOU CARRY YOUR THEENGS!
SHUCKS! I WOULDN'T WANT A LI'L FELLER LIKE YOU TUH LUG THESE BIG SUIT-CASES!
MAYBE WE BETTER LET HIM, GOOFY!
AW, HECK! I CAN HANDLE 'EM OKAY! SEE?
(GULP!)
WHOOO, BOY! GIT ME OFF THIS MERRY-GO-ROUND! EVERYTHING'S SPINNIN' 'ROUND AND 'ROUND!
FLOP!
YIPE! LOOK OUT!
?
(GASP!) THERE GOES DR. ARTIFACT'S PICTURE!
I GO GET IT, SEÑOR!
GOSH, I SHOULD HAVE WARNED GOOFY ABOUT EXERTING HIMSELF TOO MUCH AT THIS ALTITUDE! WE'RE OVER 16,000 FEET ABOVE SEA LEVEL!
THE SKEENY SEÑOR HAS THE MOUNTAIN SICKNESS, EH? I BREENG SOME WATER! HE BE HOKAY!

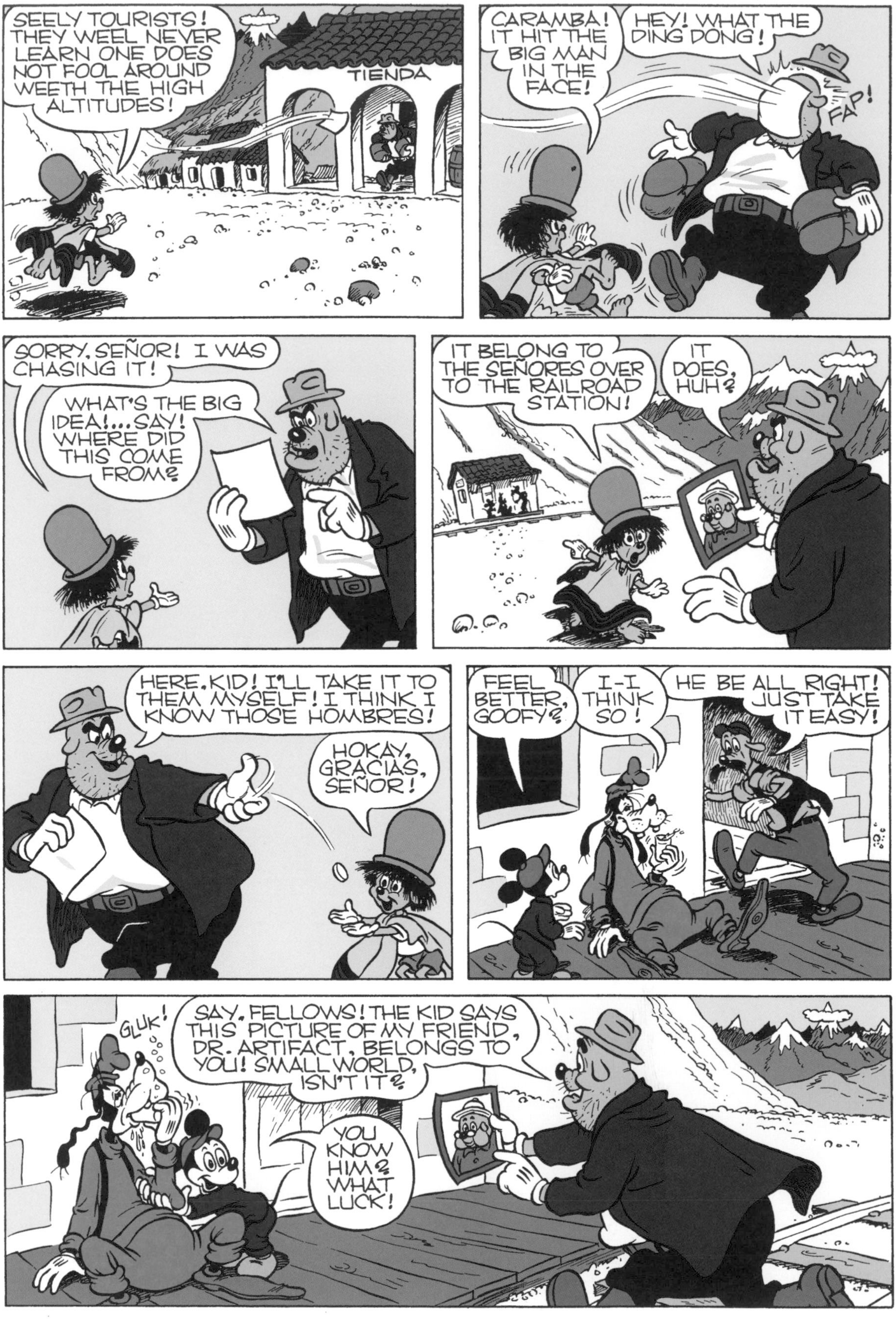
SEELY TOURISTS! THEY WEEL NEVER LEARN ONE DOES NOT FOOL AROUND WEETH THE HIGH ALTITUDES!
TIENDA
CARAMBA! IT HIT THE BIG MAN IN THE FACE!
HEY! WHAT THE DING DONG!
FAP!
SORRY, SEÑOR! I WAS CHASING IT!
WHAT'S THE BIG IDEA!...SAY! WHERE DID THIS COME FROM?
IT BELONG TO THE SEÑORES OVER TO THE RAILROAD STATION!
IT DOES, HUH?
HERE, KID! I'LL TAKE IT TO THEM MYSELF! I THINK I KNOW THOSE HOMBRES!
HOKAY, GRACIAS, SEÑOR!
FEEL BETTER, GOOFY?
I-I THINK SO!
HE BE ALL RIGHT! JUST TAKE IT EASY!
GLUK!
SAY, FELLOWS! THE KID SAYS THIS PICTURE OF MY FRIEND, DR. ARTIFACT, BELONGS TO YOU! SMALL WORLD, ISN'T IT?
YOU KNOW HIM? WHAT LUCK!

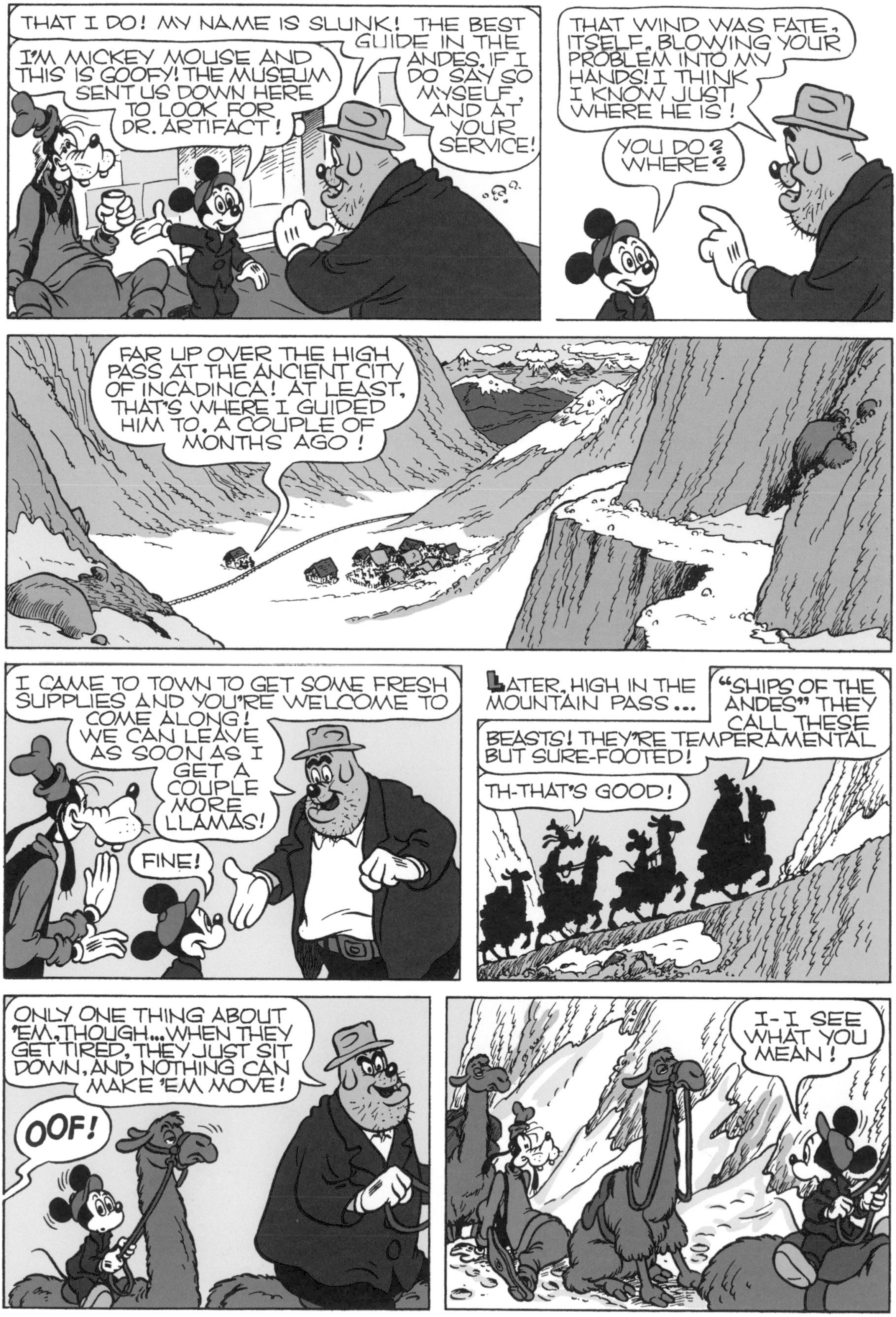
THAT I DO! MY NAME IS SLUNK! THE BEST GUIDE IN THE ANDES, IF I DO SAY SO MYSELF, AND AT YOUR SERVICE!
I'M MICKEY MOUSE AND THIS IS GOOFY! THE MUSEUM SENT US DOWN HERE TO LOOK FOR DR. ARTIFACT!
THAT WIND WAS FATE, ITSELF, BLOWING YOUR PROBLEM INTO MY HANDS! I THINK I KNOW JUST WHERE HE IS!
YOU DO?? WHERE??
FAR UP OVER THE HIGH PASS AT THE ANCIENT CITY OF INCADINCA! AT LEAST, THAT'S WHERE I GUIDED HIM TO. A COUPLE OF MONTHS AGO!
I CAME TO TOWN TO GET SOME FRESH SUPPLIES AND YOU'RE WELCOME TO COME ALONG! WE CAN LEAVE AS SOON AS I GET A COUPLE MORE LLAMAS!
FINE!
LATER, HIGH IN THE MOUNTAIN PASS...
"SHIPS OF THE ANDES" THEY CALL THESE BEASTS! THEY'RE TEMPERAMENTAL BUT SURE-FOOTED!
TH-THAT'S GOOD!
ONLY ONE THING ABOUT 'EM, THOUGH... WHEN THEY GET TIRED, THEY JUST SIT DOWN, AND NOTHING CAN MAKE 'EM MOVE!
OOF!
I-I SEE WHAT YOU MEAN!

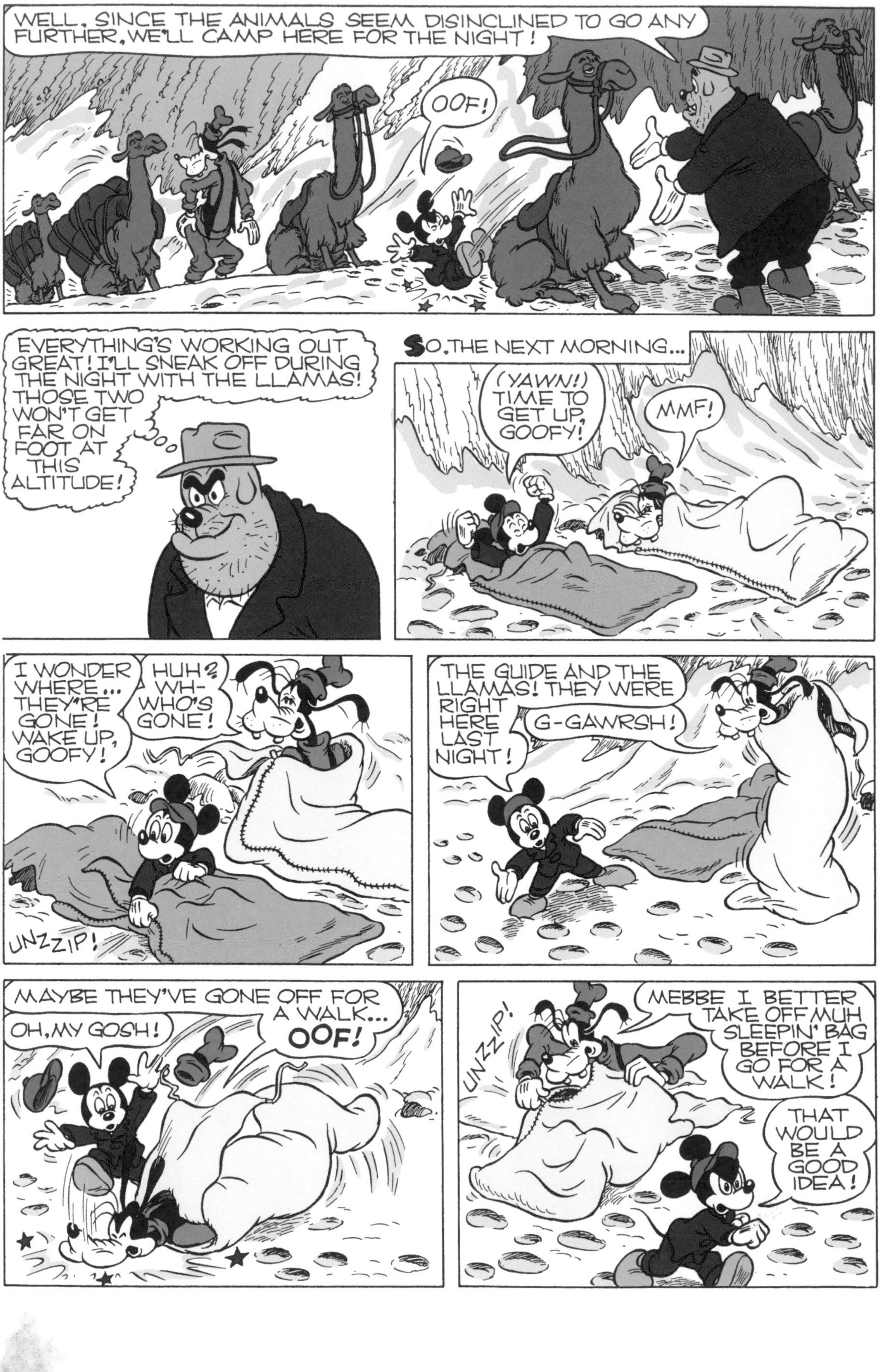
WELL, SINCE THE ANIMALS SEEM DISINCLINED TO GO ANY FURTHER, WE'LL CAMP HERE FOR THE NIGHT!
OOF!
EVERYTHING'S WORKING OUT GREAT! I'LL SNEAK OFF DURING THE NIGHT WITH THE LLAMAS! THOSE TWO WON'T GET FAR ON FOOT AT THIS ALTITUDE!
SO, THE NEXT MORNING...
(YAWN!) TIME TO GET UP, GOOFY!
MMF!
I WONDER WHERE... THEY'RE GONE! WAKE UP, GOOFY!
HUH?! WH- WHO'S GONE!
UNZZIP!
THE GUIDE AND THE LLAMAS! THEY WERE RIGHT HERE LAST NIGHT!
G-GAWRSH!
MAYBE THEY'VE GONE OFF FOR A WALK...
OH, MY GOSH!
OOF!
UNZZIP!
MEBBE I BETTER TAKE OFF MUH SLEEPIN' BAG BEFORE I GO FOR A WALK!
THAT WOULD BE A GOOD IDEA!

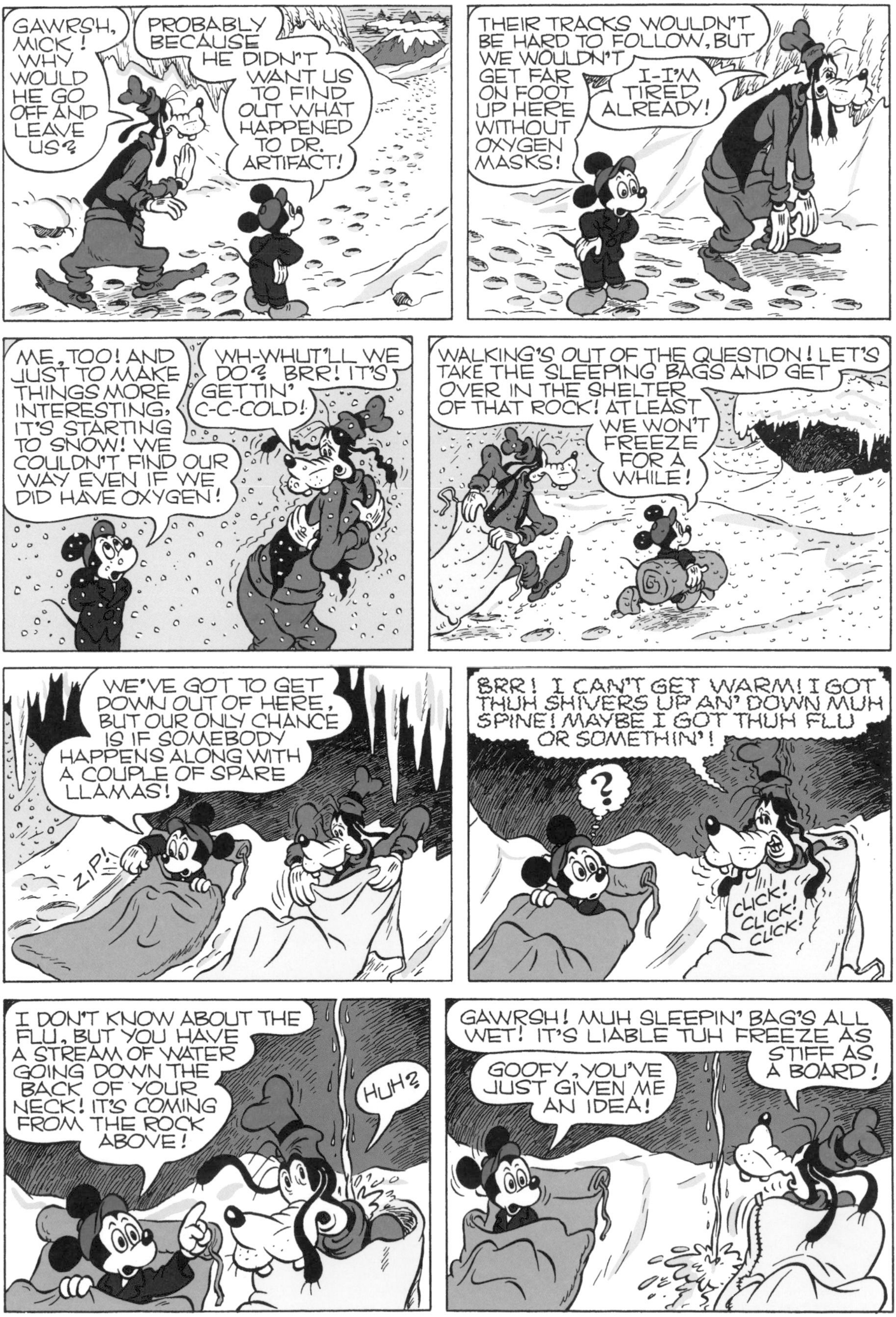
GAWRSH, MICK! WHY WOULD HE GO OFF AND LEAVE US?
PROBABLY BECAUSE HE DIDN'T WANT US TO FIND OUT WHAT HAPPENED TO DR. ARTIFACT!
THEIR TRACKS WOULDN'T BE HARD TO FOLLOW, BUT WE WOULDN'T GET FAR ON FOOT UP HERE WITHOUT OXYGEN MASKS!
I-I'M TIRED ALREADY!
ME, TOO! AND JUST TO MAKE THINGS MORE INTERESTING, IT'S STARTING TO SNOW! WE COULDN'T FIND OUR WAY EVEN IF WE DID HAVE OXYGEN!
WH-WHUT'LL WE DO? BRR! IT'S GETTIN' C-C-COLD!
WALKING'S OUT OF THE QUESTION! LET'S TAKE THE SLEEPING BAGS AND GET OVER IN THE SHELTER OF THAT ROCK! AT LEAST WE WON'T FREEZE FOR A WHILE!
WE'VE GOT TO GET DOWN OUT OF HERE, BUT OUR ONLY CHANCE IS IF SOMEBODY HAPPENS ALONG WITH A COUPLE OF SPARE LLAMAS!
ZIP!
BRR! I CAN'T GET WARM! I GOT THUH SHIVERS UP AN' DOWN MUH SPINE! MAYBE I GOT THUH FLU OR SOMETHIN'!
?
CLICK! CLICK! CLICK!
I DON'T KNOW ABOUT THE FLU, BUT YOU HAVE A STREAM OF WATER GOING DOWN THE BACK OF YOUR NECK! IT'S COMING FROM THE ROCK ABOVE!
HUH?
GAWRSH! MUH SLEEPIN' BAG'S ALL WET! IT'S LIABLE TUH FREEZE AS STIFF AS A BOARD!
GOOFY, YOU'VE JUST GIVEN ME AN IDEA!

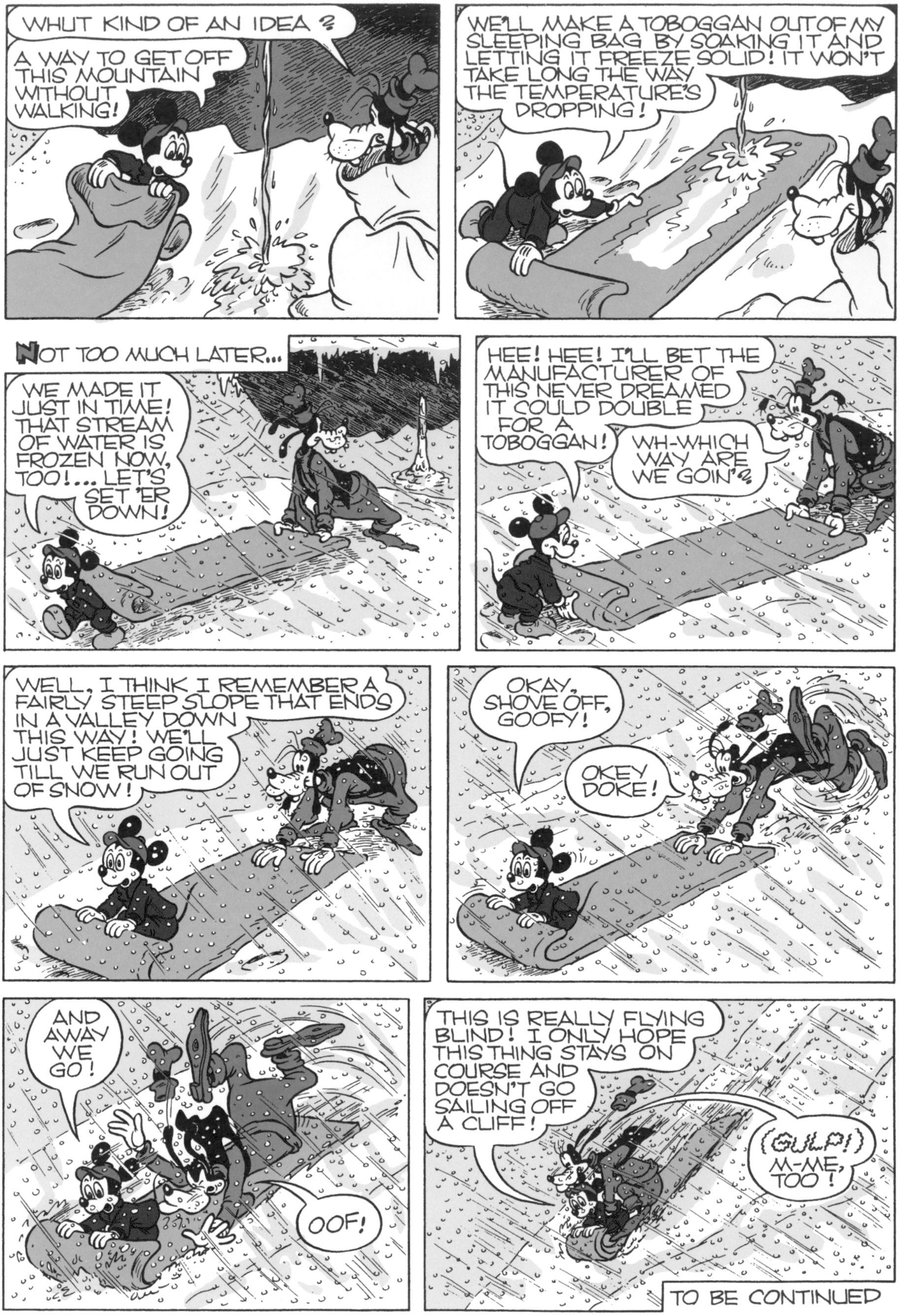
WHUT KIND OF AN IDEA?
A WAY TO GET OFF THIS MOUNTAIN WITHOUT WALKING!
WE'LL MAKE A TOBOGGAN OUT OF MY SLEEPING BAG BY SOAKING IT AND LETTING IT FREEZE SOLID! IT WON'T TAKE LONG THE WAY THE TEMPERATURE'S DROPPING!
NOT TOO MUCH LATER...
WE MADE IT JUST IN TIME! THAT STREAM OF WATER IS FROZEN NOW, TOO!... LET'S SET 'ER DOWN!
HEE! HEE! I'LL BET THE MANUFACTURER OF THIS NEVER DREAMED IT COULD DOUBLE FOR A TOBOGGAN!
WH-WHICH WAY ARE WE GOIN'?
WELL, I THINK I REMEMBER A FAIRLY STEEP SLOPE THAT ENDS IN A VALLEY DOWN THIS WAY! WE'LL JUST KEEP GOING TILL WE RUN OUT OF SNOW!
OKAY, SHOVE OFF, GOOFY!
OKEY DOKE!
AND AWAY WE GO!
OOF!
THIS IS REALLY FLYING BLIND! I ONLY HOPE THIS THING STAYS ON COURSE AND DOESN'T GO SAILING OFF A CLIFF!
(GULP!) M-ME, TOO!
TO BE CONTINUED

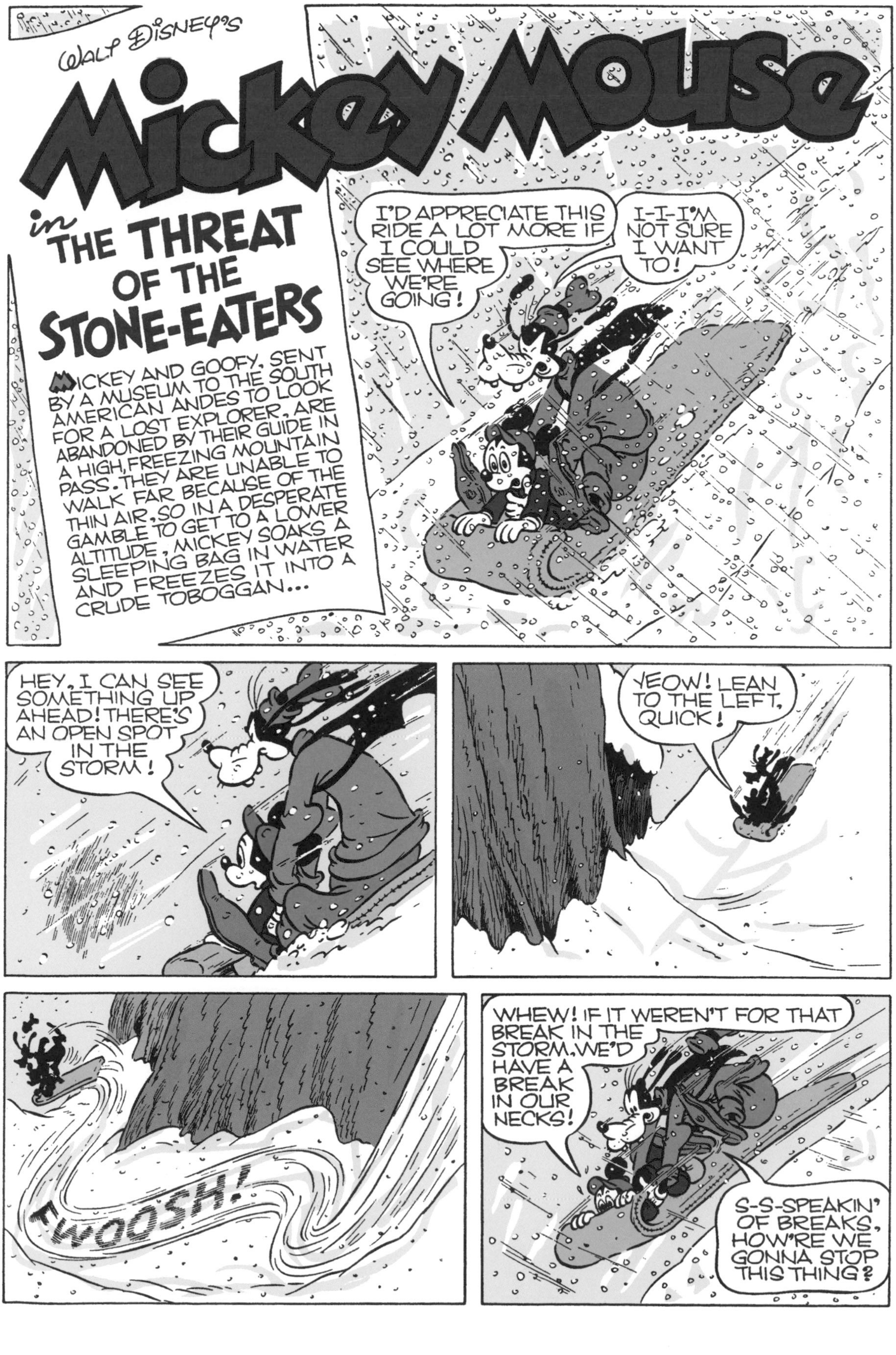

WALT DISNEY'S
Mickey Mouse
in THE THREAT OF THE STONE-EATERS
MICKEY AND GOOFY, SENT BY A MUSEUM TO THE SOUTH AMERICAN ANDES TO LOOK FOR A LOST EXPLORER, ARE ABANDONED BY THEIR GUIDE IN A HIGH, FREEZING MOUNTAIN PASS. THEY ARE UNABLE TO WALK FAR BECAUSE OF THE THIN AIR, SO IN A DESPERATE GAMBLE TO GET TO A LOWER ALTITUDE, MICKEY SOAKS A SLEEPING BAG IN WATER AND FREEZES IT INTO A CRUDE TOBOGGAN...
I'D APPRECIATE THIS RIDE A LOT MORE IF I COULD SEE WHERE WE'RE GOING!
I-I-I'M NOT SURE I WANT TO!
HEY, I CAN SEE SOMETHING UP AHEAD! THERE'S AN OPEN SPOT IN THE STORM!
YEOW! LEAN TO THE LEFT, QUICK!
FWOOSH!
WHEW! IF IT WEREN'T FOR THAT BREAK IN THE STORM, WE'D HAVE A BREAK IN OUR NECKS!
S-S-SPEAKIN' OF BREAKS, HOW'RE WE GONNA STOP THIS THING?

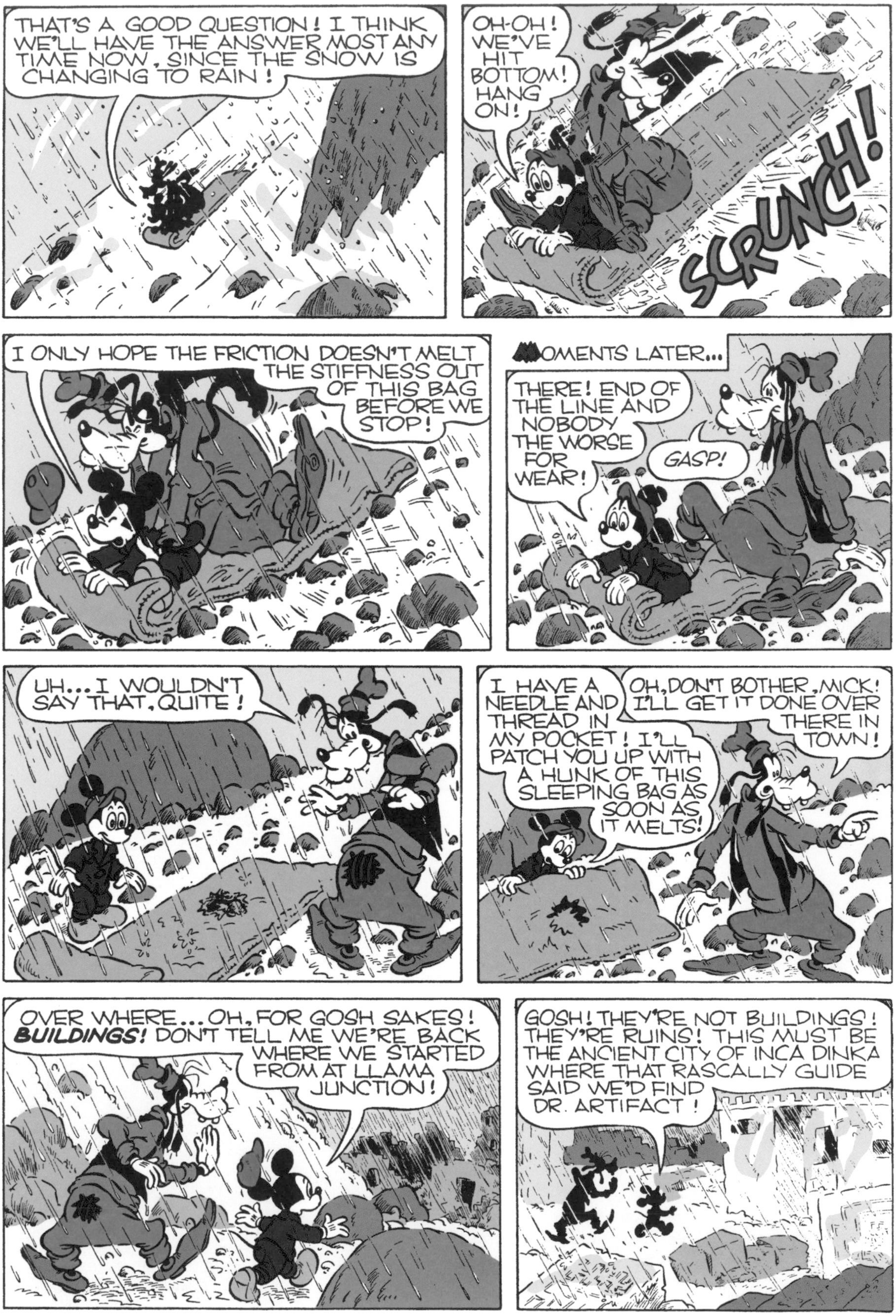
THAT'S A GOOD QUESTION! I THINK WE'LL HAVE THE ANSWER MOST ANY TIME NOW, SINCE THE SNOW IS CHANGING TO RAIN!
OH-OH! WE'VE HIT BOTTOM! HANG ON!
SCRUNCH!
I ONLY HOPE THE FRICTION DOESN'T MELT THE STIFFNESS OUT OF THIS BAG BEFORE WE STOP!
MOMENTS LATER...
THERE! END OF THE LINE AND NOBODY THE WORSE FOR WEAR!
GASP!
UH... I WOULDN'T SAY THAT, QUITE!
I HAVE A NEEDLE AND THREAD IN MY POCKET! I'LL PATCH YOU UP WITH A HUNK OF THIS SLEEPING BAG AS SOON AS IT MELTS!
OH, DON'T BOTHER, MICK! I'LL GET IT DONE OVER THERE IN TOWN!
OVER WHERE... OH, FOR GOSH SAKES! **BUILDINGS!** DON'T TELL ME WE'RE BACK WHERE WE STARTED FROM AT LLAMA JUNCTION!
GOSH! THEY'RE NOT BUILDINGS! THEY'RE RUINS! THIS MUST BE THE ANCIENT CITY OF INCA DINKA WHERE THAT RASCALLY GUIDE SAID WE'D FIND DR. ARTIFACT!

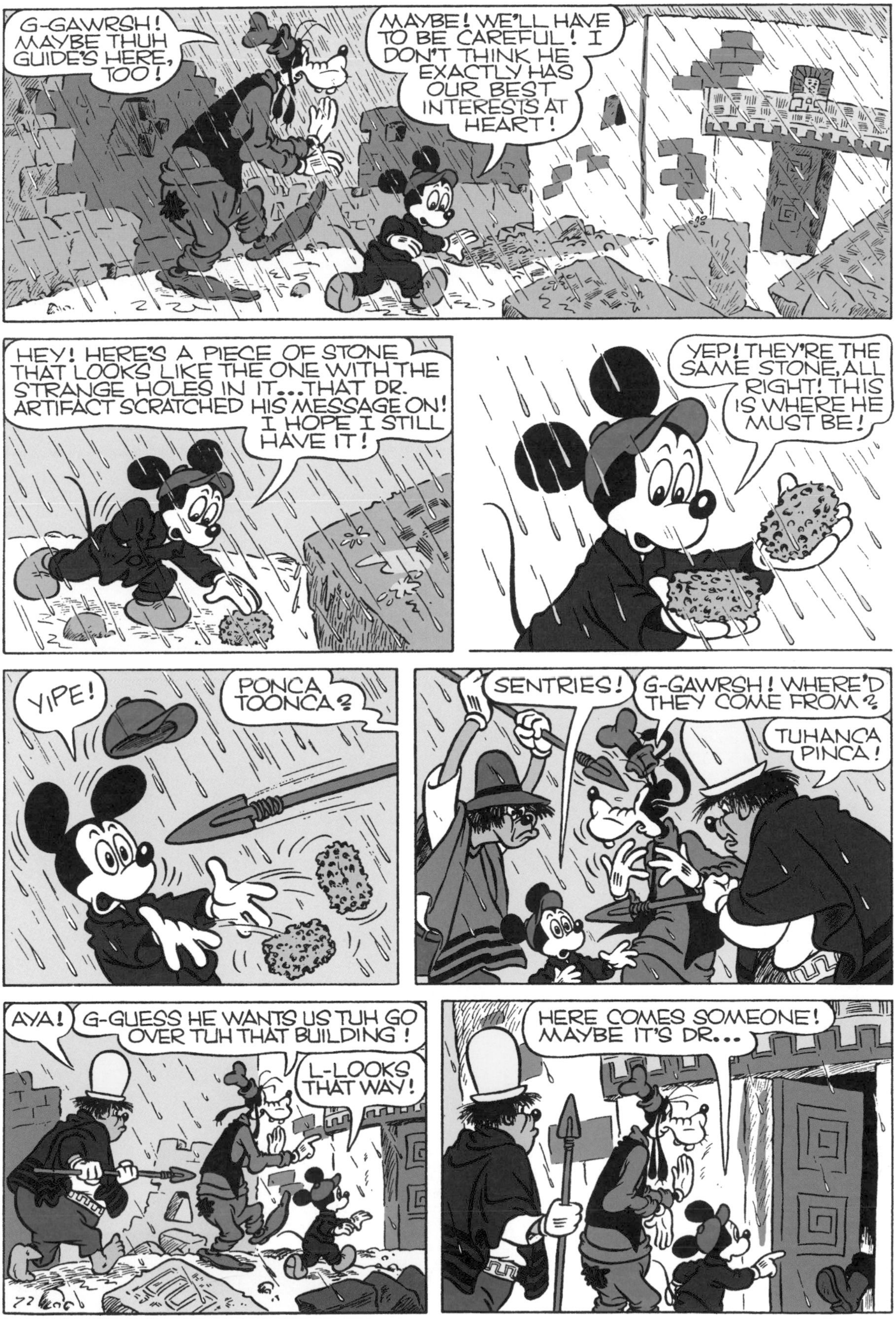
G-GAWRSH! MAYBE THUH GUIDE'S HERE, TOO!
MAYBE! WE'LL HAVE TO BE CAREFUL! I DON'T THINK HE EXACTLY HAS OUR BEST INTERESTS AT HEART!
HEY! HERE'S A PIECE OF STONE THAT LOOKS LIKE THE ONE WITH THE STRANGE HOLES IN IT...THAT DR. ARTIFACT SCRATCHED HIS MESSAGE ON! I HOPE I STILL HAVE IT!
YEP! THEY'RE THE SAME STONE, ALL RIGHT! THIS IS WHERE HE MUST BE!
YIPE!
PONCA TOONCA?
SENTRIES!
G-GAWRSH! WHERE'D THEY COME FROM?
TUHANCA PINCA!
AYA!
G-GUESS HE WANTS US TUH GO OVER TUH THAT BUILDING!
L-LOOKS THAT WAY!
HERE COMES SOMEONE! MAYBE IT'S DR...

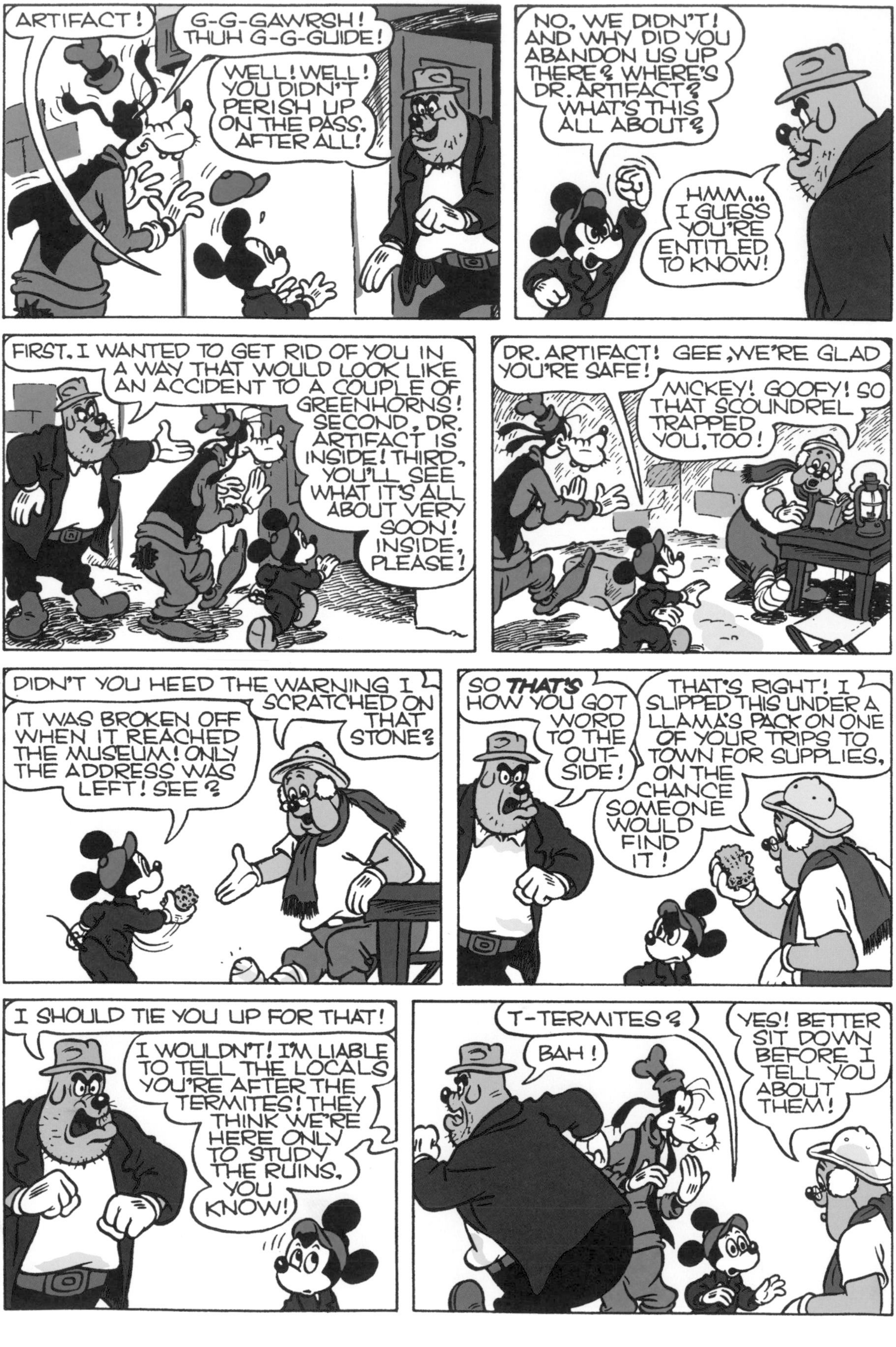
ARTIFACT!
G-G-GAWRSH! THUH G-G-GUIDE!
WELL! WELL! YOU DIDN'T PERISH UP ON THE PASS, AFTER ALL!
NO, WE DIDN'T! AND WHY DID YOU ABANDON US UP THERE? WHERE'S DR. ARTIFACT? WHAT'S THIS ALL ABOUT?
HMM... I GUESS YOU'RE ENTITLED TO KNOW!
FIRST, I WANTED TO GET RID OF YOU IN A WAY THAT WOULD LOOK LIKE AN ACCIDENT TO A COUPLE OF GREENHORNS! SECOND, DR. ARTIFACT IS INSIDE! THIRD, YOU'LL SEE WHAT IT'S ALL ABOUT VERY SOON! INSIDE, PLEASE!
DR. ARTIFACT! GEE, WE'RE GLAD YOU'RE SAFE!
MICKEY! GOOFY! SO THAT SCOUNDREL TRAPPED YOU, TOO!
DIDN'T YOU HEED THE WARNING I SCRATCHED ON THAT STONE?
IT WAS BROKEN OFF WHEN IT REACHED THE MUSEUM! ONLY THE ADDRESS WAS LEFT! SEE?
SO THAT'S HOW YOU GOT WORD TO THE OUT-SIDE!
THAT'S RIGHT! I SLIPPED THIS UNDER A LLAMA'S PACK ON ONE OF YOUR TRIPS TO TOWN FOR SUPPLIES, ON THE CHANCE SOMEONE WOULD FIND IT!
I SHOULD TIE YOU UP FOR THAT!
I WOULDN'T! I'M LIABLE TO TELL THE LOCALS YOU'RE AFTER THE TERMITES! THEY THINK WE'RE HERE ONLY TO STUDY THE RUINS, YOU KNOW!
T-TERMITES?
BAH!
YES! BETTER SIT DOWN BEFORE I TELL YOU ABOUT THEM!

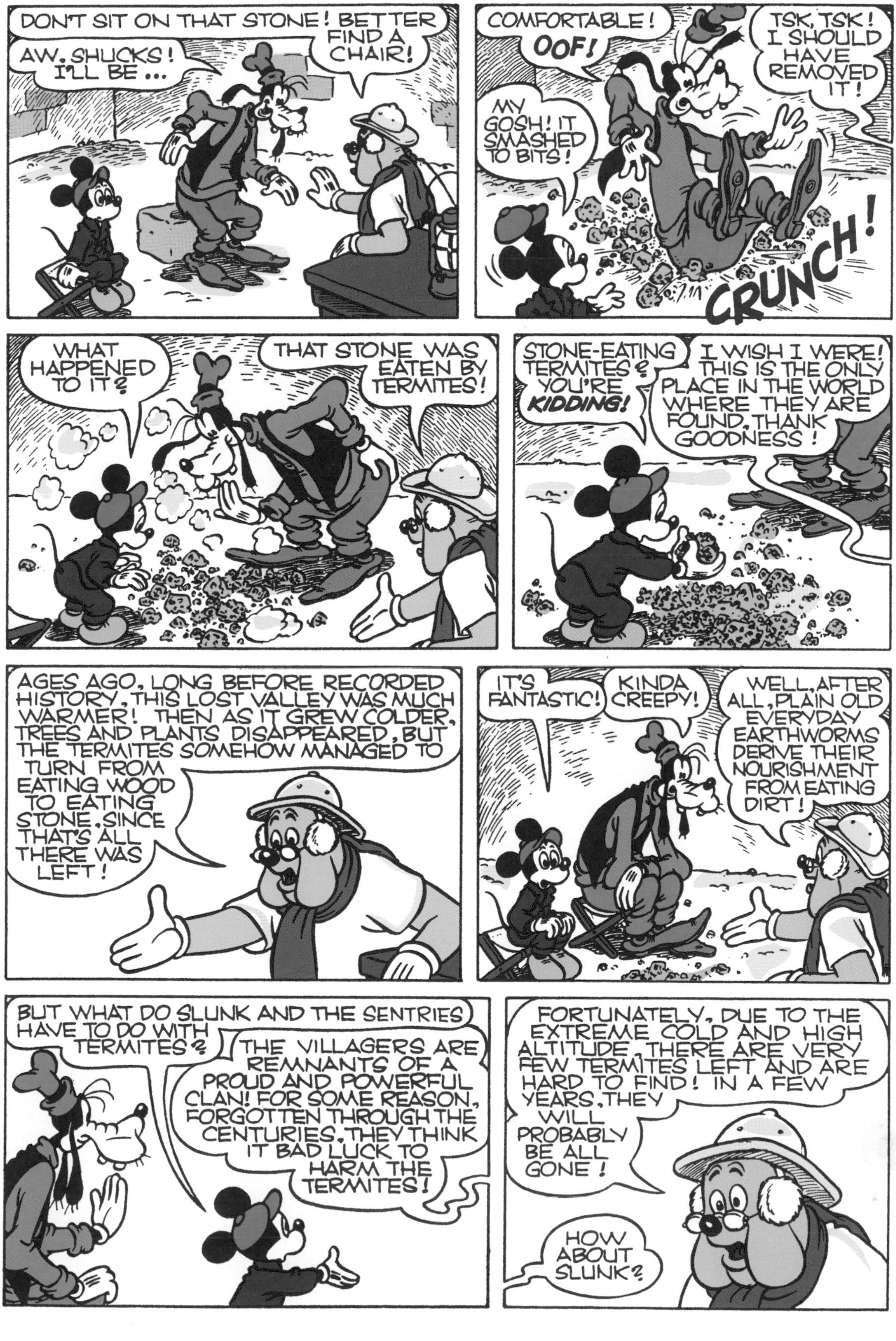
DON'T SIT ON THAT STONE! BETTER FIND A CHAIR!
AW, SHUCKS! I'LL BE ...
COMFORTABLE! OOF!
TSK, TSK! I SHOULD HAVE REMOVED IT!
MY GOSH! IT SMASHED TO BITS!
CRUNCH!
WHAT HAPPENED TO IT?
THAT STONE WAS EATEN BY TERMITES!
STONE-EATING TERMITES? YOU'RE KIDDING!
I WISH I WERE! THIS IS THE ONLY PLACE IN THE WORLD WHERE THEY ARE FOUND, THANK GOODNESS!
AGES AGO, LONG BEFORE RECORDED HISTORY, THIS LOST VALLEY WAS MUCH WARMER! THEN AS IT GREW COLDER, TREES AND PLANTS DISAPPEARED, BUT THE TERMITES SOMEHOW MANAGED TO TURN FROM EATING WOOD TO EATING STONE, SINCE THAT'S ALL THERE WAS LEFT!
IT'S FANTASTIC!
KINDA CREEPY!
WELL, AFTER ALL, PLAIN OLD EVERYDAY EARTHWORMS DERIVE THEIR NOURISHMENT FROM EATING DIRT!
BUT WHAT DO SLUNK AND THE SENTRIES HAVE TO DO WITH TERMITES?
THE VILLAGERS ARE REMNANTS OF A PROUD AND POWERFUL CLAN! FOR SOME REASON, FORGOTTEN THROUGH THE CENTURIES, THEY THINK IT BAD LUCK TO HARM THE TERMITES!
FORTUNATELY, DUE TO THE EXTREME COLD AND HIGH ALTITUDE, THERE ARE VERY FEW TERMITES LEFT AND ARE HARD TO FIND! IN A FEW YEARS, THEY WILL PROBABLY BE ALL GONE!
HOW ABOUT SLUNK?

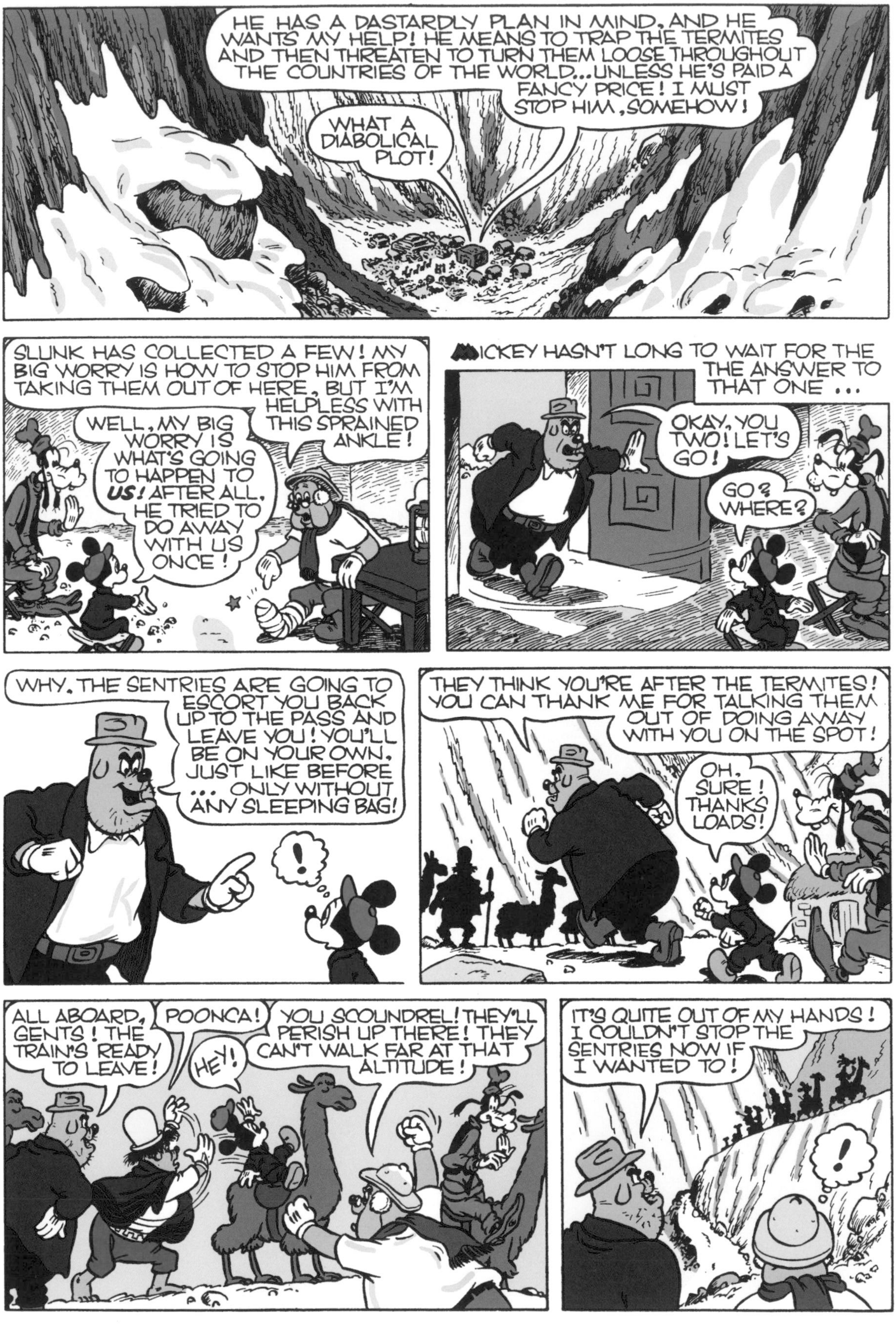
HE HAS A DASTARDLY PLAN IN MIND, AND HE WANTS MY HELP! HE MEANS TO TRAP THE TERMITES AND THEN THREATEN TO TURN THEM LOOSE THROUGHOUT THE COUNTRIES OF THE WORLD... UNLESS HE'S PAID A FANCY PRICE! I MUST STOP HIM, SOMEHOW!
WHAT A DIABOLICAL PLOT!
SLUNK HAS COLLECTED A FEW! MY BIG WORRY IS HOW TO STOP HIM FROM TAKING THEM OUT OF HERE, BUT I'M HELPLESS WITH THIS SPRAINED ANKLE!
WELL, MY BIG WORRY IS WHAT'S GOING TO HAPPEN TO US! AFTER ALL, HE TRIED TO DO AWAY WITH US ONCE!
MICKEY HASN'T LONG TO WAIT FOR THE THE ANSWER TO THAT ONE ...
OKAY, YOU TWO! LET'S GO!
GO? WHERE?
WHY, THE SENTRIES ARE GOING TO ESCORT YOU BACK UP TO THE PASS AND LEAVE YOU! YOU'LL BE ON YOUR OWN, JUST LIKE BEFORE ... ONLY WITHOUT ANY SLEEPING BAG!
!
THEY THINK YOU'RE AFTER THE TERMITES! YOU CAN THANK ME FOR TALKING THEM OUT OF DOING AWAY WITH YOU ON THE SPOT!
OH, SURE! THANKS LOADS!
ALL ABOARD, GENTS! THE TRAIN'S READY TO LEAVE!
POONCA!
HEY!
YOU SCOUNDREL! THEY'LL PERISH UP THERE! THEY CAN'T WALK FAR AT THAT ALTITUDE!
IT'S QUITE OUT OF MY HANDS! I COULDN'T STOP THE SENTRIES NOW IF I WANTED TO!
!

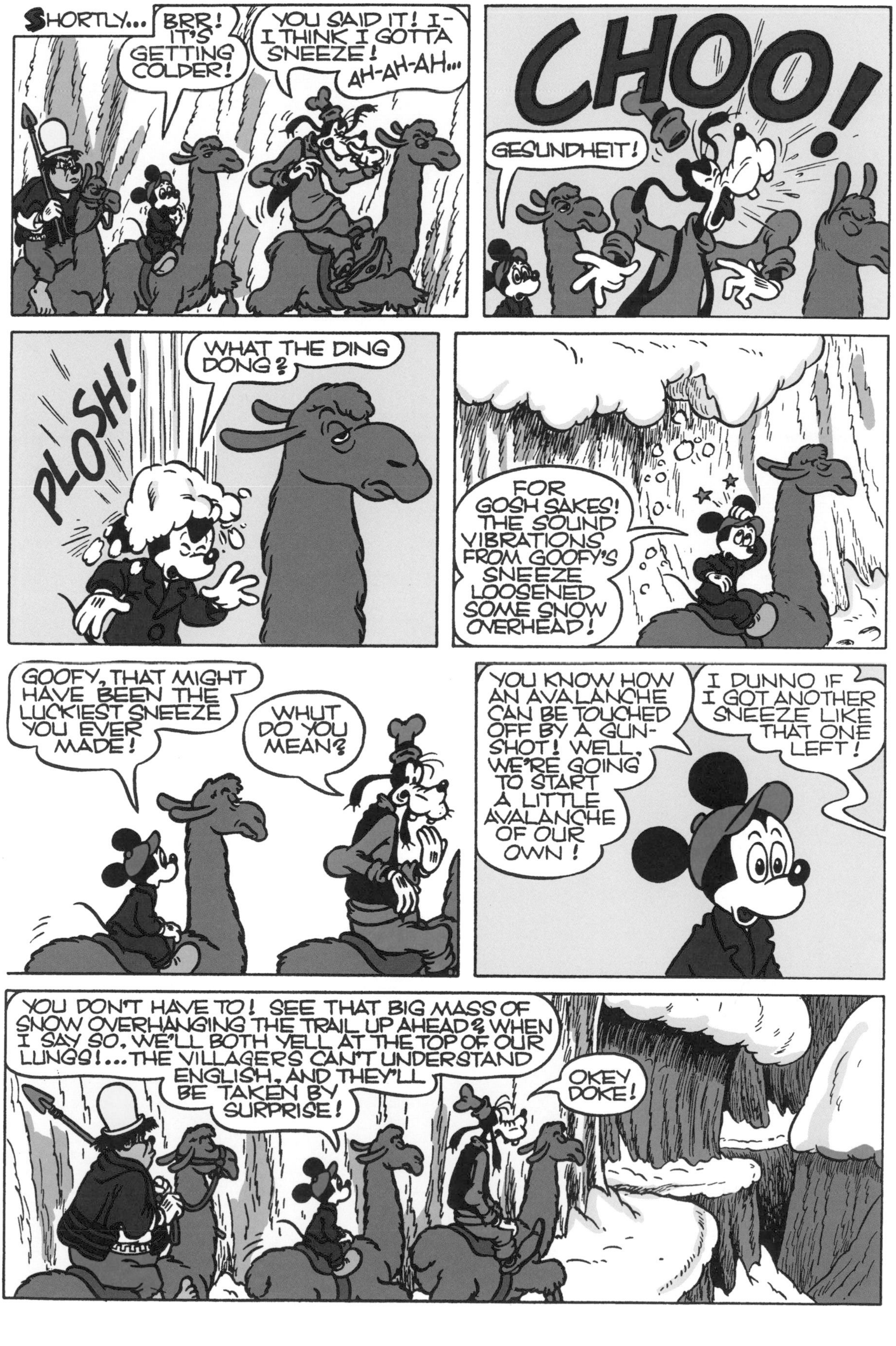
SHORTLY...
BRR! IT'S GETTING COLDER!
YOU SAID IT! I-I THINK I GOTTA SNEEZE! AH-AH-AH...
CHOO!
GESUNDHEIT!
PLOSH!
WHAT THE DING DONG?
FOR GOSH SAKES! THE SOUND VIBRATIONS FROM GOOFY'S SNEEZE LOOSENED SOME SNOW OVERHEAD!
GOOFY, THAT MIGHT HAVE BEEN THE LUCKIEST SNEEZE YOU EVER MADE!
WHUT DO YOU MEAN?
YOU KNOW HOW AN AVALANCHE CAN BE TOUCHED OFF BY A GUN-SHOT! WELL, WE'RE GOING TO START A LITTLE AVALANCHE OF OUR OWN!
I DUNNO IF I GOT ANOTHER SNEEZE LIKE THAT ONE LEFT!
YOU DON'T HAVE TO! SEE THAT BIG MASS OF SNOW OVERHANGING THE TRAIL UP AHEAD? WHEN I SAY SO, WE'LL BOTH YELL AT THE TOP OF OUR LUNGS! ... THE VILLAGERS CAN'T UNDERSTAND ENGLISH, AND THEY'LL BE TAKEN BY SURPRISE!
OKEY DOKE!

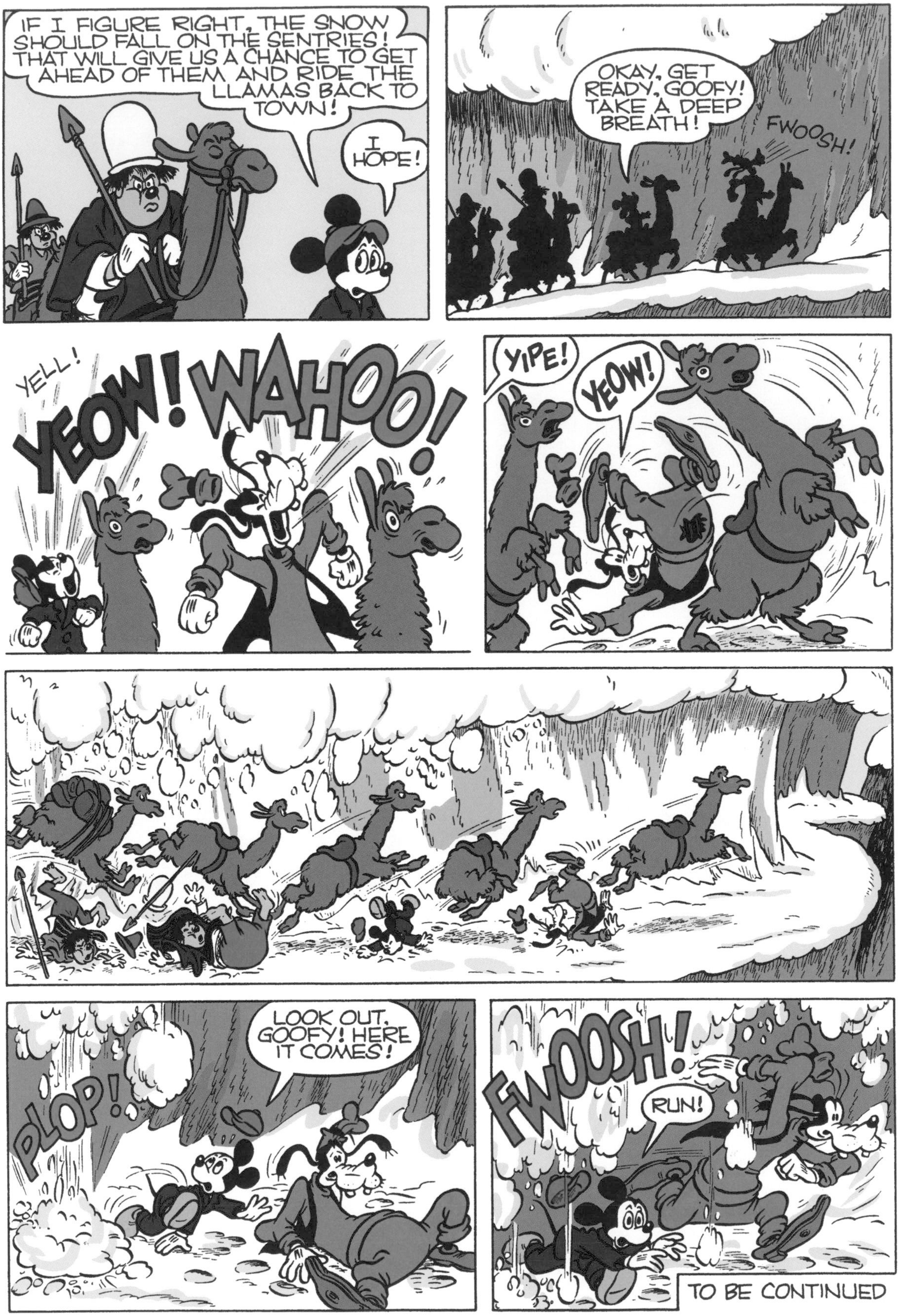
IF I FIGURE RIGHT, THE SNOW SHOULD FALL ON THE SENTRIES! THAT WILL GIVE US A CHANCE TO GET AHEAD OF THEM AND RIDE THE LLAMAS BACK TO TOWN!
I HOPE!
OKAY, GET READY, GOOFY! TAKE A DEEP BREATH!
FWOOSH!
YELL!
YEOW!
WAHOO!
YIPE!
YEOW!
LOOK OUT, GOOFY! HERE IT COMES!
PLOP!
FWOOSH!
RUN!
TO BE CONTINUED

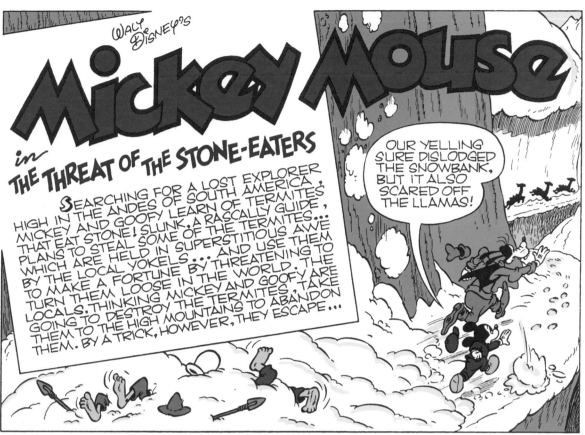

WALT DISNEY'S
Mickey Mouse
in THE THREAT OF THE STONE-EATERS

SEARCHING FOR A LOST EXPLORER HIGH IN THE ANDES OF SOUTH AMERICA, MICKEY AND GOOFY LEARN OF TERMITES THAT EAT STONE! SLUNK, A RASCALLY GUIDE, PLANS TO STEAL SOME OF THE TERMITES.... WHICH ARE HELD IN SUPERSTITIOUS AWE BY THE LOCAL YOKELS.... AND USE THEM TO MAKE A FORTUNE BY THREATENING TO TURN THEM LOOSE IN THE WORLD. THE LOCALS, THINKING MICKEY AND GOOFY ARE GOING TO DESTROY THE TERMITES, TAKE THEM TO THE HIGH MOUNTAINS TO ABANDON THEM. BY A TRICK, HOWEVER, THEY ESCAPE....

OUR YELLING SURE DISLODGED THE SNOWBANK, BUT IT ALSO SCARED OFF THE LLAMAS!

(PUFF! PUFF!) WE COULD NEVER MAKE IT BACK TO CIVILIZATION ON FOOT! IF THIS ALTITUDE DIDN'T GET US, THE WEATHER WOULD!

(GASP!) — IT'S GOT ME ALREADY!

(PUFF! GASP!) M-ME TOO! I THINK W-WE BETTER SLOW DOWN!

(WHEEZE!) C-CAN'T WE STOP?

WE DON'T DARE! THOSE TWO SENTRIES ARE ALREADY DIGGING OUT OF THAT SNOW-SLIDE! THEY'LL BE ON OUR TAIL IN MINUTES!

WHUT'LL WE DO?

WE CAN'T OUTRUN THEM! THEY'RE CONDITIONED TO THIS RARIFIED AIR, AND WE'RE NOT! C'MON!

WHERE YUH GOIN'?

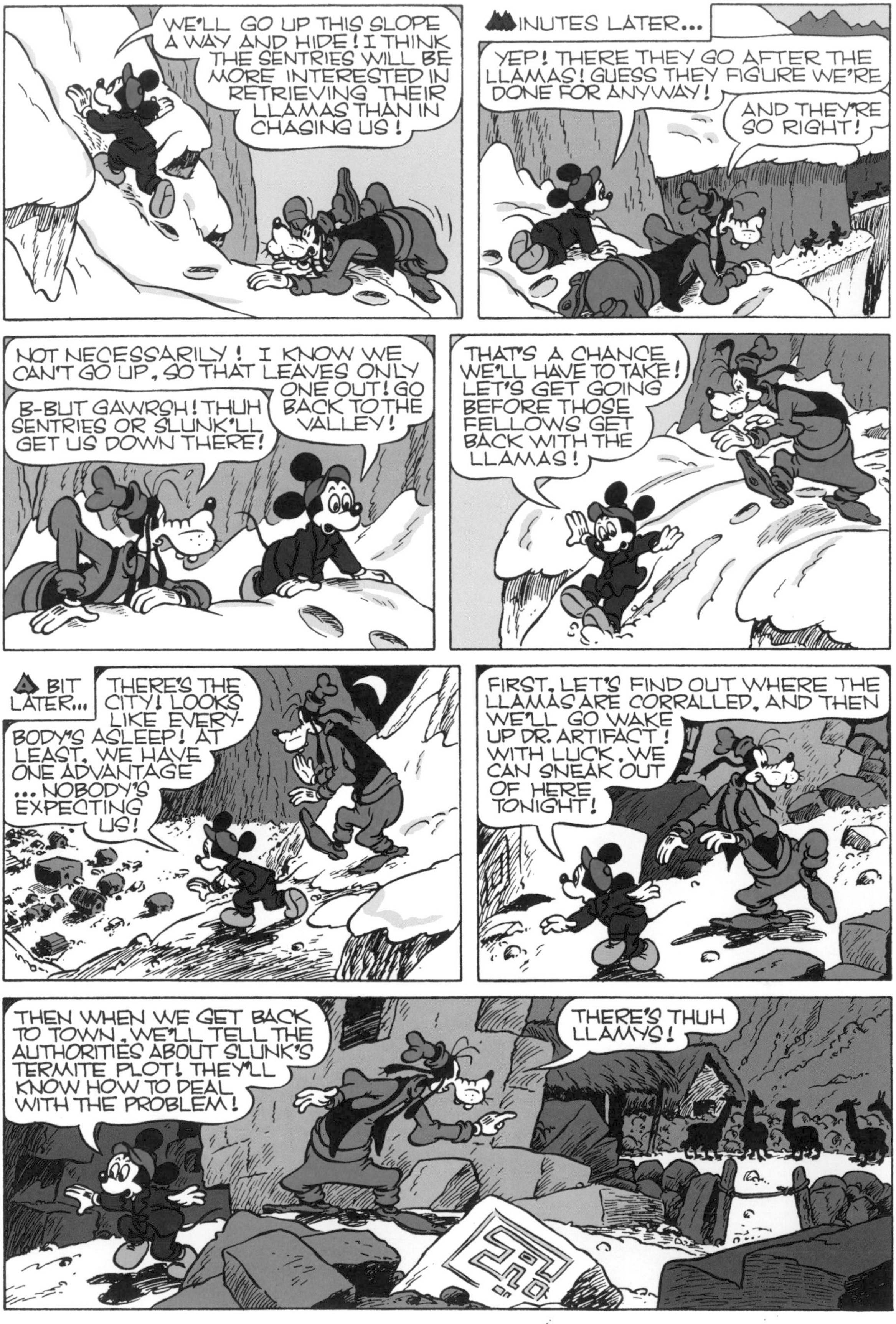
WE'LL GO UP THIS SLOPE A WAY AND HIDE! I THINK THE SENTRIES WILL BE MORE INTERESTED IN RETRIEVING THEIR LLAMAS THAN IN CHASING US!
MINUTES LATER...
YEP! THERE THEY GO AFTER THE LLAMAS! GUESS THEY FIGURE WE'RE DONE FOR ANYWAY!
AND THEY'RE SO RIGHT!
NOT NECESSARILY! I KNOW WE CAN'T GO UP, SO THAT LEAVES ONLY ONE OUT! GO BACK TO THE VALLEY!
B-BUT GAWRSH! THUH SENTRIES OR SLUNK'LL GET US DOWN THERE!
THAT'S A CHANCE WE'LL HAVE TO TAKE! LET'S GET GOING BEFORE THOSE FELLOWS GET BACK WITH THE LLAMAS!
A BIT LATER...
THERE'S THE CITY! LOOKS LIKE EVERYBODY'S ASLEEP! AT LEAST, WE HAVE ONE ADVANTAGE ... NOBODY'S EXPECTING US!
FIRST, LET'S FIND OUT WHERE THE LLAMAS ARE CORRALLED, AND THEN WE'LL GO WAKE UP DR. ARTIFACT! WITH LUCK, WE CAN SNEAK OUT OF HERE TONIGHT!
THEN WHEN WE GET BACK TO TOWN, WE'LL TELL THE AUTHORITIES ABOUT SLUNK'S TERMITE PLOT! THEY'LL KNOW HOW TO DEAL WITH THE PROBLEM!
THERE'S THUH LLAMYS!

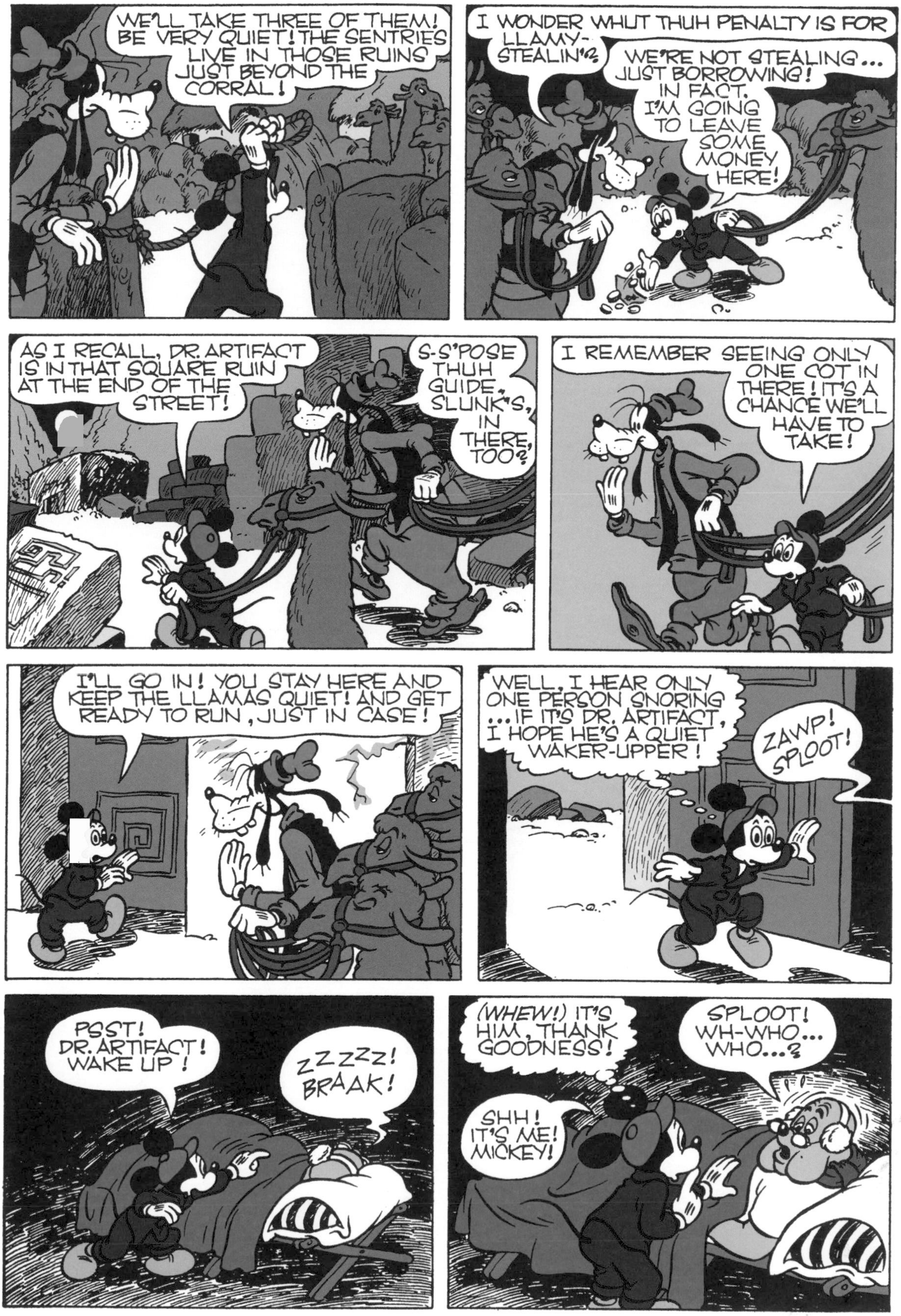
WE'LL TAKE THREE OF THEM! BE VERY QUIET! THE SENTRIES LIVE IN THOSE RUINS JUST BEYOND THE CORRAL!
I WONDER WHUT THUH PENALTY IS FOR LLAMY-STEALIN'?
WE'RE NOT STEALING... JUST BORROWING! IN FACT, I'M GOING TO LEAVE SOME MONEY HERE!
AS I RECALL, DR. ARTIFACT IS IN THAT SQUARE RUIN AT THE END OF THE STREET!
S-S'POSE THUH GUIDE, SLUNK'S, IN THERE, TOO?
I REMEMBER SEEING ONLY ONE COT IN THERE! IT'S A CHANCE WE'LL HAVE TO TAKE!
I'LL GO IN! YOU STAY HERE AND KEEP THE LLAMAS QUIET! AND GET READY TO RUN, JUST IN CASE!
WELL, I HEAR ONLY ONE PERSON SNORING ...IF IT'S DR. ARTIFACT, I HOPE HE'S A QUIET WAKER-UPPER!
ZAWP! SPLOOT!
PSST! DR. ARTIFACT! WAKE UP!
ZZZZZ! BRAAK!
(WHEW!) IT'S HIM, THANK GOODNESS!
SPLOOT! WH-WHO... WHO...?
SHH! IT'S ME! MICKEY!

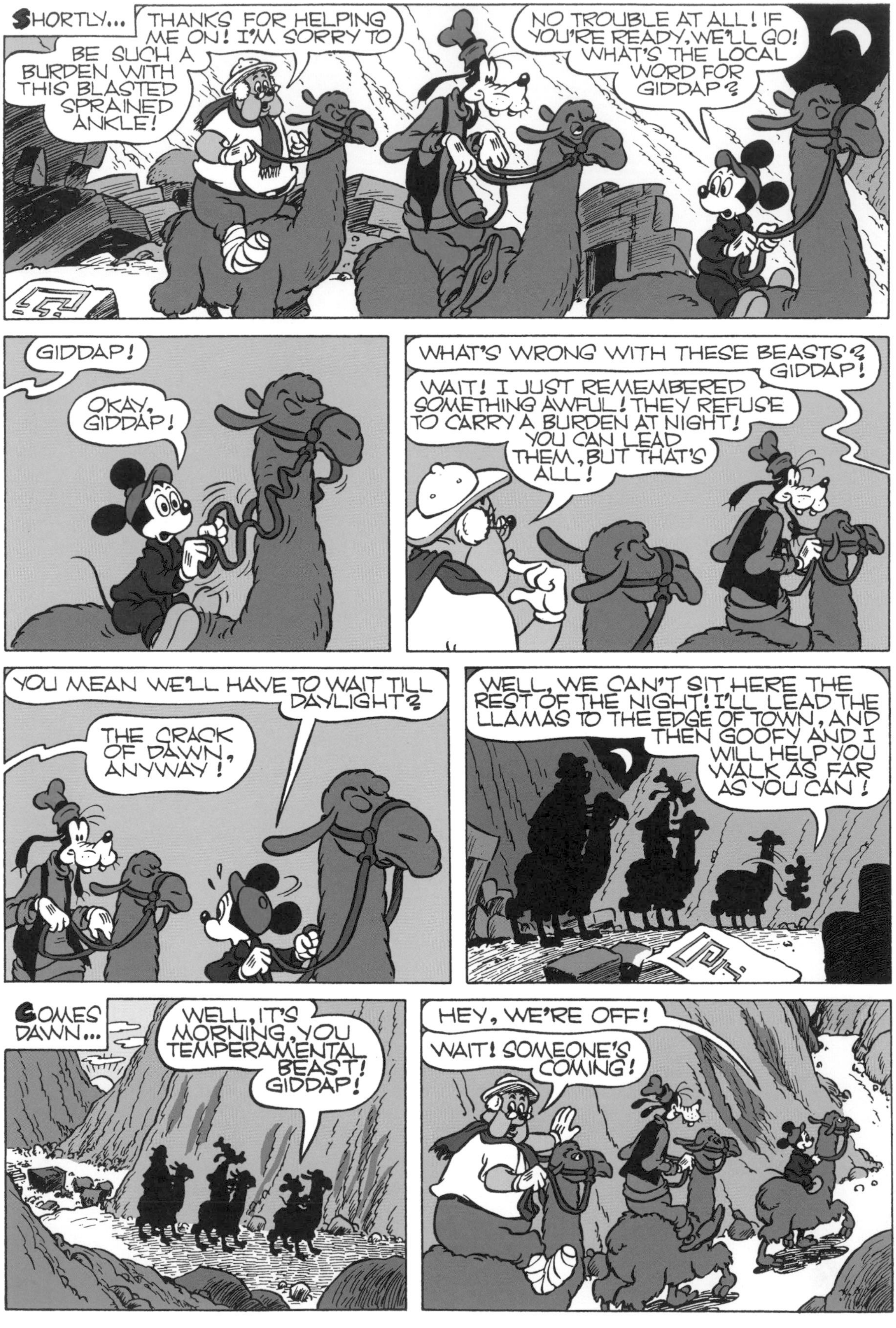
SHORTLY...
THANKS FOR HELPING ME ON! I'M SORRY TO BE SUCH A BURDEN WITH THIS BLASTED SPRAINED ANKLE!
NO TROUBLE AT ALL! IF YOU'RE READY, WE'LL GO! WHAT'S THE LOCAL WORD FOR GIDDAP?
GIDDAP!
OKAY, GIDDAP!
WHAT'S WRONG WITH THESE BEASTS? GIDDAP!
WAIT! I JUST REMEMBERED SOMETHING AWFUL! THEY REFUSE TO CARRY A BURDEN AT NIGHT! YOU CAN LEAD THEM, BUT THAT'S ALL!
YOU MEAN WE'LL HAVE TO WAIT TILL DAYLIGHT?
THE CRACK OF DAWN, ANYWAY!
WELL, WE CAN'T SIT HERE THE REST OF THE NIGHT! I'LL LEAD THE LLAMAS TO THE EDGE OF TOWN, AND THEN GOOFY AND I WILL HELP YOU WALK AS FAR AS YOU CAN!
COMES DAWN...
WELL, IT'S MORNING, YOU TEMPERAMENTAL BEAST! GIDDAP!
HEY, WE'RE OFF!
WAIT! SOMEONE'S COMING!

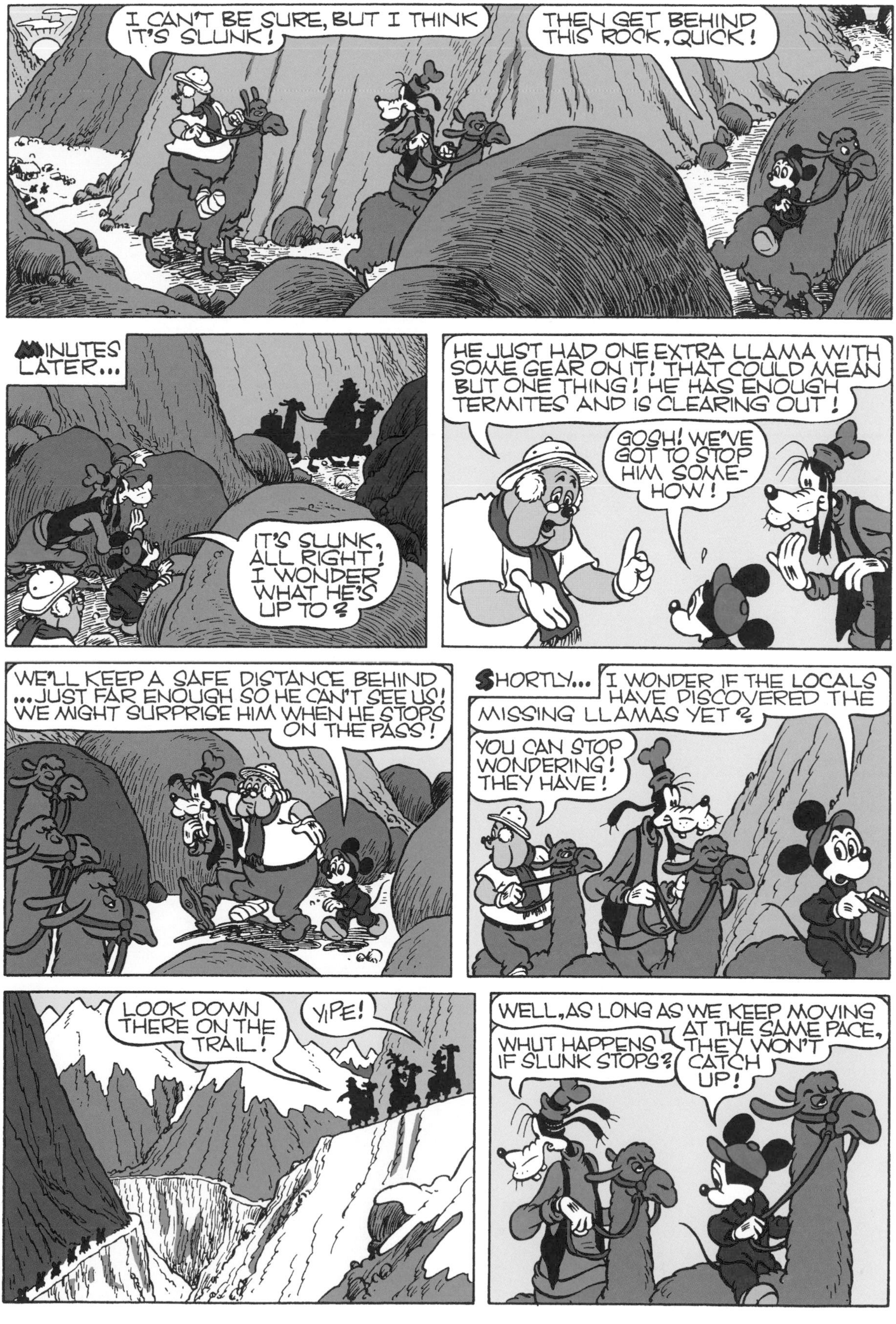
I CAN'T BE SURE, BUT I THINK IT'S SLUNK!
THEN GET BEHIND THIS ROCK, QUICK!
MINUTES LATER...
IT'S SLUNK, ALL RIGHT! I WONDER WHAT HE'S UP TO?
HE JUST HAD ONE EXTRA LLAMA WITH SOME GEAR ON IT! THAT COULD MEAN BUT ONE THING! HE HAS ENOUGH TERMITES AND IS CLEARING OUT!
GOSH! WE'VE GOT TO STOP HIM SOME-HOW!
WE'LL KEEP A SAFE DISTANCE BEHIND ...JUST FAR ENOUGH SO HE CAN'T SEE US! WE MIGHT SURPRISE HIM WHEN HE STOPS ON THE PASS!
SHORTLY...
I WONDER IF THE LOCALS HAVE DISCOVERED THE MISSING LLAMAS YET?
YOU CAN STOP WONDERING! THEY HAVE!
LOOK DOWN THERE ON THE TRAIL!
YIPE!
WELL, AS LONG AS WE KEEP MOVING AT THE SAME PACE, THEY WON'T CATCH UP!
WHUT HAPPENS IF SLUNK STOPS?

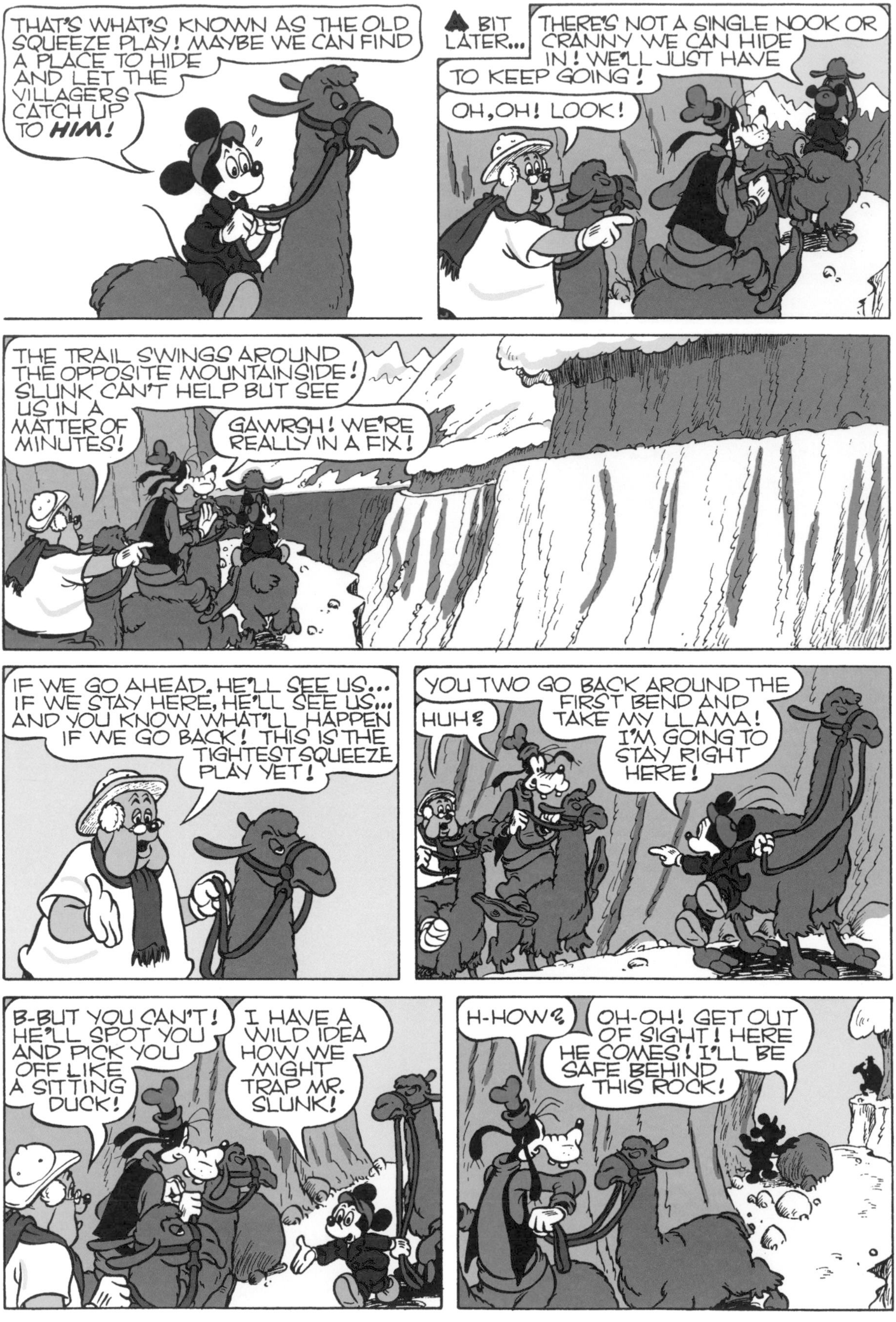
THAT'S WHAT'S KNOWN AS THE OLD SQUEEZE PLAY! MAYBE WE CAN FIND A PLACE TO HIDE AND LET THE VILLAGERS CATCH UP TO HIM!
A BIT LATER...
THERE'S NOT A SINGLE NOOK OR CRANNY WE CAN HIDE IN! WE'LL JUST HAVE TO KEEP GOING!
OH, OH! LOOK!
THE TRAIL SWINGS AROUND THE OPPOSITE MOUNTAINSIDE! SLUNK CAN'T HELP BUT SEE US IN A MATTER OF MINUTES!
GAWRSH! WE'RE REALLY IN A FIX!
IF WE GO AHEAD, HE'LL SEE US... IF WE STAY HERE, HE'LL SEE US... AND YOU KNOW WHAT'LL HAPPEN IF WE GO BACK! THIS IS THE TIGHTEST SQUEEZE PLAY YET!
YOU TWO GO BACK AROUND THE FIRST BEND AND TAKE MY LLAMA! I'M GOING TO STAY RIGHT HERE!
HUH?
B-BUT YOU CAN'T! HE'LL SPOT YOU AND PICK YOU OFF LIKE A SITTING DUCK!
I HAVE A WILD IDEA HOW WE MIGHT TRAP MR. SLUNK!
H-HOW?
OH-OH! GET OUT OF SIGHT! HERE HE COMES! I'LL BE SAFE BEHIND THIS ROCK!

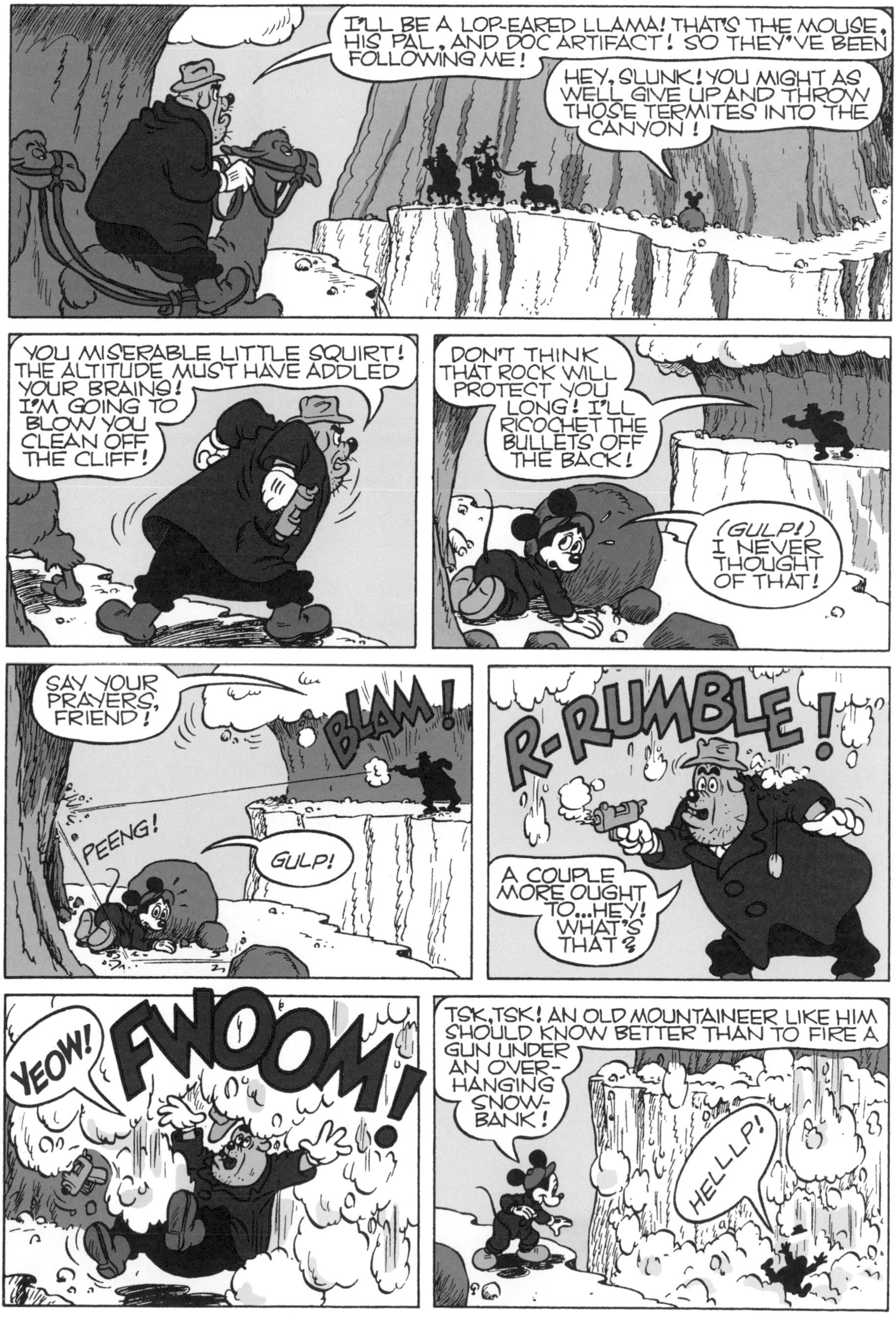
I'LL BE A LOP-EARED LLAMA! THAT'S THE MOUSE, HIS PAL, AND DOC ARTIFACT! SO THEY'VE BEEN FOLLOWING ME!
HEY, SLUNK! YOU MIGHT AS WELL GIVE UP AND THROW THOSE TERMITES INTO THE CANYON!
YOU MISERABLE LITTLE SQUIRT! THE ALTITUDE MUST HAVE ADDLED YOUR BRAINS! I'M GOING TO BLOW YOU CLEAN OFF THE CLIFF!
DON'T THINK THAT ROCK WILL PROTECT YOU LONG! I'LL RICOCHET THE BULLETS OFF THE BACK!
(GULP!) I NEVER THOUGHT OF THAT!
SAY YOUR PRAYERS, FRIEND!
BLAM!
PEENG!
GULP!
R-RUMBLE!
A COUPLE MORE OUGHT TO...HEY! WHAT'S THAT?
YEOW!
FWOOM!
TSK, TSK! AN OLD MOUNTAINEER LIKE HIM SHOULD KNOW BETTER THAN TO FIRE A GUN UNDER AN OVER-HANGING SNOW-BANK!
HELLLP!

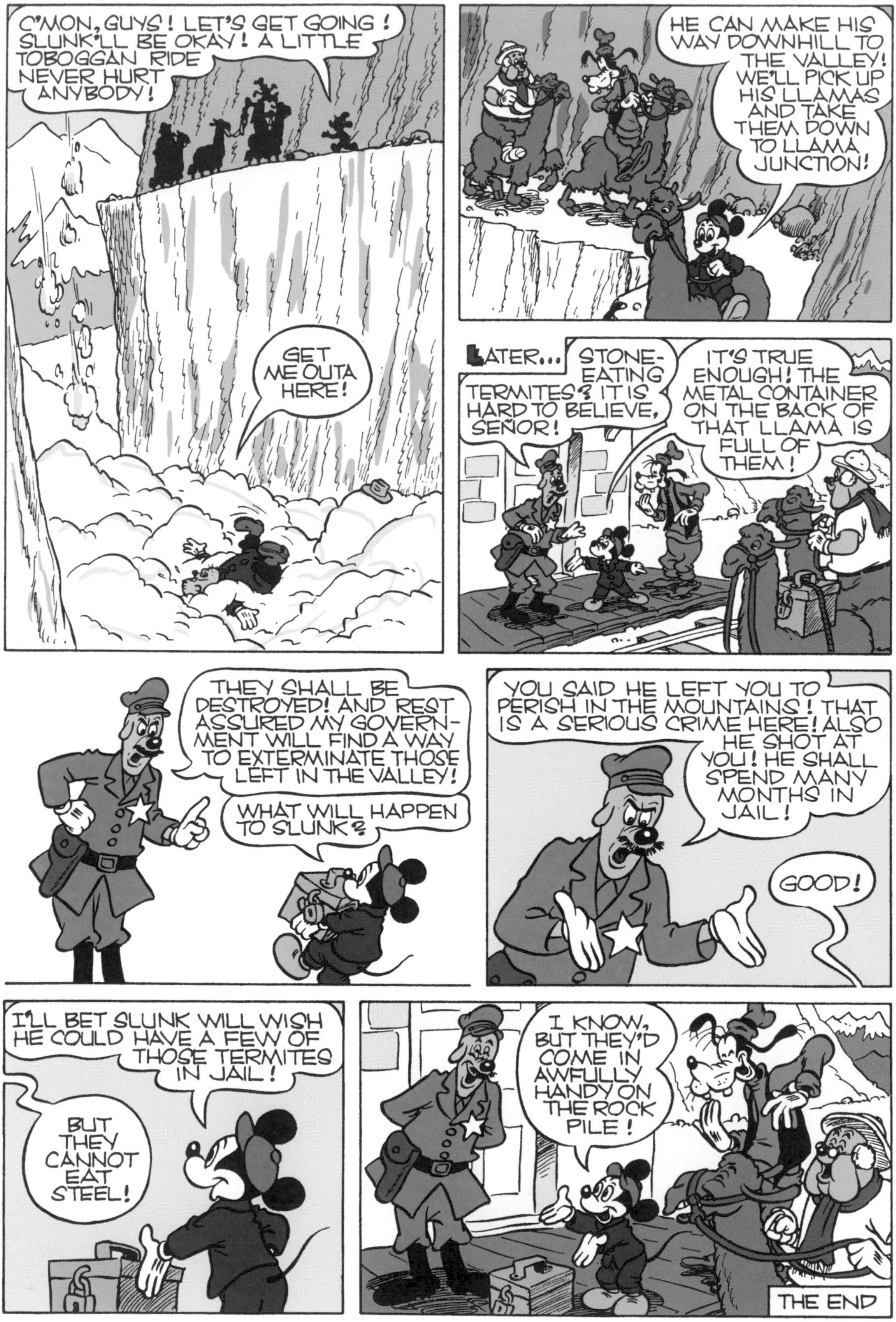
C'MON, GUYS! LET'S GET GOING! SLUNK'LL BE OKAY! A LITTLE TOBOGGAN RIDE NEVER HURT ANYBODY!
GET ME OUTA HERE!
HE CAN MAKE HIS WAY DOWNHILL TO THE VALLEY! WE'LL PICK UP HIS LLAMAS AND TAKE THEM DOWN TO LLAMA JUNCTION!
LATER...
STONE-EATING TERMITES? IT IS HARD TO BELIEVE, SEÑOR!
IT'S TRUE ENOUGH! THE METAL CONTAINER ON THE BACK OF THAT LLAMA IS FULL OF THEM!
THEY SHALL BE DESTROYED! AND REST ASSURED MY GOVERNMENT WILL FIND A WAY TO EXTERMINATE THOSE LEFT IN THE VALLEY!
WHAT WILL HAPPEN TO SLUNK?
YOU SAID HE LEFT YOU TO PERISH IN THE MOUNTAINS! THAT IS A SERIOUS CRIME HERE! ALSO HE SHOT AT YOU! HE SHALL SPEND MANY MONTHS IN JAIL!
GOOD!
I'LL BET SLUNK WILL WISH HE COULD HAVE A FEW OF THOSE TERMITES IN JAIL!
BUT THEY CANNOT EAT STEEL!
I KNOW, BUT THEY'D COME IN AWFULLY HANDY ON THE ROCK PILE!
THE END

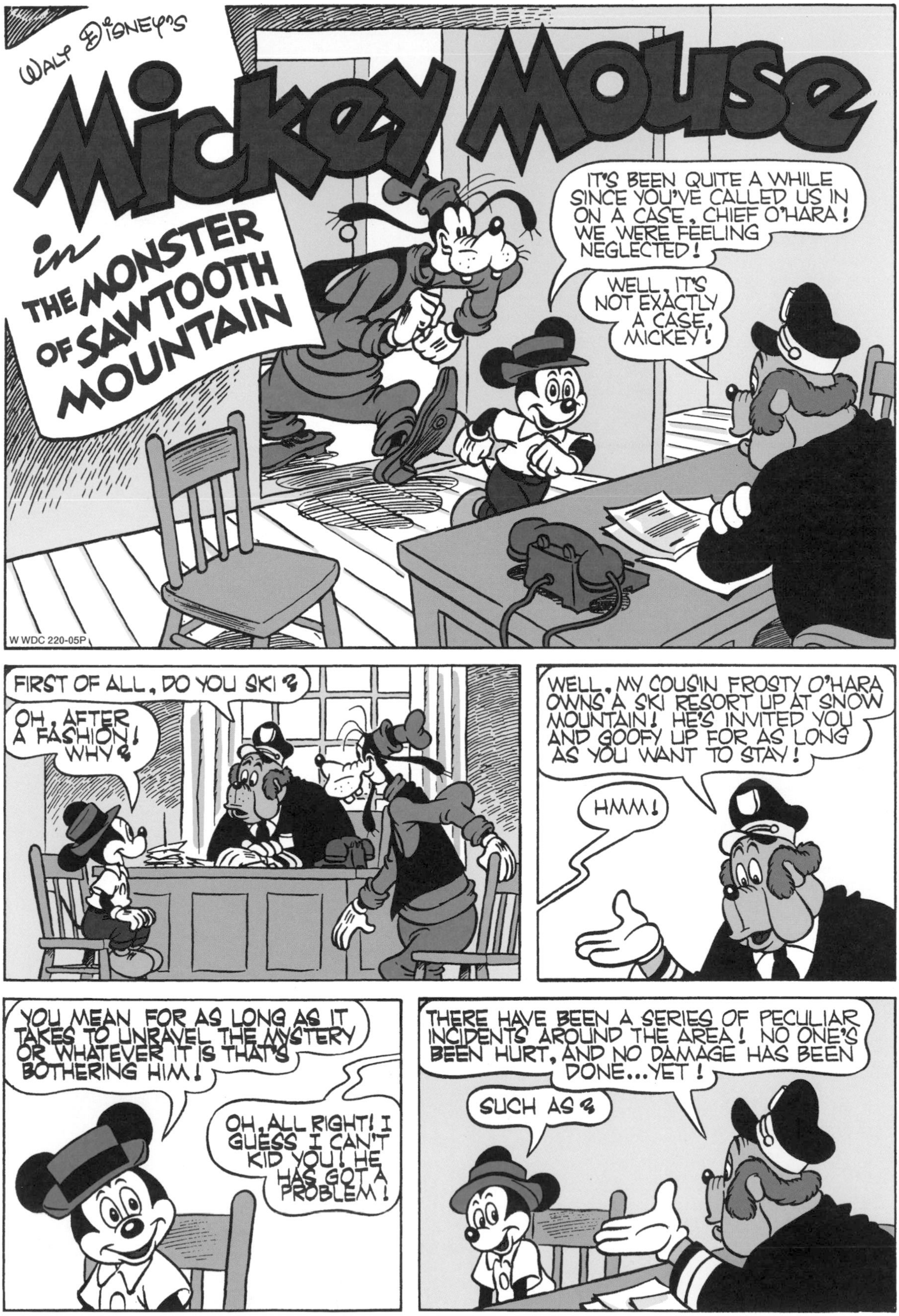

WALT DISNEY'S
Mickey Mouse
in THE MONSTER OF SAWTOOTH MOUNTAIN
IT'S BEEN QUITE A WHILE SINCE YOU'VE CALLED US IN ON A CASE, CHIEF O'HARA! WE WERE FEELING NEGLECTED!
WELL, IT'S NOT EXACTLY A CASE, MICKEY!
W WDC 220-05P
FIRST OF ALL, DO YOU SKI?
OH, AFTER A FASHION! WHY?
WELL, MY COUSIN FROSTY O'HARA OWNS A SKI RESORT UP AT SNOW MOUNTAIN! HE'S INVITED YOU AND GOOFY UP FOR AS LONG AS YOU WANT TO STAY!
HMM!
YOU MEAN FOR AS LONG AS IT TAKES TO UNRAVEL THE MYSTERY OR WHATEVER IT IS THAT'S BOTHERING HIM!
OH, ALL RIGHT! I GUESS I CAN'T KID YOU! HE HAS GOT A PROBLEM!
THERE HAVE BEEN A SERIES OF PECULIAR INCIDENTS AROUND THE AREA! NO ONE'S BEEN HURT, AND NO DAMAGE HAS BEEN DONE...YET!
SUCH AS?

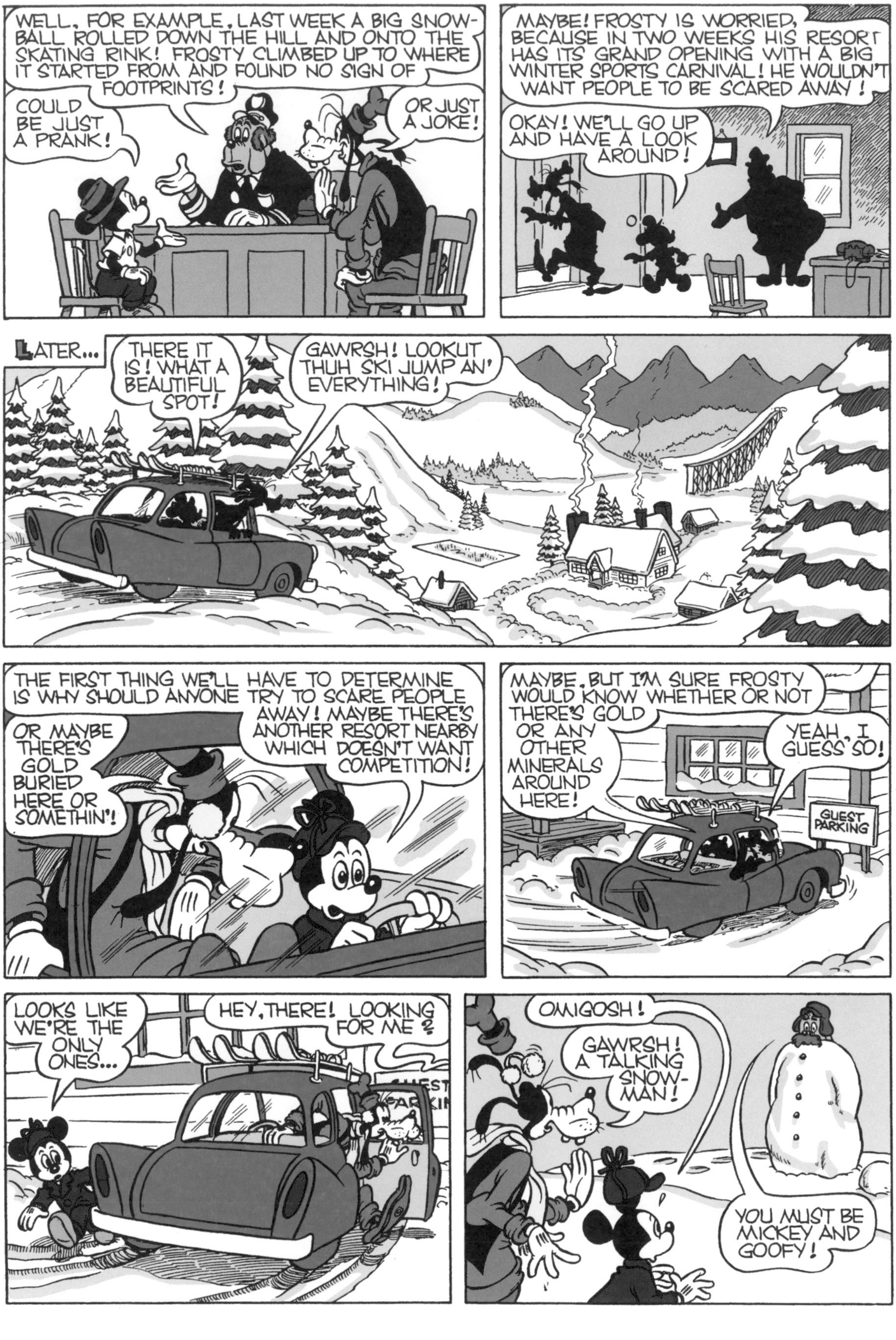

WELL, FOR EXAMPLE, LAST WEEK A BIG SNOW-BALL ROLLED DOWN THE HILL AND ONTO THE SKATING RINK! FROSTY CLIMBED UP TO WHERE IT STARTED FROM AND FOUND NO SIGN OF FOOTPRINTS!
COULD BE JUST A PRANK!
OR JUST A JOKE!
MAYBE! FROSTY IS WORRIED, BECAUSE IN TWO WEEKS HIS RESORT HAS ITS GRAND OPENING WITH A BIG WINTER SPORTS CARNIVAL! HE WOULDN'T WANT PEOPLE TO BE SCARED AWAY!
OKAY! WE'LL GO UP AND HAVE A LOOK AROUND!
LATER...
THERE IT IS! WHAT A BEAUTIFUL SPOT!
GAWRSH! LOOKUT THUH SKI JUMP AN' EVERYTHING!
THE FIRST THING WE'LL HAVE TO DETERMINE IS WHY SHOULD ANYONE TRY TO SCARE PEOPLE AWAY! MAYBE THERE'S ANOTHER RESORT NEARBY WHICH DOESN'T WANT COMPETITION!
OR MAYBE THERE'S GOLD BURIED HERE OR SOMETHIN'!
MAYBE, BUT I'M SURE FROSTY WOULD KNOW WHETHER OR NOT THERE'S GOLD OR ANY OTHER MINERALS AROUND HERE!
YEAH, I GUESS SO!
GUEST PARKING
LOOKS LIKE WE'RE THE ONLY ONES...
HEY, THERE! LOOKING FOR ME?
OMIGOSH!
GAWRSH! A TALKING SNOW-MAN!
YOU MUST BE MICKEY AND GOOFY!

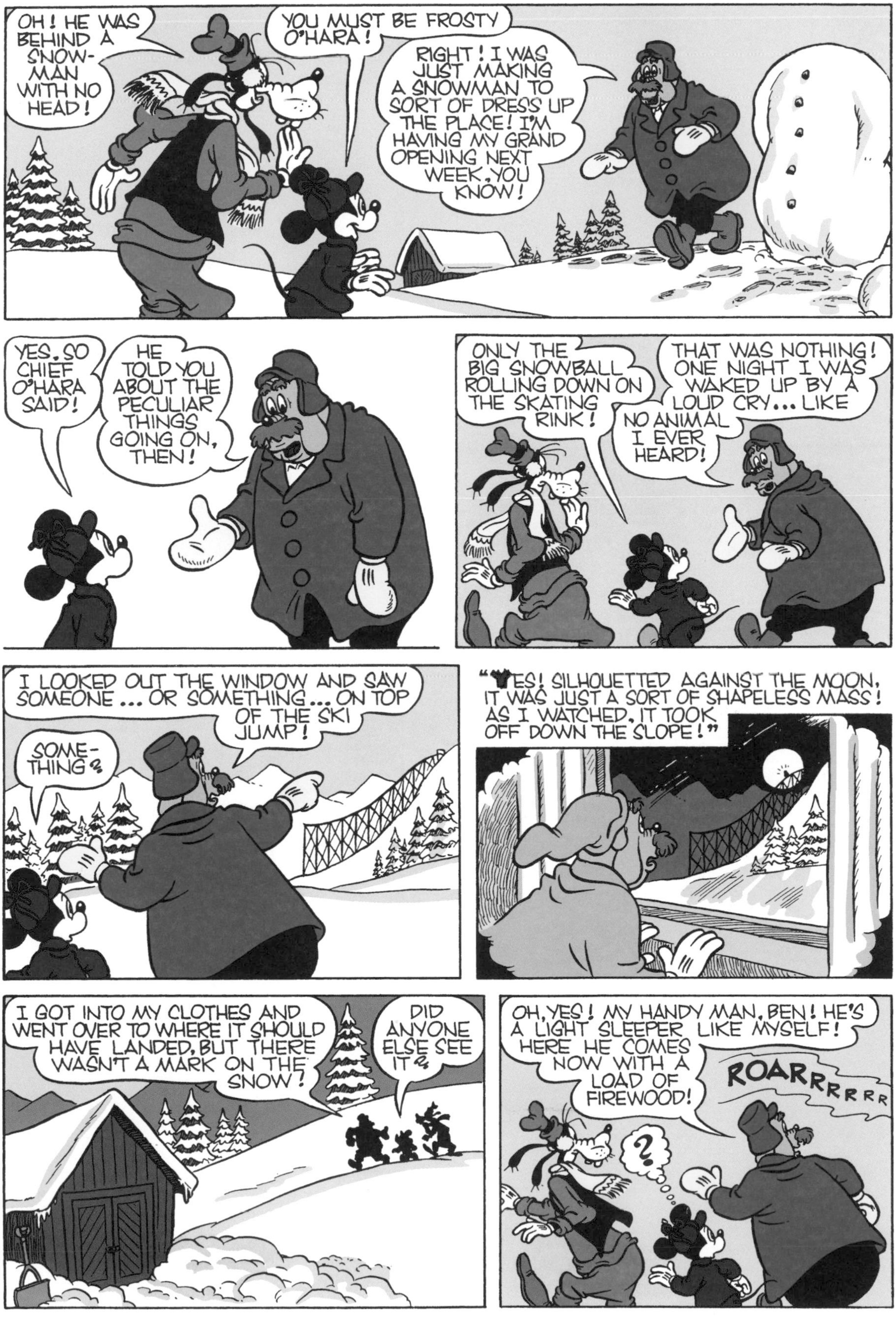
OH! HE WAS BEHIND A SNOW-MAN WITH NO HEAD!
YOU MUST BE FROSTY O'HARA!
RIGHT! I WAS JUST MAKING A SNOWMAN TO SORT OF DRESS UP THE PLACE! I'M HAVING MY GRAND OPENING NEXT WEEK, YOU KNOW!
YES. SO CHIEF O'HARA SAID!
HE TOLD YOU ABOUT THE PECULIAR THINGS GOING ON, THEN!
ONLY THE BIG SNOWBALL ROLLING DOWN ON THE SKATING RINK!
THAT WAS NOTHING! ONE NIGHT I WAS WAKED UP BY A LOUD CRY... LIKE NO ANIMAL I EVER HEARD!
I LOOKED OUT THE WINDOW AND SAW SOMEONE ... OR SOMETHING ... ON TOP OF THE SKI JUMP!
SOME-THING?
"YES! SILHOUETTED AGAINST THE MOON, IT WAS JUST A SORT OF SHAPELESS MASS! AS I WATCHED, IT TOOK OFF DOWN THE SLOPE!"
I GOT INTO MY CLOTHES AND WENT OVER TO WHERE IT SHOULD HAVE LANDED, BUT THERE WASN'T A MARK ON THE SNOW!
DID ANYONE ELSE SEE IT?
OH, YES! MY HANDY MAN, BEN! HE'S A LIGHT SLEEPER LIKE MYSELF! HERE HE COMES NOW WITH A LOAD OF FIREWOOD!
ROARRRRRR
?

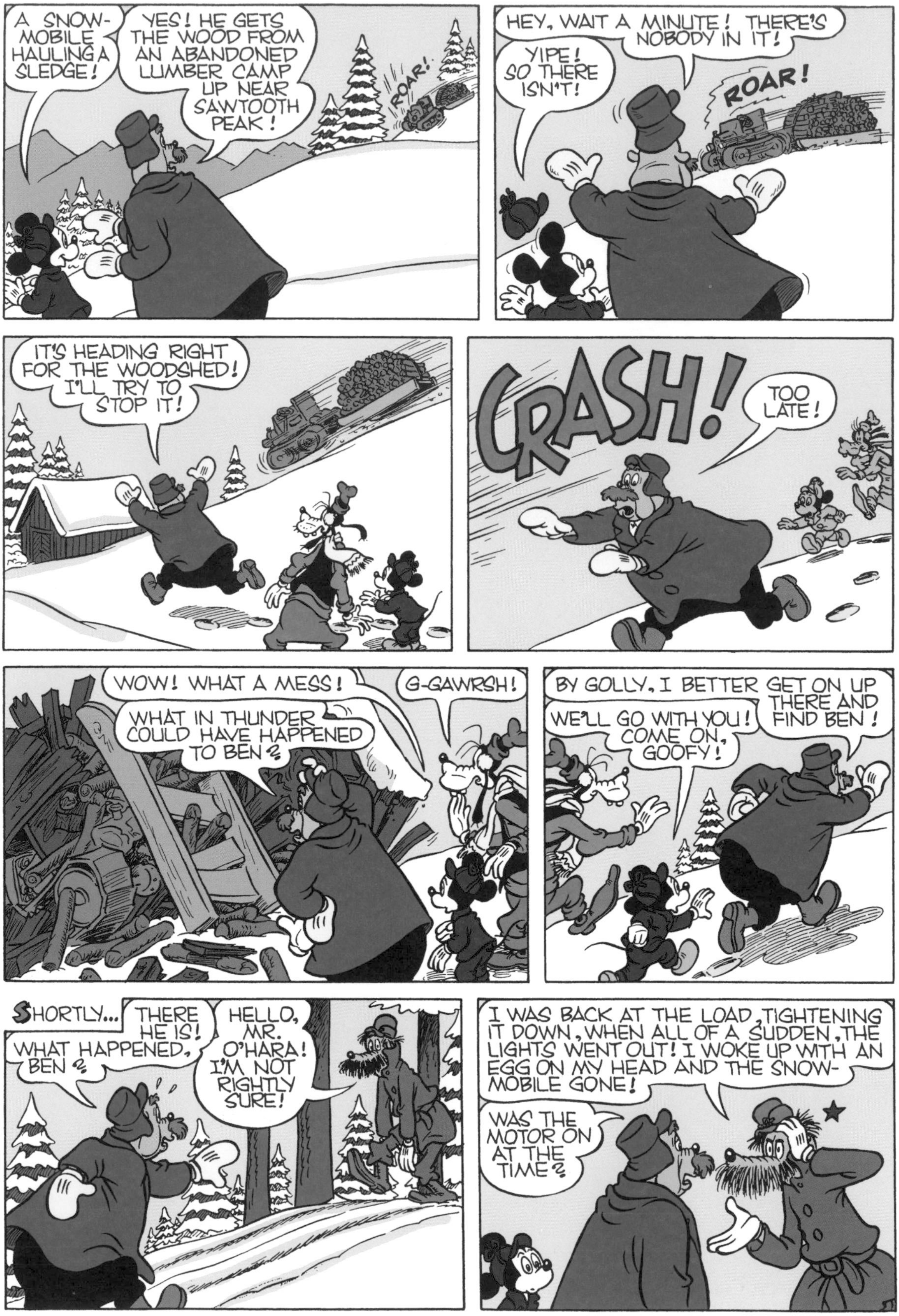
A SNOW-MOBILE HAULING A SLEDGE!
YES! HE GETS THE WOOD FROM AN ABANDONED LUMBER CAMP UP NEAR SAWTOOTH PEAK!
ROAR!
HEY, WAIT A MINUTE! THERE'S NOBODY IN IT!
YIPE! SO THERE ISN'T!
ROAR!
IT'S HEADING RIGHT FOR THE WOODSHED! I'LL TRY TO STOP IT!
CRASH!
TOO LATE!
WOW! WHAT A MESS!
WHAT IN THUNDER COULD HAVE HAPPENED TO BEN?
G-GAWRSH!
BY GOLLY, I BETTER GET ON UP THERE AND FIND BEN!
WE'LL GO WITH YOU! COME ON, GOOFY!
SHORTLY...
THERE HE IS! WHAT HAPPENED, BEN?
HELLO, MR. O'HARA! I'M NOT RIGHTLY SURE!
I WAS BACK AT THE LOAD, TIGHTENING IT DOWN, WHEN ALL OF A SUDDEN, THE LIGHTS WENT OUT! I WOKE UP WITH AN EGG ON MY HEAD AND THE SNOW-MOBILE GONE!
WAS THE MOTOR ON AT THE TIME?

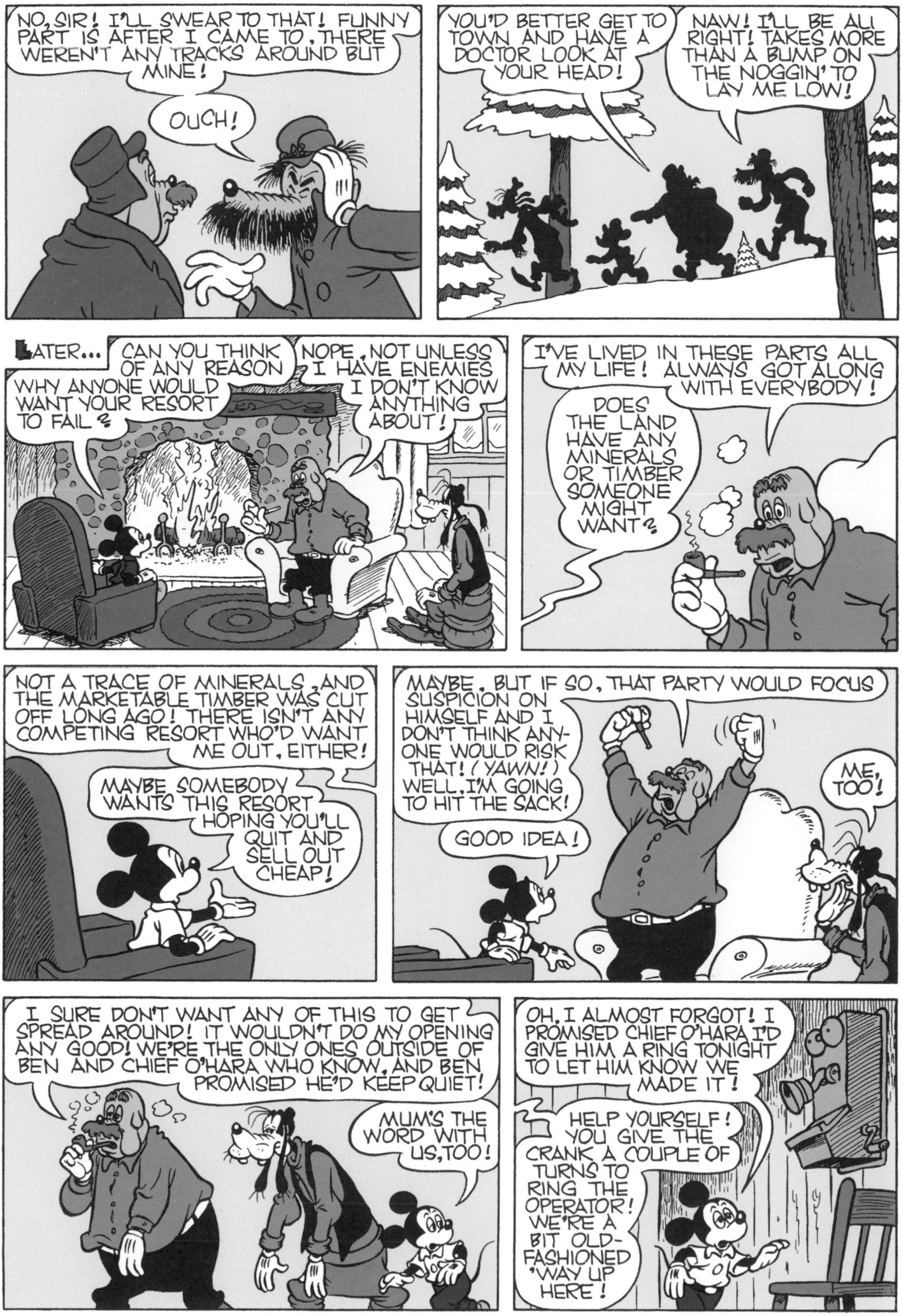
NO, SIR! I'LL SWEAR TO THAT! FUNNY PART IS AFTER I CAME TO, THERE WEREN'T ANY TRACKS AROUND BUT MINE!
OUCH!
YOU'D BETTER GET TO TOWN AND HAVE A DOCTOR LOOK AT YOUR HEAD!
NAW! I'LL BE ALL RIGHT! TAKES MORE THAN A BUMP ON THE NOGGIN' TO LAY ME LOW!
LATER...
CAN YOU THINK OF ANY REASON WHY ANYONE WOULD WANT YOUR RESORT TO FAIL?
NOPE, NOT UNLESS I HAVE ENEMIES I DON'T KNOW ANYTHING ABOUT!
I'VE LIVED IN THESE PARTS ALL MY LIFE! ALWAYS GOT ALONG WITH EVERYBODY!
DOES THE LAND HAVE ANY MINERALS OR TIMBER SOMEONE MIGHT WANT?
NOT A TRACE OF MINERALS, AND THE MARKETABLE TIMBER WAS CUT OFF LONG AGO! THERE ISN'T ANY COMPETING RESORT WHO'D WANT ME OUT, EITHER!
MAYBE SOMEBODY WANTS THIS RESORT HOPING YOU'LL QUIT AND SELL OUT CHEAP!
MAYBE, BUT IF SO, THAT PARTY WOULD FOCUS SUSPICION ON HIMSELF AND I DON'T THINK ANYONE WOULD RISK THAT! (YAWN!) WELL, I'M GOING TO HIT THE SACK!
GOOD IDEA!
ME, TOO!
I SURE DON'T WANT ANY OF THIS TO GET SPREAD AROUND! IT WOULDN'T DO MY OPENING ANY GOOD! WE'RE THE ONLY ONES OUTSIDE OF BEN AND CHIEF O'HARA WHO KNOW, AND BEN PROMISED HE'D KEEP QUIET!
MUM'S THE WORD WITH US, TOO!
OH, I ALMOST FORGOT! I PROMISED CHIEF O'HARA I'D GIVE HIM A RING TONIGHT TO LET HIM KNOW WE MADE IT!
HELP YOURSELF! YOU GIVE THE CRANK A COUPLE OF TURNS TO RING THE OPERATOR! WE'RE A BIT OLD-FASHIONED 'WAY UP HERE!

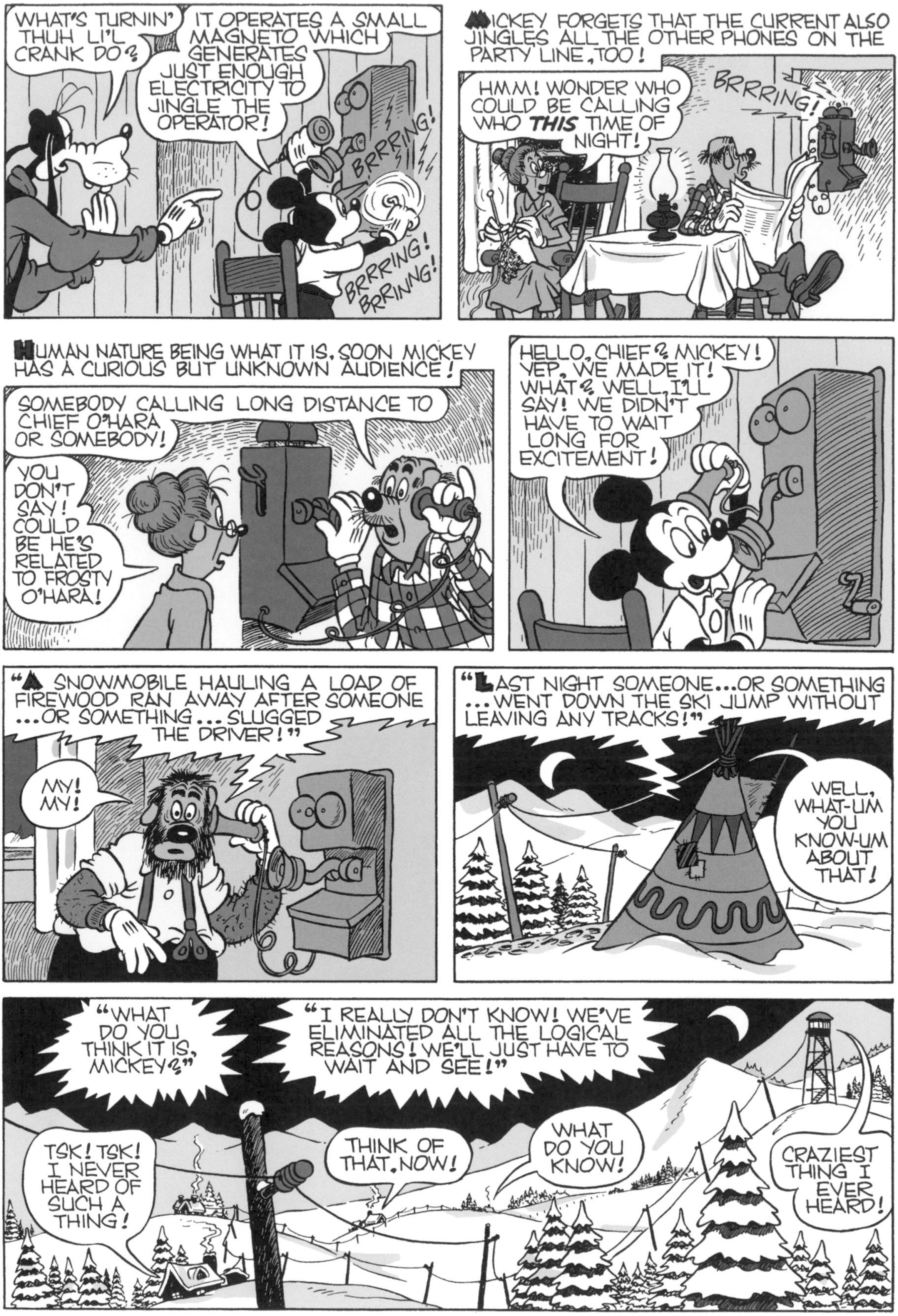
WHAT'S TURNIN' THUH LI'L CRANK DO?
IT OPERATES A SMALL MAGNETO WHICH GENERATES JUST ENOUGH ELECTRICITY TO JINGLE THE OPERATOR!
BRRRING!
BRRRING! BRRING!
MICKEY FORGETS THAT THE CURRENT ALSO JINGLES ALL THE OTHER PHONES ON THE PARTY LINE, TOO!
HMM! WONDER WHO COULD BE CALLING WHO THIS TIME OF NIGHT!
BRRRING!
HUMAN NATURE BEING WHAT IT IS, SOON MICKEY HAS A CURIOUS BUT UNKNOWN AUDIENCE!
SOMEBODY CALLING LONG DISTANCE TO CHIEF O'HARA OR SOMEBODY!
YOU DON'T SAY! COULD BE HE'S RELATED TO FROSTY O'HARA!
HELLO, CHIEF? MICKEY! YEP, WE MADE IT! WHAT? WELL, I'LL SAY! WE DIDN'T HAVE TO WAIT LONG FOR EXCITEMENT!
"A SNOWMOBILE HAULING A LOAD OF FIREWOOD RAN AWAY AFTER SOMEONE ...OR SOMETHING... SLUGGED THE DRIVER!"
MY! MY!
"LAST NIGHT SOMEONE...OR SOMETHING ...WENT DOWN THE SKI JUMP WITHOUT LEAVING ANY TRACKS!"
WELL, WHAT-UM YOU KNOW-UM ABOUT THAT!
"WHAT DO YOU THINK IT IS, MICKEY?"
"I REALLY DON'T KNOW! WE'VE ELIMINATED ALL THE LOGICAL REASONS! WE'LL JUST HAVE TO WAIT AND SEE!"
TSK! TSK! I NEVER HEARD OF SUCH A THING!
THINK OF THAT, NOW!
WHAT DO YOU KNOW!
CRAZIEST THING I EVER HEARD!

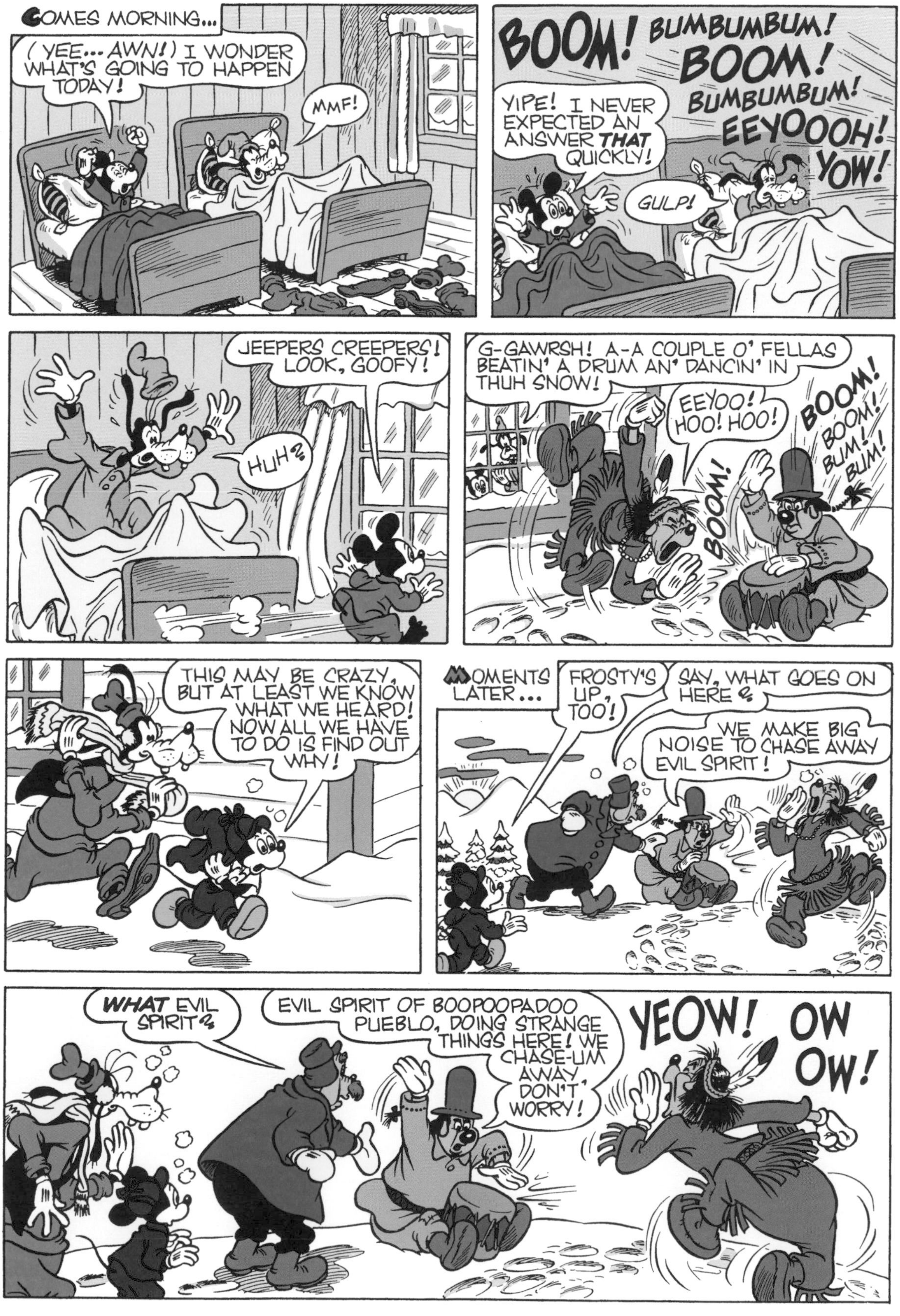
COMES MORNING...
(YEE... AWN!) I WONDER WHAT'S GOING TO HAPPEN TODAY!
MMF!
BOOM! BUMBUMBUM! BOOM! BUMBUMBUM! EEYOOOH! YOW!
YIPE! I NEVER EXPECTED AN ANSWER THAT QUICKLY!
GULP!
JEEPERS CREEPERS! LOOK, GOOFY!
HUH?
G-GAWRSH! A-A COUPLE O' FELLAS BEATIN' A DRUM AN' DANCIN' IN THUH SNOW!
EEYOO! HOO! HOO!
BOOM! BOOM! BUM! BUM!
BOOM!
THIS MAY BE CRAZY, BUT AT LEAST WE KNOW WHAT WE HEARD! NOW ALL WE HAVE TO DO IS FIND OUT WHY!
MOMENTS LATER...
FROSTY'S UP, TOO!
SAY, WHAT GOES ON HERE?
WE MAKE BIG NOISE TO CHASE AWAY EVIL SPIRIT!
WHAT EVIL SPIRIT?
EVIL SPIRIT OF BOOPOOPADOO PUEBLO, DOING STRANGE THINGS HERE! WE CHASE-UM AWAY, DON'T WORRY!
YEOW! OW OW!

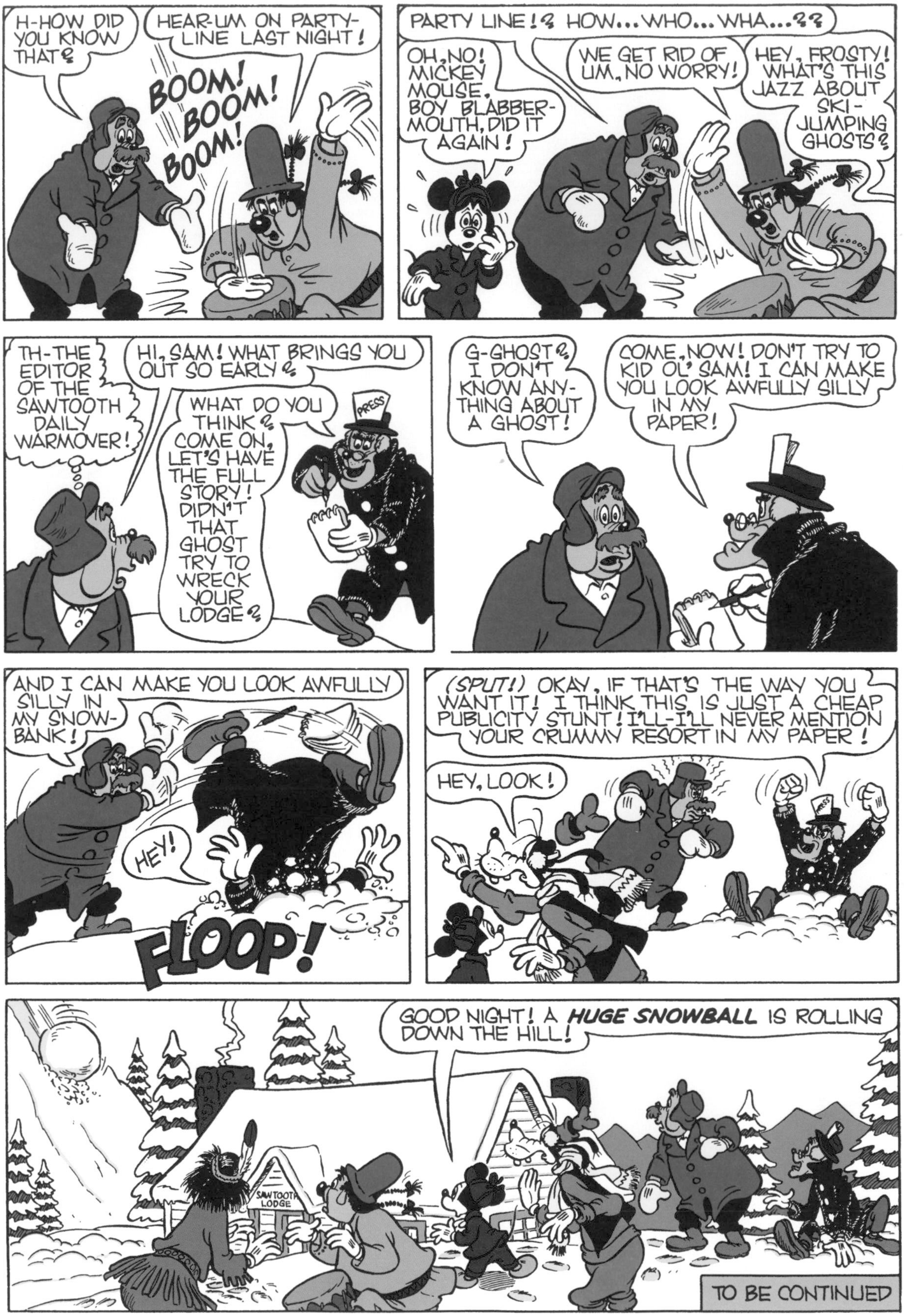
H-HOW DID YOU KNOW THAT?
HEAR-UM ON PARTY-LINE LAST NIGHT!
BOOM! BOOM! BOOM!
PARTY LINE!? HOW... WHO... WHA...??
OH, NO! MICKEY MOUSE, BOY BLABBER-MOUTH, DID IT AGAIN!
WE GET RID OF UM, NO WORRY!
HEY, FROSTY! WHAT'S THIS JAZZ ABOUT SKI-JUMPING GHOSTS?
TH-THE EDITOR OF THE SAWTOOTH DAILY WARMOVER!
HI, SAM! WHAT BRINGS YOU OUT SO EARLY?
WHAT DO YOU THINK? COME ON, LET'S HAVE THE FULL STORY! DIDN'T THAT GHOST TRY TO WRECK YOUR LODGE?
PRESS
G-GHOST? I DON'T KNOW ANY-THING ABOUT A GHOST!
COME, NOW! DON'T TRY TO KID OL' SAM! I CAN MAKE YOU LOOK AWFULLY SILLY IN MY PAPER!
AND I CAN MAKE YOU LOOK AWFULLY SILLY IN MY SNOW-BANK!
HEY!
FLOOP!
(SPUT!) OKAY, IF THAT'S THE WAY YOU WANT IT! I THINK THIS IS JUST A CHEAP PUBLICITY STUNT! I'LL-I'LL NEVER MENTION YOUR CRUMMY RESORT IN MY PAPER!
HEY, LOOK!
PRESS
GOOD NIGHT! A **HUGE SNOWBALL** IS ROLLING DOWN THE HILL!
SAWTOOTH LODGE
TO BE CONTINUED

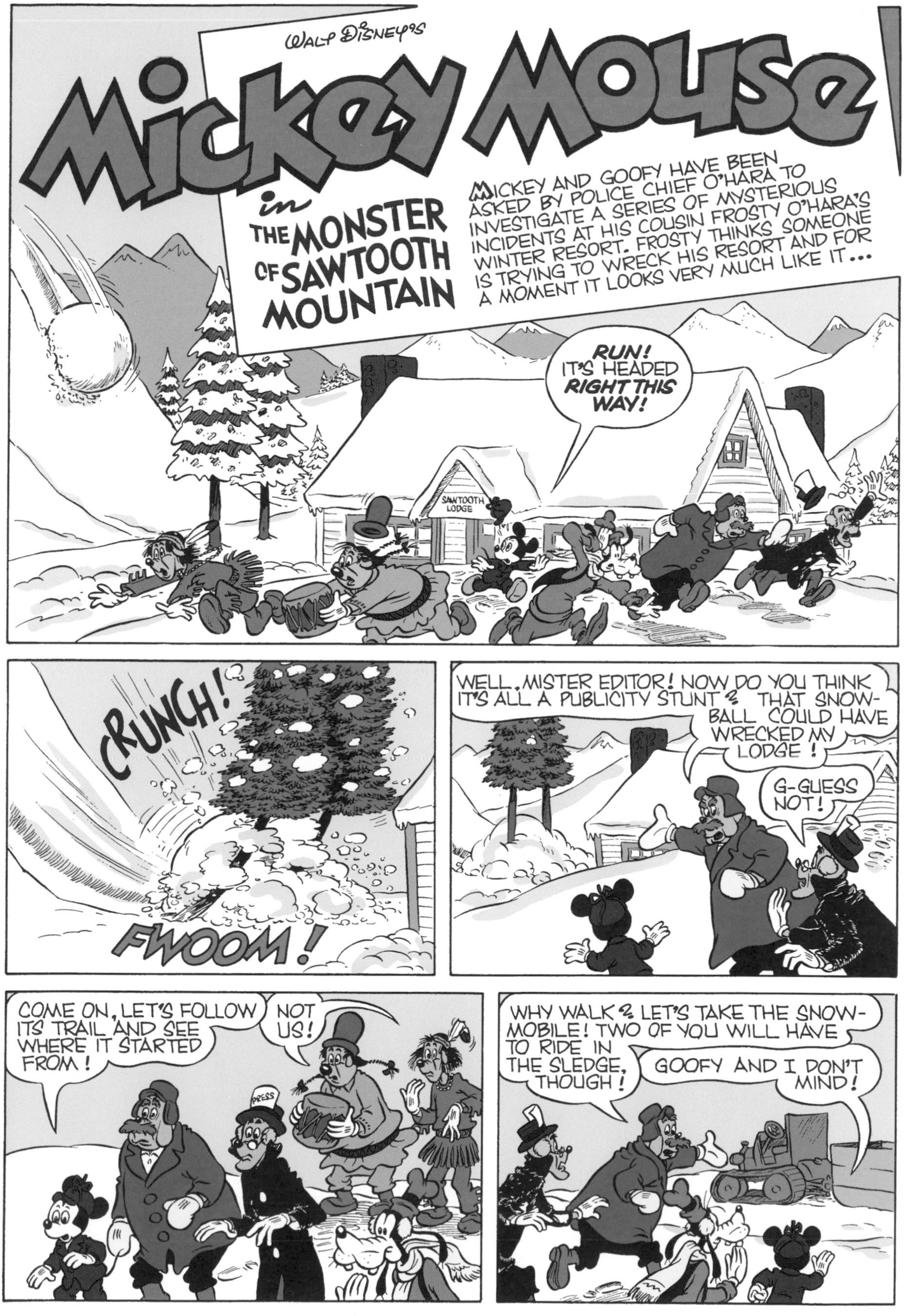
WALT DISNEY'S
MICKEY MOUSE
in THE MONSTER OF SAWTOOTH MOUNTAIN
MICKEY AND GOOFY HAVE BEEN ASKED BY POLICE CHIEF O'HARA TO INVESTIGATE A SERIES OF MYSTERIOUS INCIDENTS AT HIS COUSIN FROSTY O'HARA'S WINTER RESORT. FROSTY THINKS SOMEONE IS TRYING TO WRECK HIS RESORT AND FOR A MOMENT IT LOOKS VERY MUCH LIKE IT...
RUN! IT'S HEADED RIGHT THIS WAY!
SAWTOOTH LODGE
CRUNCH!
FWOOM!
WELL, MISTER EDITOR! NOW DO YOU THINK IT'S ALL A PUBLICITY STUNT? THAT SNOWBALL COULD HAVE WRECKED MY LODGE!
G-GUESS NOT!
COME ON, LET'S FOLLOW ITS TRAIL AND SEE WHERE IT STARTED FROM!
NOT US!
PRESS
WHY WALK? LET'S TAKE THE SNOWMOBILE! TWO OF YOU WILL HAVE TO RIDE IN THE SLEDGE, THOUGH!
GOOFY AND I DON'T MIND!

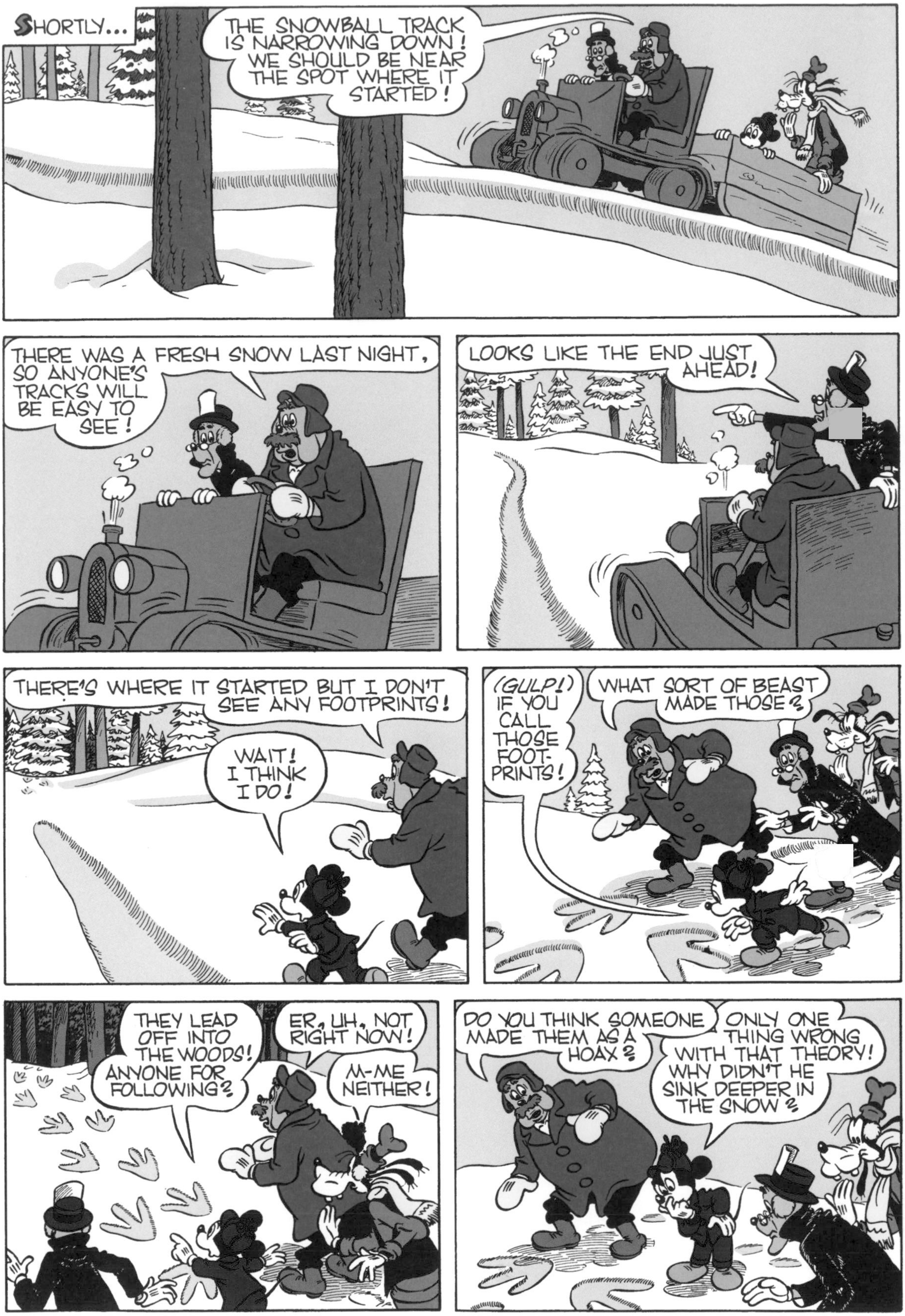
SHORTLY...
THE SNOWBALL TRACK IS NARROWING DOWN! WE SHOULD BE NEAR THE SPOT WHERE IT STARTED!
THERE WAS A FRESH SNOW LAST NIGHT, SO ANYONE'S TRACKS WILL BE EASY TO SEE!
LOOKS LIKE THE END JUST AHEAD!
THERE'S WHERE IT STARTED BUT I DON'T SEE ANY FOOTPRINTS!
WAIT! I THINK I DO!
(GULP!) IF YOU CALL THOSE FOOT-PRINTS!
WHAT SORT OF BEAST MADE THOSE?
THEY LEAD OFF INTO THE WOODS! ANYONE FOR FOLLOWING?
ER, UH, NOT RIGHT NOW!
M-ME NEITHER!
DO YOU THINK SOMEONE MADE THEM AS A HOAX?
ONLY ONE THING WRONG WITH THAT THEORY! WHY DIDN'T HE SINK DEEPER IN THE SNOW?

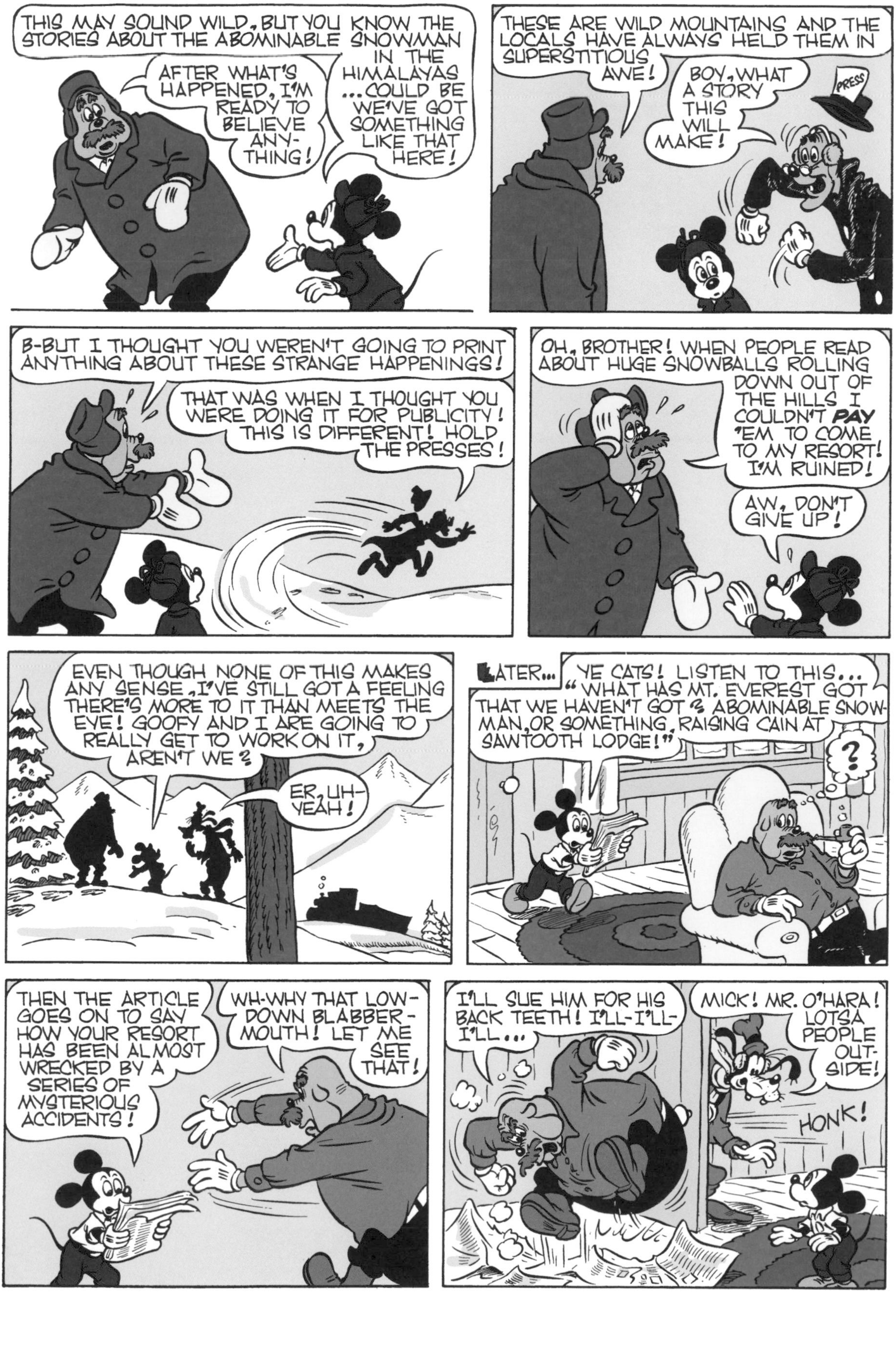
THIS MAY SOUND WILD, BUT YOU KNOW THE STORIES ABOUT THE ABOMINABLE SNOWMAN IN THE HIMALAYAS ...COULD BE WE'VE GOT SOMETHING LIKE THAT HERE!
AFTER WHAT'S HAPPENED, I'M READY TO BELIEVE ANY-THING!
THESE ARE WILD MOUNTAINS AND THE LOCALS HAVE ALWAYS HELD THEM IN SUPERSTITIOUS AWE!
BOY, WHAT A STORY THIS WILL MAKE!
PRESS
B-BUT I THOUGHT YOU WEREN'T GOING TO PRINT ANYTHING ABOUT THESE STRANGE HAPPENINGS!
THAT WAS WHEN I THOUGHT YOU WERE DOING IT FOR PUBLICITY! THIS IS DIFFERENT! HOLD THE PRESSES!
OH, BROTHER! WHEN PEOPLE READ ABOUT HUGE SNOWBALLS ROLLING DOWN OUT OF THE HILLS I COULDN'T PAY 'EM TO COME TO MY RESORT! I'M RUINED!
AW, DON'T GIVE UP!
EVEN THOUGH NONE OF THIS MAKES ANY SENSE, I'VE STILL GOT A FEELING THERE'S MORE TO IT THAN MEETS THE EYE! GOOFY AND I ARE GOING TO REALLY GET TO WORK ON IT, AREN'T WE?
ER, UH- YEAH!
LATER...
YE CATS! LISTEN TO THIS... "WHAT HAS MT. EVEREST GOT THAT WE HAVEN'T GOT? ABOMINABLE SNOW-MAN, OR SOMETHING, RAISING CAIN AT SAWTOOTH LODGE!"
?
THEN THE ARTICLE GOES ON TO SAY HOW YOUR RESORT HAS BEEN ALMOST WRECKED BY A SERIES OF MYSTERIOUS ACCIDENTS!
WH-WHY THAT LOW-DOWN BLABBER-MOUTH! LET ME SEE THAT!
I'LL SUE HIM FOR HIS BACK TEETH! I'LL-I'LL-I'LL...
MICK! MR. O'HARA! LOTSA PEOPLE OUT-SIDE!
HONK!

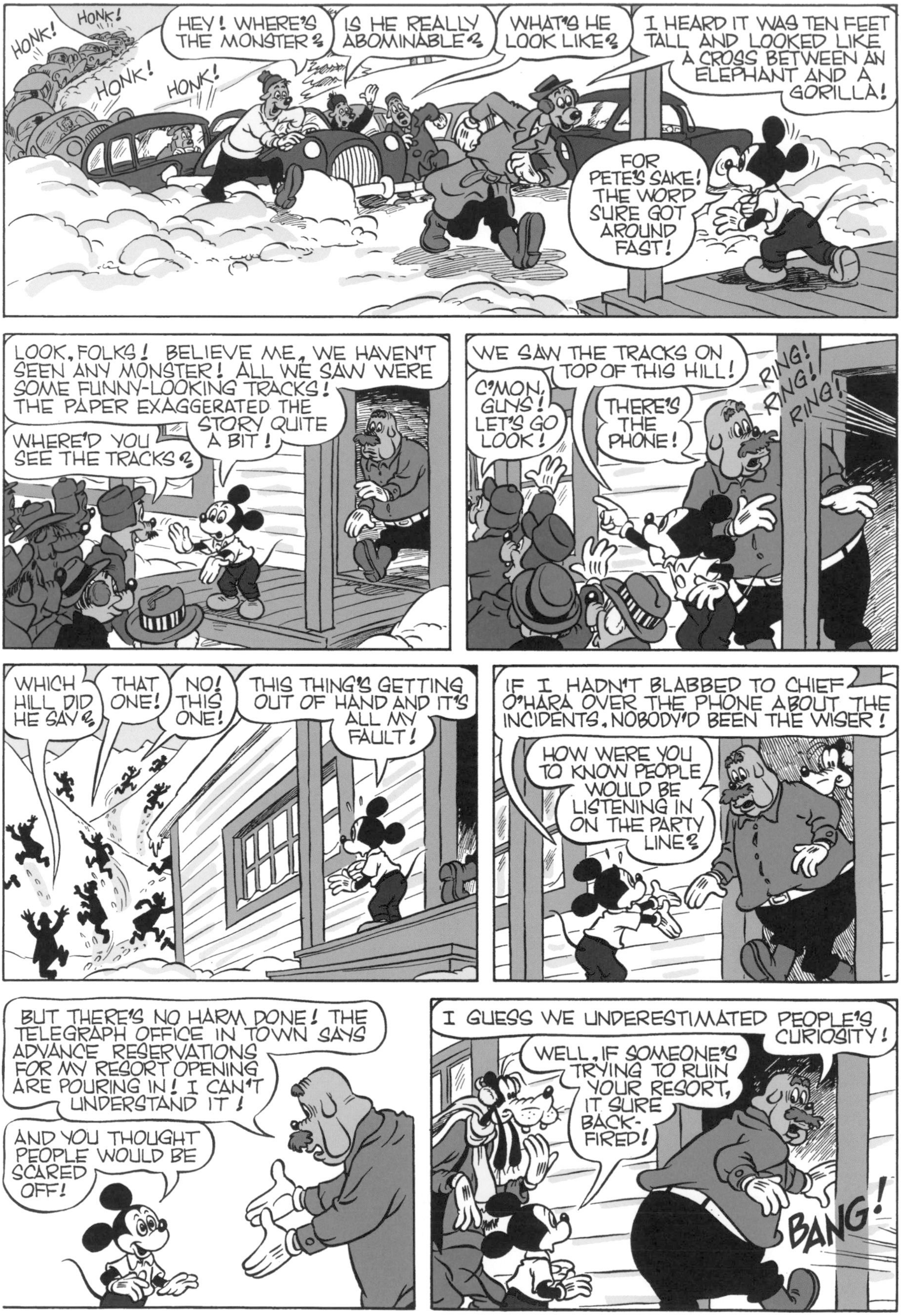
HONK!
HONK!
HONK!
HONK!
HEY! WHERE'S THE MONSTER?
IS HE REALLY ABOMINABLE?
WHAT'S HE LOOK LIKE?
I HEARD IT WAS TEN FEET TALL AND LOOKED LIKE A CROSS BETWEEN AN ELEPHANT AND A GORILLA!
FOR PETE'S SAKE! THE WORD SURE GOT AROUND FAST!
LOOK, FOLKS! BELIEVE ME, WE HAVEN'T SEEN ANY MONSTER! ALL WE SAW WERE SOME FUNNY-LOOKING TRACKS! THE PAPER EXAGGERATED THE STORY QUITE A BIT!
WHERE'D YOU SEE THE TRACKS?
WE SAW THE TRACKS ON TOP OF THIS HILL!
C'MON, GUYS! LET'S GO LOOK!
THERE'S THE PHONE!
RING! RING! RING!
WHICH HILL DID HE SAY?
THAT ONE!
NO! THIS ONE!
THIS THING'S GETTING OUT OF HAND AND IT'S ALL MY FAULT!
IF I HADN'T BLABBED TO CHIEF O'HARA OVER THE PHONE ABOUT THE INCIDENTS, NOBODY'D BEEN THE WISER!
HOW WERE YOU TO KNOW PEOPLE WOULD BE LISTENING IN ON THE PARTY LINE?
BUT THERE'S NO HARM DONE! THE TELEGRAPH OFFICE IN TOWN SAYS ADVANCE RESERVATIONS FOR MY RESORT OPENING ARE POURING IN! I CAN'T UNDERSTAND IT!
AND YOU THOUGHT PEOPLE WOULD BE SCARED OFF!
I GUESS WE UNDERESTIMATED PEOPLE'S CURIOSITY!
WELL, IF SOMEONE'S TRYING TO RUIN YOUR RESORT, IT SURE BACK-FIRED!
BANG!

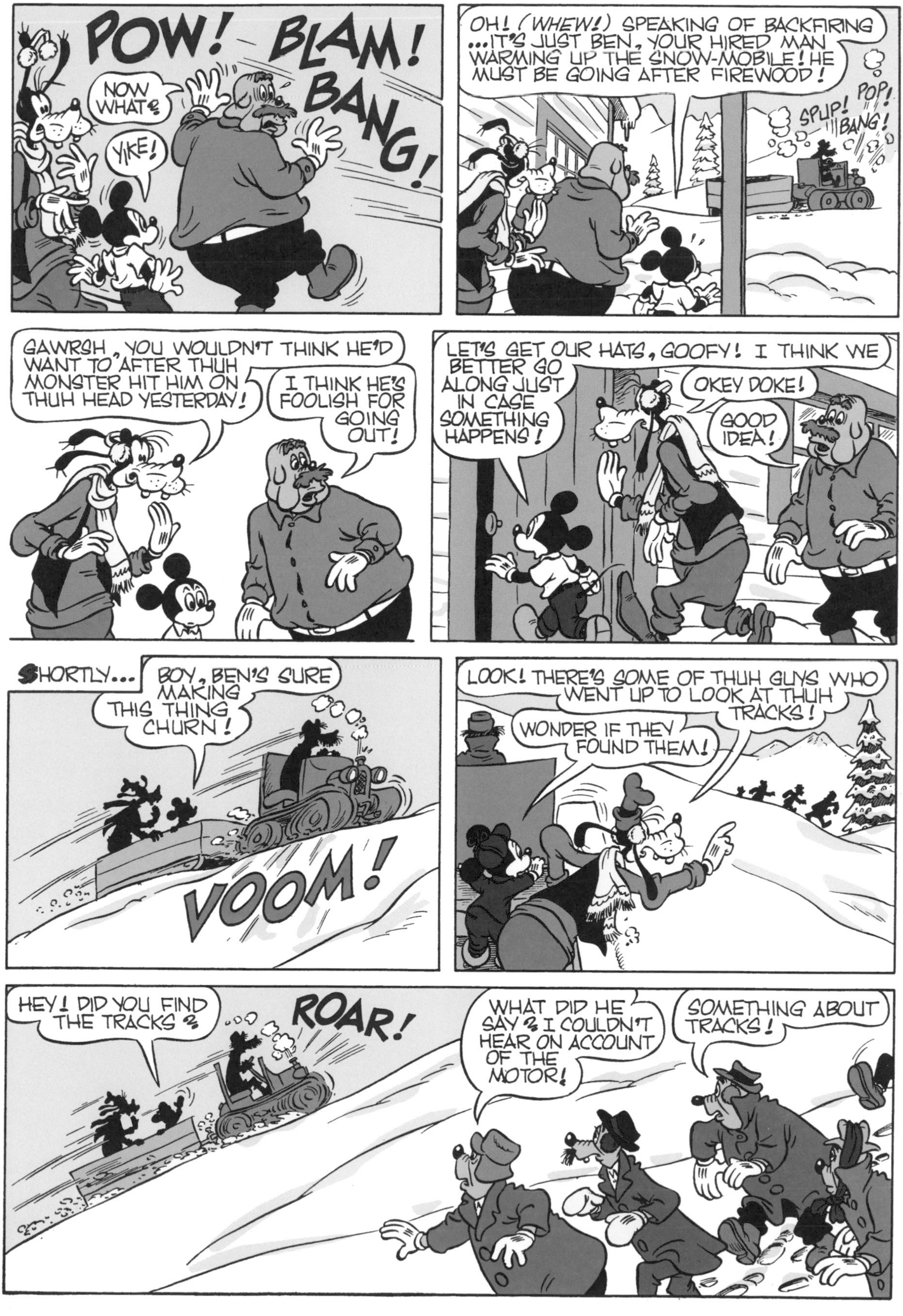
POW! BLAM!
NOW WHAT?
YIKE!
BANG!
OH! (WHEW!) SPEAKING OF BACKFIRING ...IT'S JUST BEN, YOUR HIRED MAN WARMING UP THE SNOW-MOBILE! HE MUST BE GOING AFTER FIREWOOD!
SPUP! POP! BANG!
GAWRSH, YOU WOULDN'T THINK HE'D WANT TO AFTER THUH MONSTER HIT HIM ON THUH HEAD YESTERDAY!
I THINK HE'S FOOLISH FOR GOING OUT!
LET'S GET OUR HATS, GOOFY! I THINK WE BETTER GO ALONG JUST IN CASE SOMETHING HAPPENS!
OKEY DOKE!
GOOD IDEA!
SHORTLY...
BOY, BEN'S SURE MAKING THIS THING CHURN!
VOOM!
LOOK! THERE'S SOME OF THUH GUYS WHO WENT UP TO LOOK AT THUH TRACKS!
WONDER IF THEY FOUND THEM!
HEY! DID YOU FIND THE TRACKS?
ROAR!
WHAT DID HE SAY? I COULDN'T HEAR ON ACCOUNT OF THE MOTOR!
SOMETHING ABOUT TRACKS!

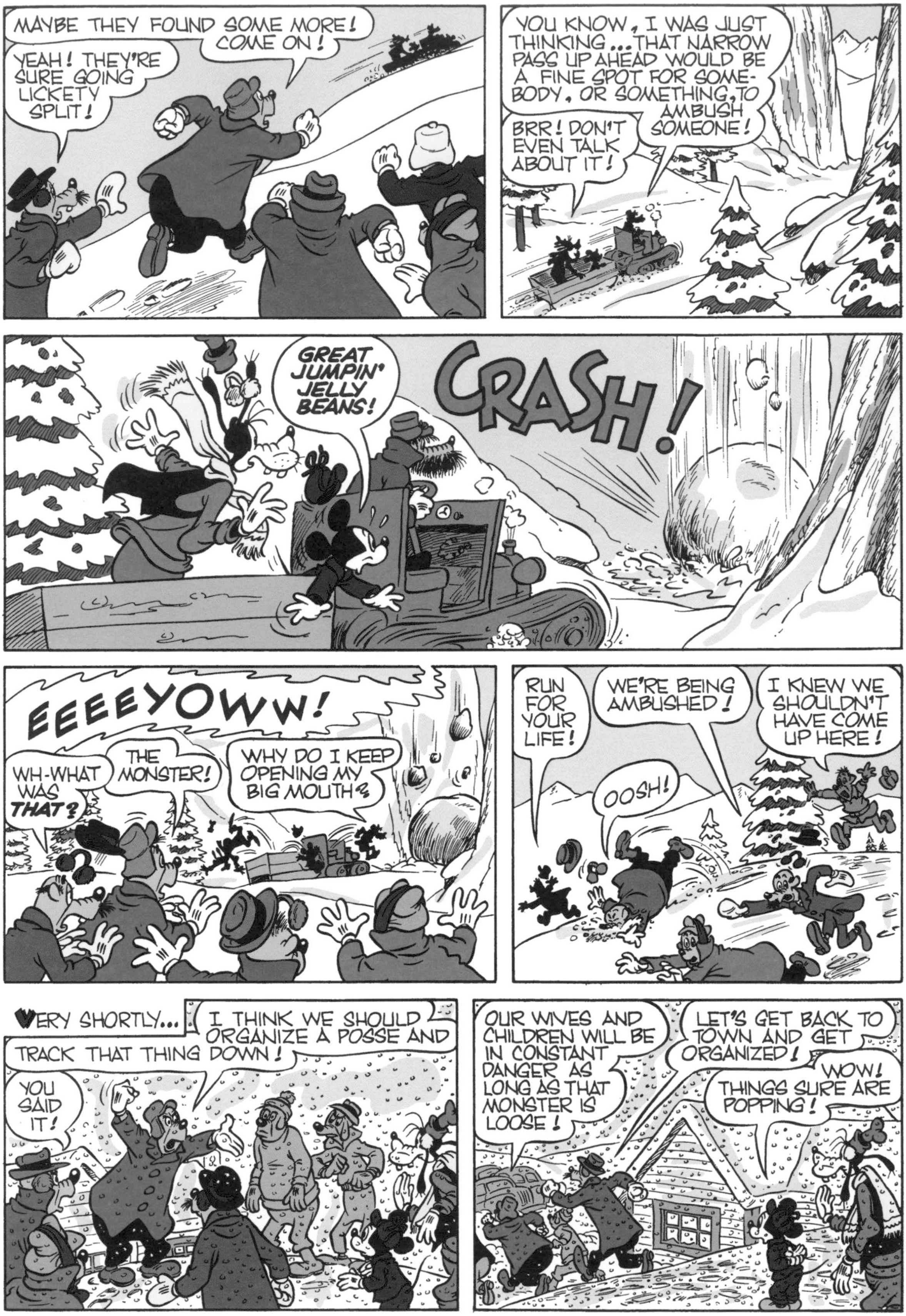
MAYBE THEY FOUND SOME MORE! COME ON!
YEAH! THEY'RE SURE GOING LICKETY SPLIT!
YOU KNOW, I WAS JUST THINKING... THAT NARROW PASS UP AHEAD WOULD BE A FINE SPOT FOR SOMEBODY, OR SOMETHING, TO AMBUSH SOMEONE!
BRR! DON'T EVEN TALK ABOUT IT!
GREAT JUMPIN' JELLY BEANS!
CRASH!
EEEEYOWW!
WH-WHAT WAS THAT?
THE MONSTER!
WHY DO I KEEP OPENING MY BIG MOUTH?
RUN FOR YOUR LIFE!
WE'RE BEING AMBUSHED!
I KNEW WE SHOULDN'T HAVE COME UP HERE!
OOSH!
VERY SHORTLY...
I THINK WE SHOULD ORGANIZE A POSSE AND TRACK THAT THING DOWN!
YOU SAID IT!
OUR WIVES AND CHILDREN WILL BE IN CONSTANT DANGER AS LONG AS THAT MONSTER IS LOOSE!
LET'S GET BACK TO TOWN AND GET ORGANIZED!
WOW! THINGS SURE ARE POPPING!

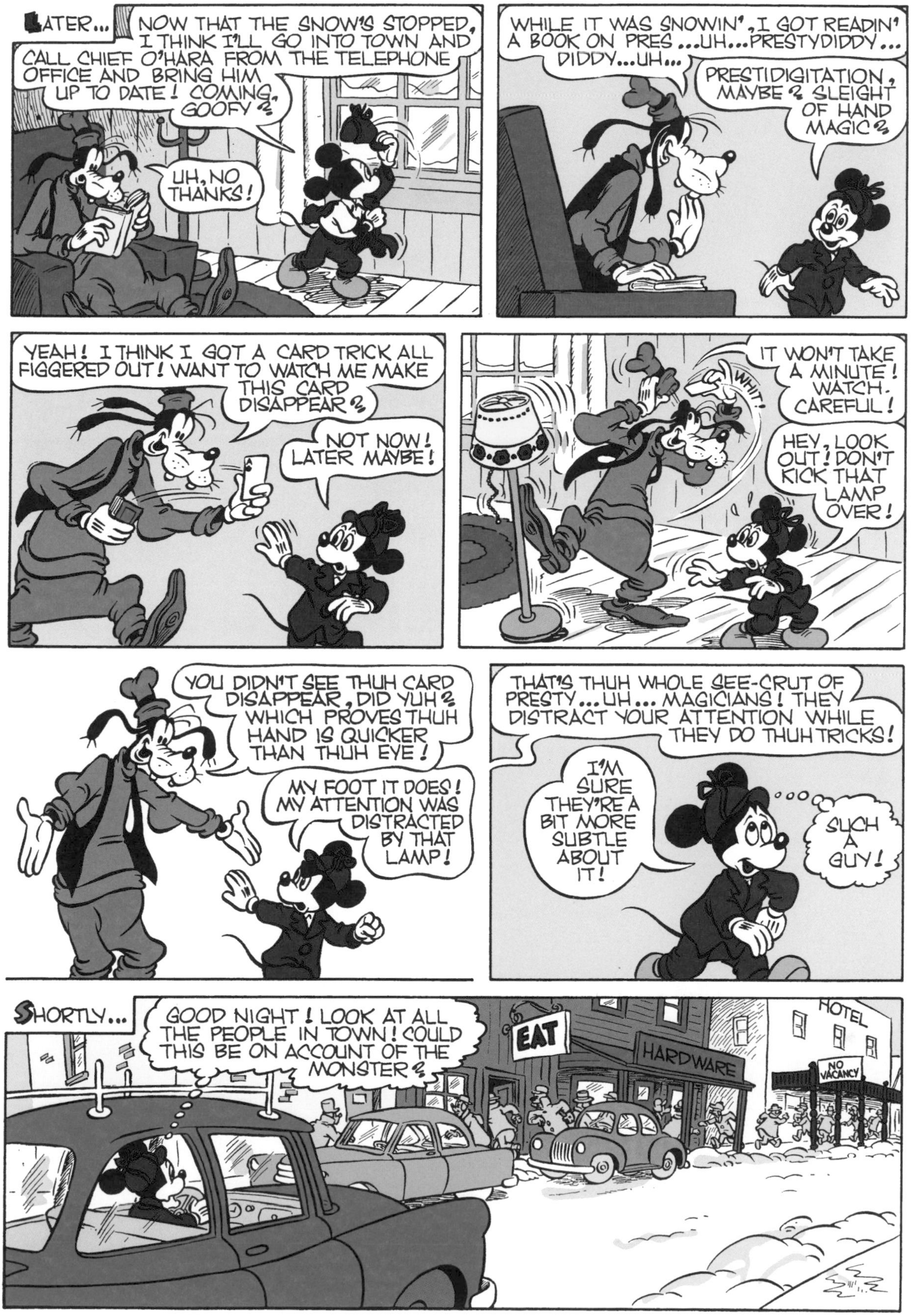
LATER...
NOW THAT THE SNOW'S STOPPED, I THINK I'LL GO INTO TOWN AND CALL CHIEF O'HARA FROM THE TELEPHONE OFFICE AND BRING HIM UP TO DATE! COMING, GOOFY?
UH, NO THANKS!
WHILE IT WAS SNOWIN', I GOT READIN' A BOOK ON PRES...UH...PRESTYDIDDY...DIDDY...UH...
PRESTIDIGITATION, MAYBE? SLEIGHT OF HAND MAGIC?
YEAH! I THINK I GOT A CARD TRICK ALL FIGGERED OUT! WANT TO WATCH ME MAKE THIS CARD DISAPPEAR?
NOT NOW! LATER MAYBE!
IT WON'T TAKE A MINUTE! WATCH. CAREFUL!
WHIT!
HEY, LOOK OUT! DON'T KICK THAT LAMP OVER!
YOU DIDN'T SEE THUH CARD DISAPPEAR, DID YUH? WHICH PROVES THUH HAND IS QUICKER THAN THUH EYE!
MY FOOT IT DOES! MY ATTENTION WAS DISTRACTED BY THAT LAMP!
THAT'S THUH WHOLE SEE-CRUT OF PRESTY...UH...MAGICIANS! THEY DISTRACT YOUR ATTENTION WHILE THEY DO THUH TRICKS!
I'M SURE THEY'RE A BIT MORE SUBTLE ABOUT IT!
SUCH A GUY!
SHORTLY...
GOOD NIGHT! LOOK AT ALL THE PEOPLE IN TOWN! COULD THIS BE ON ACCOUNT OF THE MONSTER?
EAT
HARDWARE
HOTEL
NO VACANCY

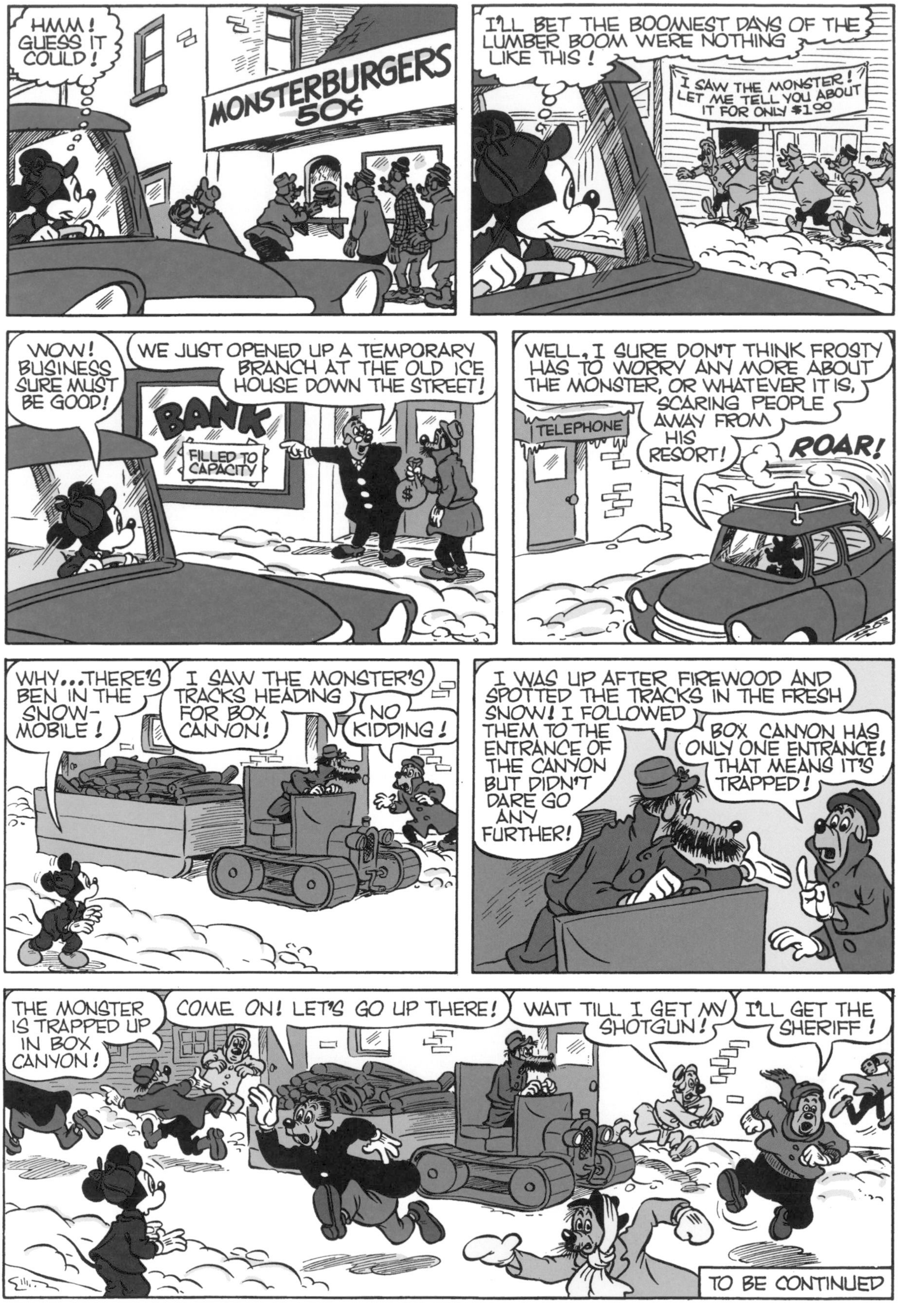
HMM! GUESS IT COULD!
MONSTERBURGERS 50¢
I'LL BET THE BOOMIEST DAYS OF THE LUMBER BOOM WERE NOTHING LIKE THIS!
I SAW THE MONSTER! LET ME TELL YOU ABOUT IT FOR ONLY $1.00
WOW! BUSINESS SURE MUST BE GOOD!
WE JUST OPENED UP A TEMPORARY BRANCH AT THE OLD ICE HOUSE DOWN THE STREET!
BANK
FILLED TO CAPACITY
WELL, I SURE DON'T THINK FROSTY HAS TO WORRY ANY MORE ABOUT THE MONSTER, OR WHATEVER IT IS, SCARING PEOPLE AWAY FROM HIS RESORT!
TELEPHONE
ROAR!
WHY...THERE'S BEN IN THE SNOW-MOBILE!
I SAW THE MONSTER'S TRACKS HEADING FOR BOX CANYON!
NO KIDDING!
I WAS UP AFTER FIREWOOD AND SPOTTED THE TRACKS IN THE FRESH SNOW! I FOLLOWED THEM TO THE ENTRANCE OF THE CANYON BUT DIDN'T DARE GO ANY FURTHER!
BOX CANYON HAS ONLY ONE ENTRANCE! THAT MEANS IT'S TRAPPED!
THE MONSTER IS TRAPPED UP IN BOX CANYON!
COME ON! LET'S GO UP THERE!
WAIT TILL I GET MY SHOTGUN!
I'LL GET THE SHERIFF!
TO BE CONTINUED

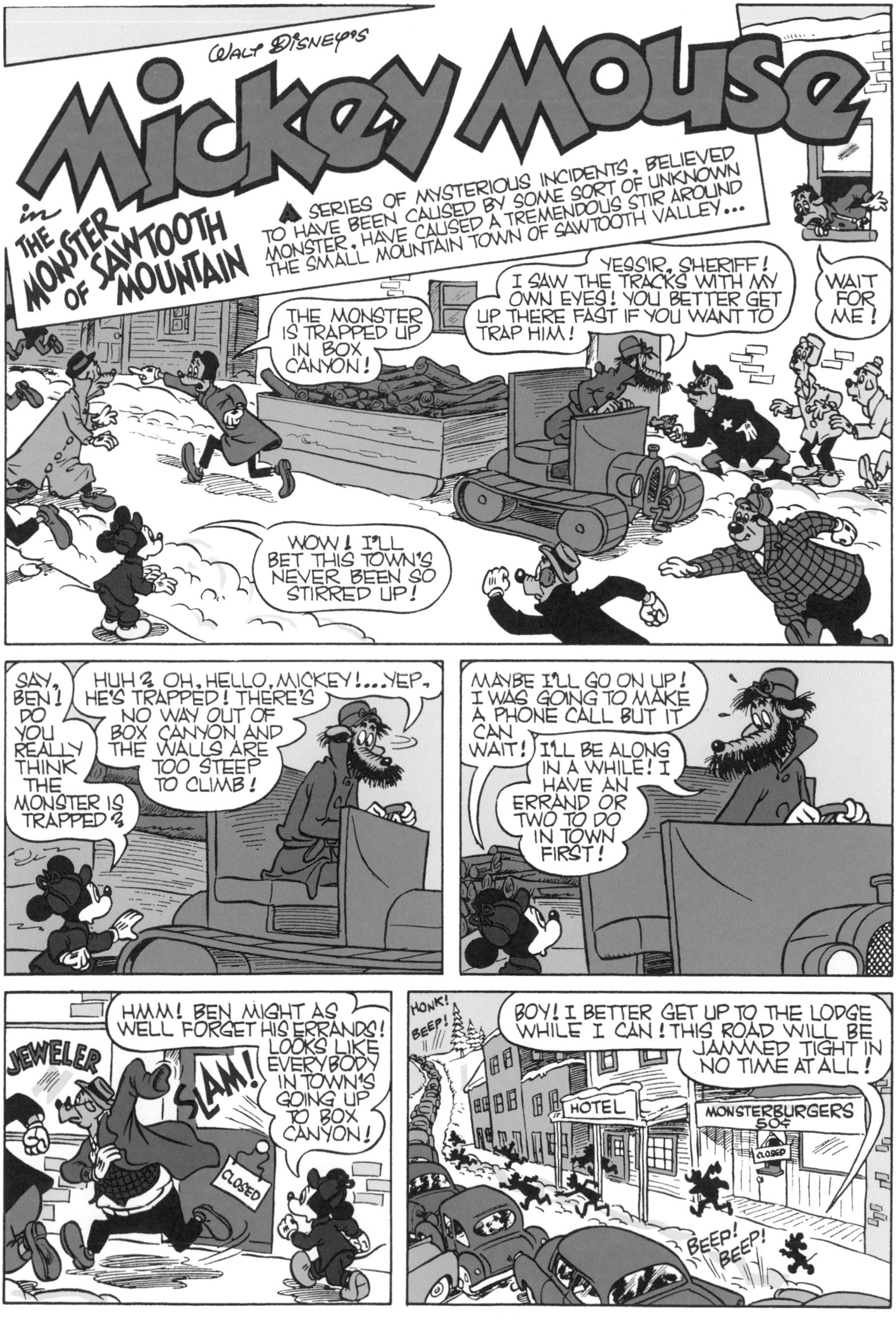
WALT DISNEY'S
Mickey Mouse
in THE MONSTER OF SAWTOOTH MOUNTAIN
A SERIES OF MYSTERIOUS INCIDENTS, BELIEVED TO HAVE BEEN CAUSED BY SOME SORT OF UNKNOWN MONSTER, HAVE CAUSED A TREMENDOUS STIR AROUND THE SMALL MOUNTAIN TOWN OF SAWTOOTH VALLEY...
THE MONSTER IS TRAPPED UP IN BOX CANYON!
YESSIR, SHERIFF! I SAW THE TRACKS WITH MY OWN EYES! YOU BETTER GET UP THERE FAST IF YOU WANT TO TRAP HIM!
WAIT FOR ME!
WOW! I'LL BET THIS TOWN'S NEVER BEEN SO STIRRED UP!
SAY, BEN! DO YOU REALLY THINK THE MONSTER IS TRAPPED?
HUH? OH, HELLO, MICKEY!...YEP, HE'S TRAPPED! THERE'S NO WAY OUT OF BOX CANYON AND THE WALLS ARE TOO STEEP TO CLIMB!
MAYBE I'LL GO ON UP! I WAS GOING TO MAKE A PHONE CALL BUT IT CAN WAIT!
I'LL BE ALONG IN A WHILE! I HAVE AN ERRAND OR TWO TO DO IN TOWN FIRST!
JEWELER
SLAM!
CLOSED
HMM! BEN MIGHT AS WELL FORGET HIS ERRANDS! LOOKS LIKE EVERYBODY IN TOWN'S GOING UP TO BOX CANYON!
HONK!
BEEP!
BOY! I BETTER GET UP TO THE LODGE WHILE I CAN! THIS ROAD WILL BE JAMMED TIGHT IN NO TIME AT ALL!
HOTEL
MONSTERBURGERS 50¢
CLOSED
BEEP! BEEP!

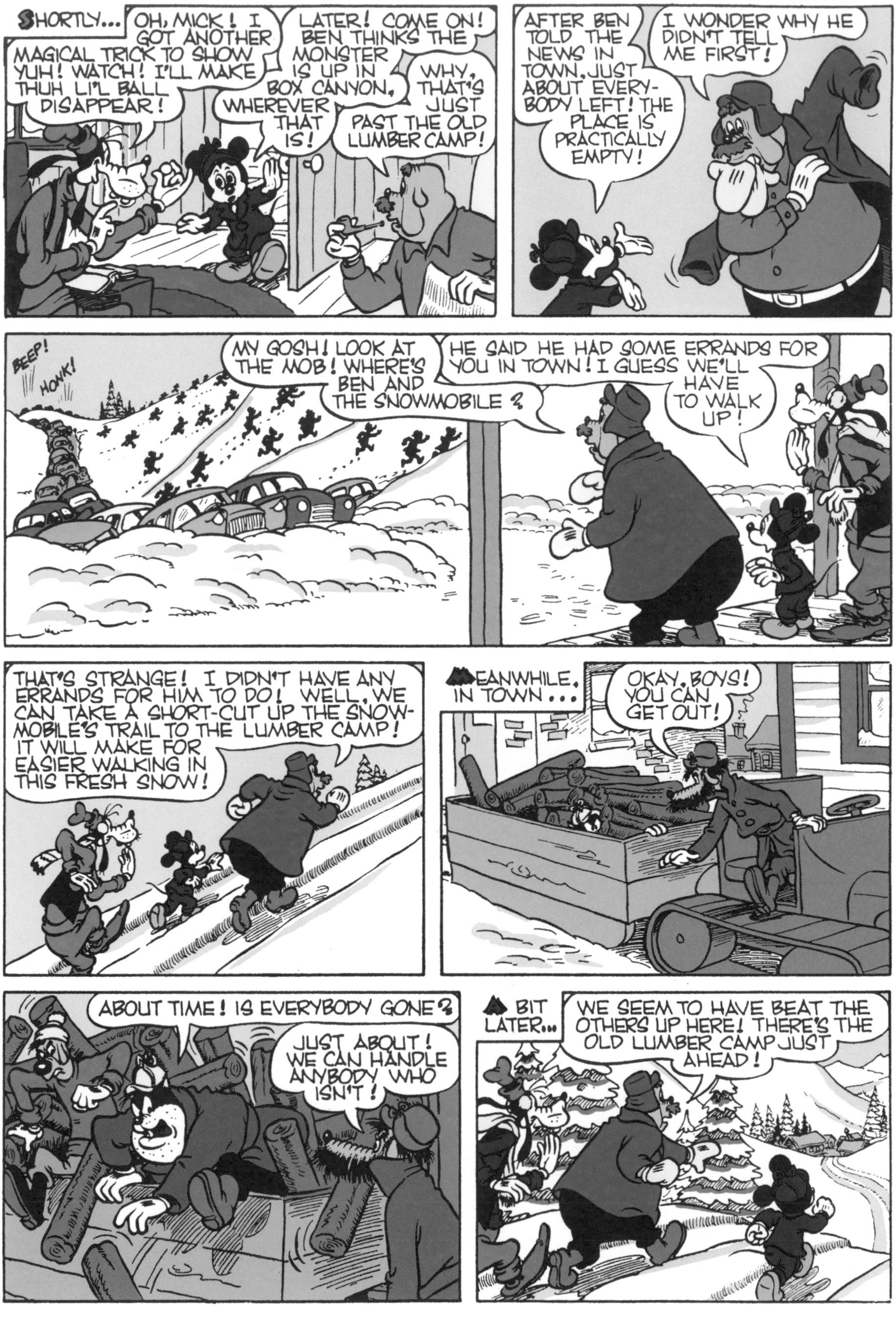
SHORTLY...
OH, MICK! I GOT ANOTHER MAGICAL TRICK TO SHOW YUH! WATCH! I'LL MAKE THUH LI'L BALL DISAPPEAR!
LATER! COME ON! BEN THINKS THE MONSTER IS UP IN BOX CANYON, WHEREVER THAT IS!
WHY, THAT'S JUST PAST THE OLD LUMBER CAMP!
AFTER BEN TOLD THE NEWS IN TOWN, JUST ABOUT EVERYBODY LEFT! THE PLACE IS PRACTICALLY EMPTY!
I WONDER WHY HE DIDN'T TELL ME FIRST!
BEEP!
HONK!
MY GOSH! LOOK AT THE MOB! WHERE'S BEN AND THE SNOWMOBILE?
HE SAID HE HAD SOME ERRANDS FOR YOU IN TOWN! I GUESS WE'LL HAVE TO WALK UP!
THAT'S STRANGE! I DIDN'T HAVE ANY ERRANDS FOR HIM TO DO! WELL, WE CAN TAKE A SHORT-CUT UP THE SNOWMOBILE'S TRAIL TO THE LUMBER CAMP! IT WILL MAKE FOR EASIER WALKING IN THIS FRESH SNOW!
MEANWHILE, IN TOWN...
OKAY, BOYS! YOU CAN GET OUT!
ABOUT TIME! IS EVERYBODY GONE?
JUST ABOUT! WE CAN HANDLE ANYBODY WHO ISN'T!
A BIT LATER...
WE SEEM TO HAVE BEAT THE OTHERS UP HERE! THERE'S THE OLD LUMBER CAMP JUST AHEAD!

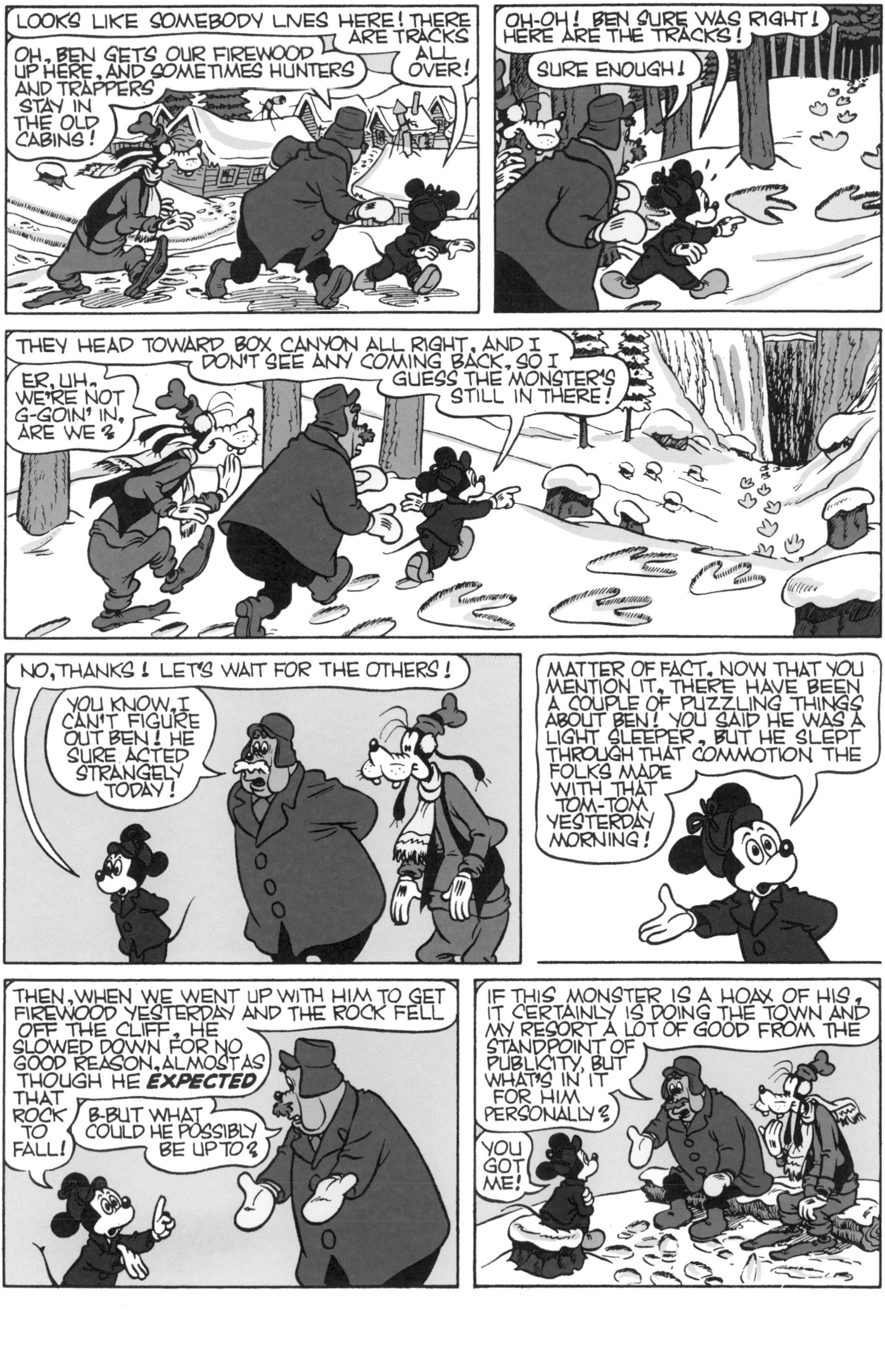

LOOKS LIKE SOMEBODY LIVES HERE! THERE ARE TRACKS ALL OVER!
OH, BEN GETS OUR FIREWOOD UP HERE, AND SOMETIMES HUNTERS AND TRAPPERS STAY IN THE OLD CABINS!
OH-OH! BEN SURE WAS RIGHT! HERE ARE THE TRACKS!
SURE ENOUGH!
THEY HEAD TOWARD BOX CANYON ALL RIGHT, AND I DON'T SEE ANY COMING BACK, SO I GUESS THE MONSTER'S STILL IN THERE!
ER, UH, WE'RE NOT G-GOIN' IN, ARE WE?
NO, THANKS! LET'S WAIT FOR THE OTHERS!
YOU KNOW, I CAN'T FIGURE OUT BEN! HE SURE ACTED STRANGELY TODAY!
MATTER OF FACT, NOW THAT YOU MENTION IT, THERE HAVE BEEN A COUPLE OF PUZZLING THINGS ABOUT BEN! YOU SAID HE WAS A LIGHT SLEEPER, BUT HE SLEPT THROUGH THAT COMMOTION THE FOLKS MADE WITH THAT TOM-TOM YESTERDAY MORNING!
THEN, WHEN WE WENT UP WITH HIM TO GET FIREWOOD YESTERDAY AND THE ROCK FELL OFF THE CLIFF, HE SLOWED DOWN FOR NO GOOD REASON, ALMOST AS THOUGH HE EXPECTED THAT ROCK TO FALL!
B-BUT WHAT COULD HE POSSIBLY BE UP TO?
IF THIS MONSTER IS A HOAX OF HIS, IT CERTAINLY IS DOING THE TOWN AND MY RESORT A LOT OF GOOD FROM THE STANDPOINT OF PUBLICITY, BUT WHAT'S IN IT FOR HIM PERSONALLY?
YOU GOT ME!

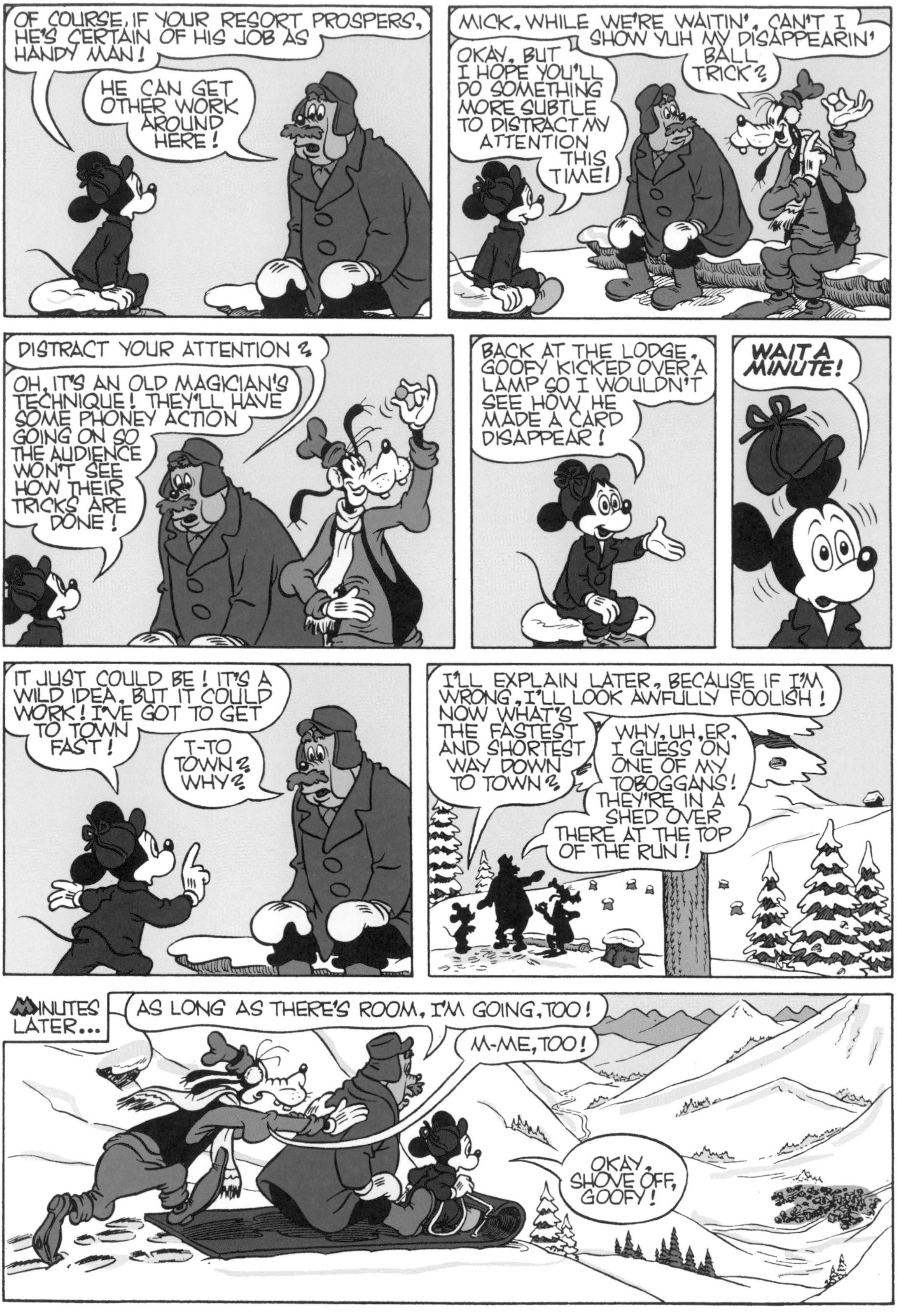

OF COURSE, IF YOUR RESORT PROSPERS, HE'S CERTAIN OF HIS JOB AS HANDY MAN!
HE CAN GET OTHER WORK AROUND HERE!
MICK, WHILE WE'RE WAITIN', CAN'T I SHOW YUH MY DISAPPEARIN' BALL TRICK?
OKAY, BUT I HOPE YOU'LL DO SOMETHING MORE SUBTLE TO DISTRACT MY ATTENTION THIS TIME!
DISTRACT YOUR ATTENTION?
OH, IT'S AN OLD MAGICIAN'S TECHNIQUE! THEY'LL HAVE SOME PHONEY ACTION GOING ON SO THE AUDIENCE WON'T SEE HOW THEIR TRICKS ARE DONE!
BACK AT THE LODGE, GOOFY KICKED OVER A LAMP SO I WOULDN'T SEE HOW HE MADE A CARD DISAPPEAR!
WAIT A MINUTE!
IT JUST COULD BE! IT'S A WILD IDEA, BUT IT COULD WORK! I'VE GOT TO GET TO TOWN FAST!
T-TO TOWN? WHY?
I'LL EXPLAIN LATER, BECAUSE IF I'M WRONG, I'LL LOOK AWFULLY FOOLISH! NOW WHAT'S THE FASTEST AND SHORTEST WAY DOWN TO TOWN?
WHY, UH, ER, I GUESS ON ONE OF MY TOBOGGANS! THEY'RE IN A SHED OVER THERE AT THE TOP OF THE RUN!
MINUTES LATER...
AS LONG AS THERE'S ROOM, I'M GOING, TOO!
M-ME, TOO!
OKAY, SHOVE OFF, GOOFY!

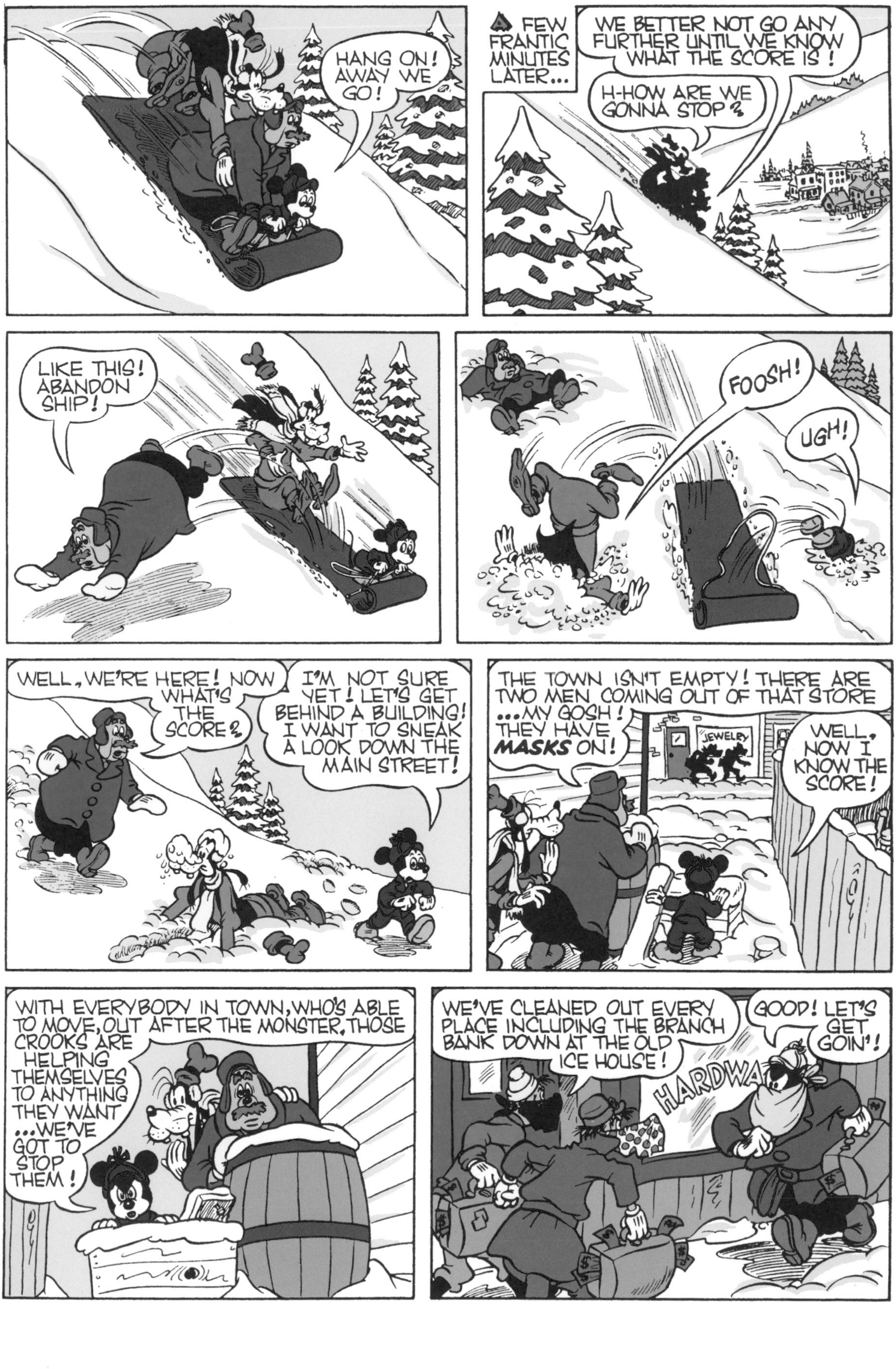
HANG ON! AWAY WE GO!
A FEW FRANTIC MINUTES LATER...
WE BETTER NOT GO ANY FURTHER UNTIL WE KNOW WHAT THE SCORE IS!
H-HOW ARE WE GONNA STOP?
LIKE THIS! ABANDON SHIP!
FOOSH!
UGH!
WELL, WE'RE HERE! NOW WHAT'S THE SCORE?
I'M NOT SURE YET! LET'S GET BEHIND A BUILDING! I WANT TO SNEAK A LOOK DOWN THE MAIN STREET!
THE TOWN ISN'T EMPTY! THERE ARE TWO MEN COMING OUT OF THAT STORE ...MY GOSH! THEY HAVE **MASKS** ON!
JEWELRY
WELL, NOW I KNOW THE SCORE!
WITH EVERYBODY IN TOWN, WHO'S ABLE TO MOVE, OUT AFTER THE MONSTER, THOSE CROOKS ARE HELPING THEMSELVES TO ANYTHING THEY WANT ...WE'VE GOT TO STOP THEM!
WE'VE CLEANED OUT EVERY PLACE INCLUDING THE BRANCH BANK DOWN AT THE OLD ICE HOUSE!
GOOD! LET'S GET GOIN'!
HARDWA

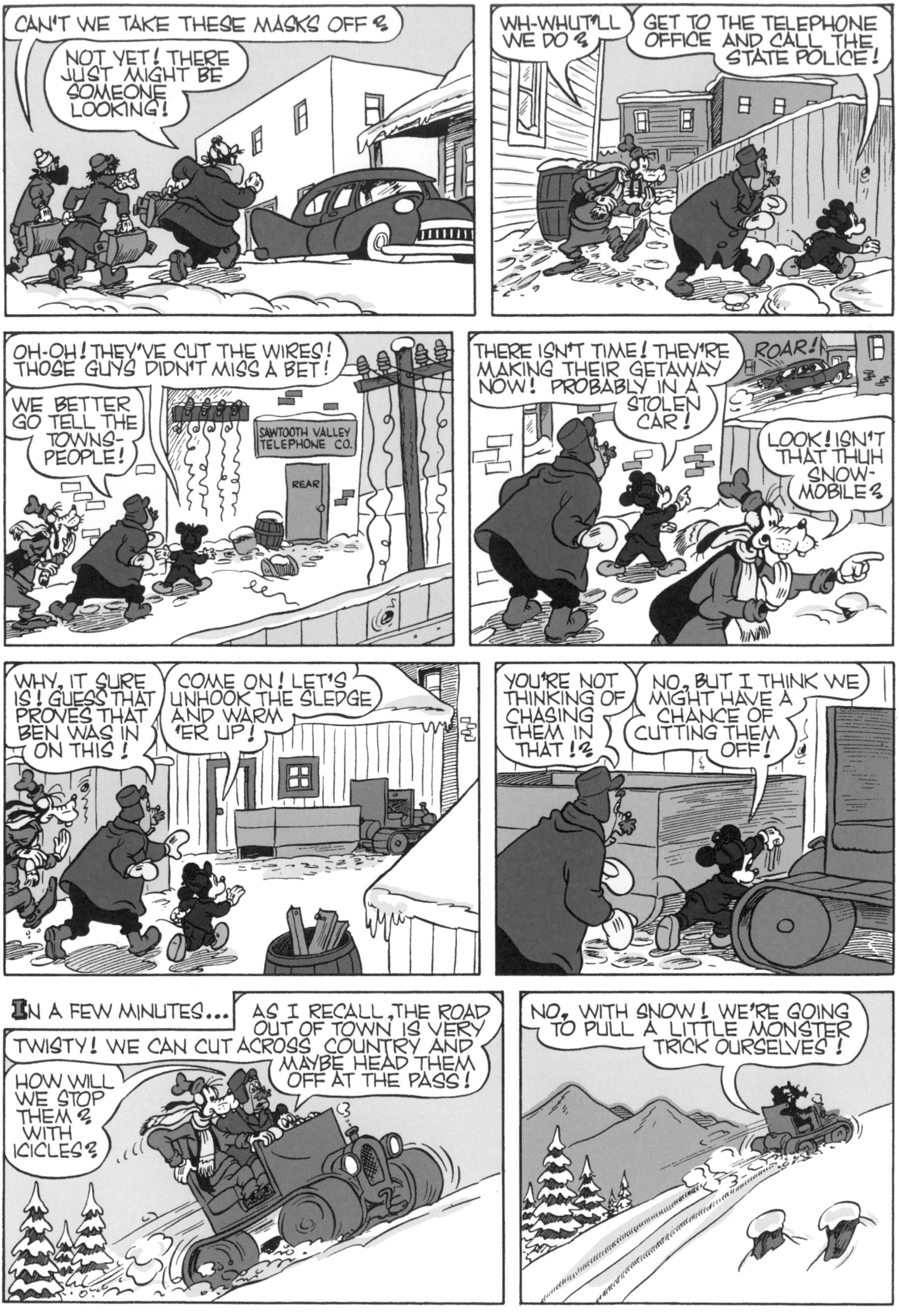
CAN'T WE TAKE THESE MASKS OFF?
NOT YET! THERE JUST MIGHT BE SOMEONE LOOKING!
WH-WHUT'LL WE DO?
GET TO THE TELEPHONE OFFICE AND CALL THE STATE POLICE!
OH-OH! THEY'VE CUT THE WIRES! THOSE GUYS DIDN'T MISS A BET!
WE BETTER GO TELL THE TOWNS-PEOPLE!
SAWTOOTH VALLEY TELEPHONE CO.
REAR
THERE ISN'T TIME! THEY'RE MAKING THEIR GETAWAY NOW! PROBABLY IN A STOLEN CAR!
ROAR!
LOOK! ISN'T THAT THUH SNOW-MOBILE?
WHY, IT SURE IS! GUESS THAT PROVES THAT BEN WAS IN ON THIS!
COME ON! LET'S UNHOOK THE SLEDGE AND WARM 'ER UP!
YOU'RE NOT THINKING OF CHASING THEM IN THAT!?
NO, BUT I THINK WE MIGHT HAVE A CHANCE OF CUTTING THEM OFF!
IN A FEW MINUTES...
AS I RECALL, THE ROAD OUT OF TOWN IS VERY TWISTY! WE CAN CUT ACROSS COUNTRY AND MAYBE HEAD THEM OFF AT THE PASS!
HOW WILL WE STOP THEM? WITH ICICLES?
NO, WITH SNOW! WE'RE GOING TO PULL A LITTLE MONSTER TRICK OURSELVES!

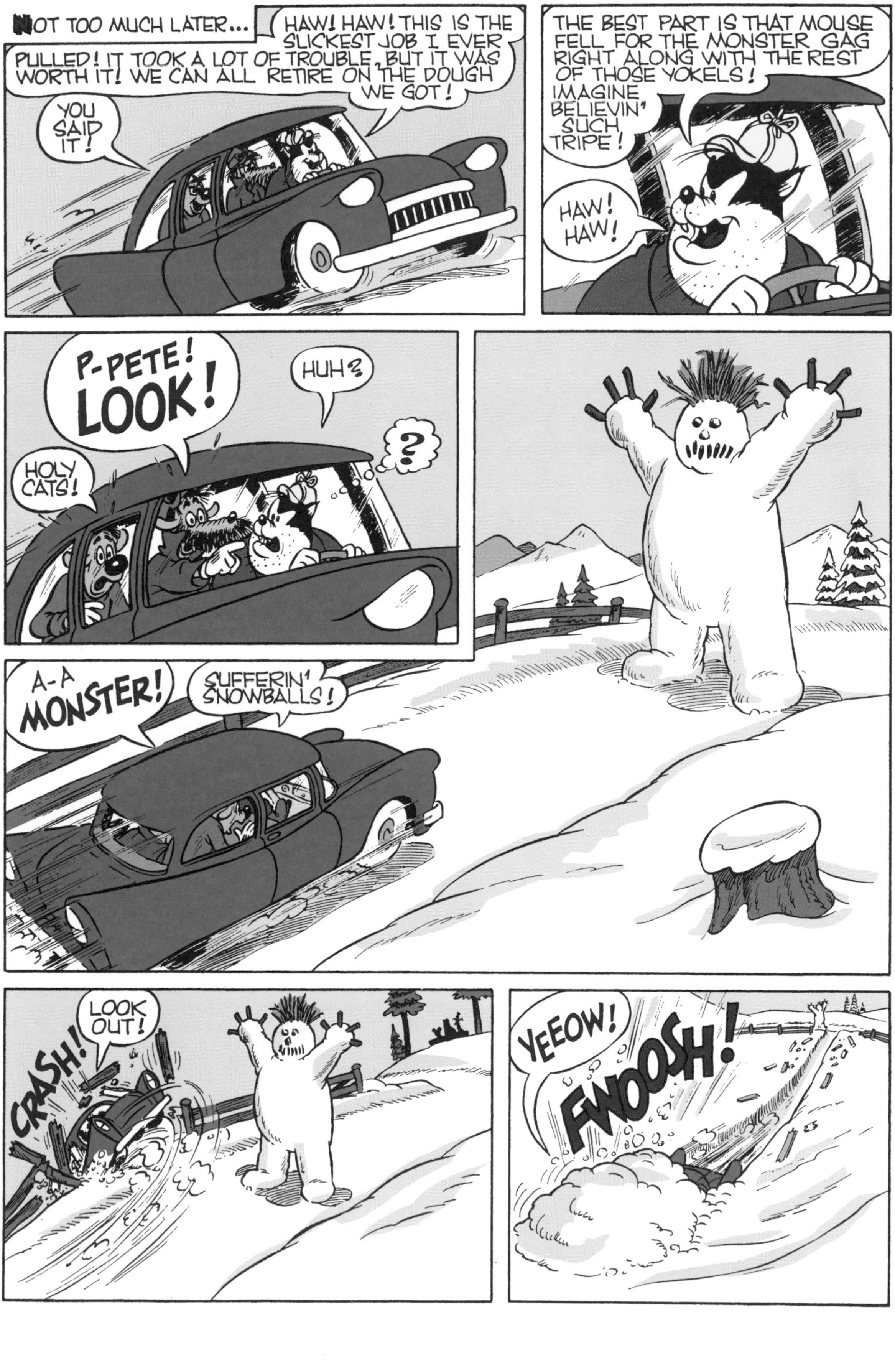
NOT TOO MUCH LATER...
HAW! HAW! THIS IS THE SLICKEST JOB I EVER PULLED! IT TOOK A LOT OF TROUBLE, BUT IT WAS WORTH IT! WE CAN ALL RETIRE ON THE DOUGH WE GOT!
YOU SAID IT!
THE BEST PART IS THAT MOUSE FELL FOR THE MONSTER GAG RIGHT ALONG WITH THE REST OF THOSE YOKELS!
IMAGINE BELIEVIN' SUCH TRIPE!
HAW! HAW!
P-PETE! LOOK!
HUH?
HOLY CATS!
?
A-A MONSTER!
SUFFERIN' SNOWBALLS!
LOOK OUT!
CRASH!
YEEOW!
FWOOSH!

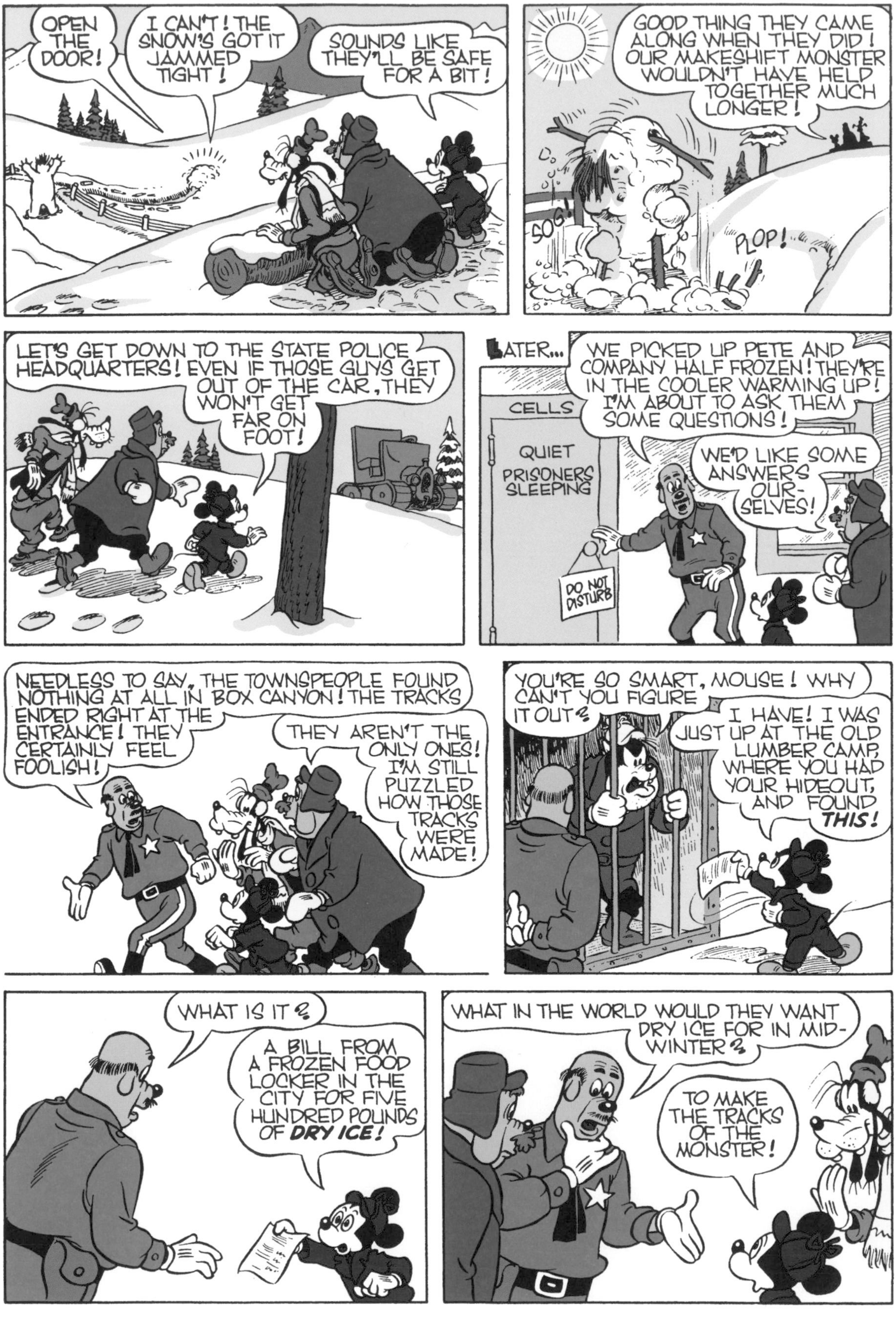

OPEN THE DOOR!
I CAN'T! THE SNOW'S GOT IT JAMMED TIGHT!
SOUNDS LIKE THEY'LL BE SAFE FOR A BIT!
GOOD THING THEY CAME ALONG WHEN THEY DID! OUR MAKESHIFT MONSTER WOULDN'T HAVE HELD TOGETHER MUCH LONGER!
SOG!
PLOP!
LET'S GET DOWN TO THE STATE POLICE HEADQUARTERS! EVEN IF THOSE GUYS GET OUT OF THE CAR, THEY WON'T GET FAR ON FOOT!
LATER...
CELLS
QUIET PRISONERS SLEEPING
DO NOT DISTURB
WE PICKED UP PETE AND COMPANY HALF FROZEN! THEY'RE IN THE COOLER WARMING UP! I'M ABOUT TO ASK THEM SOME QUESTIONS!
WE'D LIKE SOME ANSWERS OUR-SELVES!
NEEDLESS TO SAY, THE TOWNSPEOPLE FOUND NOTHING AT ALL IN BOX CANYON! THE TRACKS ENDED RIGHT AT THE ENTRANCE! THEY CERTAINLY FEEL FOOLISH!
THEY AREN'T THE ONLY ONES! I'M STILL PUZZLED HOW THOSE TRACKS WERE MADE!
YOU'RE SO SMART, MOUSE! WHY CAN'T YOU FIGURE IT OUT?
I HAVE! I WAS JUST UP AT THE OLD LUMBER CAMP, WHERE YOU HAD YOUR HIDEOUT, AND FOUND THIS!
WHAT IS IT?
A BILL FROM A FROZEN FOOD LOCKER IN THE CITY FOR FIVE HUNDRED POUNDS OF DRY ICE!
WHAT IN THE WORLD WOULD THEY WANT DRY ICE FOR IN MID-WINTER?
TO MAKE THE TRACKS OF THE MONSTER!

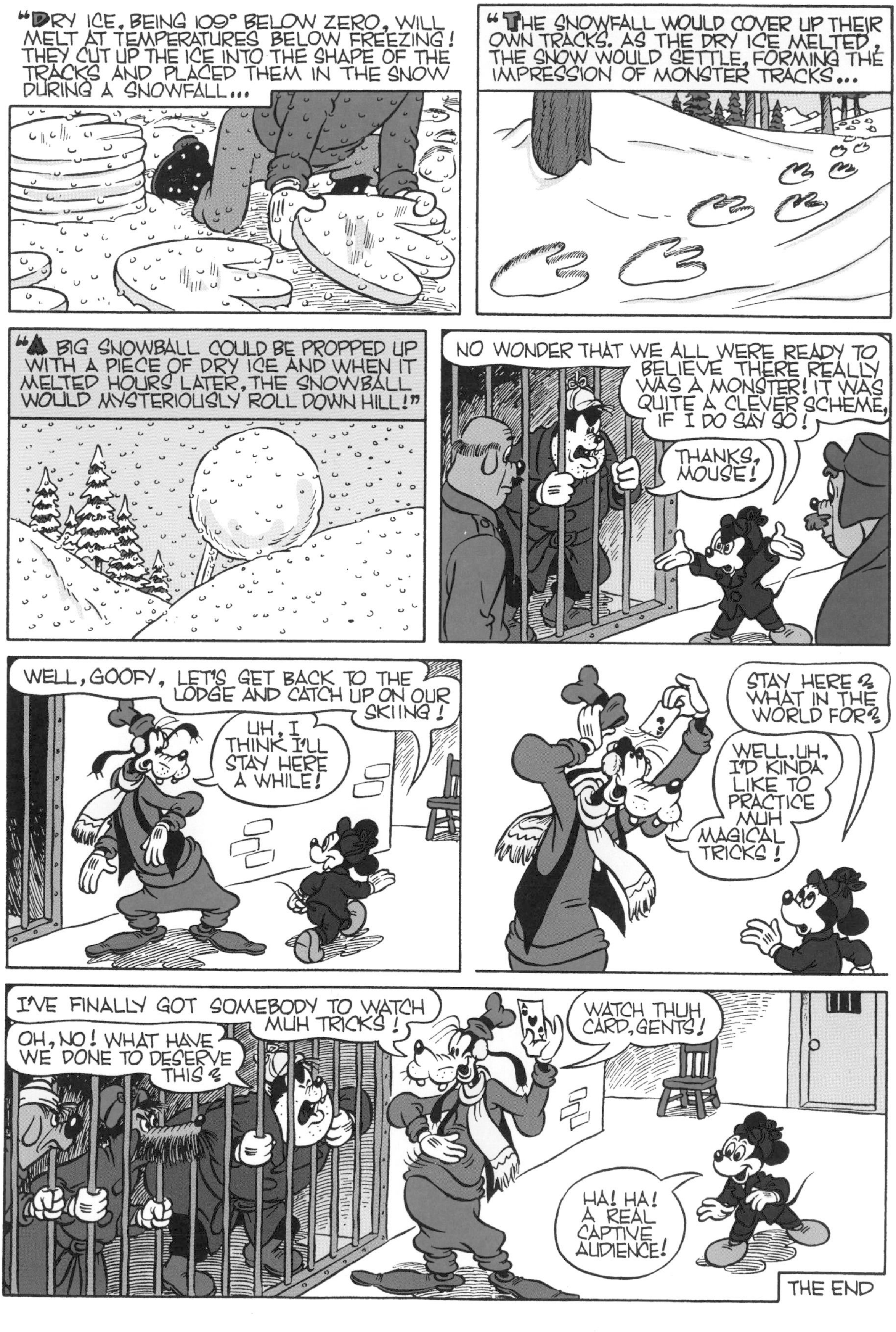
"DRY ICE, BEING 109° BELOW ZERO, WILL MELT AT TEMPERATURES BELOW FREEZING! THEY CUT UP THE ICE INTO THE SHAPE OF THE TRACKS AND PLACED THEM IN THE SNOW DURING A SNOWFALL...
"THE SNOWFALL WOULD COVER UP THEIR OWN TRACKS. AS THE DRY ICE MELTED, THE SNOW WOULD SETTLE, FORMING THE IMPRESSION OF MONSTER TRACKS...
"A BIG SNOWBALL COULD BE PROPPED UP WITH A PIECE OF DRY ICE AND WHEN IT MELTED HOURS LATER, THE SNOWBALL WOULD MYSTERIOUSLY ROLL DOWN HILL!"
NO WONDER THAT WE ALL WERE READY TO BELIEVE THERE REALLY WAS A MONSTER! IT WAS QUITE A CLEVER SCHEME, IF I DO SAY SO!
THANKS, MOUSE!
WELL, GOOFY, LET'S GET BACK TO THE LODGE AND CATCH UP ON OUR SKIING!
UH, I THINK I'LL STAY HERE A WHILE!
STAY HERE? WHAT IN THE WORLD FOR?
WELL, UH, I'D KINDA LIKE TO PRACTICE MUH MAGICAL TRICKS!
I'VE FINALLY GOT SOMEBODY TO WATCH MUH TRICKS!
WATCH THUH CARD, GENTS!
OH, NO! WHAT HAVE WE DONE TO DESERVE THIS?
HA! HA! A REAL CAPTIVE AUDIENCE!
THE END

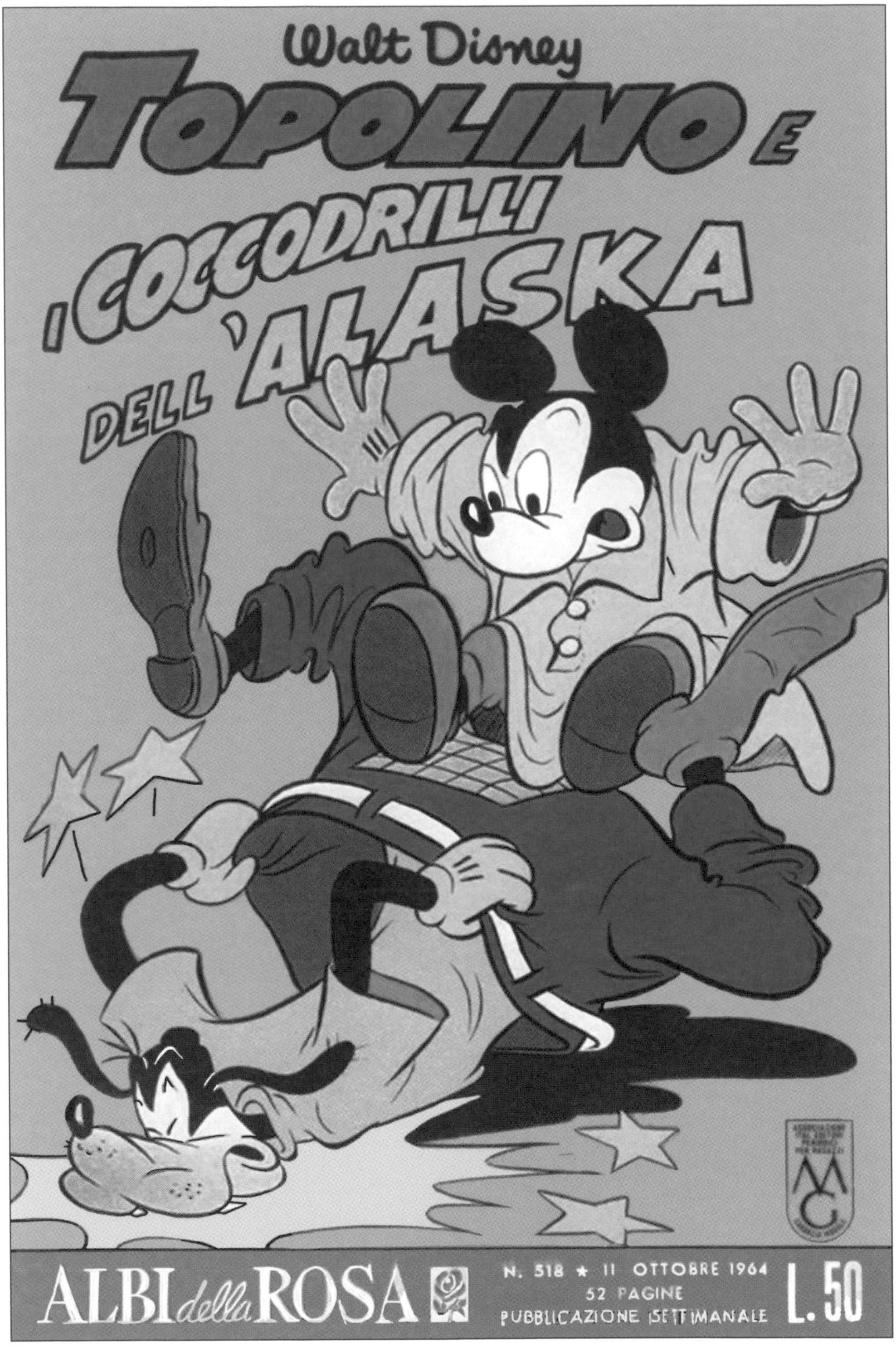
Walt Disney
TOPOLINO E
I COCCODRILLI
DELL'ALASKA
ALBI della ROSA
N. 518 ★ 11 OTTOBRE 1964
52 PAGINE
PUBBLICAZIONE SETTIMANALE
L. 50

Paul Murry didn't create his own cover for "Alaskan Adventure," the story you're about to read—but Italian artist Giuseppe Perego drew this one for a local edition (*Walt Disney Albi della Rosa* 518, 1964). Tasked with illustrating an epic quest full of dangerous bandits and crocodiles, Perego fearlessly chose to focus on a random pratfall. Gawrsh!

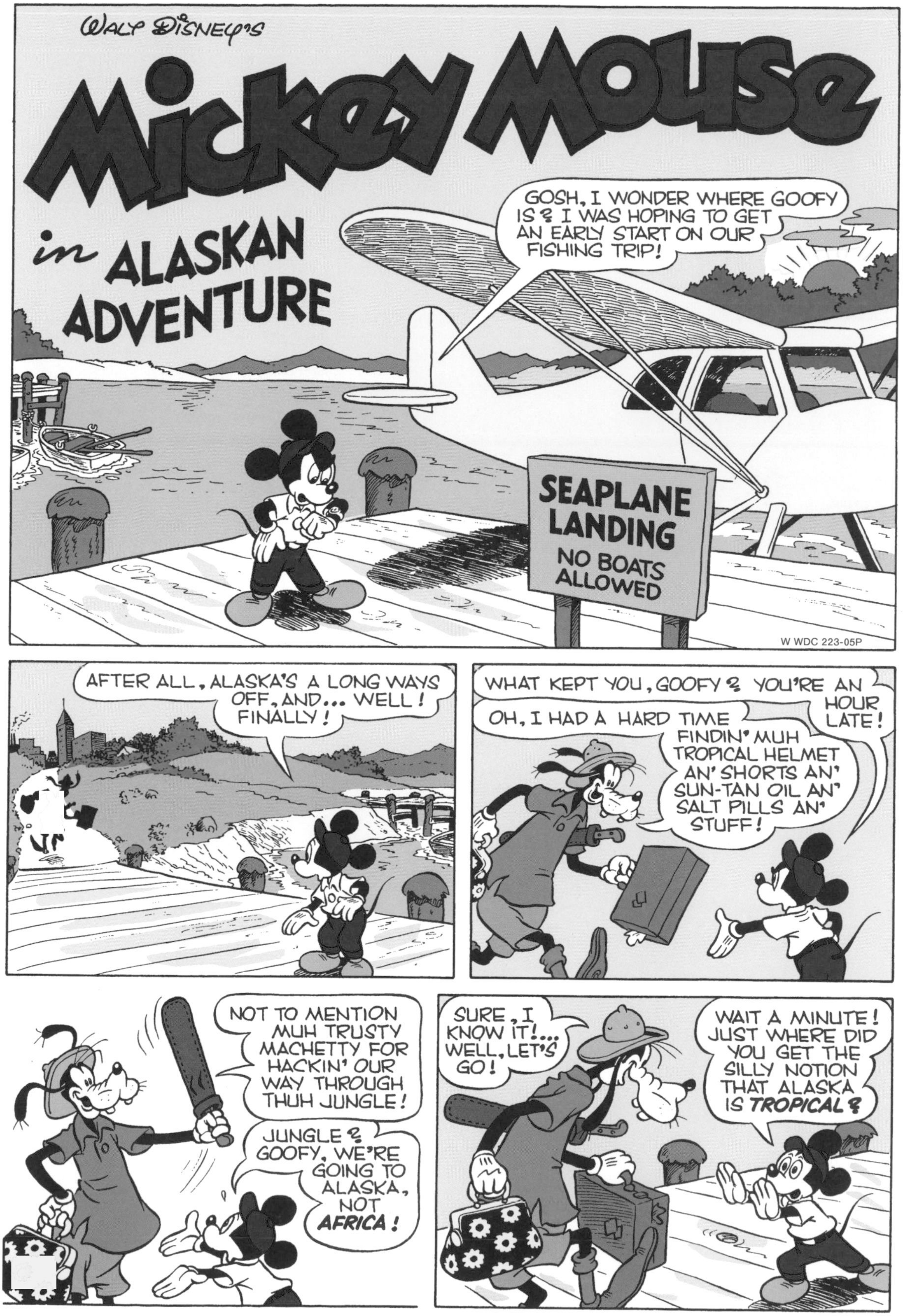
WALT DISNEY'S
Mickey Mouse
in ALASKAN ADVENTURE
GOSH, I WONDER WHERE GOOFY IS? I WAS HOPING TO GET AN EARLY START ON OUR FISHING TRIP!
SEAPLANE LANDING
NO BOATS ALLOWED
W WDC 223-05P
AFTER ALL, ALASKA'S A LONG WAYS OFF, AND... WELL! FINALLY!
WHAT KEPT YOU, GOOFY? YOU'RE AN HOUR LATE!
OH, I HAD A HARD TIME FINDIN' MUH TROPICAL HELMET AN' SHORTS AN' SUN-TAN OIL AN' SALT PILLS AN' STUFF!
NOT TO MENTION MUH TRUSTY MACHETTY FOR HACKIN' OUR WAY THROUGH THUH JUNGLE!
JUNGLE? GOOFY, WE'RE GOING TO ALASKA, NOT AFRICA!
SURE, I KNOW IT!... WELL, LET'S GO!
WAIT A MINUTE! JUST WHERE DID YOU GET THE SILLY NOTION THAT ALASKA IS TROPICAL?

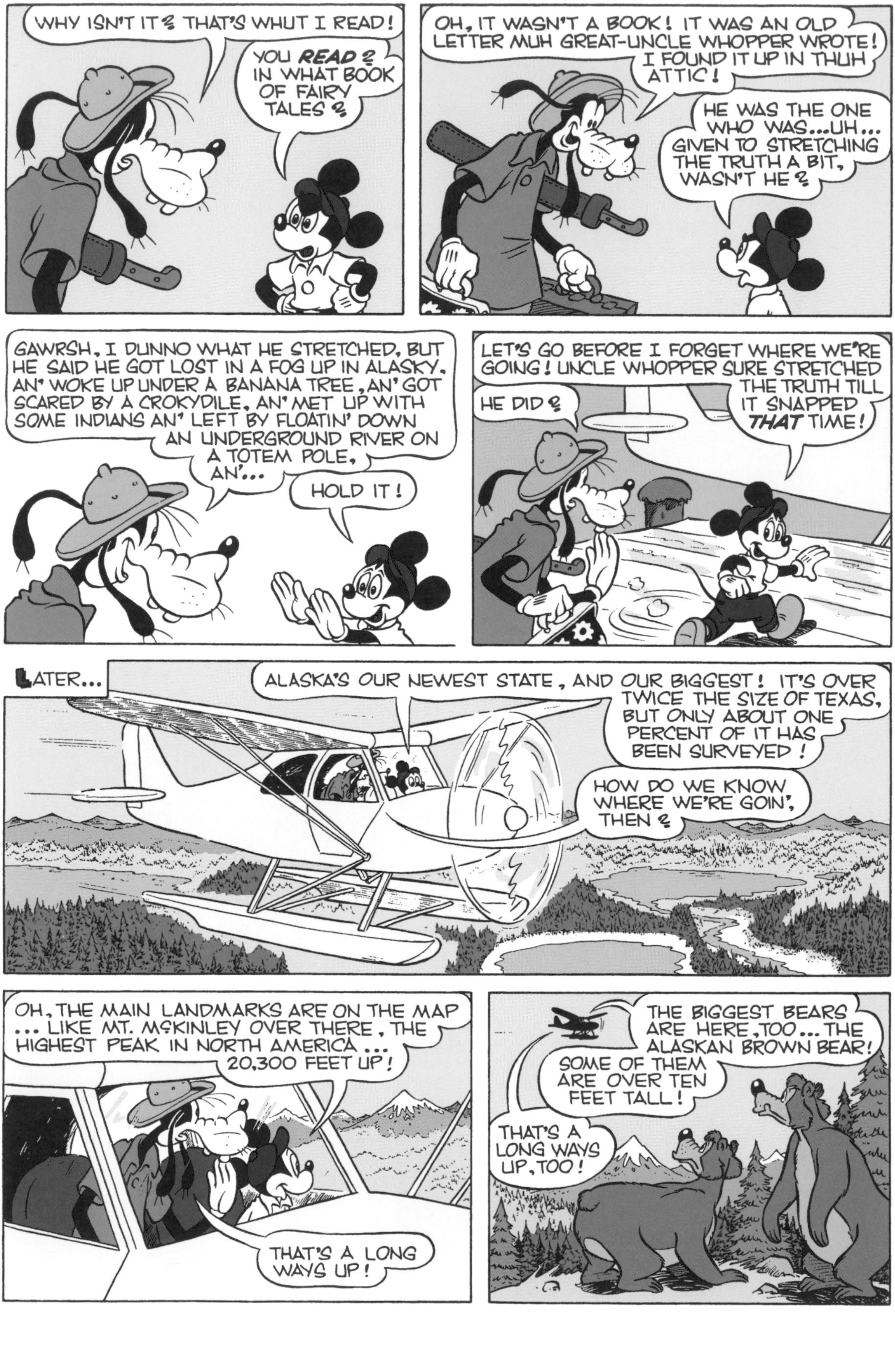
WHY ISN'T IT? THAT'S WHUT I READ!
YOU READ? IN WHAT BOOK OF FAIRY TALES?
OH, IT WASN'T A BOOK! IT WAS AN OLD LETTER MUH GREAT-UNCLE WHOPPER WROTE! I FOUND IT UP IN THUH ATTIC!
HE WAS THE ONE WHO WAS...UH... GIVEN TO STRETCHING THE TRUTH A BIT, WASN'T HE?
GAWRSH, I DUNNO WHAT HE STRETCHED, BUT HE SAID HE GOT LOST IN A FOG UP IN ALASKY, AN' WOKE UP UNDER A BANANA TREE, AN' GOT SCARED BY A CROKYDILE, AN' MET UP WITH SOME INDIANS AN' LEFT BY FLOATIN' DOWN AN UNDERGROUND RIVER ON A TOTEM POLE, AN'...
HOLD IT!
LET'S GO BEFORE I FORGET WHERE WE'RE GOING! UNCLE WHOPPER SURE STRETCHED THE TRUTH TILL IT SNAPPED THAT TIME!
HE DID?
LATER...
ALASKA'S OUR NEWEST STATE, AND OUR BIGGEST! IT'S OVER TWICE THE SIZE OF TEXAS, BUT ONLY ABOUT ONE PERCENT OF IT HAS BEEN SURVEYED!
HOW DO WE KNOW WHERE WE'RE GOIN', THEN?
OH, THE MAIN LANDMARKS ARE ON THE MAP ... LIKE MT. McKINLEY OVER THERE, THE HIGHEST PEAK IN NORTH AMERICA ... 20,300 FEET UP!
THAT'S A LONG WAYS UP!
THE BIGGEST BEARS ARE HERE, TOO... THE ALASKAN BROWN BEAR!
SOME OF THEM ARE OVER TEN FEET TALL!
THAT'S A LONG WAYS UP, TOO!

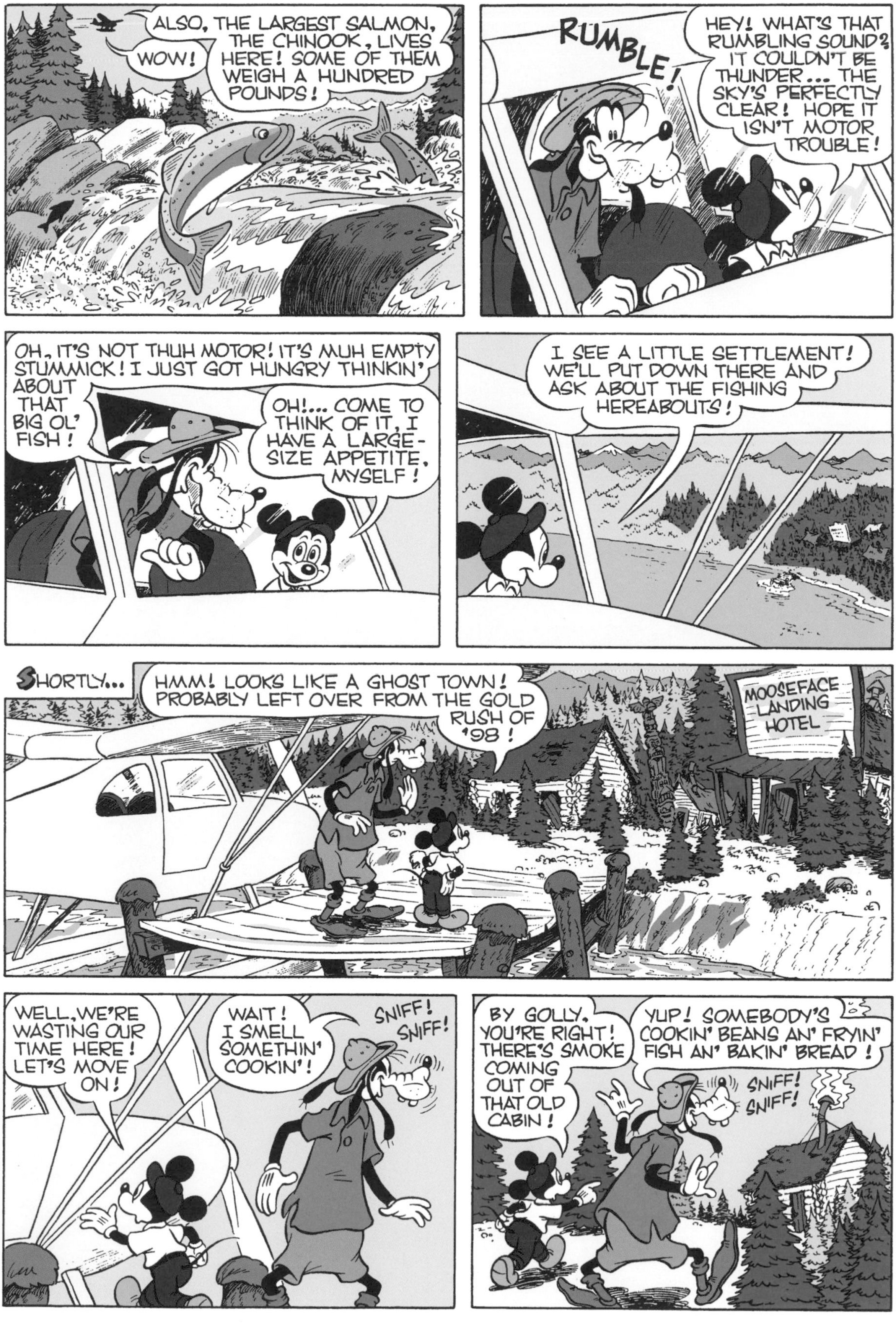
ALSO, THE LARGEST SALMON, THE CHINOOK, LIVES HERE! SOME OF THEM WEIGH A HUNDRED POUNDS!
WOW!
RUMBLE!
HEY! WHAT'S THAT RUMBLING SOUND? IT COULDN'T BE THUNDER... THE SKY'S PERFECTLY CLEAR! HOPE IT ISN'T MOTOR TROUBLE!
OH, IT'S NOT THUH MOTOR! IT'S MUH EMPTY STUMMICK! I JUST GOT HUNGRY THINKIN' ABOUT THAT BIG OL' FISH!
OH!... COME TO THINK OF IT, I HAVE A LARGE-SIZE APPETITE, MYSELF!
I SEE A LITTLE SETTLEMENT! WE'LL PUT DOWN THERE AND ASK ABOUT THE FISHING HEREABOUTS!
SHORTLY...
HMM! LOOKS LIKE A GHOST TOWN! PROBABLY LEFT OVER FROM THE GOLD RUSH OF '98!
MOOSEFACE LANDING HOTEL
WELL, WE'RE WASTING OUR TIME HERE! LET'S MOVE ON!
WAIT! I SMELL SOMETHIN' COOKIN'!
SNIFF! SNIFF!
BY GOLLY, YOU'RE RIGHT! THERE'S SMOKE COMING OUT OF THAT OLD CABIN!
YUP! SOMEBODY'S COOKIN' BEANS AN' FRYIN' FISH AN' BAKIN' BREAD!
SNIFF! SNIFF!

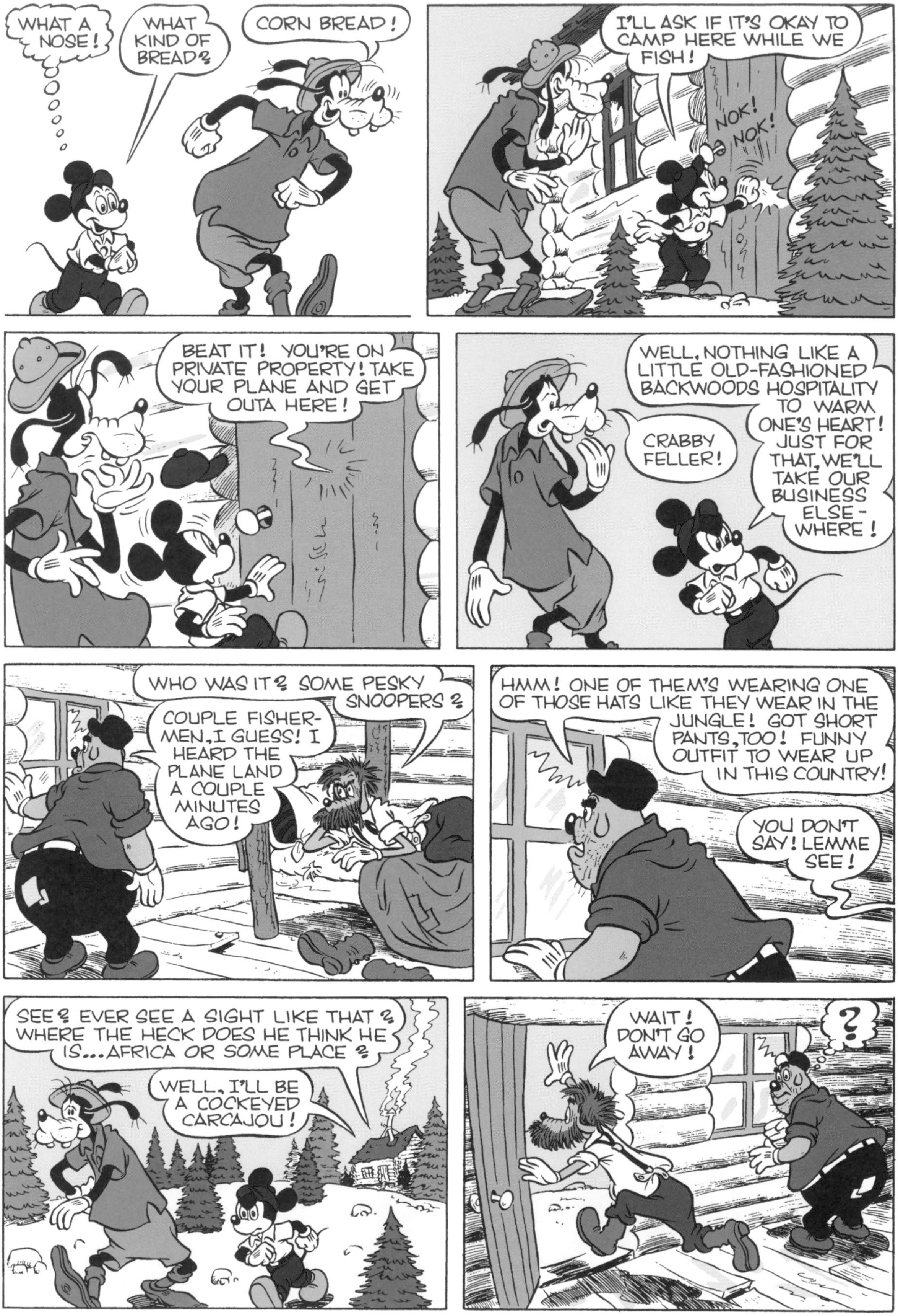
WHAT A NOSE!
WHAT KIND OF BREAD?
CORN BREAD!
I'LL ASK IF IT'S OKAY TO CAMP HERE WHILE WE FISH!
NOK! NOK!
BEAT IT! YOU'RE ON PRIVATE PROPERTY! TAKE YOUR PLANE AND GET OUTA HERE!
WELL, NOTHING LIKE A LITTLE OLD-FASHIONED BACKWOODS HOSPITALITY TO WARM ONE'S HEART! JUST FOR THAT, WE'LL TAKE OUR BUSINESS ELSE-WHERE!
CRABBY FELLER!
WHO WAS IT? SOME PESKY SNOOPERS?
COUPLE FISHER-MEN, I GUESS! I HEARD THE PLANE LAND A COUPLE MINUTES AGO!
HMM! ONE OF THEM'S WEARING ONE OF THOSE HATS LIKE THEY WEAR IN THE JUNGLE! GOT SHORT PANTS, TOO! FUNNY OUTFIT TO WEAR UP IN THIS COUNTRY!
YOU DON'T SAY! LEMME SEE!
SEE? EVER SEE A SIGHT LIKE THAT? WHERE THE HECK DOES HE THINK HE IS... AFRICA OR SOME PLACE?
WELL, I'LL BE A COCKEYED CARCAJOU!
WAIT! DON'T GO AWAY!
?

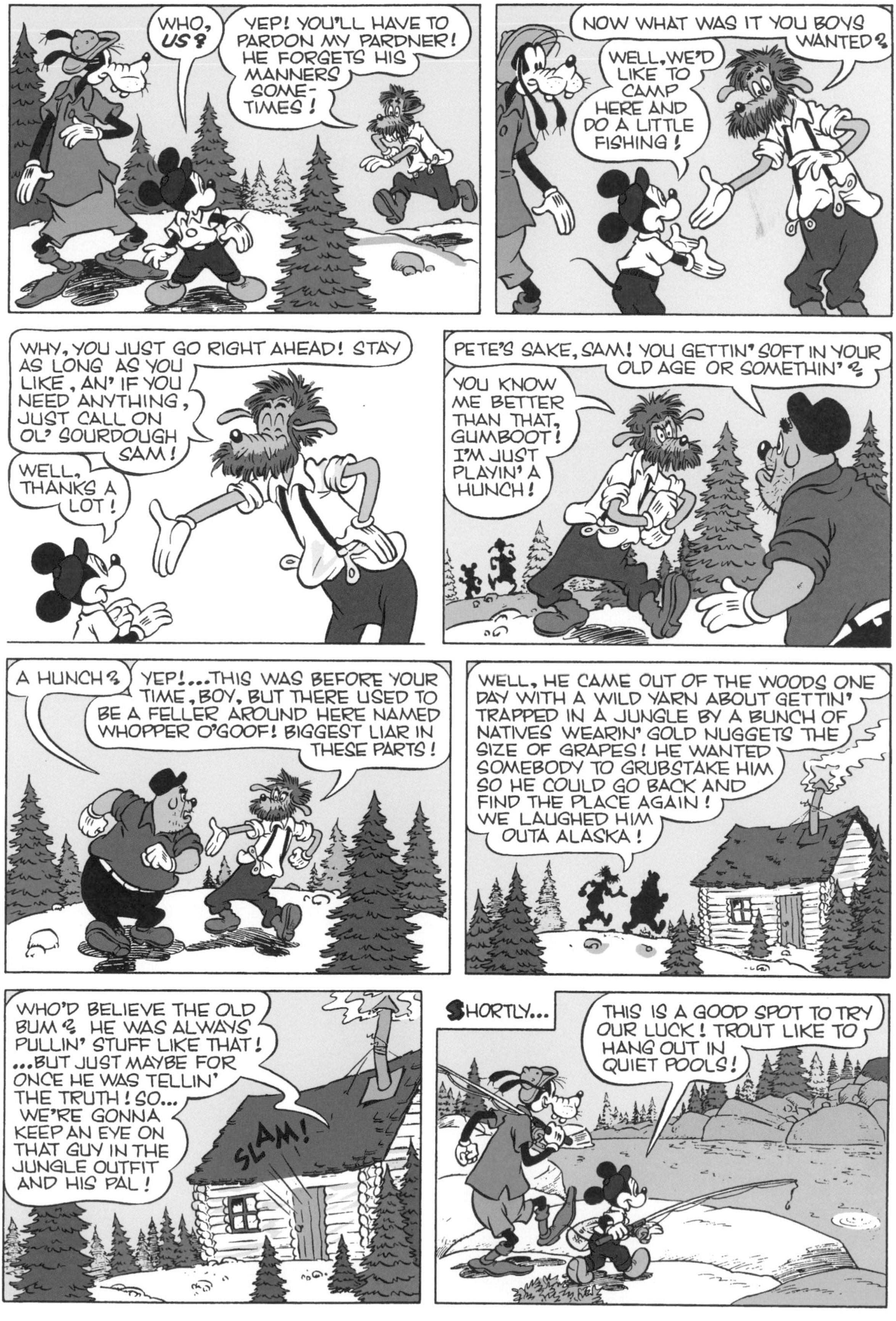
WHO, US?
YEP! YOU'LL HAVE TO PARDON MY PARDNER! HE FORGETS HIS MANNERS SOME-TIMES!
NOW WHAT WAS IT YOU BOYS WANTED?
WELL, WE'D LIKE TO CAMP HERE AND DO A LITTLE FISHING!
WHY, YOU JUST GO RIGHT AHEAD! STAY AS LONG AS YOU LIKE, AN' IF YOU NEED ANYTHING, JUST CALL ON OL' SOURDOUGH SAM!
WELL, THANKS A LOT!
PETE'S SAKE, SAM! YOU GETTIN' SOFT IN YOUR OLD AGE OR SOMETHIN'?
YOU KNOW ME BETTER THAN THAT, GUMBOOT! I'M JUST PLAYIN' A HUNCH!
A HUNCH?
YEP!...THIS WAS BEFORE YOUR TIME, BOY, BUT THERE USED TO BE A FELLER AROUND HERE NAMED WHOPPER O'GOOF! BIGGEST LIAR IN THESE PARTS!
WELL, HE CAME OUT OF THE WOODS ONE DAY WITH A WILD YARN ABOUT GETTIN' TRAPPED IN A JUNGLE BY A BUNCH OF NATIVES WEARIN' GOLD NUGGETS THE SIZE OF GRAPES! HE WANTED SOMEBODY TO GRUBSTAKE HIM SO HE COULD GO BACK AND FIND THE PLACE AGAIN! WE LAUGHED HIM OUTA ALASKA!
WHO'D BELIEVE THE OLD BUM? HE WAS ALWAYS PULLIN' STUFF LIKE THAT! ...BUT JUST MAYBE FOR ONCE HE WAS TELLIN' THE TRUTH! SO... WE'RE GONNA KEEP AN EYE ON THAT GUY IN THE JUNGLE OUTFIT AND HIS PAL!
SLAM!
SHORTLY...
THIS IS A GOOD SPOT TO TRY OUR LUCK! TROUT LIKE TO HANG OUT IN QUIET POOLS!

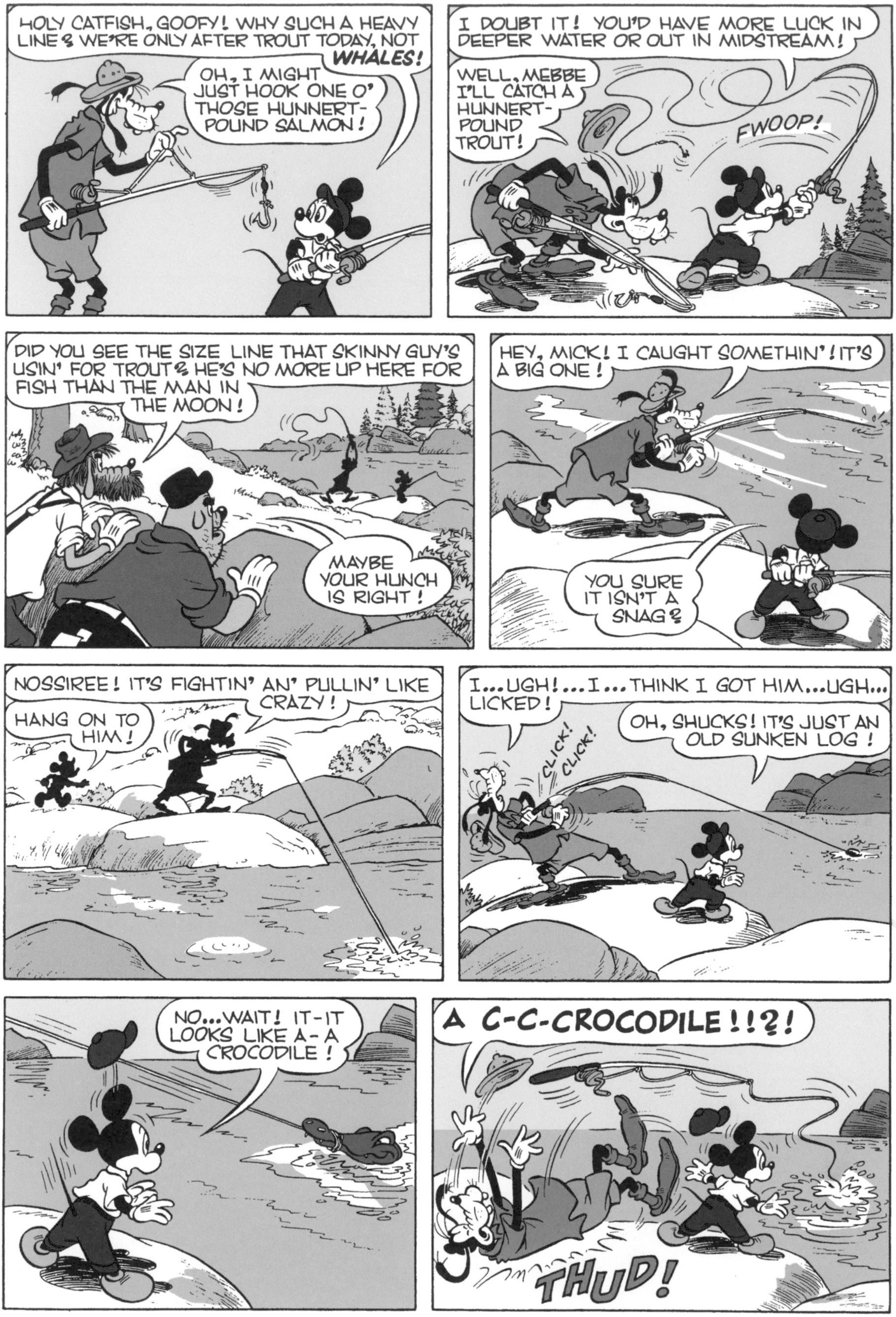

HOLY CATFISH, GOOFY! WHY SUCH A HEAVY LINE? WE'RE ONLY AFTER TROUT TODAY, NOT WHALES!
OH, I MIGHT JUST HOOK ONE O' THOSE HUNNERT-POUND SALMON!
I DOUBT IT! YOU'D HAVE MORE LUCK IN DEEPER WATER OR OUT IN MIDSTREAM!
WELL, MEBBE I'LL CATCH A HUNNERT-POUND TROUT!
FWOOP!
DID YOU SEE THE SIZE LINE THAT SKINNY GUY'S US'IN' FOR TROUT? HE'S NO MORE UP HERE FOR FISH THAN THE MAN IN THE MOON!
MAYBE YOUR HUNCH IS RIGHT!
HEY, MICK! I CAUGHT SOMETHIN'! IT'S A BIG ONE!
YOU SURE IT ISN'T A SNAG?
NOSSIREE! IT'S FIGHTIN' AN' PULLIN' LIKE CRAZY!
HANG ON TO HIM!
I...UGH!...I...THINK I GOT HIM...UGH... LICKED!
CLICK! CLICK!
OH, SHUCKS! IT'S JUST AN OLD SUNKEN LOG!
NO...WAIT! IT-IT LOOKS LIKE A-A CROCODILE!
A C-C-CROCODILE!!?!
THUD!

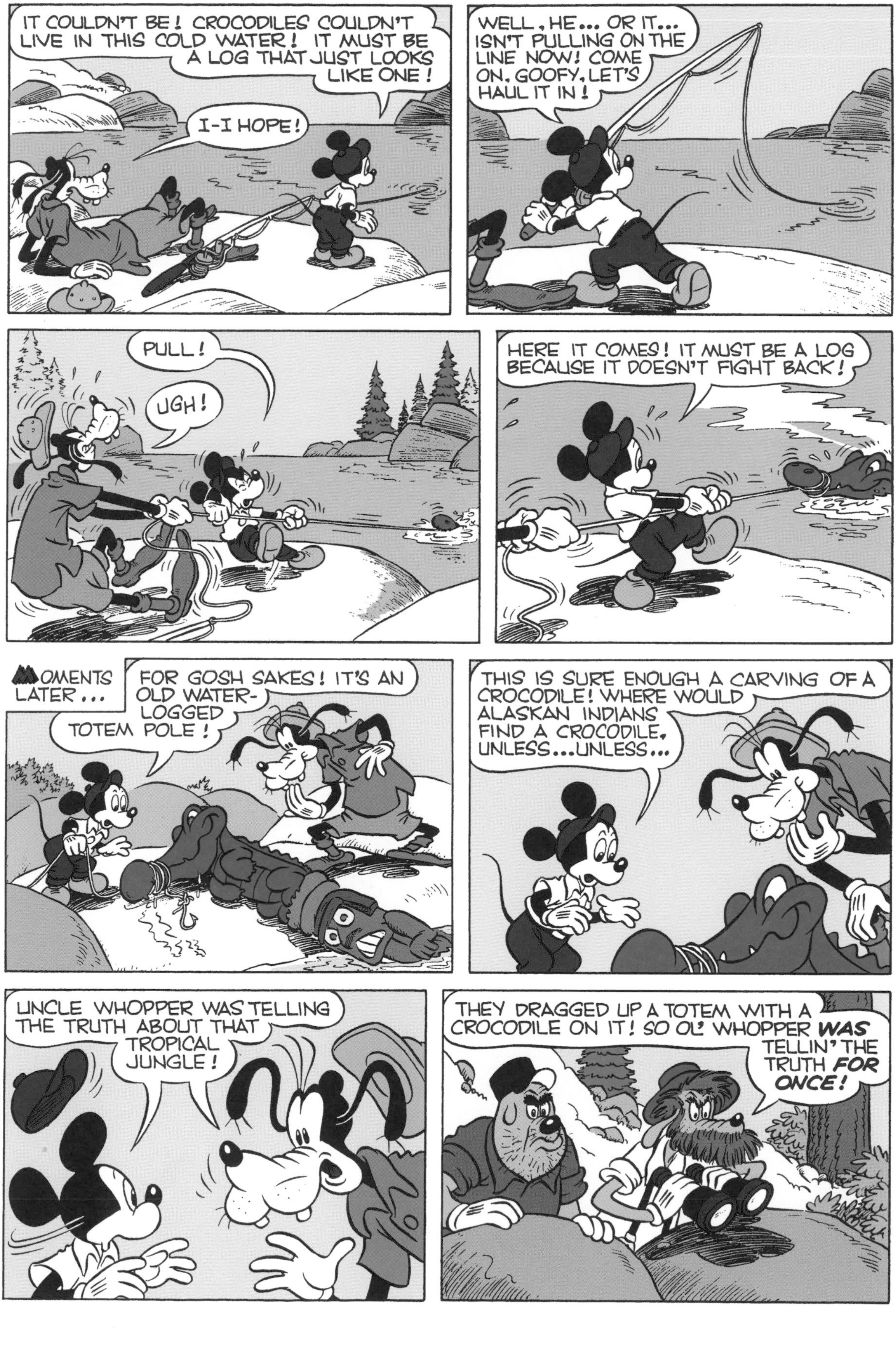
IT COULDN'T BE! CROCODILES COULDN'T LIVE IN THIS COLD WATER! IT MUST BE A LOG THAT JUST LOOKS LIKE ONE!
I-I HOPE!
WELL, HE... OR IT... ISN'T PULLING ON THE LINE NOW! COME ON, GOOFY, LET'S HAUL IT IN!
PULL!
UGH!
HERE IT COMES! IT MUST BE A LOG BECAUSE IT DOESN'T FIGHT BACK!
MOMENTS LATER...
FOR GOSH SAKES! IT'S AN OLD WATER-LOGGED TOTEM POLE!
THIS IS SURE ENOUGH A CARVING OF A CROCODILE! WHERE WOULD ALASKAN INDIANS FIND A CROCODILE, UNLESS...UNLESS...
UNCLE WHOPPER WAS TELLING THE TRUTH ABOUT THAT TROPICAL JUNGLE!
THEY DRAGGED UP A TOTEM WITH A CROCODILE ON IT! SO OL' WHOPPER WAS TELLIN' THE TRUTH FOR ONCE!

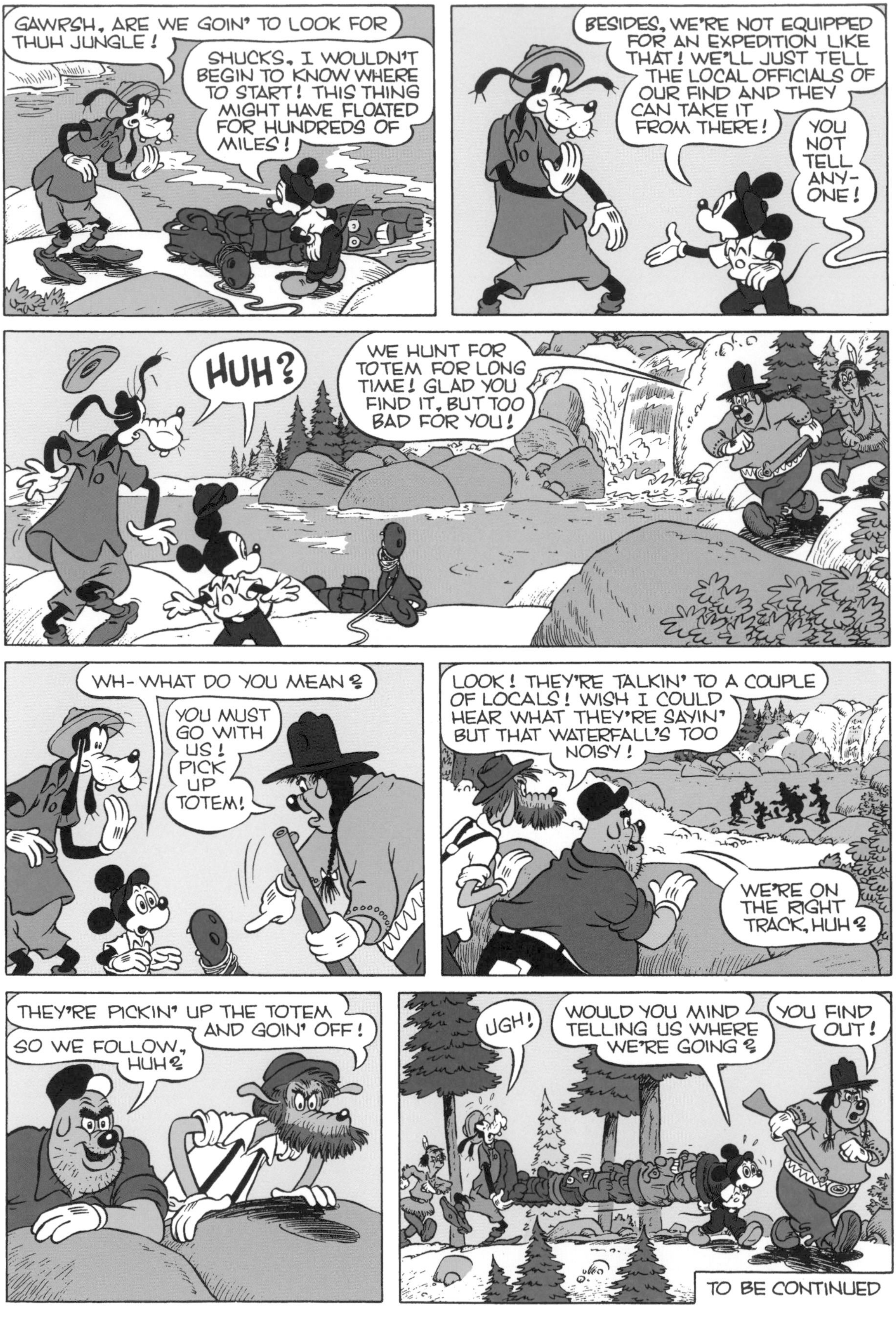
GAWRSH, ARE WE GOIN' TO LOOK FOR THUH JUNGLE!
SHUCKS, I WOULDN'T BEGIN TO KNOW WHERE TO START! THIS THING MIGHT HAVE FLOATED FOR HUNDREDS OF MILES!
BESIDES, WE'RE NOT EQUIPPED FOR AN EXPEDITION LIKE THAT! WE'LL JUST TELL THE LOCAL OFFICIALS OF OUR FIND AND THEY CAN TAKE IT FROM THERE!
YOU NOT TELL ANY-ONE!
HUH?
WE HUNT FOR TOTEM FOR LONG TIME! GLAD YOU FIND IT, BUT TOO BAD FOR YOU!
WH-WHAT DO YOU MEAN?
YOU MUST GO WITH US! PICK UP TOTEM!
LOOK! THEY'RE TALKIN' TO A COUPLE OF LOCALS! WISH I COULD HEAR WHAT THEY'RE SAYIN' BUT THAT WATERFALL'S TOO NOISY!
WE'RE ON THE RIGHT TRACK, HUH?
THEY'RE PICKIN' UP THE TOTEM AND GOIN' OFF!
SO WE FOLLOW, HUH?
UGH!
WOULD YOU MIND TELLING US WHERE WE'RE GOING?
YOU FIND OUT!
TO BE CONTINUED

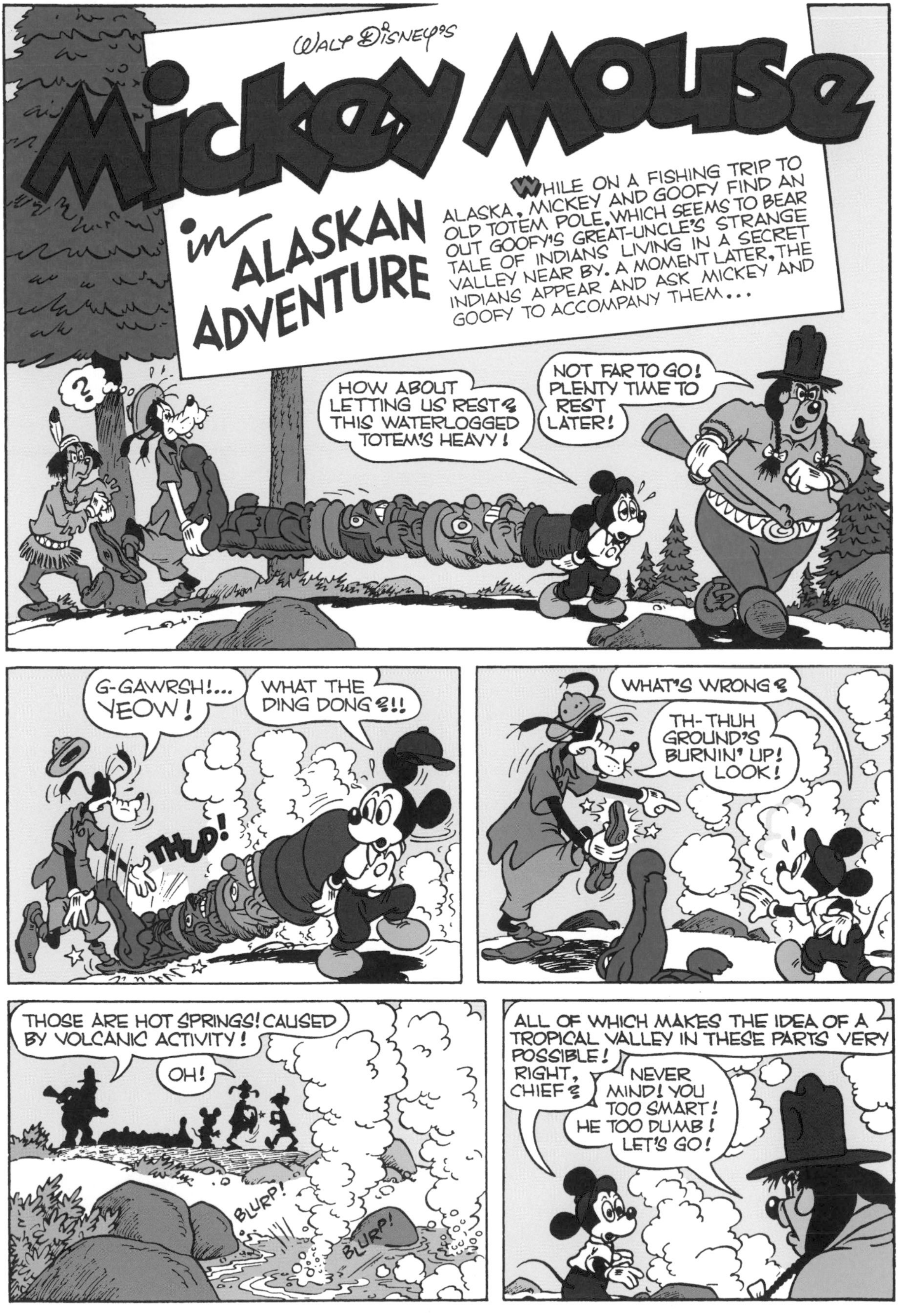
WALT DISNEY'S
Mickey Mouse
in ALASKAN ADVENTURE
WHILE ON A FISHING TRIP TO ALASKA, MICKEY AND GOOFY FIND AN OLD TOTEM POLE, WHICH SEEMS TO BEAR OUT GOOFY'S GREAT-UNCLE'S STRANGE TALE OF INDIANS LIVING IN A SECRET VALLEY NEAR BY. A MOMENT LATER, THE INDIANS APPEAR AND ASK MICKEY AND GOOFY TO ACCOMPANY THEM...
HOW ABOUT LETTING US REST? THIS WATERLOGGED TOTEM'S HEAVY!
NOT FAR TO GO! PLENTY TIME TO REST LATER!
G-GAWRSH!... YEOW!
WHAT THE DING DONG?!!
THUD!
WHAT'S WRONG?
TH-THUH GROUND'S BURNIN' UP! LOOK!
THOSE ARE HOT SPRINGS! CAUSED BY VOLCANIC ACTIVITY!
OH!
BLURP!
BLURP!
ALL OF WHICH MAKES THE IDEA OF A TROPICAL VALLEY IN THESE PARTS VERY POSSIBLE! RIGHT, CHIEF?
NEVER MIND! YOU TOO SMART! HE TOO DUMB! LET'S GO!

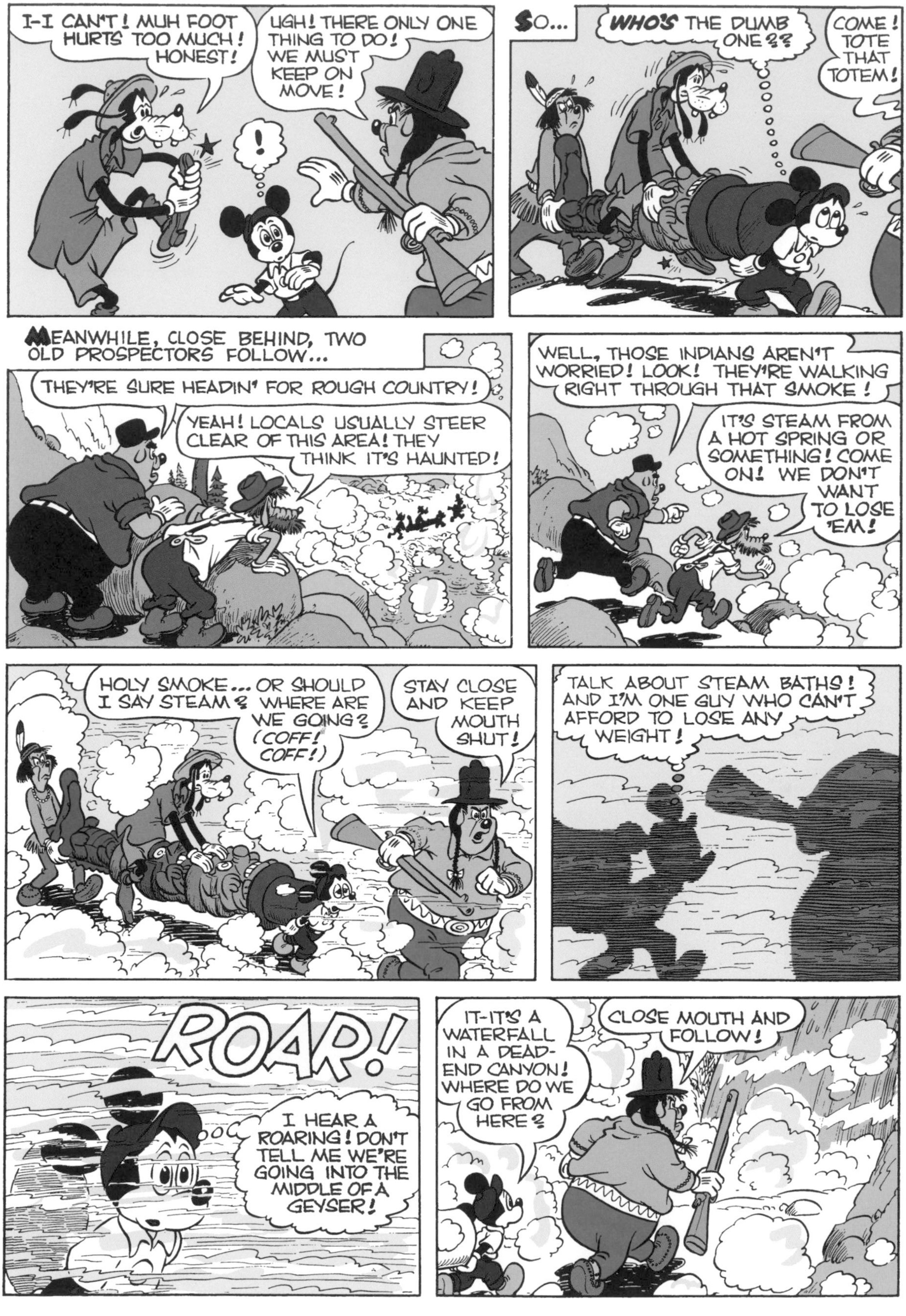
I-I CAN'T! MUH FOOT HURTS TOO MUCH! HONEST!
UGH! THERE ONLY ONE THING TO DO! WE MUST KEEP ON MOVE!
!
SO...
WHO'S THE DUMB ONE??
COME! TOTE THAT TOTEM!
MEANWHILE, CLOSE BEHIND, TWO OLD PROSPECTORS FOLLOW...
THEY'RE SURE HEADIN' FOR ROUGH COUNTRY!
YEAH! LOCALS USUALLY STEER CLEAR OF THIS AREA! THEY THINK IT'S HAUNTED!
WELL, THOSE INDIANS AREN'T WORRIED! LOOK! THEY'RE WALKING RIGHT THROUGH THAT SMOKE!
IT'S STEAM FROM A HOT SPRING OR SOMETHING! COME ON! WE DON'T WANT TO LOSE 'EM!
HOLY SMOKE... OR SHOULD I SAY STEAM? WHERE ARE WE GOING? (COFF! COFF!)
STAY CLOSE AND KEEP MOUTH SHUT!
TALK ABOUT STEAM BATHS! AND I'M ONE GUY WHO CAN'T AFFORD TO LOSE ANY WEIGHT!
ROAR!
I HEAR A ROARING! DON'T TELL ME WE'RE GOING INTO THE MIDDLE OF A GEYSER!
IT-IT'S A WATERFALL IN A DEAD-END CANYON! WHERE DO WE GO FROM HERE?
CLOSE MOUTH AND FOLLOW!

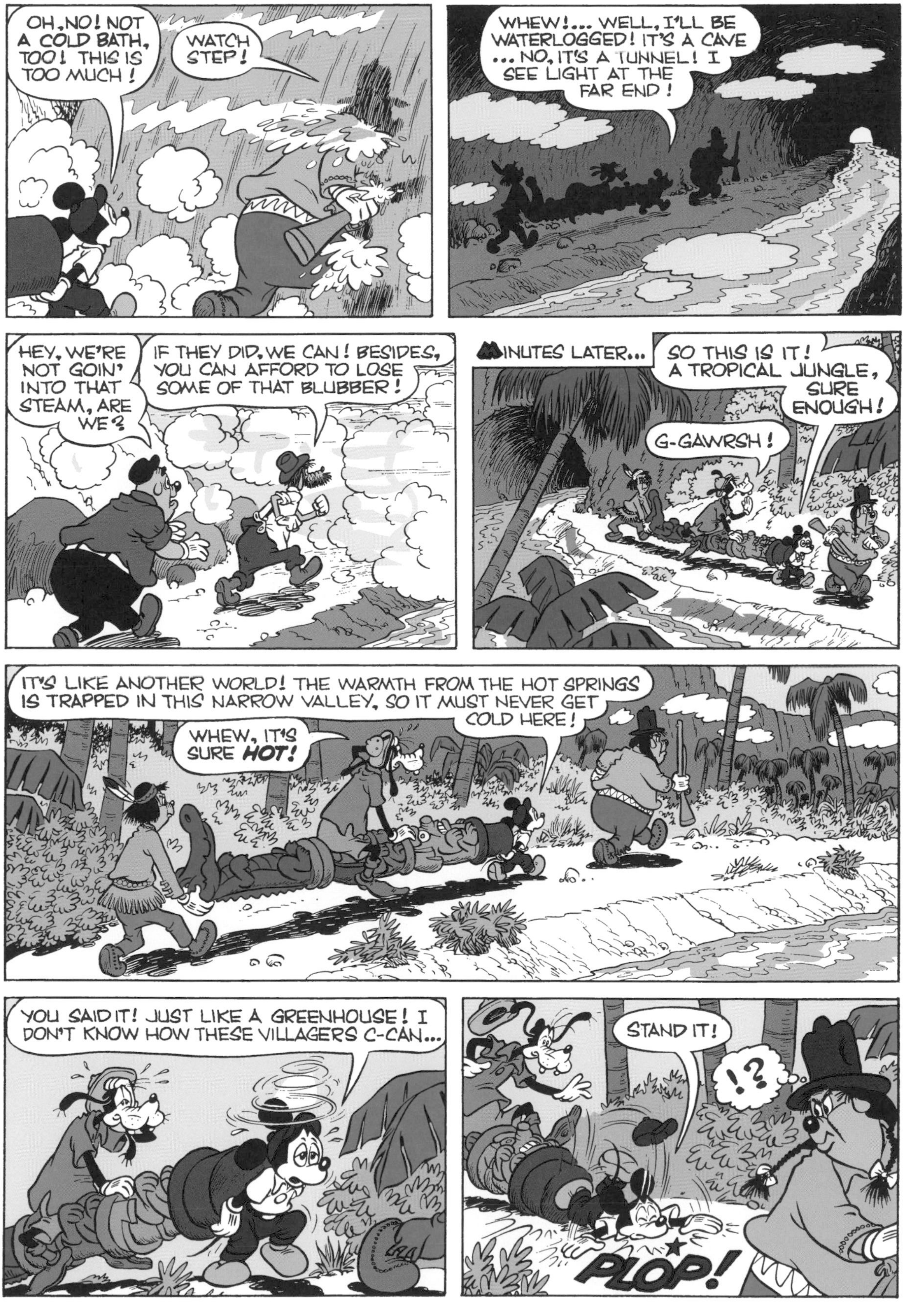
OH, NO! NOT A COLD BATH, TOO! THIS IS TOO MUCH!
WATCH STEP!
WHEW!... WELL, I'LL BE WATERLOGGED! IT'S A CAVE ... NO, IT'S A TUNNEL! I SEE LIGHT AT THE FAR END!
HEY, WE'RE NOT GOIN' INTO THAT STEAM, ARE WE?
IF THEY DID, WE CAN! BESIDES, YOU CAN AFFORD TO LOSE SOME OF THAT BLUBBER!
MINUTES LATER...
SO THIS IS IT! A TROPICAL JUNGLE, SURE ENOUGH!
G-GAWRSH!
IT'S LIKE ANOTHER WORLD! THE WARMTH FROM THE HOT SPRINGS IS TRAPPED IN THIS NARROW VALLEY, SO IT MUST NEVER GET COLD HERE!
WHEW, IT'S SURE HOT!
YOU SAID IT! JUST LIKE A GREENHOUSE! I DON'T KNOW HOW THESE VILLAGERS C-CAN...
STAND IT!
!?
PLOP!

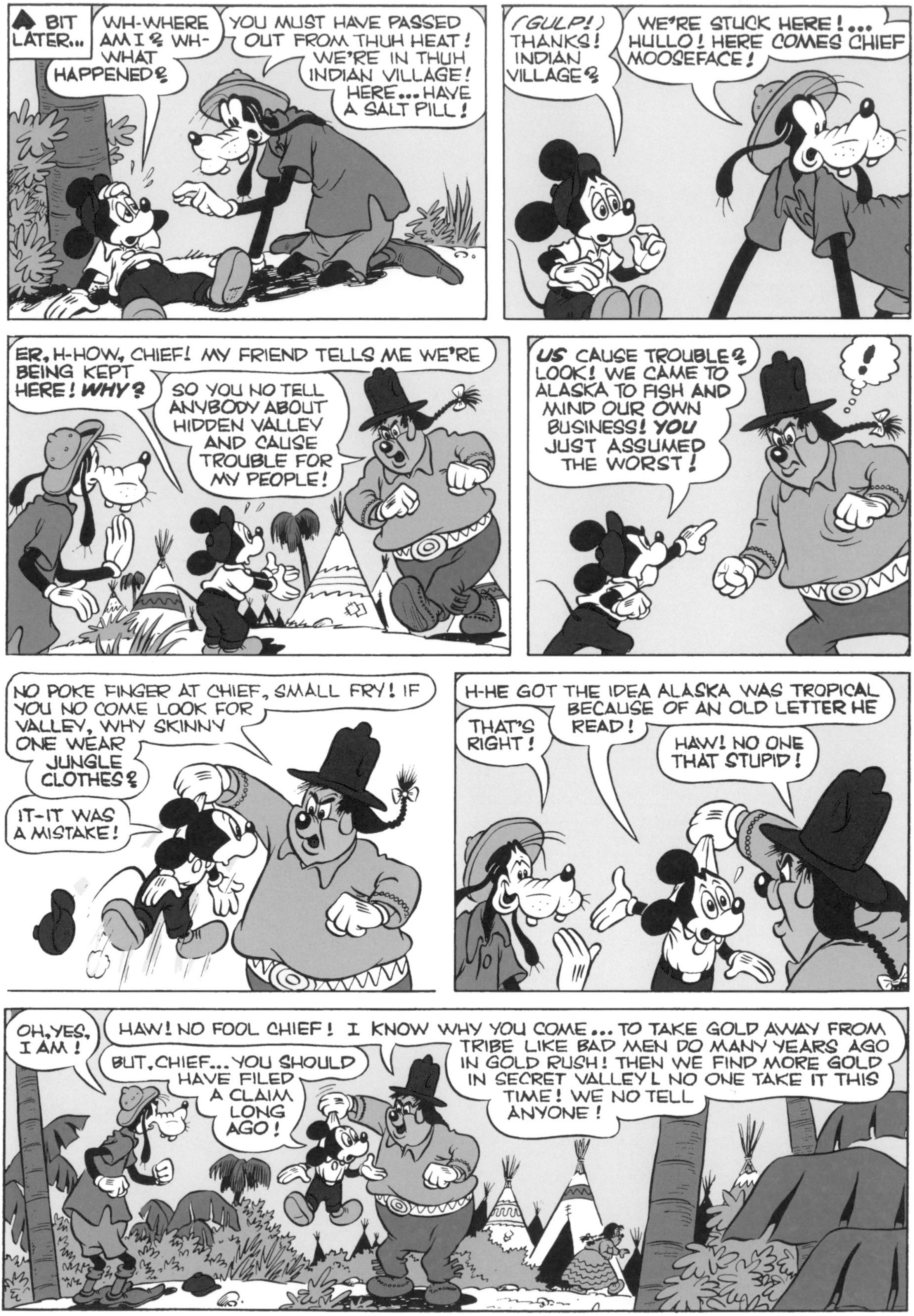
A BIT LATER...
WH-WHERE AM I? WH-WHAT HAPPENED?
YOU MUST HAVE PASSED OUT FROM THUH HEAT! WE'RE IN THUH INDIAN VILLAGE! HERE... HAVE A SALT PILL!
(GULP!) THANKS! INDIAN VILLAGE?
WE'RE STUCK HERE!... HULLO! HERE COMES CHIEF MOOSEFACE!
ER, H-HOW, CHIEF! MY FRIEND TELLS ME WE'RE BEING KEPT HERE! WHY?
SO YOU NO TELL ANYBODY ABOUT HIDDEN VALLEY AND CAUSE TROUBLE FOR MY PEOPLE!
US CAUSE TROUBLE? LOOK! WE CAME TO ALASKA TO FISH AND MIND OUR OWN BUSINESS! YOU JUST ASSUMED THE WORST!
!
NO POKE FINGER AT CHIEF, SMALL FRY! IF YOU NO COME LOOK FOR VALLEY, WHY SKINNY ONE WEAR JUNGLE CLOTHES?
IT-IT WAS A MISTAKE!
H-HE GOT THE IDEA ALASKA WAS TROPICAL BECAUSE OF AN OLD LETTER HE READ!
THAT'S RIGHT!
HAW! NO ONE THAT STUPID!
OH, YES, I AM!
HAW! NO FOOL CHIEF! I KNOW WHY YOU COME... TO TAKE GOLD AWAY FROM TRIBE LIKE BAD MEN DO MANY YEARS AGO IN GOLD RUSH! THEN WE FIND MORE GOLD IN SECRET VALLEY! NO ONE TAKE IT THIS TIME! WE NO TELL ANYONE!
BUT, CHIEF... YOU SHOULD HAVE FILED A CLAIM LONG AGO!

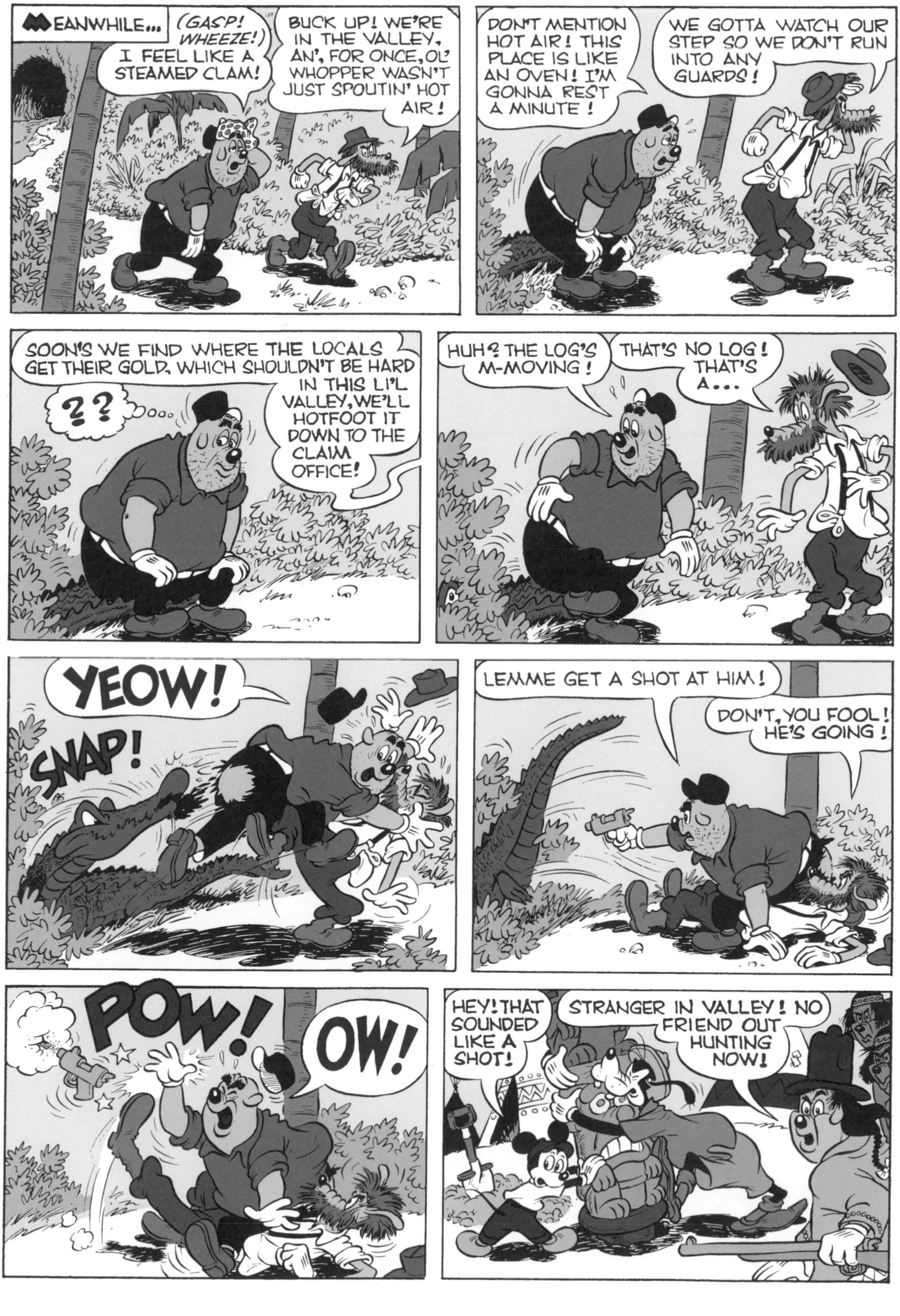
MEANWHILE...
(GASP! WHEEZE!) I FEEL LIKE A STEAMED CLAM!
BUCK UP! WE'RE IN THE VALLEY, AN', FOR ONCE, OL' WHOPPER WASN'T JUST SPOUTIN' HOT AIR!
DON'T MENTION HOT AIR! THIS PLACE IS LIKE AN OVEN! I'M GONNA REST A MINUTE!
WE GOTTA WATCH OUR STEP SO WE DON'T RUN INTO ANY GUARDS!
SOON'S WE FIND WHERE THE LOCALS GET THEIR GOLD, WHICH SHOULDN'T BE HARD IN THIS LI'L VALLEY, WE'LL HOTFOOT IT DOWN TO THE CLAIM OFFICE!
??
HUH? THE LOG'S M-MOVING!
THAT'S NO LOG! THAT'S A...
YEOW!
SNAP!
LEMME GET A SHOT AT HIM!
DON'T, YOU FOOL! HE'S GOING!
POW!
OW!
HEY! THAT SOUNDED LIKE A SHOT!
STRANGER IN VALLEY! NO FRIEND OUT HUNTING NOW!

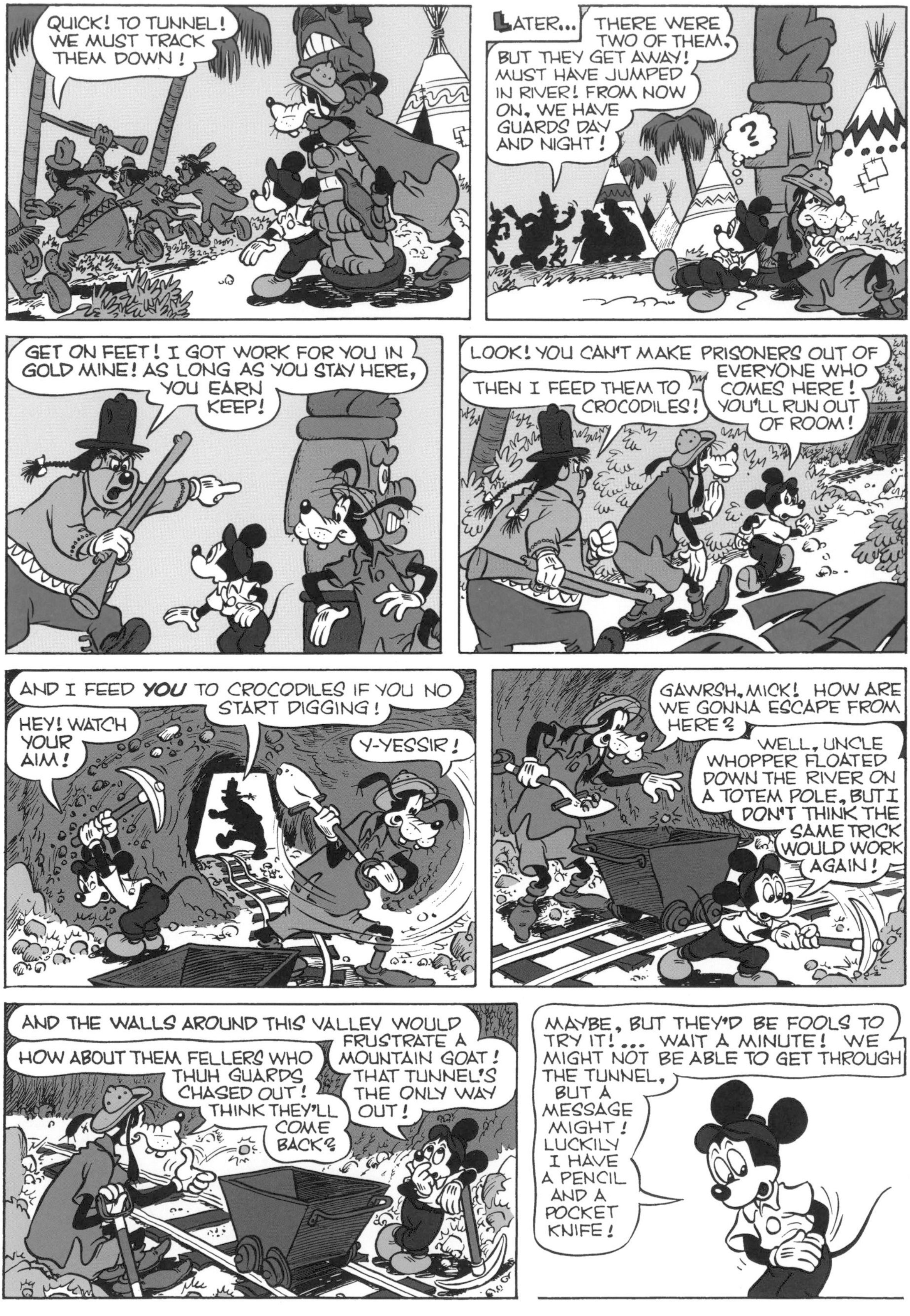
QUICK! TO TUNNEL! WE MUST TRACK THEM DOWN!
LATER...
THERE WERE TWO OF THEM, BUT THEY GET AWAY! MUST HAVE JUMPED IN RIVER! FROM NOW ON, WE HAVE GUARDS DAY AND NIGHT!
?
GET ON FEET! I GOT WORK FOR YOU IN GOLD MINE! AS LONG AS YOU STAY HERE, YOU EARN KEEP!
LOOK! YOU CAN'T MAKE PRISONERS OUT OF EVERYONE WHO COMES HERE! YOU'LL RUN OUT OF ROOM!
THEN I FEED THEM TO CROCODILES!
AND I FEED *YOU* TO CROCODILES IF YOU NO START DIGGING!
HEY! WATCH YOUR AIM!
Y-YESSIR!
GAWRSH, MICK! HOW ARE WE GONNA ESCAPE FROM HERE?
WELL, UNCLE WHOPPER FLOATED DOWN THE RIVER ON A TOTEM POLE, BUT I DON'T THINK THE SAME TRICK WOULD WORK AGAIN!
AND THE WALLS AROUND THIS VALLEY WOULD FRUSTRATE A MOUNTAIN GOAT! THAT TUNNEL'S THE ONLY WAY OUT!
HOW ABOUT THEM FELLERS WHO THUH GUARDS CHASED OUT! THINK THEY'LL COME BACK?
MAYBE, BUT THEY'D BE FOOLS TO TRY IT! ... WAIT A MINUTE! WE MIGHT NOT BE ABLE TO GET THROUGH THE TUNNEL,
BUT A MESSAGE MIGHT! LUCKILY I HAVE A PENCIL AND A POCKET KNIFE!

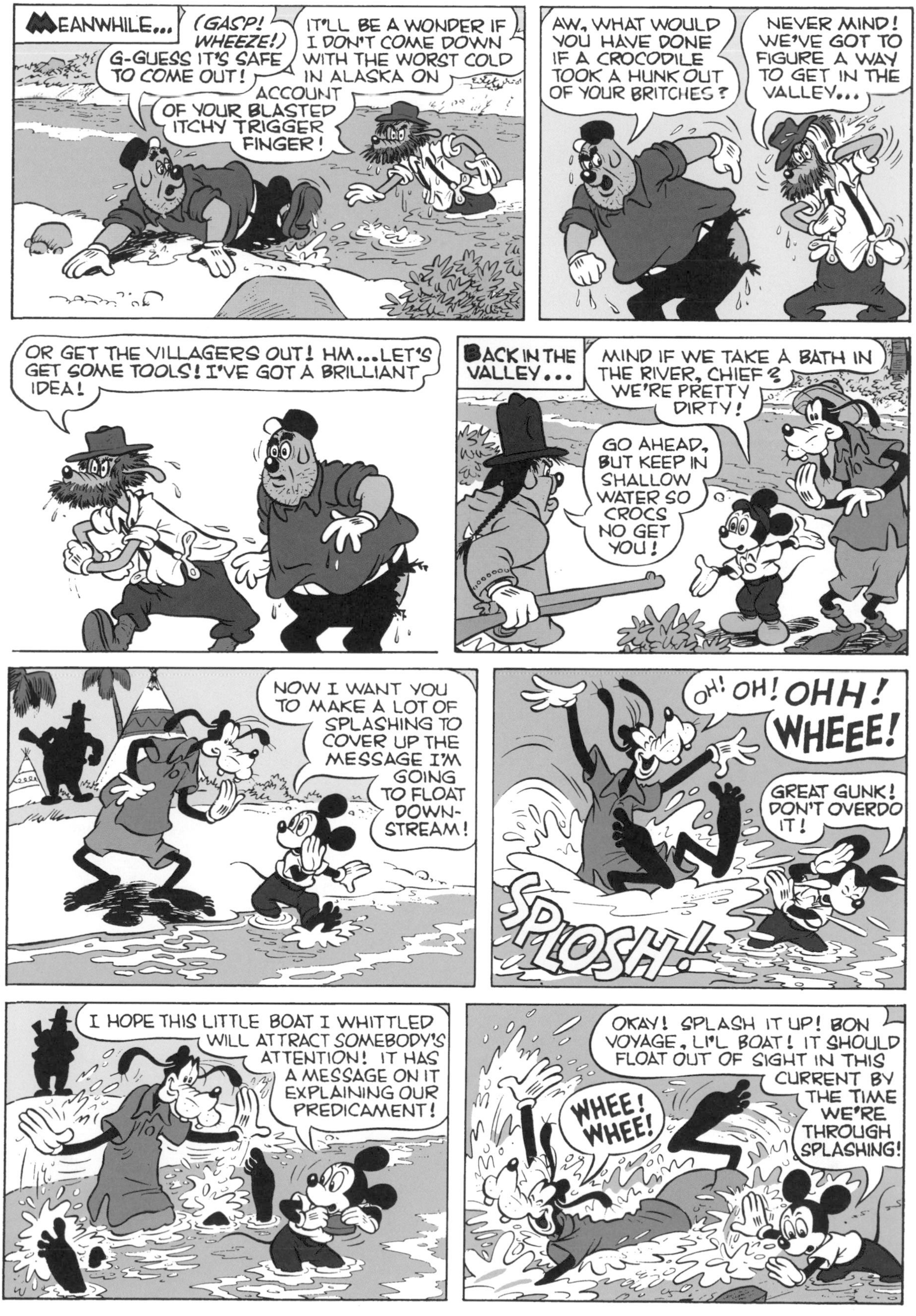
MEANWHILE...
(GASP! WHEEZE!) G-GUESS IT'S SAFE TO COME OUT!
IT'LL BE A WONDER IF I DON'T COME DOWN WITH THE WORST COLD IN ALASKA ON ACCOUNT OF YOUR BLASTED ITCHY TRIGGER FINGER!
AW, WHAT WOULD YOU HAVE DONE IF A CROCODILE TOOK A HUNK OUT OF YOUR BRITCHES?
NEVER MIND! WE'VE GOT TO FIGURE A WAY TO GET IN THE VALLEY...
OR GET THE VILLAGERS OUT! HM...LET'S GET SOME TOOLS! I'VE GOT A BRILLIANT IDEA!
BACK IN THE VALLEY...
MIND IF WE TAKE A BATH IN THE RIVER, CHIEF? WE'RE PRETTY DIRTY!
GO AHEAD, BUT KEEP IN SHALLOW WATER SO CROCS NO GET YOU!
NOW I WANT YOU TO MAKE A LOT OF SPLASHING TO COVER UP THE MESSAGE I'M GOING TO FLOAT DOWN-STREAM!
OH! OH! OHH! WHEEE!
GREAT GUNK! DON'T OVERDO IT!
SPLOSH!
I HOPE THIS LITTLE BOAT I WHITTLED WILL ATTRACT SOMEBODY'S ATTENTION! IT HAS A MESSAGE ON IT EXPLAINING OUR PREDICAMENT!
OKAY! SPLASH IT UP! BON VOYAGE, LI'L BOAT! IT SHOULD FLOAT OUT OF SIGHT IN THIS CURRENT BY THE TIME WE'RE THROUGH SPLASHING!
WHEE! WHEE!

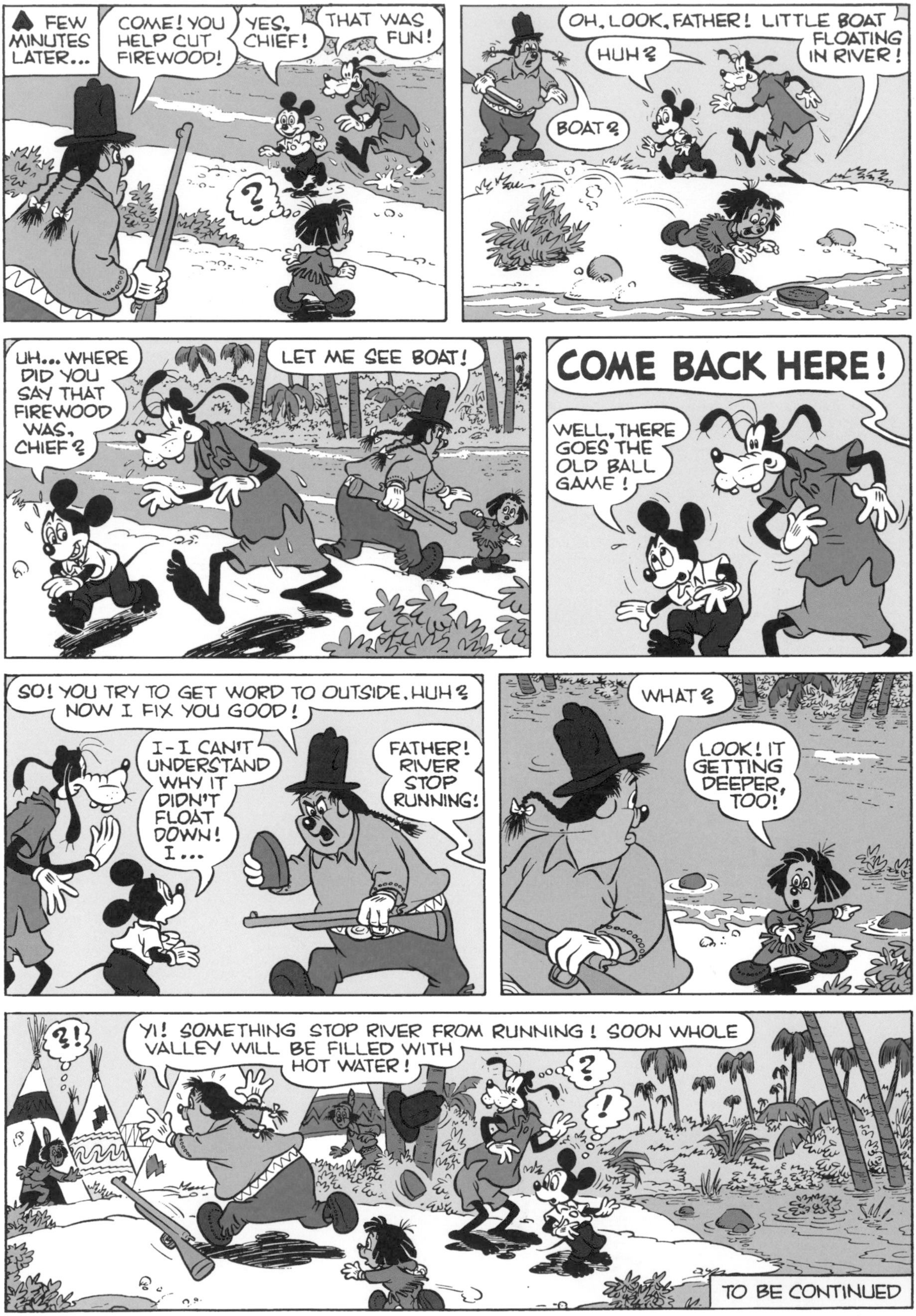
A FEW MINUTES LATER...
COME! YOU HELP CUT FIREWOOD!
YES, CHIEF!
THAT WAS FUN!
OH, LOOK, FATHER! LITTLE BOAT FLOATING IN RIVER!
HUH?
BOAT?
UH... WHERE DID YOU SAY THAT FIREWOOD WAS, CHIEF?
LET ME SEE BOAT!
COME BACK HERE!
WELL, THERE GOES THE OLD BALL GAME!
SO! YOU TRY TO GET WORD TO OUTSIDE, HUH? NOW I FIX YOU GOOD!
I-I CAN'T UNDERSTAND WHY IT DIDN'T FLOAT DOWN! I...
FATHER! RIVER STOP RUNNING!
WHAT?
LOOK! IT GETTING DEEPER, TOO!
?!
YI! SOMETHING STOP RIVER FROM RUNNING! SOON WHOLE VALLEY WILL BE FILLED WITH HOT WATER!
?
!
TO BE CONTINUED

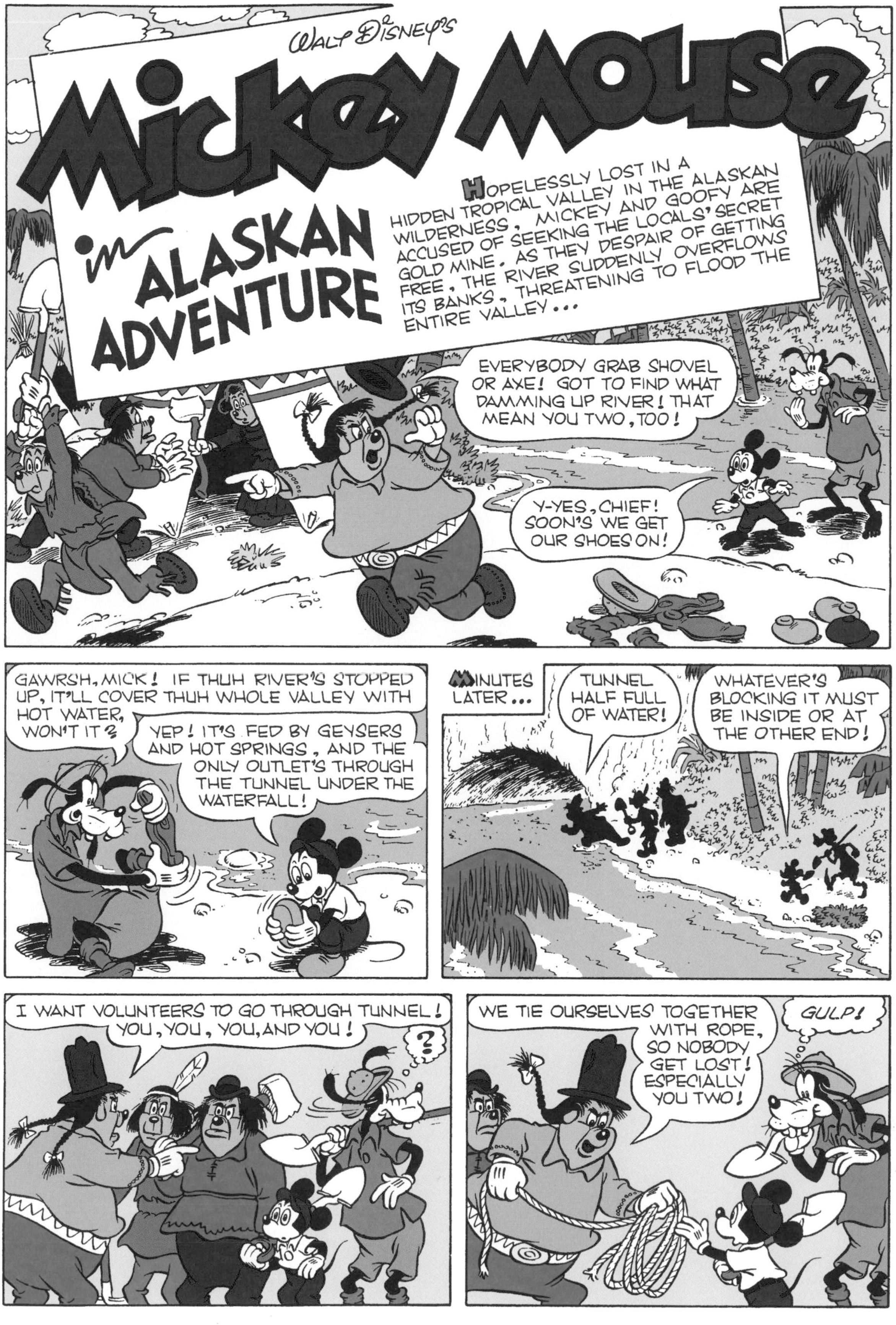
WALT DISNEY'S
Mickey Mouse
in ALASKAN ADVENTURE
HOPELESSLY LOST IN A HIDDEN TROPICAL VALLEY IN THE ALASKAN WILDERNESS, MICKEY AND GOOFY ARE ACCUSED OF SEEKING THE LOCALS' SECRET GOLD MINE. AS THEY DESPAIR OF GETTING FREE, THE RIVER SUDDENLY OVERFLOWS ITS BANKS, THREATENING TO FLOOD THE ENTIRE VALLEY...
EVERYBODY GRAB SHOVEL OR AXE! GOT TO FIND WHAT DAMMING UP RIVER! THAT MEAN YOU TWO, TOO!
Y-YES, CHIEF! SOON'S WE GET OUR SHOES ON!
GAWRSH, MICK! IF THUH RIVER'S STOPPED UP, IT'LL COVER THUH WHOLE VALLEY WITH HOT WATER, WON'T IT?
YEP! IT'S FED BY GEYSERS AND HOT SPRINGS, AND THE ONLY OUTLET'S THROUGH THE TUNNEL UNDER THE WATERFALL!
MINUTES LATER...
TUNNEL HALF FULL OF WATER!
WHATEVER'S BLOCKING IT MUST BE INSIDE OR AT THE OTHER END!
I WANT VOLUNTEERS TO GO THROUGH TUNNEL! YOU, YOU, YOU, AND YOU!
?
WE TIE OURSELVES TOGETHER WITH ROPE, SO NOBODY GET LOST! ESPECIALLY YOU TWO!
GULP!

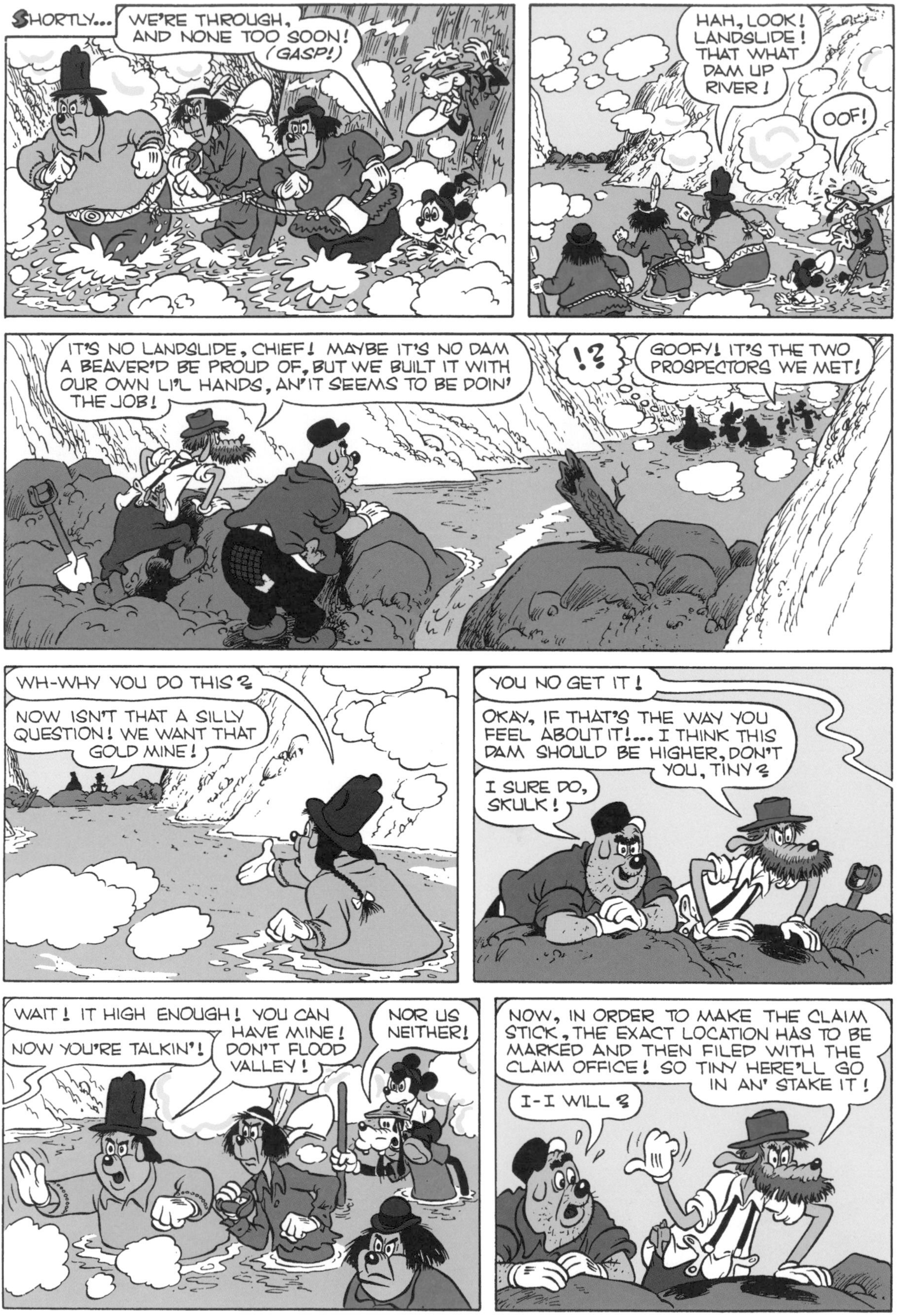
SHORTLY...
WE'RE THROUGH, AND NONE TOO SOON! (GASP!)
HAH, LOOK! LANDSLIDE! THAT WHAT DAM UP RIVER!
OOF!
IT'S NO LANDSLIDE, CHIEF! MAYBE IT'S NO DAM A BEAVER'D BE PROUD OF, BUT WE BUILT IT WITH OUR OWN LI'L HANDS, AN' IT SEEMS TO BE DOIN' THE JOB!
!?
GOOFY! IT'S THE TWO PROSPECTORS WE MET!
WH-WHY YOU DO THIS?
NOW ISN'T THAT A SILLY QUESTION! WE WANT THAT GOLD MINE!
YOU NO GET IT!
OKAY, IF THAT'S THE WAY YOU FEEL ABOUT IT!... I THINK THIS DAM SHOULD BE HIGHER, DON'T YOU, TINY?
I SURE DO, SKULK!
WAIT! IT HIGH ENOUGH! YOU CAN HAVE MINE! DON'T FLOOD VALLEY!
NOR US NEITHER!
NOW YOU'RE TALKIN'!
NOW, IN ORDER TO MAKE THE CLAIM STICK, THE EXACT LOCATION HAS TO BE MARKED AND THEN FILED WITH THE CLAIM OFFICE! SO TINY HERE'LL GO IN AN' STAKE IT!
I-I WILL?

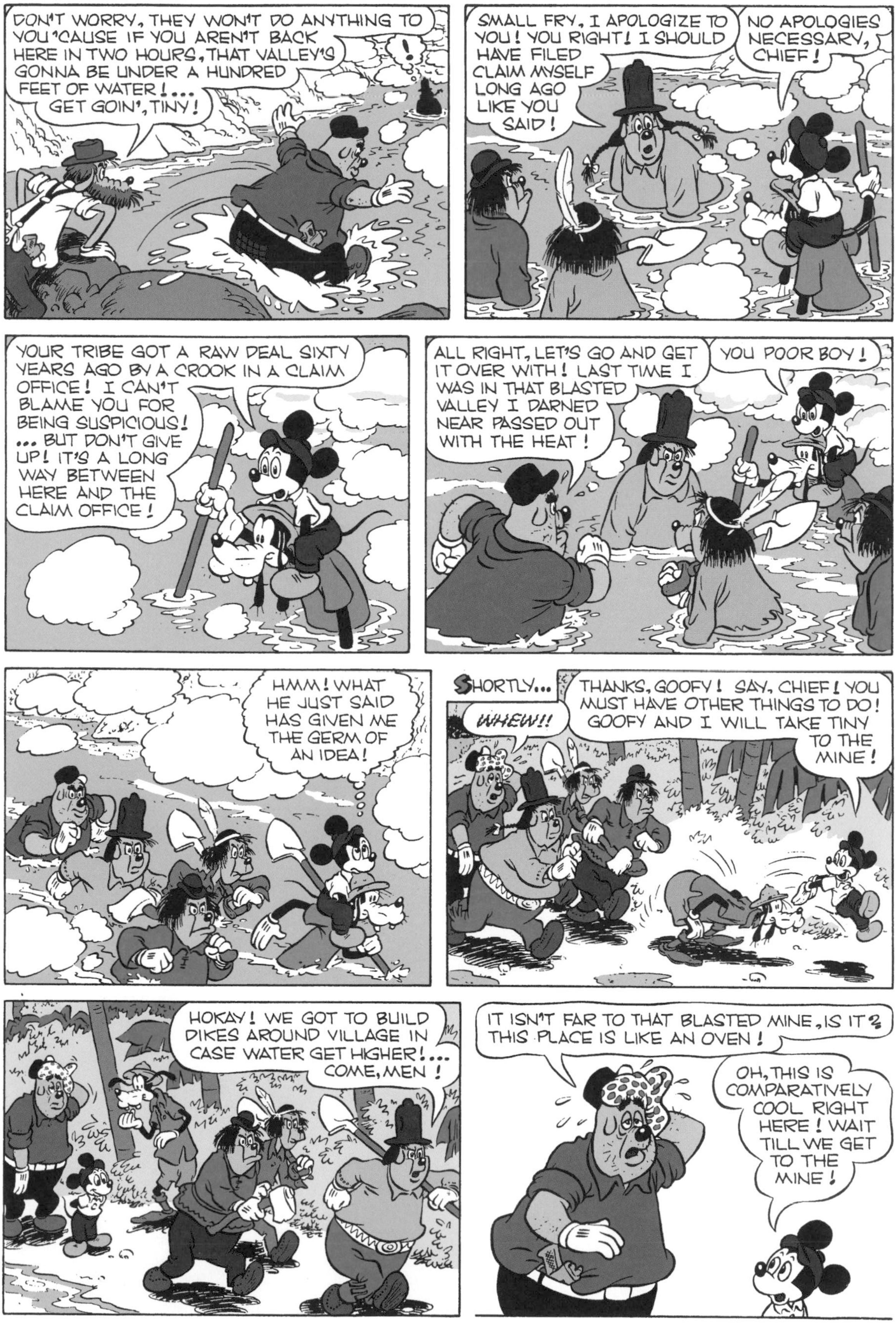
DON'T WORRY, THEY WON'T DO ANYTHING TO YOU 'CAUSE IF YOU AREN'T BACK HERE IN TWO HOURS, THAT VALLEY'S GONNA BE UNDER A HUNDRED FEET OF WATER!... GET GOIN', TINY!
!
SMALL FRY, I APOLOGIZE TO YOU! YOU RIGHT! I SHOULD HAVE FILED CLAIM MYSELF LONG AGO LIKE YOU SAID!
NO APOLOGIES NECESSARY, CHIEF!
YOUR TRIBE GOT A RAW DEAL SIXTY YEARS AGO BY A CROOK IN A CLAIM OFFICE! I CAN'T BLAME YOU FOR BEING SUSPICIOUS! ... BUT DON'T GIVE UP! IT'S A LONG WAY BETWEEN HERE AND THE CLAIM OFFICE!
ALL RIGHT, LET'S GO AND GET IT OVER WITH! LAST TIME I WAS IN THAT BLASTED VALLEY I DARNED NEAR PASSED OUT WITH THE HEAT!
YOU POOR BOY!
HMM! WHAT HE JUST SAID HAS GIVEN ME THE GERM OF AN IDEA!
SHORTLY...
WHEW!!
THANKS, GOOFY! SAY, CHIEF! YOU MUST HAVE OTHER THINGS TO DO! GOOFY AND I WILL TAKE TINY TO THE MINE!
HOKAY! WE GOT TO BUILD DIKES AROUND VILLAGE IN CASE WATER GET HIGHER!... COME, MEN!
IT ISN'T FAR TO THAT BLASTED MINE, IS IT? THIS PLACE IS LIKE AN OVEN!
OH, THIS IS COMPARATIVELY COOL RIGHT HERE! WAIT TILL WE GET TO THE MINE!

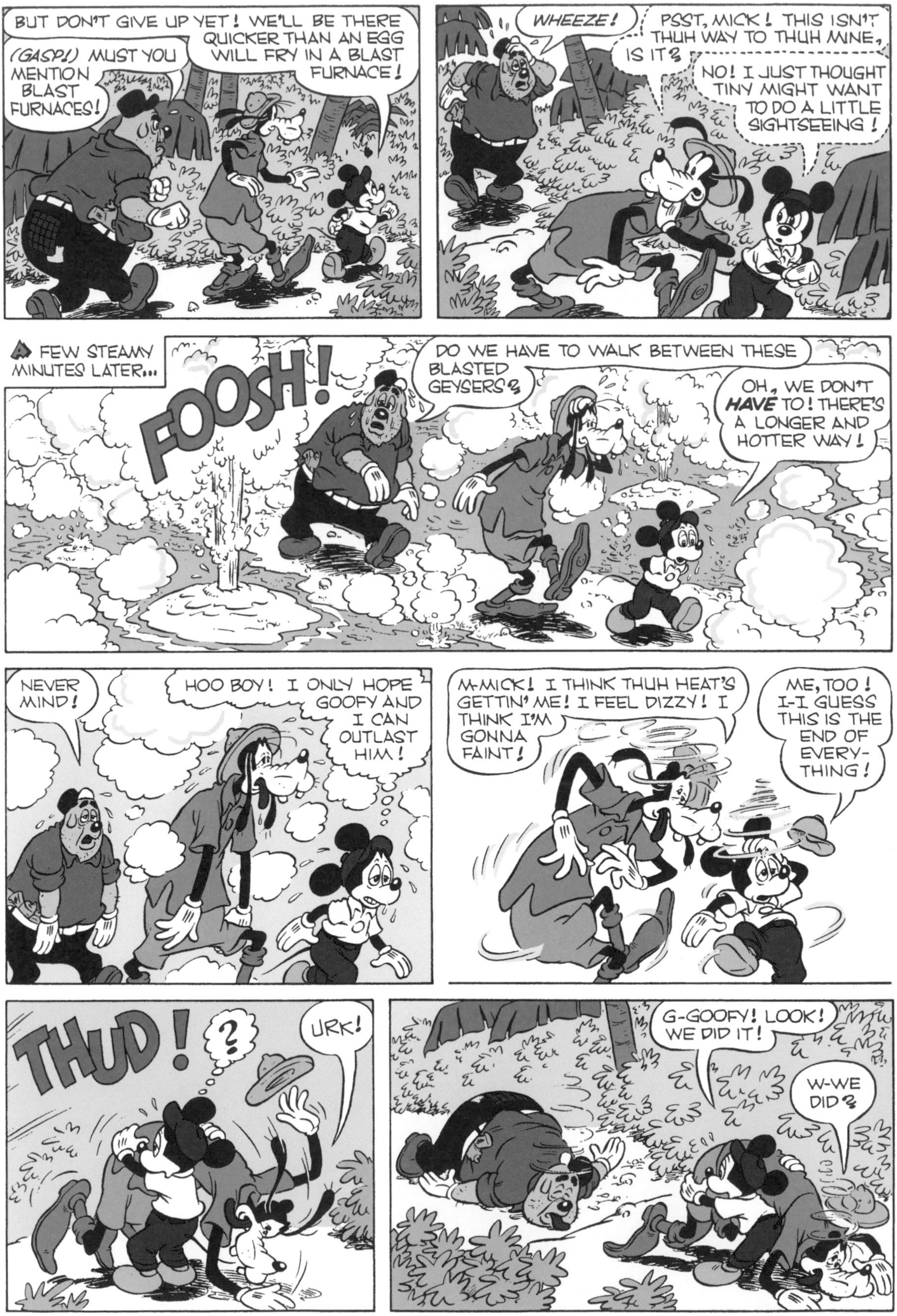

BUT DON'T GIVE UP YET! WE'LL BE THERE QUICKER THAN AN EGG WILL FRY IN A BLAST FURNACE!
(GASP!) MUST YOU MENTION BLAST FURNACES!
WHEEZE!
PSST, MICK! THIS ISN'T THUH WAY TO THUH MINE, IS IT?
NO! I JUST THOUGHT TINY MIGHT WANT TO DO A LITTLE SIGHTSEEING!
A FEW STEAMY MINUTES LATER...
FOOSH!
DO WE HAVE TO WALK BETWEEN THESE BLASTED GEYSERS?
OH, WE DON'T HAVE TO! THERE'S A LONGER AND HOTTER WAY!
NEVER MIND!
HOO BOY! I ONLY HOPE GOOFY AND I CAN OUTLAST HIM!
M-MICK! I THINK THUH HEAT'S GETTIN' ME! I FEEL DIZZY! I THINK I'M GONNA FAINT!
ME, TOO! I-I GUESS THIS IS THE END OF EVERY-THING!
THUD!
?
URK!
G-GOOFY! LOOK! WE DID IT!
W-WE DID?

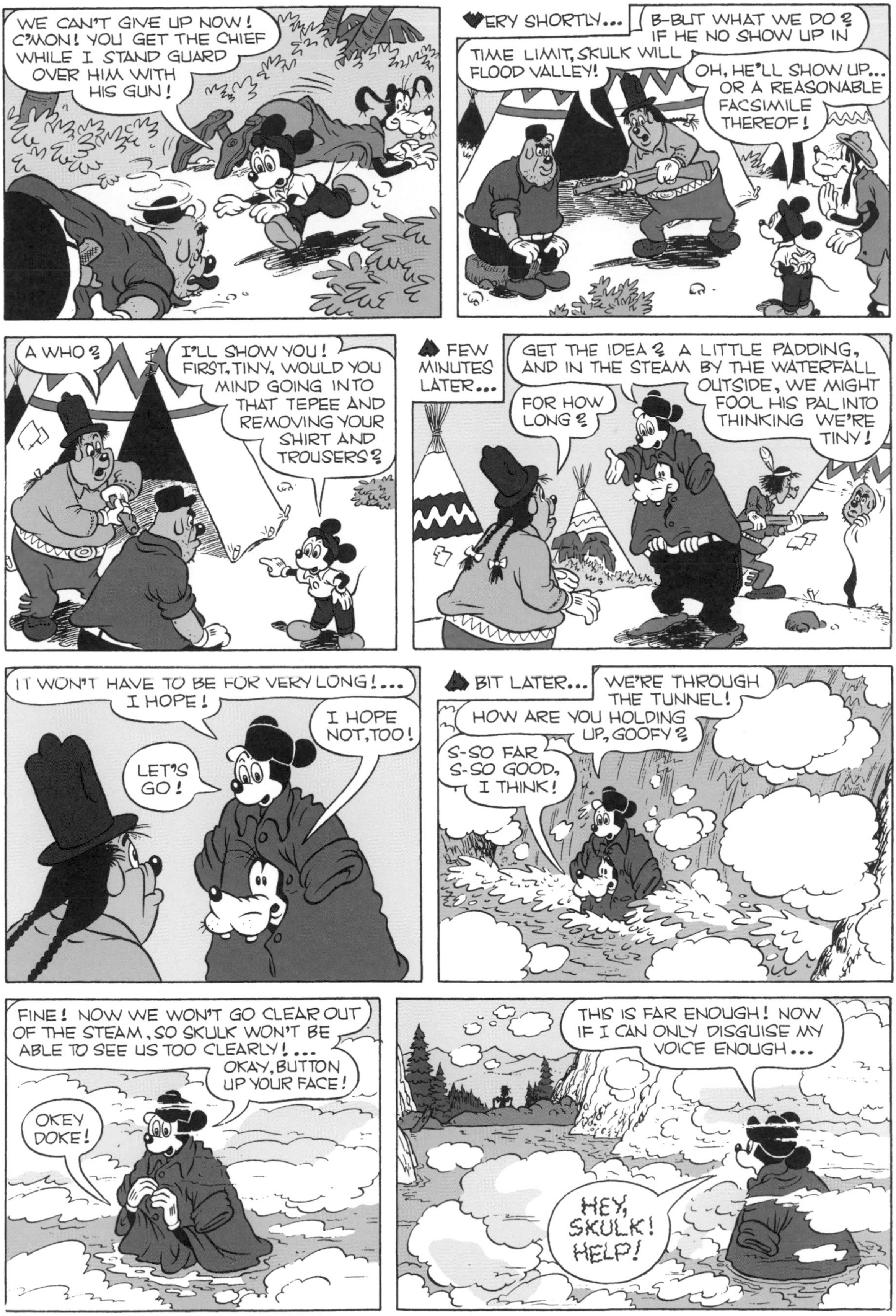
WE CAN'T GIVE UP NOW! C'MON! YOU GET THE CHIEF WHILE I STAND GUARD OVER HIM WITH HIS GUN!
VERY SHORTLY...
B-BUT WHAT WE DO? IF HE NO SHOW UP IN
TIME LIMIT, SKULK WILL FLOOD VALLEY!
OH, HE'LL SHOW UP... OR A REASONABLE FACSIMILE THEREOF!
A WHO?
I'LL SHOW YOU! FIRST, TINY, WOULD YOU MIND GOING INTO THAT TEPEE AND REMOVING YOUR SHIRT AND TROUSERS?
A FEW MINUTES LATER...
GET THE IDEA? A LITTLE PADDING, AND IN THE STEAM BY THE WATERFALL OUTSIDE, WE MIGHT FOOL HIS PAL INTO THINKING WE'RE TINY!
FOR HOW LONG?
IT WON'T HAVE TO BE FOR VERY LONG!... I HOPE!
I HOPE NOT, TOO!
LET'S GO!
A BIT LATER...
WE'RE THROUGH THE TUNNEL!
HOW ARE YOU HOLDING UP, GOOFY?
S-SO FAR S-SO GOOD, I THINK!
FINE! NOW WE WON'T GO CLEAR OUT OF THE STEAM, SO SKULK WON'T BE ABLE TO SEE US TOO CLEARLY!...
OKAY, BUTTON UP YOUR FACE!
OKEY DOKE!
THIS IS FAR ENOUGH! NOW IF I CAN ONLY DISGUISE MY VOICE ENOUGH...
HEY, SKULK! HELP!

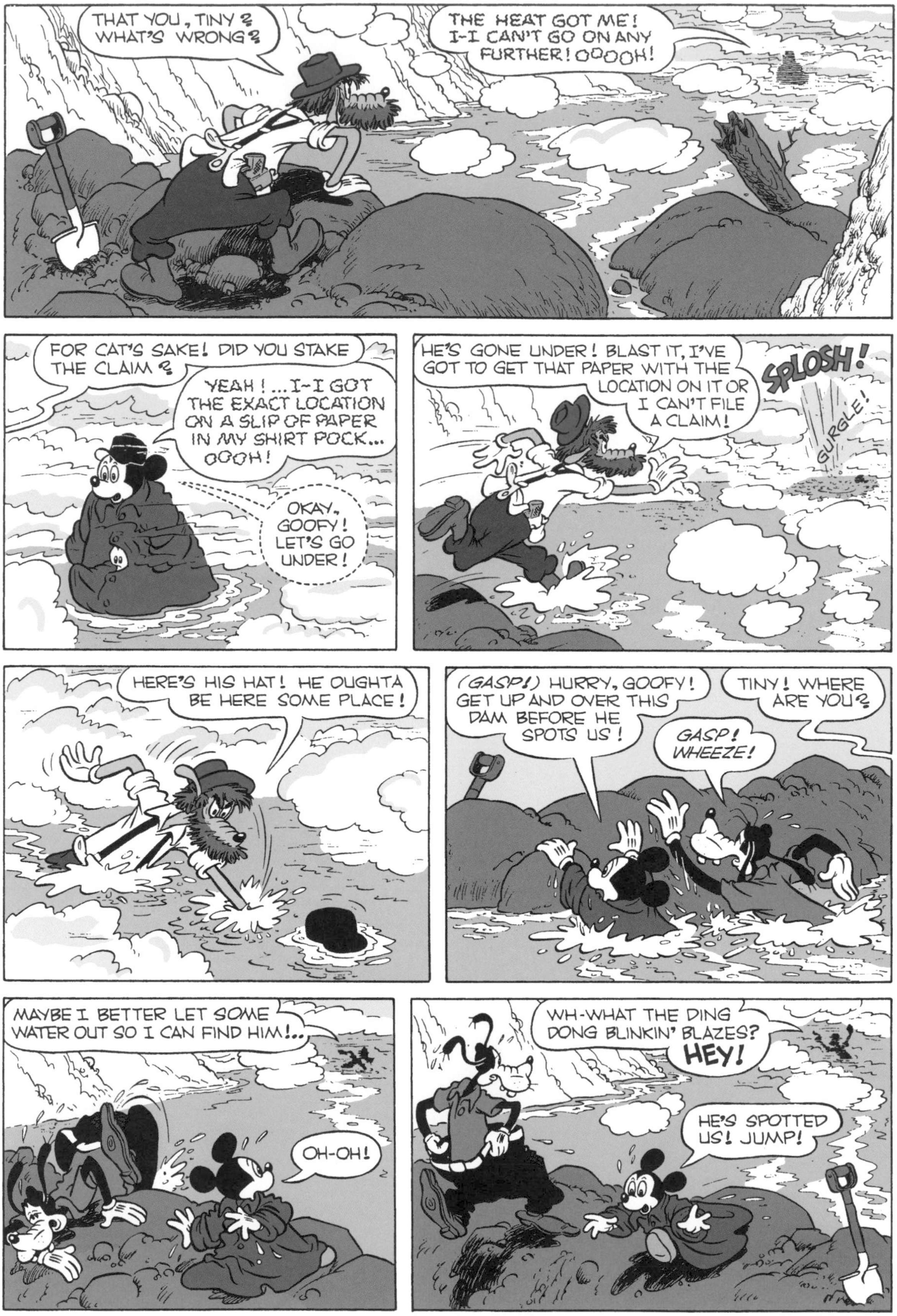
THAT YOU, TINY? WHAT'S WRONG?
THE HEAT GOT ME! I-I CAN'T GO ON ANY FURTHER! OOOOH!
FOR CAT'S SAKE! DID YOU STAKE THE CLAIM?
YEAH! ...I-I GOT THE EXACT LOCATION ON A SLIP OF PAPER IN MY SHIRT POCK... OOOH!
OKAY, GOOFY! LET'S GO UNDER!
SPLOSH!
GURGLE!
HE'S GONE UNDER! BLAST IT, I'VE GOT TO GET THAT PAPER WITH THE LOCATION ON IT OR I CAN'T FILE A CLAIM!
HERE'S HIS HAT! HE OUGHTA BE HERE SOME PLACE!
(GASP!) HURRY, GOOFY! GET UP AND OVER THIS DAM BEFORE HE SPOTS US!
GASP! WHEEZE!
TINY! WHERE ARE YOU?
MAYBE I BETTER LET SOME WATER OUT SO I CAN FIND HIM!..
OH-OH!
WH-WHAT THE DING DONG BLINKIN' BLAZES? HEY!
HE'S SPOTTED US! JUMP!

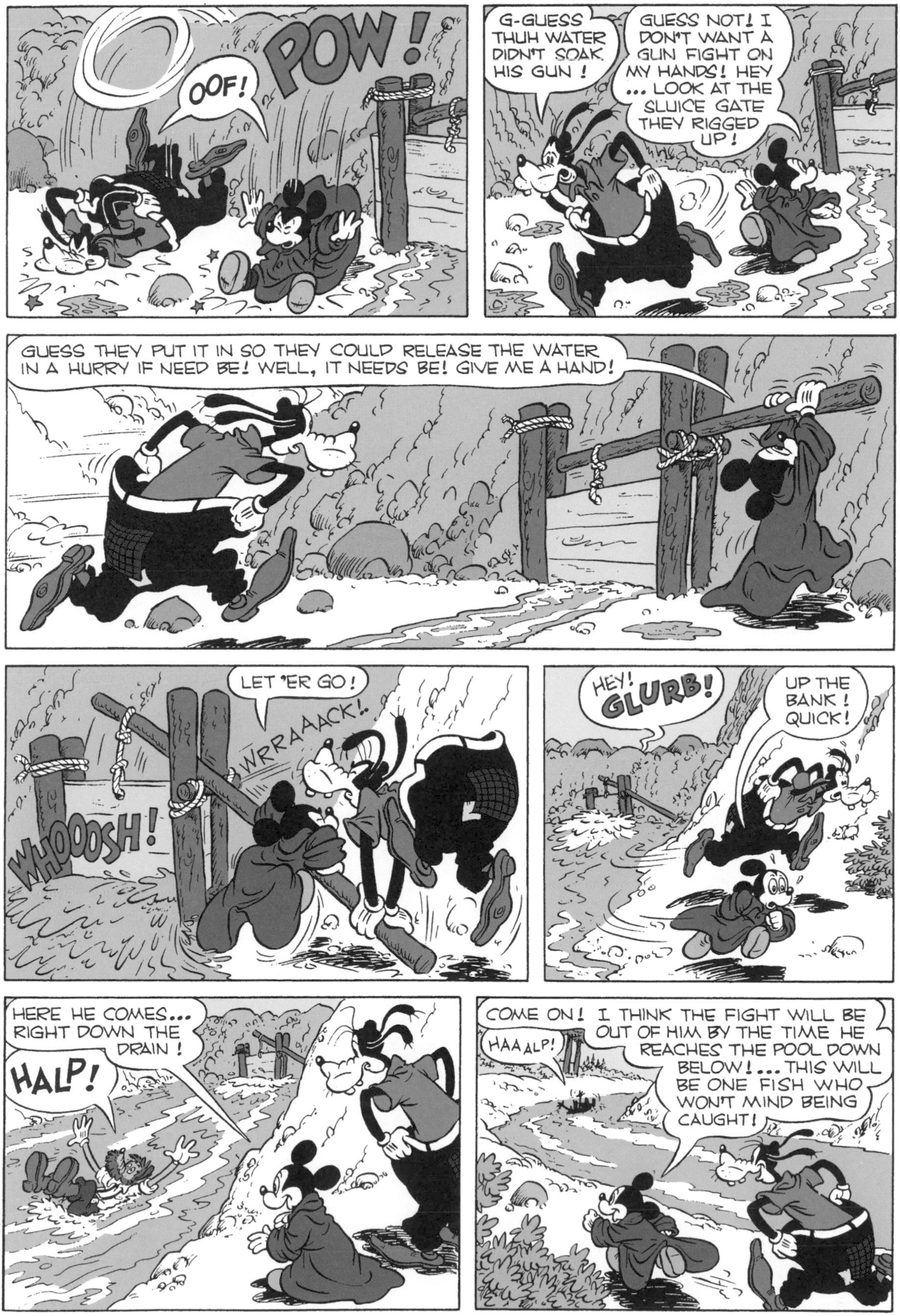

OOF!
POW!
G-GUESS THUH WATER DIDN'T SOAK HIS GUN!
GUESS NOT! I DON'T WANT A GUN FIGHT ON MY HANDS! HEY ... LOOK AT THE SLUICE GATE THEY RIGGED UP!
GUESS THEY PUT IT IN SO THEY COULD RELEASE THE WATER IN A HURRY IF NEED BE! WELL, IT NEEDS BE! GIVE ME A HAND!
LET 'ER GO!
WRRAAACK!
WHOOOSH!
HEY! GLURB!
UP THE BANK! QUICK!
HERE HE COMES... RIGHT DOWN THE DRAIN!
HALP!
COME ON! I THINK THE FIGHT WILL BE OUT OF HIM BY THE TIME HE REACHES THE POOL DOWN BELOW! ... THIS WILL BE ONE FISH WHO WON'T MIND BEING CAUGHT!
HAAALP!

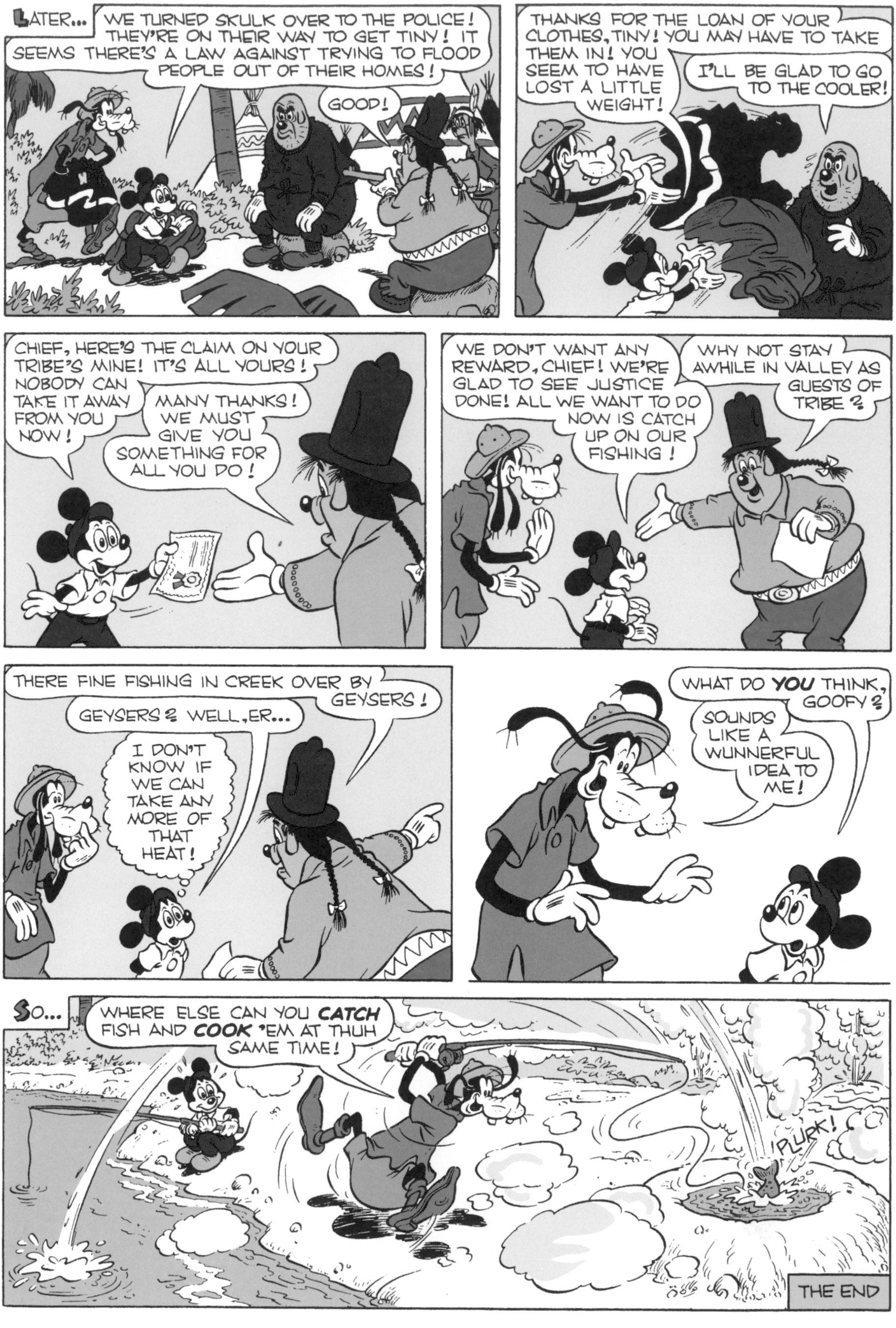
LATER...
WE TURNED SKULK OVER TO THE POLICE! THEY'RE ON THEIR WAY TO GET TINY! IT SEEMS THERE'S A LAW AGAINST TRYING TO FLOOD PEOPLE OUT OF THEIR HOMES!
GOOD!
THANKS FOR THE LOAN OF YOUR CLOTHES, TINY! YOU MAY HAVE TO TAKE THEM IN! YOU SEEM TO HAVE LOST A LITTLE WEIGHT!
I'LL BE GLAD TO GO TO THE COOLER!
CHIEF, HERE'S THE CLAIM ON YOUR TRIBE'S MINE! IT'S ALL YOURS! NOBODY CAN TAKE IT AWAY FROM YOU NOW!
MANY THANKS! WE MUST GIVE YOU SOMETHING FOR ALL YOU DO!
WE DON'T WANT ANY REWARD, CHIEF! WE'RE GLAD TO SEE JUSTICE DONE! ALL WE WANT TO DO NOW IS CATCH UP ON OUR FISHING!
WHY NOT STAY AWHILE IN VALLEY AS GUESTS OF TRIBE?
THERE FINE FISHING IN CREEK OVER BY GEYSERS!
GEYSERS? WELL, ER...
I DON'T KNOW IF WE CAN TAKE ANY MORE OF THAT HEAT!
WHAT DO YOU THINK, GOOFY?
SOUNDS LIKE A WUNNERFUL IDEA TO ME!
SO...
WHERE ELSE CAN YOU CATCH FISH AND COOK 'EM AT THUH SAME TIME!
PLURK!
THE END

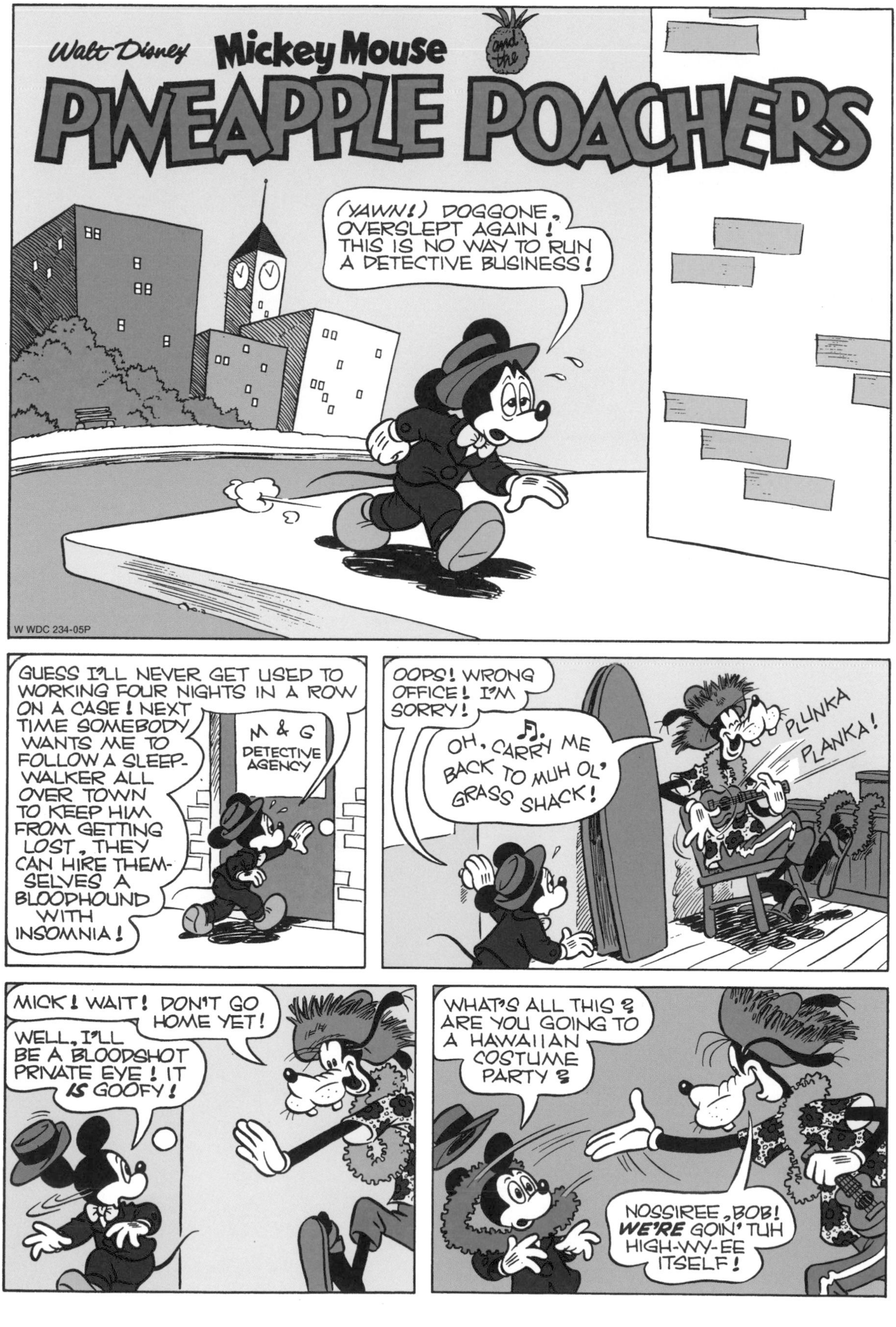
Walt Disney
Mickey Mouse and the
PINEAPPLE POACHERS
(YAWN!) DOGGONE, OVERSLEPT AGAIN! THIS IS NO WAY TO RUN A DETECTIVE BUSINESS!
W WDC 234-05P
GUESS I'LL NEVER GET USED TO WORKING FOUR NIGHTS IN A ROW ON A CASE! NEXT TIME SOMEBODY WANTS ME TO FOLLOW A SLEEP-WALKER ALL OVER TOWN TO KEEP HIM FROM GETTING LOST, THEY CAN HIRE THEM-SELVES A BLOODHOUND WITH INSOMNIA!
M & G DETECTIVE AGENCY
OOPS! WRONG OFFICE! I'M SORRY!
OH, CARRY ME BACK TO MUH OL' GRASS SHACK!
PLUNKA PLANKA!
MICK! WAIT! DON'T GO HOME YET!
WELL, I'LL BE A BLOODSHOT PRIVATE EYE! IT IS GOOFY!
WHAT'S ALL THIS? ARE YOU GOING TO A HAWAIIAN COSTUME PARTY?
NOSSIREE, BOB! WE'RE GOIN' TUH HIGH-WY-EE ITSELF!

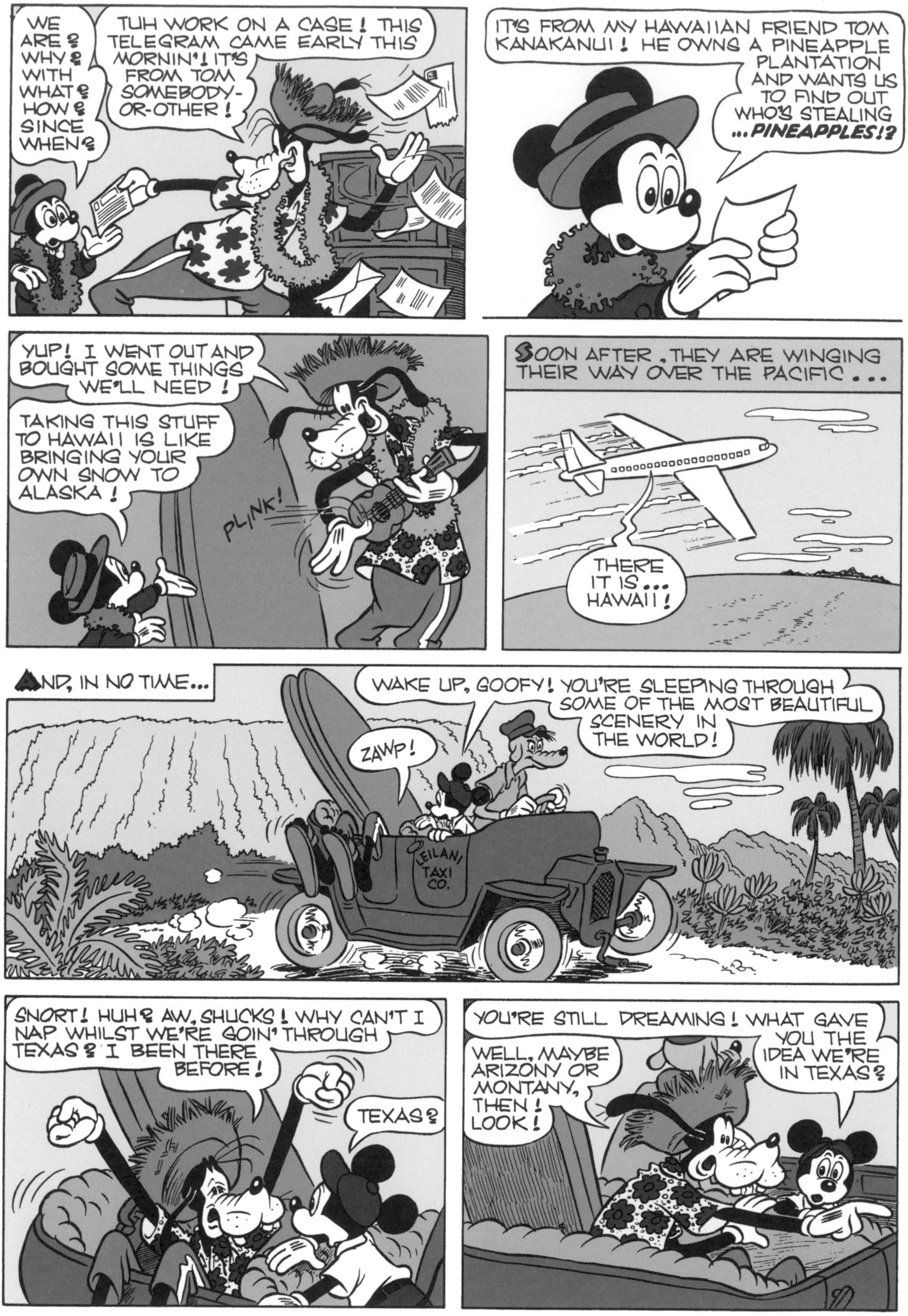
WE ARE? WHY? WITH WHAT? HOW? SINCE WHEN?
TUH WORK ON A CASE! THIS TELEGRAM CAME EARLY THIS MORNIN'! IT'S FROM TOM SOMEBODY-OR-OTHER!
IT'S FROM MY HAWAIIAN FRIEND TOM KANAKANUI! HE OWNS A PINEAPPLE PLANTATION AND WANTS US TO FIND OUT WHO'S STEALING ...PINEAPPLES!?
YUP! I WENT OUT AND BOUGHT SOME THINGS WE'LL NEED!
TAKING THIS STUFF TO HAWAII IS LIKE BRINGING YOUR OWN SNOW TO ALASKA!
PLINK!
SOON AFTER, THEY ARE WINGING THEIR WAY OVER THE PACIFIC...
THERE IT IS... HAWAII!
AND, IN NO TIME...
WAKE UP, GOOFY! YOU'RE SLEEPING THROUGH SOME OF THE MOST BEAUTIFUL SCENERY IN THE WORLD!
ZAWP!
LEILANI TAXI CO.
SNORT! HUH? AW, SHUCKS! WHY CAN'T I NAP WHILST WE'RE GOIN' THROUGH TEXAS? I BEEN THERE BEFORE!
TEXAS?
YOU'RE STILL DREAMING! WHAT GAVE YOU THE IDEA WE'RE IN TEXAS?
WELL, MAYBE ARIZONY OR MONTANY, THEN! LOOK!

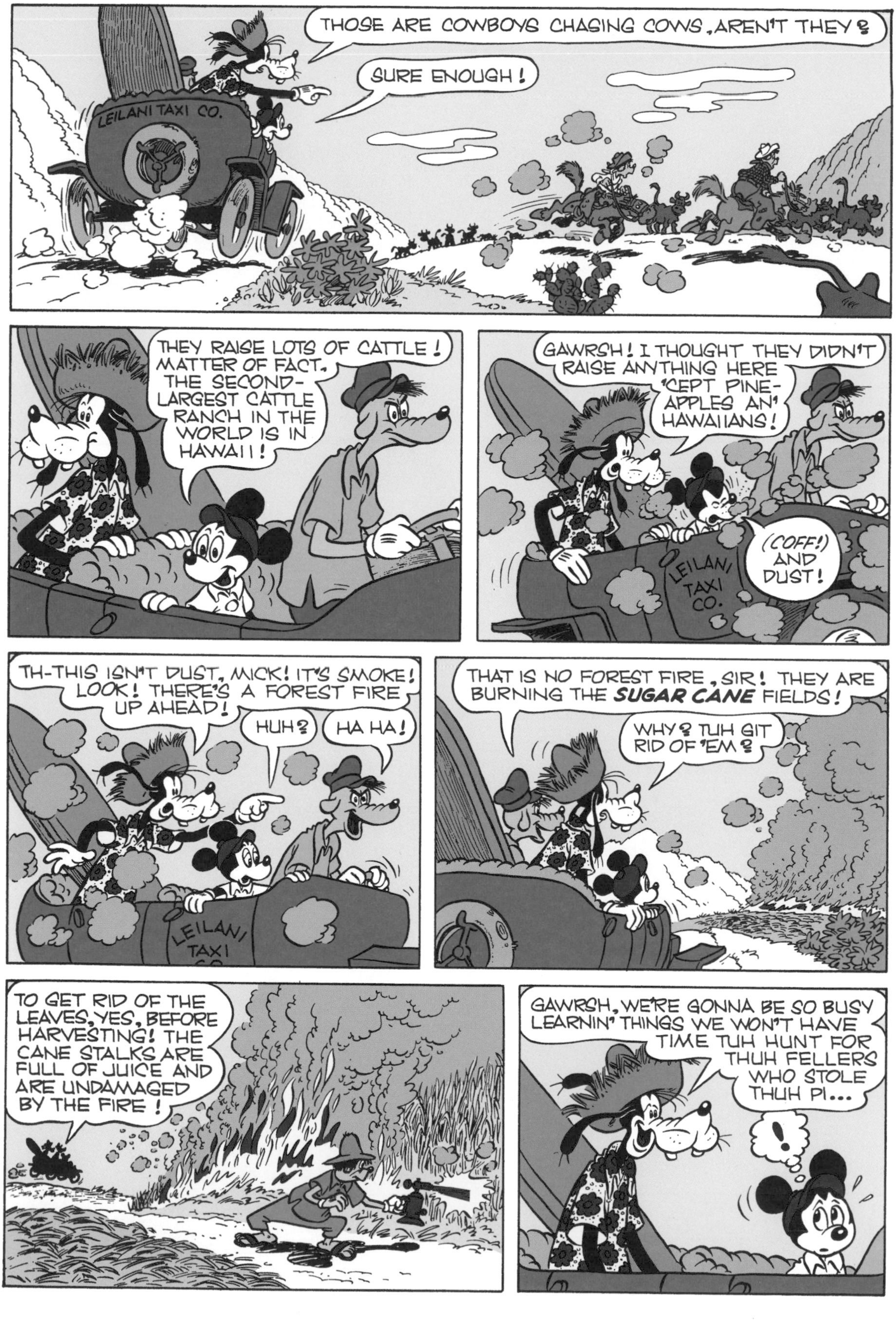
THOSE ARE COWBOYS CHASING COWS, AREN'T THEY?
SURE ENOUGH!
LEILANI TAXI CO.
THEY RAISE LOTS OF CATTLE! MATTER OF FACT, THE SECOND-LARGEST CATTLE RANCH IN THE WORLD IS IN HAWAII!
GAWRSH! I THOUGHT THEY DIDN'T RAISE ANYTHING HERE 'CEPT PINE-APPLES AN' HAWAIIANS!
(COFF!) AND DUST!
LEILANI TAXI CO.
TH-THIS ISN'T DUST, MICK! IT'S SMOKE! LOOK! THERE'S A FOREST FIRE UP AHEAD!
HUH?
HA HA!
THAT IS NO FOREST FIRE, SIR! THEY ARE BURNING THE SUGAR CANE FIELDS!
WHY? TUH GIT RID OF 'EM?
TO GET RID OF THE LEAVES, YES, BEFORE HARVESTING! THE CANE STALKS ARE FULL OF JUICE AND ARE UNDAMAGED BY THE FIRE!
GAWRSH, WE'RE GONNA BE SO BUSY LEARNIN' THINGS WE WON'T HAVE TIME TUH HUNT FOR THUH FELLERS WHO STOLE THUH PI...
!

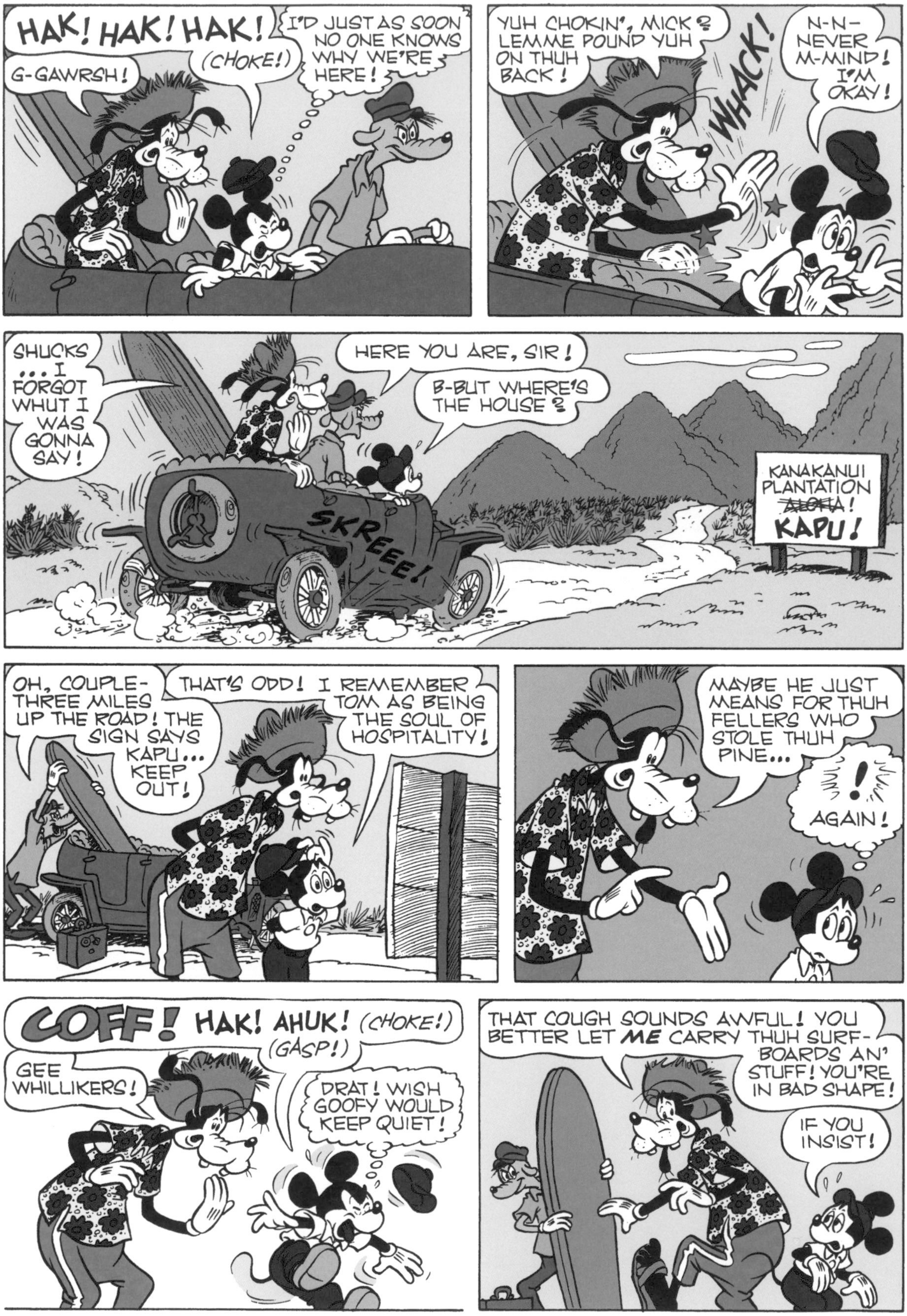
HAK! HAK! HAK!
G-GAWRSH!
(CHOKE!)
I'D JUST AS SOON NO ONE KNOWS WHY WE'RE HERE!
YUH CHOKIN', MICK? LEMME POUND YUH ON THUH BACK!
WHACK!
N-N-NEVER M-MIND! I'M OKAY!
SHUCKS ... I FORGOT WHUT I WAS GONNA SAY!
HERE YOU ARE, SIR!
B-BUT WHERE'S THE HOUSE?
KANAKANUI PLANTATION ALOHA! KAPU!
SKREEEE!
OH, COUPLE-THREE MILES UP THE ROAD! THE SIGN SAYS KAPU... KEEP OUT!
THAT'S ODD! I REMEMBER TOM AS BEING THE SOUL OF HOSPITALITY!
MAYBE HE JUST MEANS FOR THUH FELLERS WHO STOLE THUH PINE...
!
AGAIN!
COFF! HAK! AHUK! (CHOKE!)
(GASP!)
GEE WHILLIKERS!
DRAT! WISH GOOFY WOULD KEEP QUIET!
THAT COUGH SOUNDS AWFUL! YOU BETTER LET ME CARRY THUH SURF-BOARDS AN' STUFF! YOU'RE IN BAD SHAPE!
IF YOU INSIST!

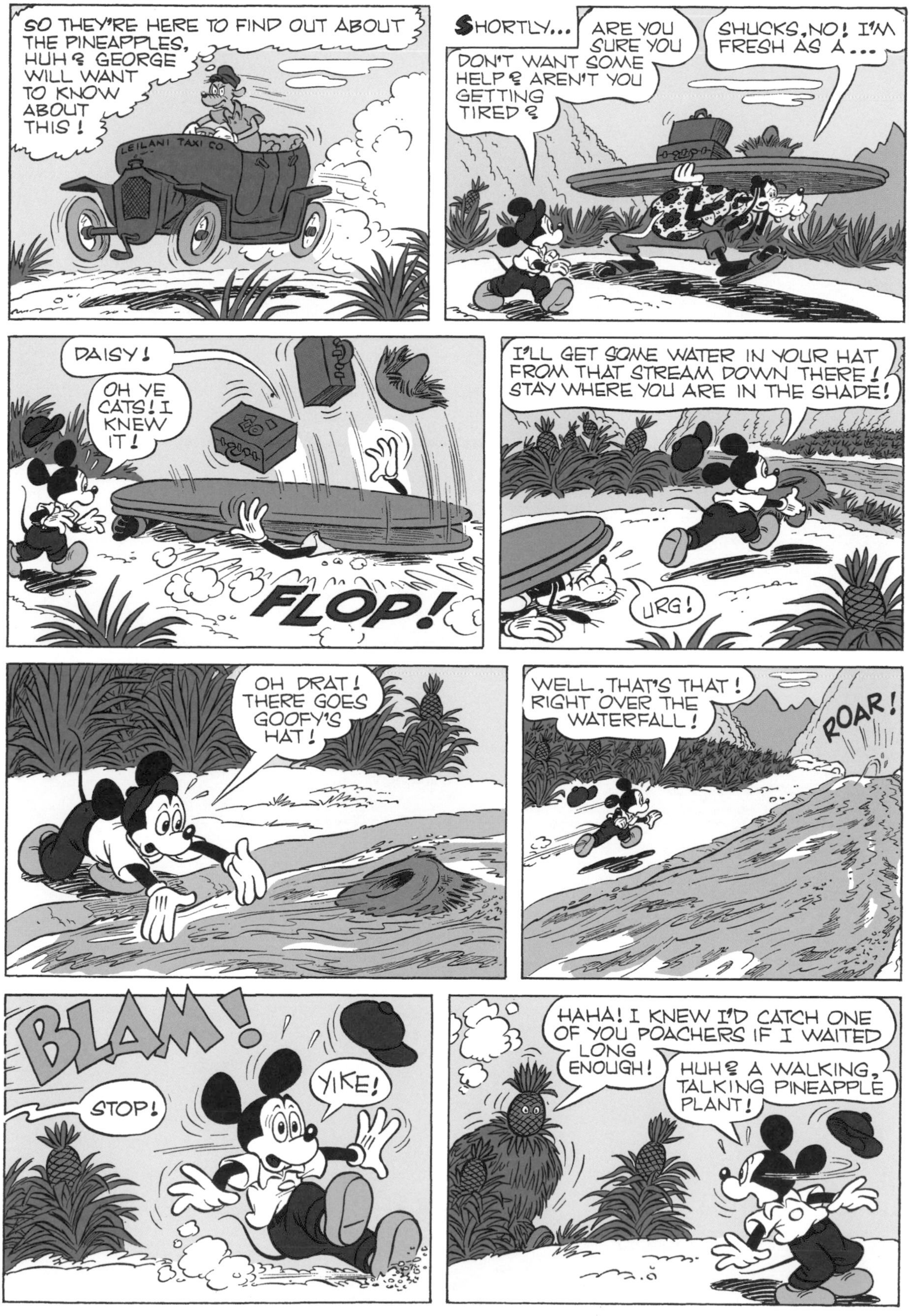
SO THEY'RE HERE TO FIND OUT ABOUT THE PINEAPPLES, HUH? GEORGE WILL WANT TO KNOW ABOUT THIS!
LEILANI TAXI CO.
SHORTLY...
ARE YOU SURE YOU DON'T WANT SOME HELP? AREN'T YOU GETTING TIRED?
SHUCKS, NO! I'M FRESH AS A...
DAISY!
OH YE CATS! I KNEW IT!
FLOP!
I'LL GET SOME WATER IN YOUR HAT FROM THAT STREAM DOWN THERE! STAY WHERE YOU ARE IN THE SHADE!
URG!
OH DRAT! THERE GOES GOOFY'S HAT!
WELL, THAT'S THAT! RIGHT OVER THE WATERFALL!
ROAR!
BLAM!
STOP!
YIKE!
HAHA! I KNEW I'D CATCH ONE OF YOU POACHERS IF I WAITED LONG ENOUGH!
HUH? A WALKING, TALKING PINEAPPLE PLANT!

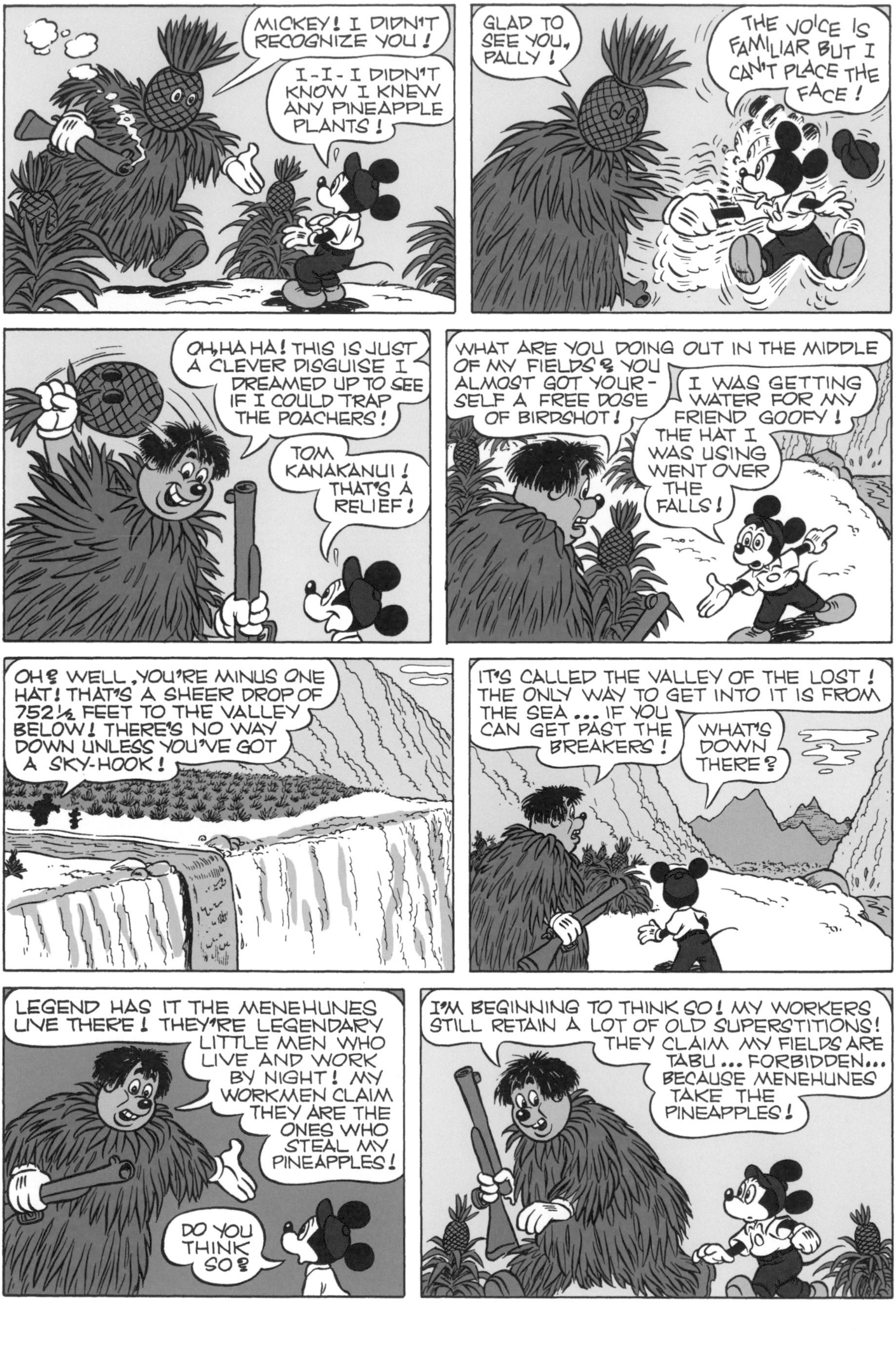
MICKEY! I DIDN'T RECOGNIZE YOU!
I-I-I DIDN'T KNOW I KNEW ANY PINEAPPLE PLANTS!
GLAD TO SEE YOU, PALLY!
THE VOICE IS FAMILIAR BUT I CAN'T PLACE THE FACE!
OH, HA HA! THIS IS JUST A CLEVER DISGUISE I DREAMED UP TO SEE IF I COULD TRAP THE POACHERS!
TOM KANAKANUI! THAT'S A RELIEF!
WHAT ARE YOU DOING OUT IN THE MIDDLE OF MY FIELDS? YOU ALMOST GOT YOURSELF A FREE DOSE OF BIRDSHOT!
I WAS GETTING WATER FOR MY FRIEND GOOFY! THE HAT I WAS USING WENT OVER THE FALLS!
OH? WELL, YOU'RE MINUS ONE HAT! THAT'S A SHEER DROP OF 752½ FEET TO THE VALLEY BELOW! THERE'S NO WAY DOWN UNLESS YOU'VE GOT A SKY-HOOK!
IT'S CALLED THE VALLEY OF THE LOST! THE ONLY WAY TO GET INTO IT IS FROM THE SEA... IF YOU CAN GET PAST THE BREAKERS!
WHAT'S DOWN THERE?
LEGEND HAS IT THE MENEHUNES LIVE THERE! THEY'RE LEGENDARY LITTLE MEN WHO LIVE AND WORK BY NIGHT! MY WORKMEN CLAIM THEY ARE THE ONES WHO STEAL MY PINEAPPLES!
DO YOU THINK SO?
I'M BEGINNING TO THINK SO! MY WORKERS STILL RETAIN A LOT OF OLD SUPERSTITIONS! THEY CLAIM MY FIELDS ARE TABU... FORBIDDEN... BECAUSE MENEHUNES TAKE THE PINEAPPLES!

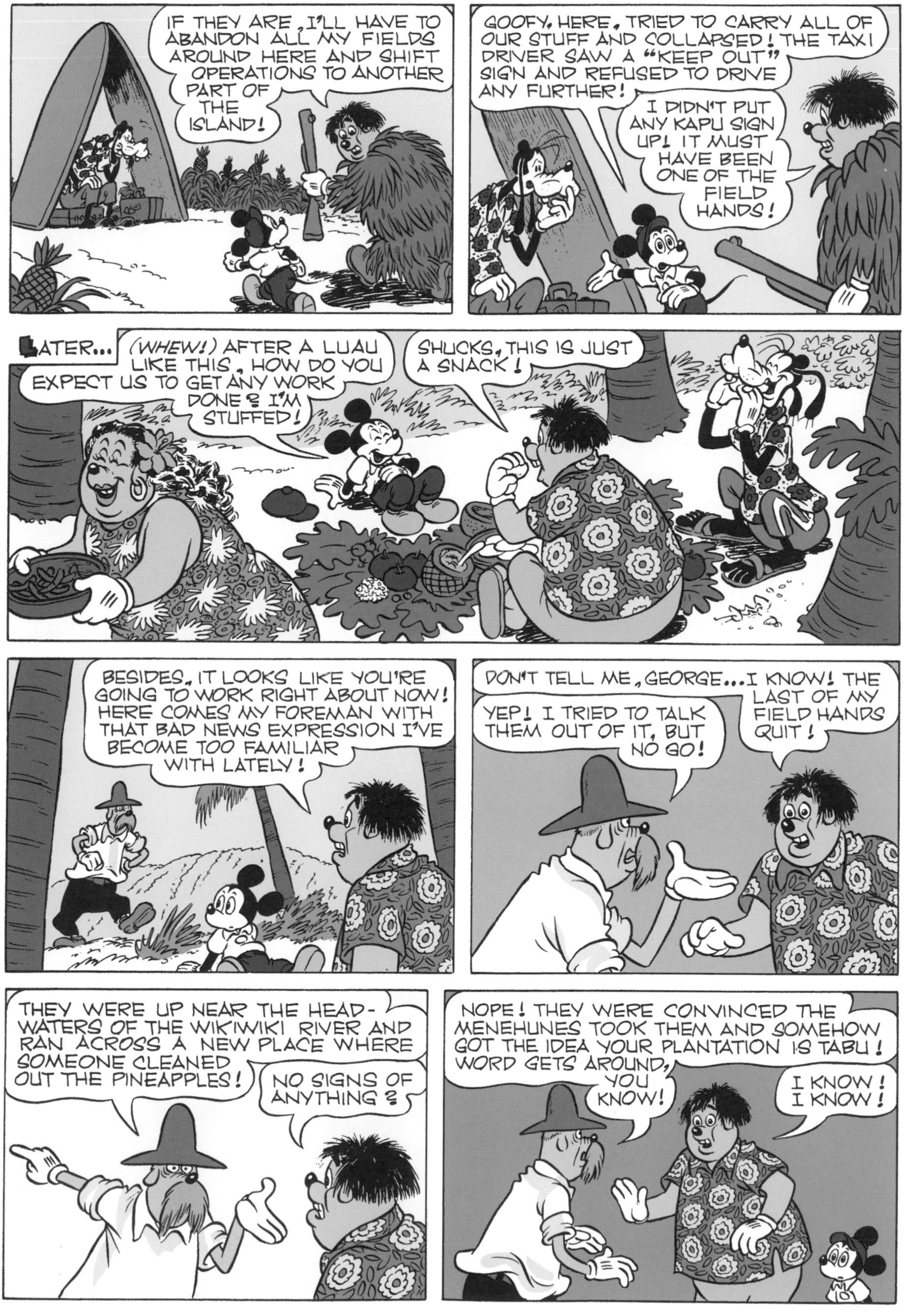
IF THEY ARE, I'LL HAVE TO ABANDON ALL MY FIELDS AROUND HERE AND SHIFT OPERATIONS TO ANOTHER PART OF THE ISLAND!
GOOFY, HERE, TRIED TO CARRY ALL OF OUR STUFF AND COLLAPSED! THE TAXI DRIVER SAW A "KEEP OUT" SIGN AND REFUSED TO DRIVE ANY FURTHER!
I DIDN'T PUT ANY KAPU SIGN UP! IT MUST HAVE BEEN ONE OF THE FIELD HANDS!
LATER...
(WHEW!) AFTER A LUAU LIKE THIS, HOW DO YOU EXPECT US TO GET ANY WORK DONE? I'M STUFFED!
SHUCKS, THIS IS JUST A SNACK!
BESIDES, IT LOOKS LIKE YOU'RE GOING TO WORK RIGHT ABOUT NOW! HERE COMES MY FOREMAN WITH THAT BAD NEWS EXPRESSION I'VE BECOME TOO FAMILIAR WITH LATELY!
DON'T TELL ME, GEORGE... I KNOW! THE LAST OF MY FIELD HANDS QUIT!
YEP! I TRIED TO TALK THEM OUT OF IT, BUT NO GO!
THEY WERE UP NEAR THE HEAD-WATERS OF THE WIKIWIKI RIVER AND RAN ACROSS A NEW PLACE WHERE SOMEONE CLEANED OUT THE PINEAPPLES!
NO SIGNS OF ANYTHING?
NOPE! THEY WERE CONVINCED THE MENEHUNES TOOK THEM AND SOMEHOW GOT THE IDEA YOUR PLANTATION IS TABU! WORD GETS AROUND, YOU KNOW!
I KNOW! I KNOW!

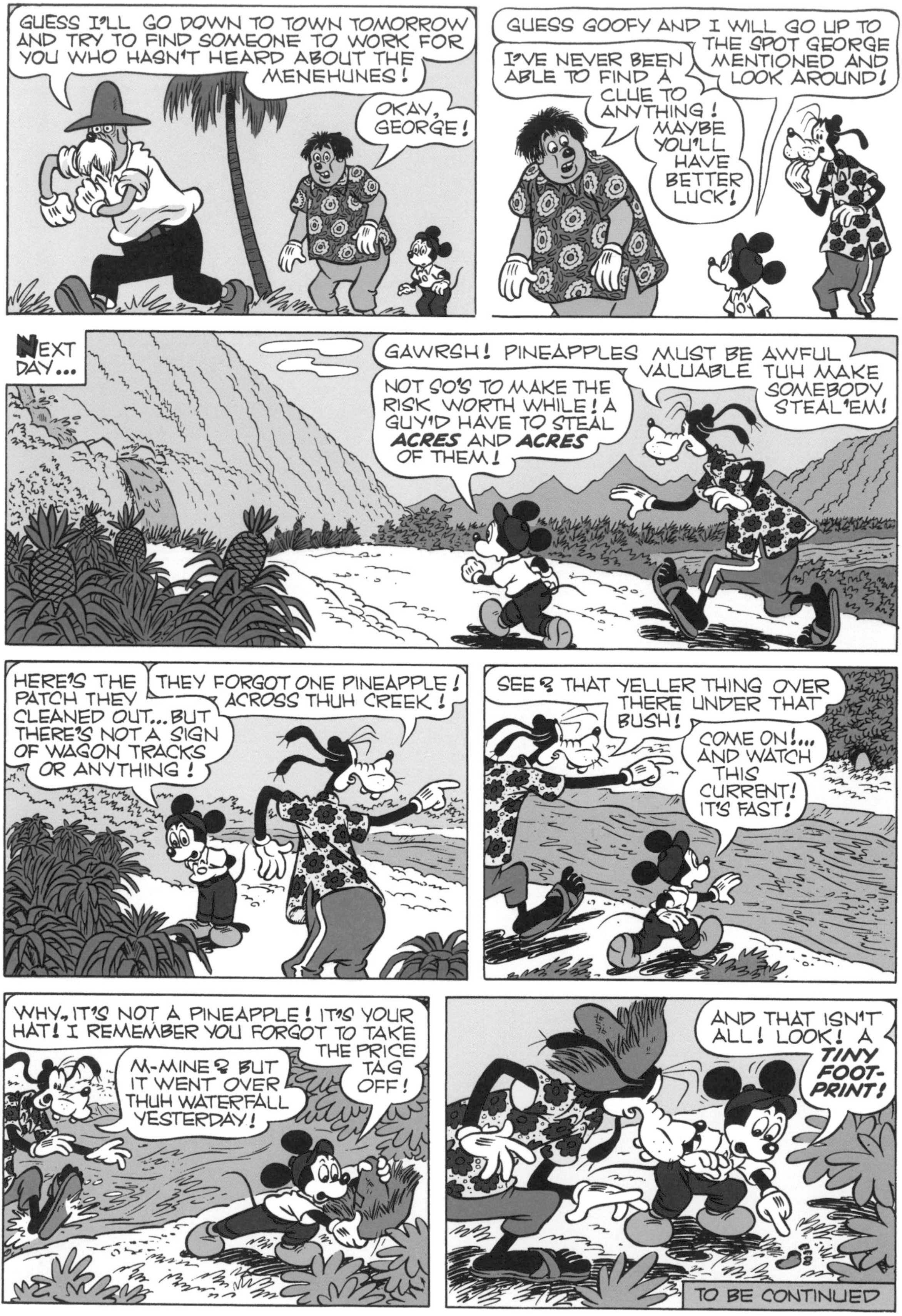

GUESS I'LL GO DOWN TO TOWN TOMORROW AND TRY TO FIND SOMEONE TO WORK FOR YOU WHO HASN'T HEARD ABOUT THE MENEHUNES!
OKAY, GEORGE!
GUESS GOOFY AND I WILL GO UP TO THE SPOT GEORGE MENTIONED AND LOOK AROUND!
I'VE NEVER BEEN ABLE TO FIND A CLUE TO ANYTHING! MAYBE YOU'LL HAVE BETTER LUCK!
NEXT DAY...
GAWRSH! PINEAPPLES MUST BE AWFUL VALUABLE TUH MAKE SOMEBODY STEAL 'EM!
NOT SO'S TO MAKE THE RISK WORTH WHILE! A GUY'D HAVE TO STEAL ACRES AND ACRES OF THEM!
HERE'S THE PATCH THEY CLEANED OUT... BUT THERE'S NOT A SIGN OF WAGON TRACKS OR ANYTHING!
THEY FORGOT ONE PINEAPPLE! ACROSS THUH CREEK!
SEE? THAT YELLER THING OVER THERE UNDER THAT BUSH!
COME ON!... AND WATCH THIS CURRENT! IT'S FAST!
WHY, IT'S NOT A PINEAPPLE! IT'S YOUR HAT! I REMEMBER YOU FORGOT TO TAKE THE PRICE TAG OFF!
M-MINE? BUT IT WENT OVER THUH WATERFALL YESTERDAY!
AND THAT ISN'T ALL! LOOK! A TINY FOOT-PRINT!
TO BE CONTINUED

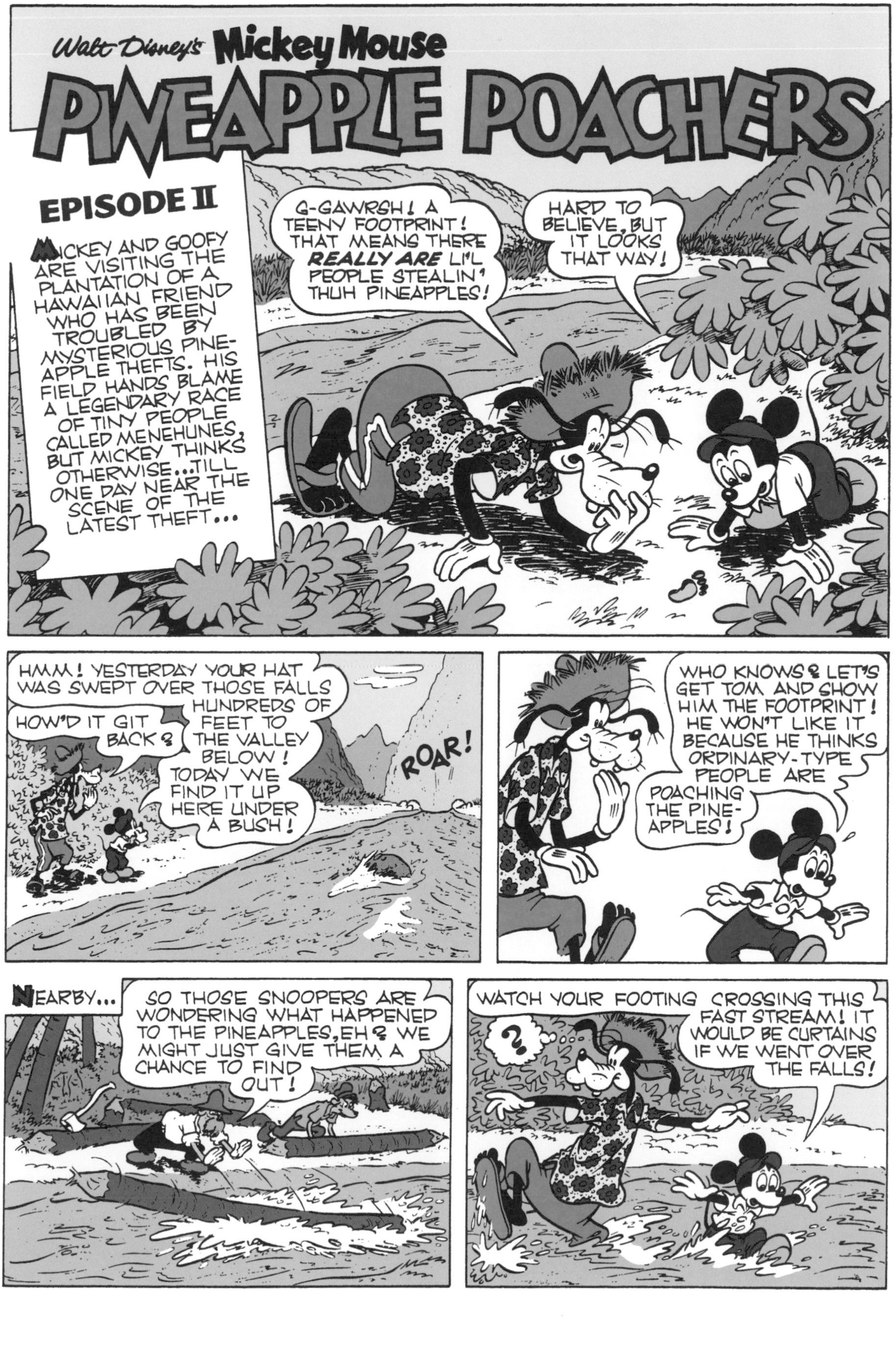
Walt Disney's Mickey Mouse
PINEAPPLE POACHERS
EPISODE II
MICKEY AND GOOFY ARE VISITING THE PLANTATION OF A HAWAIIAN FRIEND WHO HAS BEEN TROUBLED BY MYSTERIOUS PINE-APPLE THEFTS. HIS FIELD HANDS BLAME A LEGENDARY RACE OF TINY PEOPLE CALLED MENEHUNES, BUT MICKEY THINKS OTHERWISE...TILL ONE DAY NEAR THE SCENE OF THE LATEST THEFT...
G-GAWRSH! A TEENY FOOTPRINT! THAT MEANS THERE REALLY ARE LI'L PEOPLE STEALIN' THUH PINEAPPLES!
HARD TO BELIEVE, BUT IT LOOKS THAT WAY!
HMM! YESTERDAY YOUR HAT WAS SWEPT OVER THOSE FALLS HUNDREDS OF FEET TO THE VALLEY BELOW! TODAY WE FIND IT UP HERE UNDER A BUSH!
HOW'D IT GIT BACK?
ROAR!
WHO KNOWS? LET'S GET TOM AND SHOW HIM THE FOOTPRINT! HE WON'T LIKE IT BECAUSE HE THINKS ORDINARY-TYPE PEOPLE ARE POACHING THE PINE-APPLES!
NEARBY...
SO THOSE SNOOPERS ARE WONDERING WHAT HAPPENED TO THE PINEAPPLES, EH? WE MIGHT JUST GIVE THEM A CHANCE TO FIND OUT!
WATCH YOUR FOOTING CROSSING THIS FAST STREAM! IT WOULD BE CURTAINS IF WE WENT OVER THE FALLS!
?

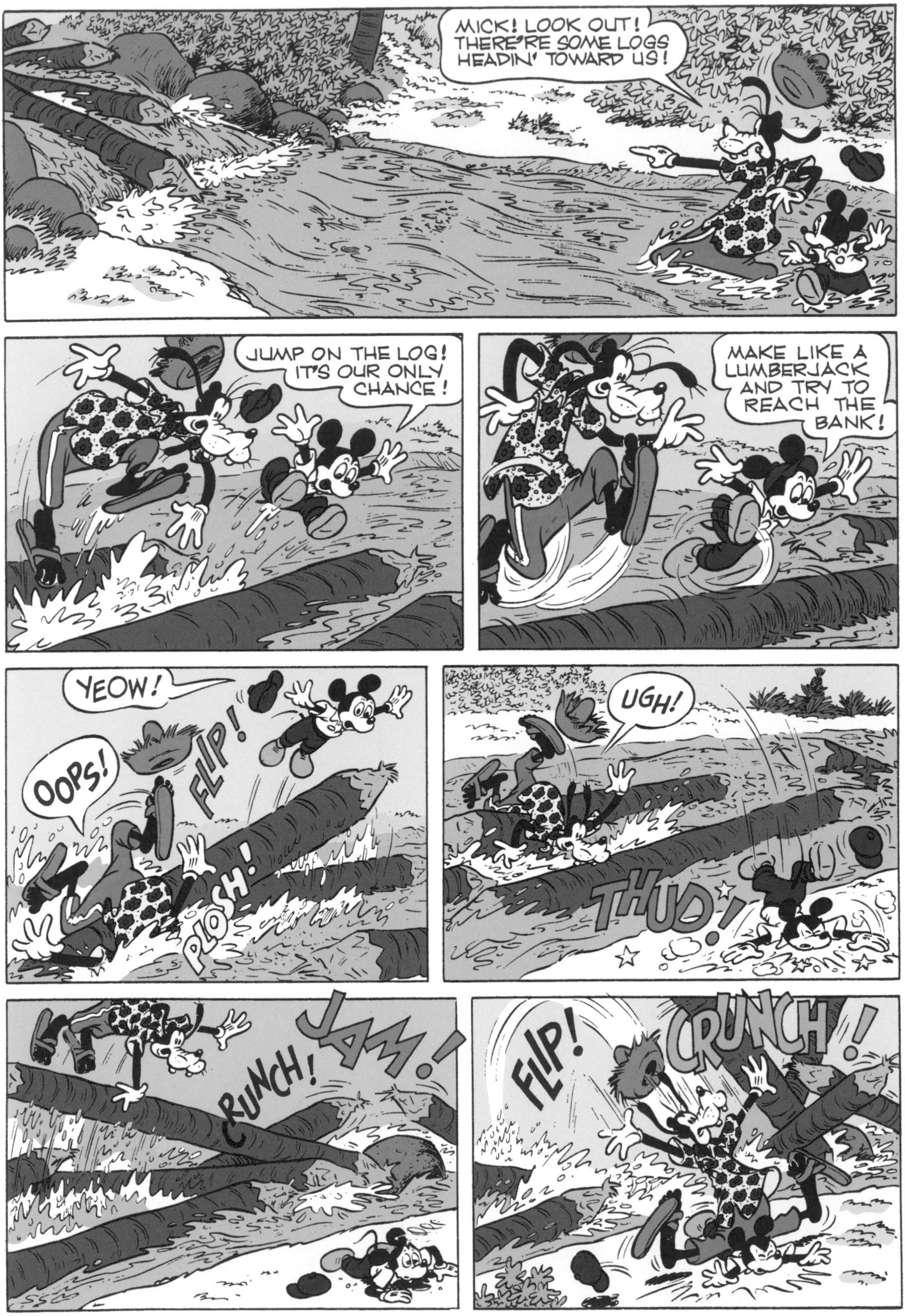
MICK! LOOK OUT! THERE'RE SOME LOGS HEADIN' TOWARD US!
JUMP ON THE LOG! IT'S OUR ONLY CHANCE!
MAKE LIKE A LUMBERJACK AND TRY TO REACH THE BANK!
YEOW!
OOPS!
FLIP!
PLOSH!
UGH!
THUD!
CRUNCH!
JAM!
FLIP!
CRUNCH!

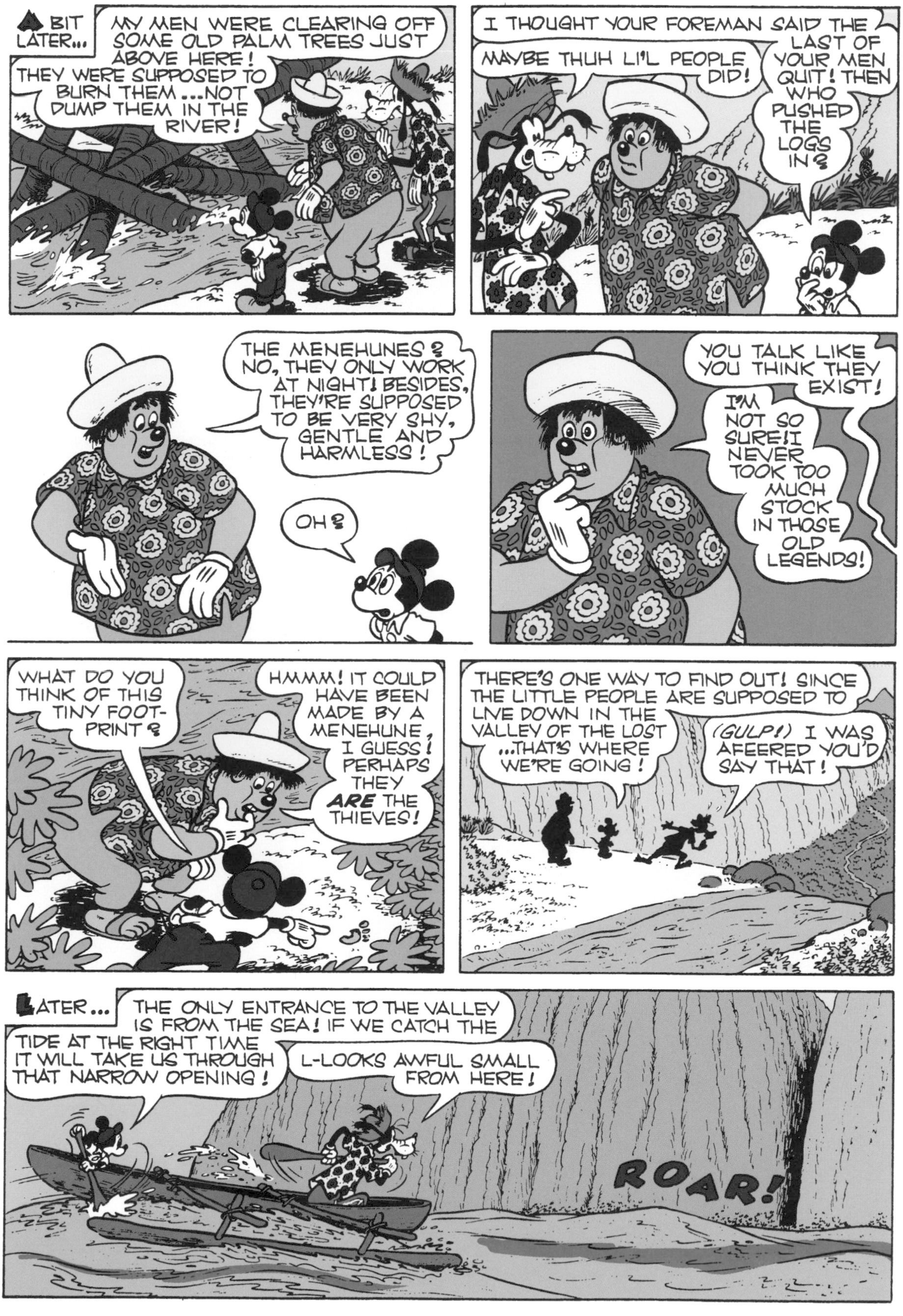
A BIT LATER...
MY MEN WERE CLEARING OFF SOME OLD PALM TREES JUST ABOVE HERE!
THEY WERE SUPPOSED TO BURN THEM ...NOT DUMP THEM IN THE RIVER!
I THOUGHT YOUR FOREMAN SAID THE LAST OF YOUR MEN QUIT! THEN WHO PUSHED THE LOGS IN?
MAYBE THUH LI'L PEOPLE DID!
THE MENEHUNES? NO, THEY ONLY WORK AT NIGHT! BESIDES, THEY'RE SUPPOSED TO BE VERY SHY, GENTLE AND HARMLESS!
OH?
YOU TALK LIKE YOU THINK THEY EXIST!
I'M NOT SO SURE! I NEVER TOOK TOO MUCH STOCK IN THOSE OLD LEGENDS!
WHAT DO YOU THINK OF THIS TINY FOOT-PRINT?
HMMM! IT COULD HAVE BEEN MADE BY A MENEHUNE, I GUESS! PERHAPS THEY ARE THE THIEVES!
THERE'S ONE WAY TO FIND OUT! SINCE THE LITTLE PEOPLE ARE SUPPOSED TO LIVE DOWN IN THE VALLEY OF THE LOST ...THAT'S WHERE WE'RE GOING!
(GULP!) I WAS AFEERED YOU'D SAY THAT!
LATER...
THE ONLY ENTRANCE TO THE VALLEY IS FROM THE SEA! IF WE CATCH THE TIDE AT THE RIGHT TIME IT WILL TAKE US THROUGH THAT NARROW OPENING!
L-LOOKS AWFUL SMALL FROM HERE!
ROAR!

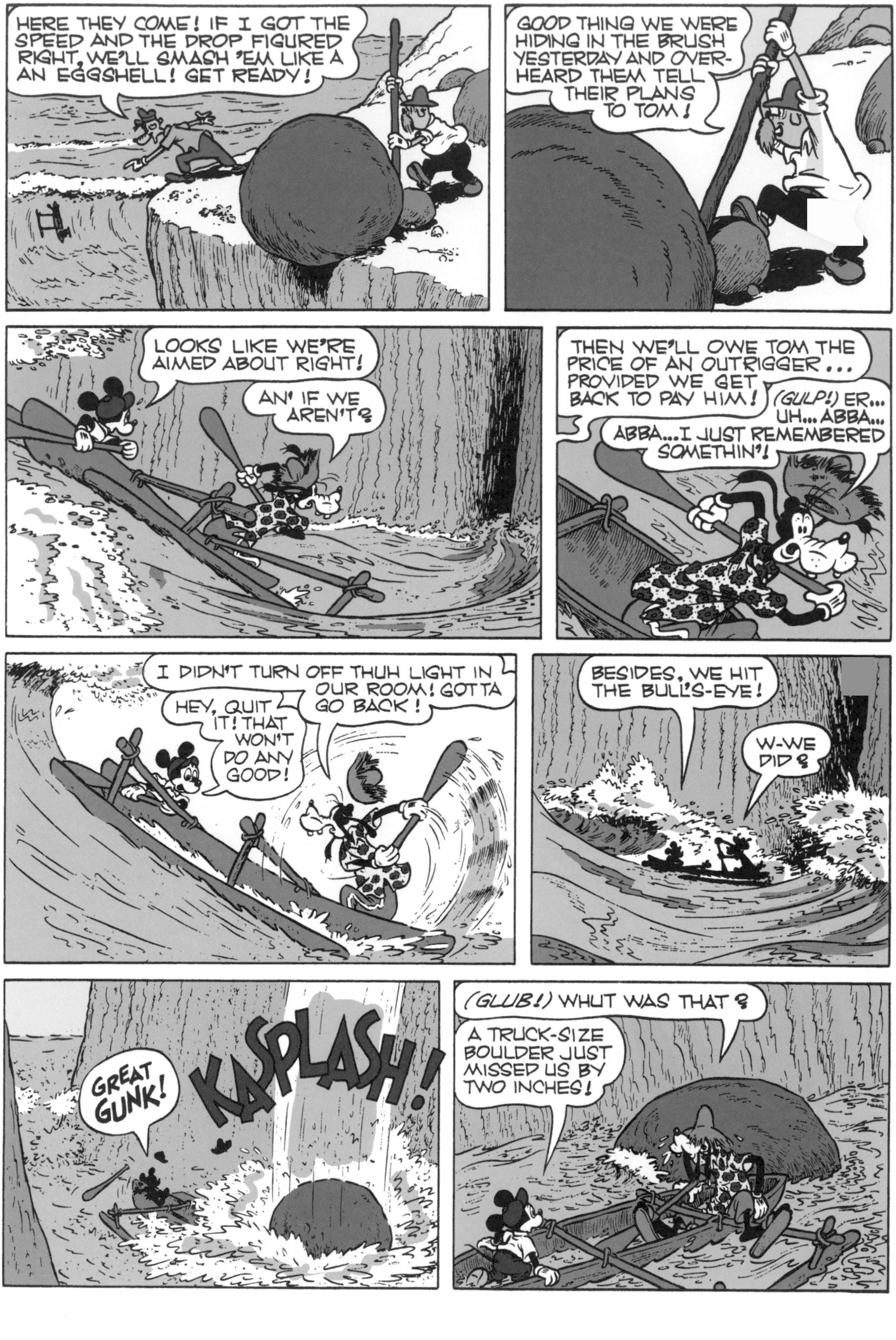
HERE THEY COME! IF I GOT THE SPEED AND THE DROP FIGURED RIGHT, WE'LL SMASH 'EM LIKE A AN EGGSHELL! GET READY!
GOOD THING WE WERE HIDING IN THE BRUSH YESTERDAY AND OVER-HEARD THEM TELL THEIR PLANS TO TOM!
LOOKS LIKE WE'RE AIMED ABOUT RIGHT!
AN' IF WE AREN'T?
THEN WE'LL OWE TOM THE PRICE OF AN OUTRIGGER... PROVIDED WE GET BACK TO PAY HIM!
(GULP!) ER... UH... ABBA... ABBA... I JUST REMEMBERED SOMETHIN'!
I DIDN'T TURN OFF THUH LIGHT IN OUR ROOM! GOTTA GO BACK!
HEY, QUIT IT! THAT WON'T DO ANY GOOD!
BESIDES, WE HIT THE BULL'S-EYE!
W-WE DID?
GREAT GUNK!
KASPLASH!
(GLUB!) WHUT WAS THAT?
A TRUCK-SIZE BOULDER JUST MISSED US BY TWO INCHES!

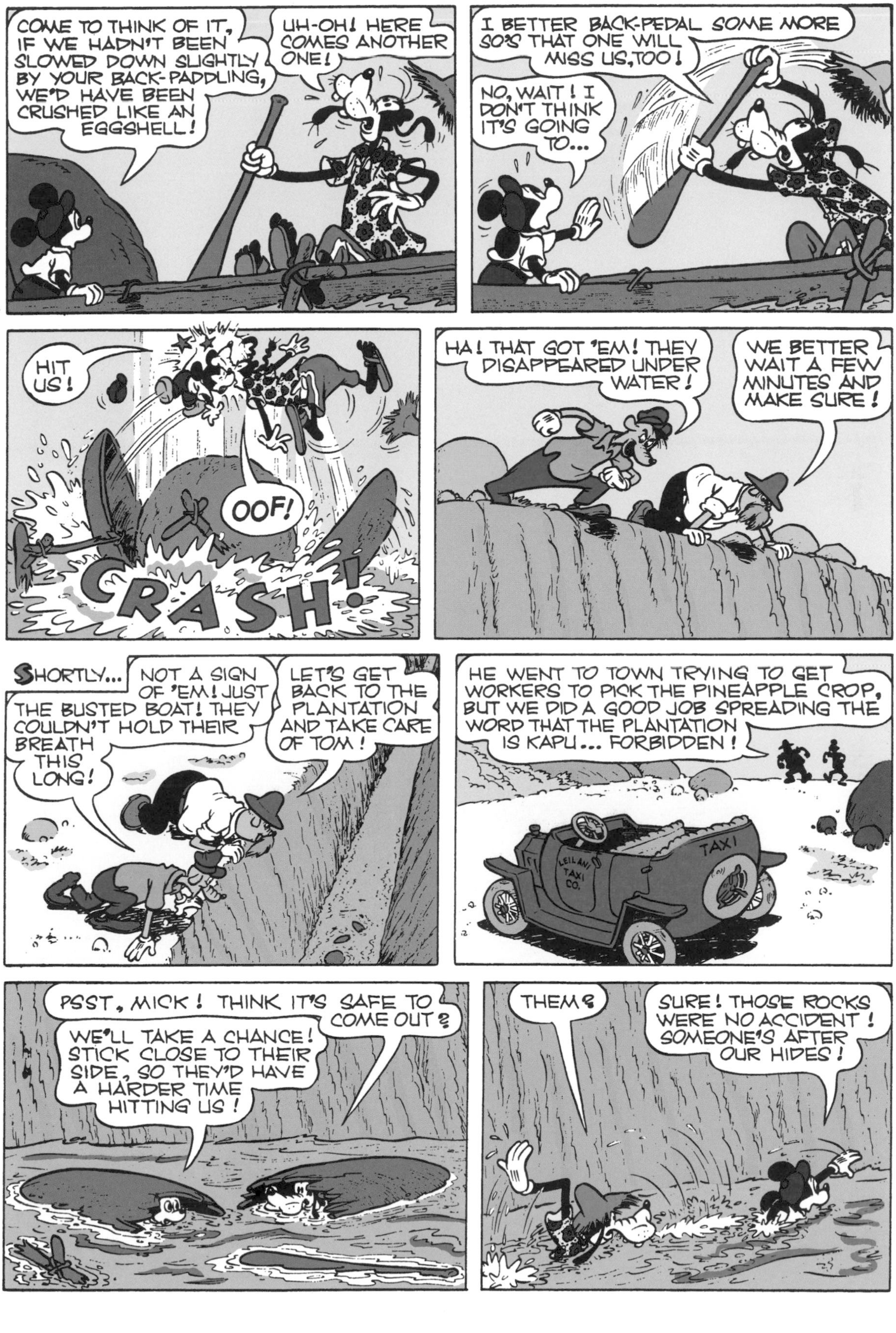
COME TO THINK OF IT, IF WE HADN'T BEEN SLOWED DOWN SLIGHTLY BY YOUR BACK-PADDLING, WE'D HAVE BEEN CRUSHED LIKE AN EGGSHELL!
UH-OH! HERE COMES ANOTHER ONE!
I BETTER BACK-PEDAL SOME MORE SO'S THAT ONE WILL MISS US, TOO!
NO, WAIT! I DON'T THINK IT'S GOING TO...
HIT US!
OOF!
CRASH!
HA! THAT GOT 'EM! THEY DISAPPEARED UNDER WATER!
WE BETTER WAIT A FEW MINUTES AND MAKE SURE!
SHORTLY...
NOT A SIGN OF 'EM! JUST THE BUSTED BOAT! THEY COULDN'T HOLD THEIR BREATH THIS LONG!
LET'S GET BACK TO THE PLANTATION AND TAKE CARE OF TOM!
HE WENT TO TOWN TRYING TO GET WORKERS TO PICK THE PINEAPPLE CROP, BUT WE DID A GOOD JOB SPREADING THE WORD THAT THE PLANTATION IS KAPU... FORBIDDEN!
TAXI
LEILANI TAXI CO.
PSST, MICK! THINK IT'S SAFE TO COME OUT?
WE'LL TAKE A CHANCE! STICK CLOSE TO THEIR SIDE, SO THEY'D HAVE A HARDER TIME HITTING US!
THEM?
SURE! THOSE ROCKS WERE NO ACCIDENT! SOMEONE'S AFTER OUR HIDES!

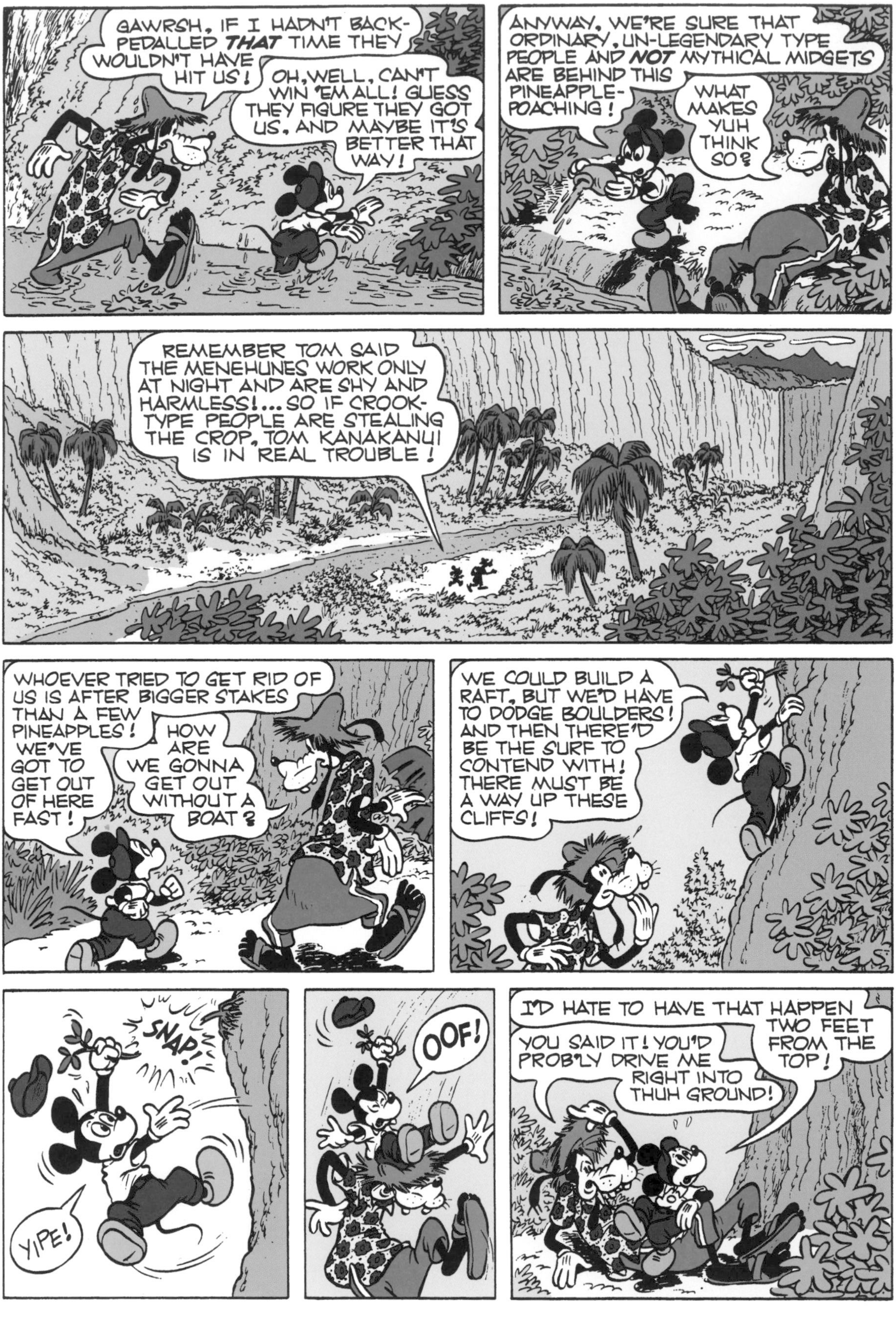
GAWRSH, IF I HADN'T BACK-PEDALLED **THAT** TIME THEY WOULDN'T HAVE HIT US!
OH, WELL, CAN'T WIN 'EM ALL! GUESS THEY FIGURE THEY GOT US, AND MAYBE IT'S BETTER THAT WAY!
ANYWAY, WE'RE SURE THAT ORDINARY, UN-LEGENDARY TYPE PEOPLE AND **NOT** MYTHICAL MIDGETS ARE BEHIND THIS PINEAPPLE-POACHING!
WHAT MAKES YUH THINK SO?
REMEMBER TOM SAID THE MENEHUNES WORK ONLY AT NIGHT AND ARE SHY AND HARMLESS!... SO IF CROOK-TYPE PEOPLE ARE STEALING THE CROP, TOM KANAKANUI IS IN REAL TROUBLE!
WHOEVER TRIED TO GET RID OF US IS AFTER BIGGER STAKES THAN A FEW PINEAPPLES! WE'VE GOT TO GET OUT OF HERE FAST!
HOW ARE WE GONNA GET OUT WITHOUT A BOAT?
WE COULD BUILD A RAFT, BUT WE'D HAVE TO DODGE BOULDERS! AND THEN THERE'D BE THE SURF TO CONTEND WITH! THERE MUST BE A WAY UP THESE CLIFFS!
SNAP!
YIPE!
OOF!
I'D HATE TO HAVE THAT HAPPEN TWO FEET FROM THE TOP!
YOU SAID IT! YOU'D PROB'LY DRIVE ME RIGHT INTO THUH GROUND!

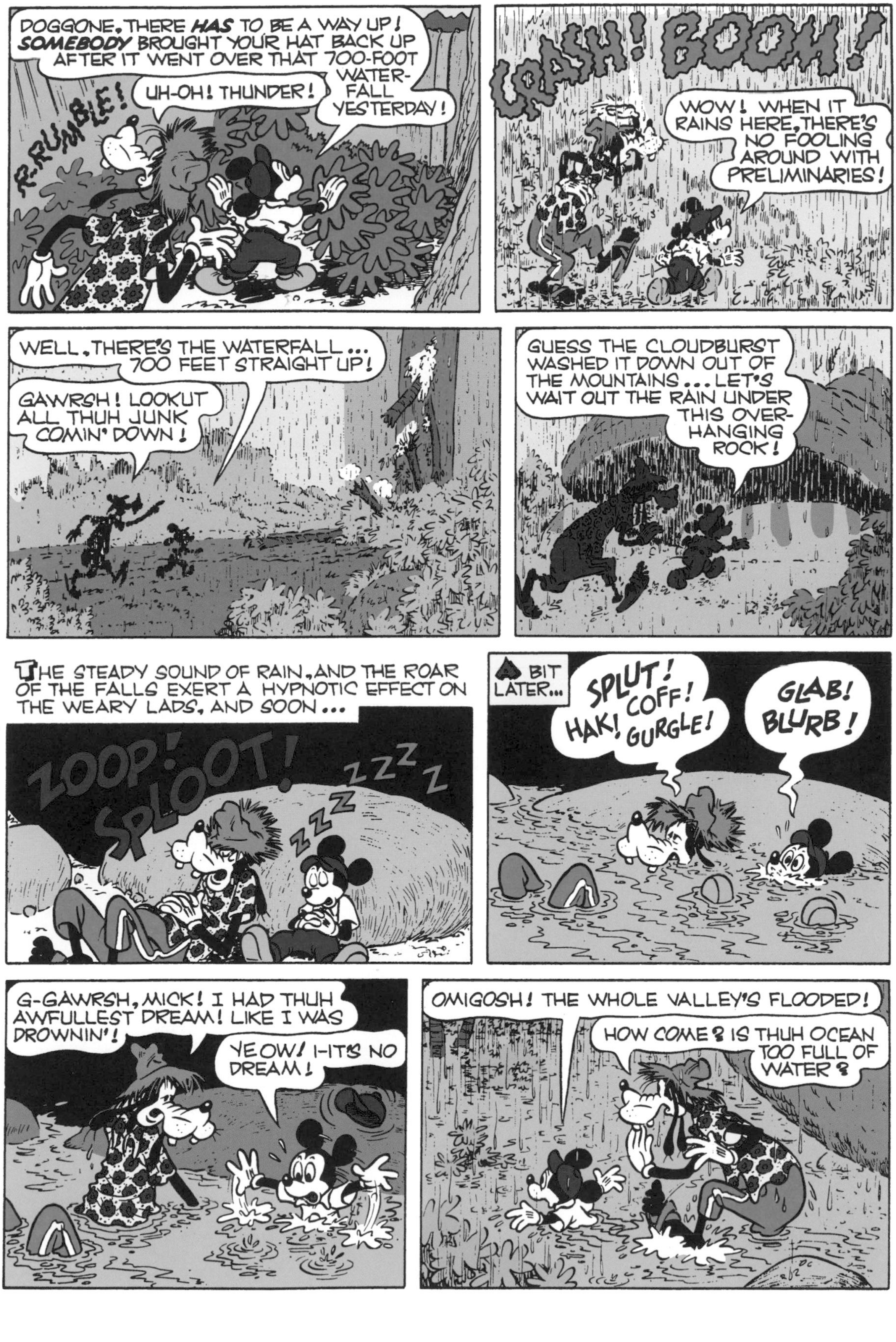
DOGGONE, THERE HAS TO BE A WAY UP! SOMEBODY BROUGHT YOUR HAT BACK UP AFTER IT WENT OVER THAT 700-FOOT WATER-FALL YESTERDAY!
UH-OH! THUNDER!
R-RUMBLE!
CRASH! BOOM!
WOW! WHEN IT RAINS HERE, THERE'S NO FOOLING AROUND WITH PRELIMINARIES!
WELL, THERE'S THE WATERFALL... 700 FEET STRAIGHT UP!
GAWRSH! LOOKUT ALL THUH JUNK COMIN' DOWN!
GUESS THE CLOUDBURST WASHED IT DOWN OUT OF THE MOUNTAINS... LET'S WAIT OUT THE RAIN UNDER THIS OVER-HANGING ROCK!
THE STEADY SOUND OF RAIN, AND THE ROAR OF THE FALLS EXERT A HYPNOTIC EFFECT ON THE WEARY LADS, AND SOON...
ZOOP! SPLOOT!
ZZZZ
ZZZ
A BIT LATER...
SPLUT! COFF! HAK! GURGLE!
GLAB! BLURB!
G-GAWRSH, MICK! I HAD THUH AWFULLEST DREAM! LIKE I WAS DROWNIN'!
YEOW! I-IT'S NO DREAM!
OMIGOSH! THE WHOLE VALLEY'S FLOODED!
HOW COME? IS THUH OCEAN TOO FULL OF WATER?

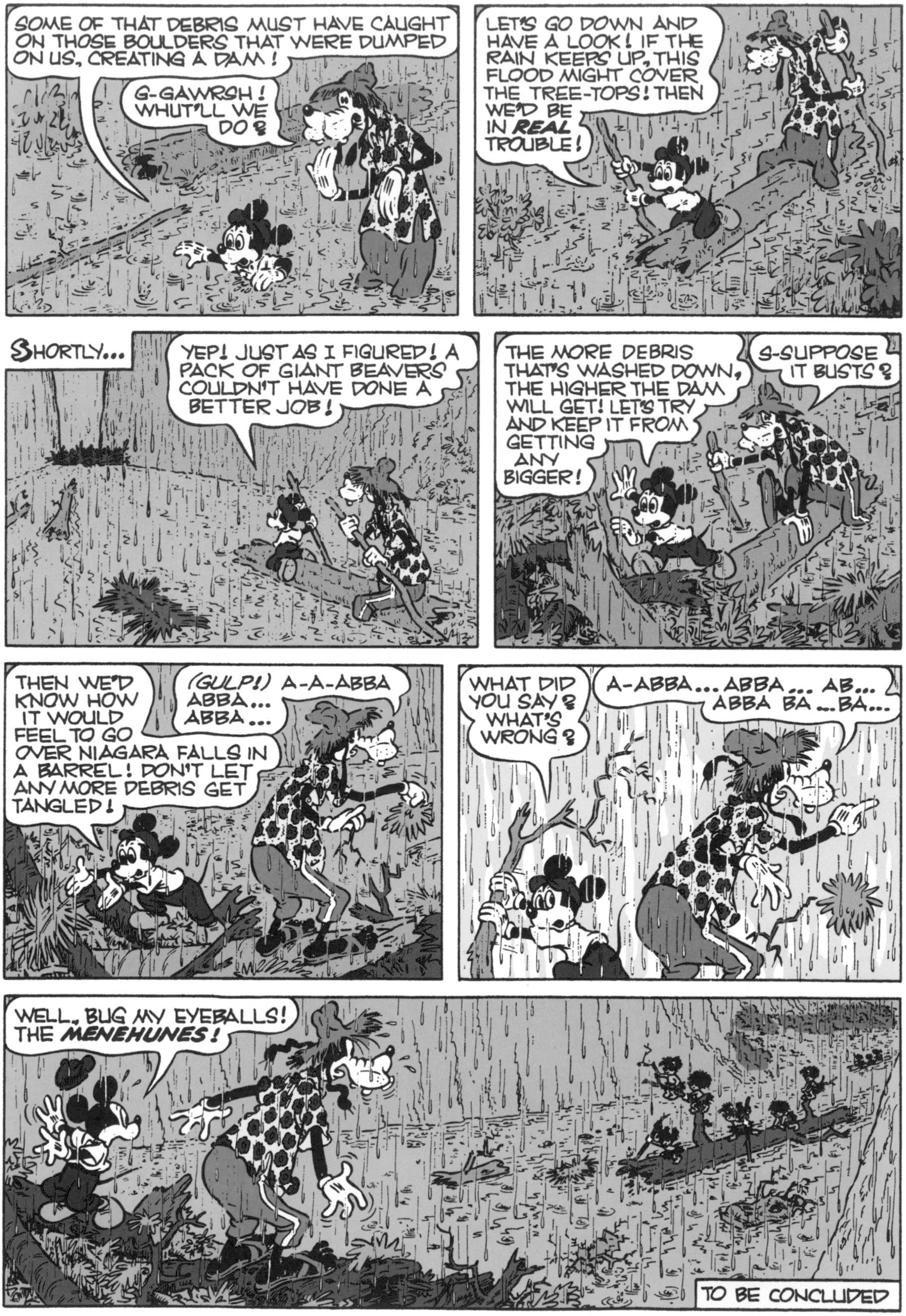
SOME OF THAT DEBRIS MUST HAVE CAUGHT ON THOSE BOULDERS THAT WERE DUMPED ON US, CREATING A DAM!
G-GAWRSH! WHUT'LL WE DO?
LET'S GO DOWN AND HAVE A LOOK! IF THE RAIN KEEPS UP, THIS FLOOD MIGHT COVER THE TREE-TOPS! THEN WE'D BE IN *REAL* TROUBLE!
SHORTLY...
YEP! JUST AS I FIGURED! A PACK OF GIANT BEAVERS COULDN'T HAVE DONE A BETTER JOB!
THE MORE DEBRIS THAT'S WASHED DOWN, THE HIGHER THE DAM WILL GET! LET'S TRY AND KEEP IT FROM GETTING ANY BIGGER!
S-SUPPOSE IT BUSTS?
THEN WE'D KNOW HOW IT WOULD FEEL TO GO OVER NIAGARA FALLS IN A BARREL! DON'T LET ANY MORE DEBRIS GET TANGLED!
(GULP!) A-A-ABBA ABBA... ABBA...
WHAT DID YOU SAY? WHAT'S WRONG?
A-ABBA... ABBA... AB... ABBA BA... BA...
WELL, BUG MY EYEBALLS! THE *MENEHUNES*!
TO BE CONCLUDED

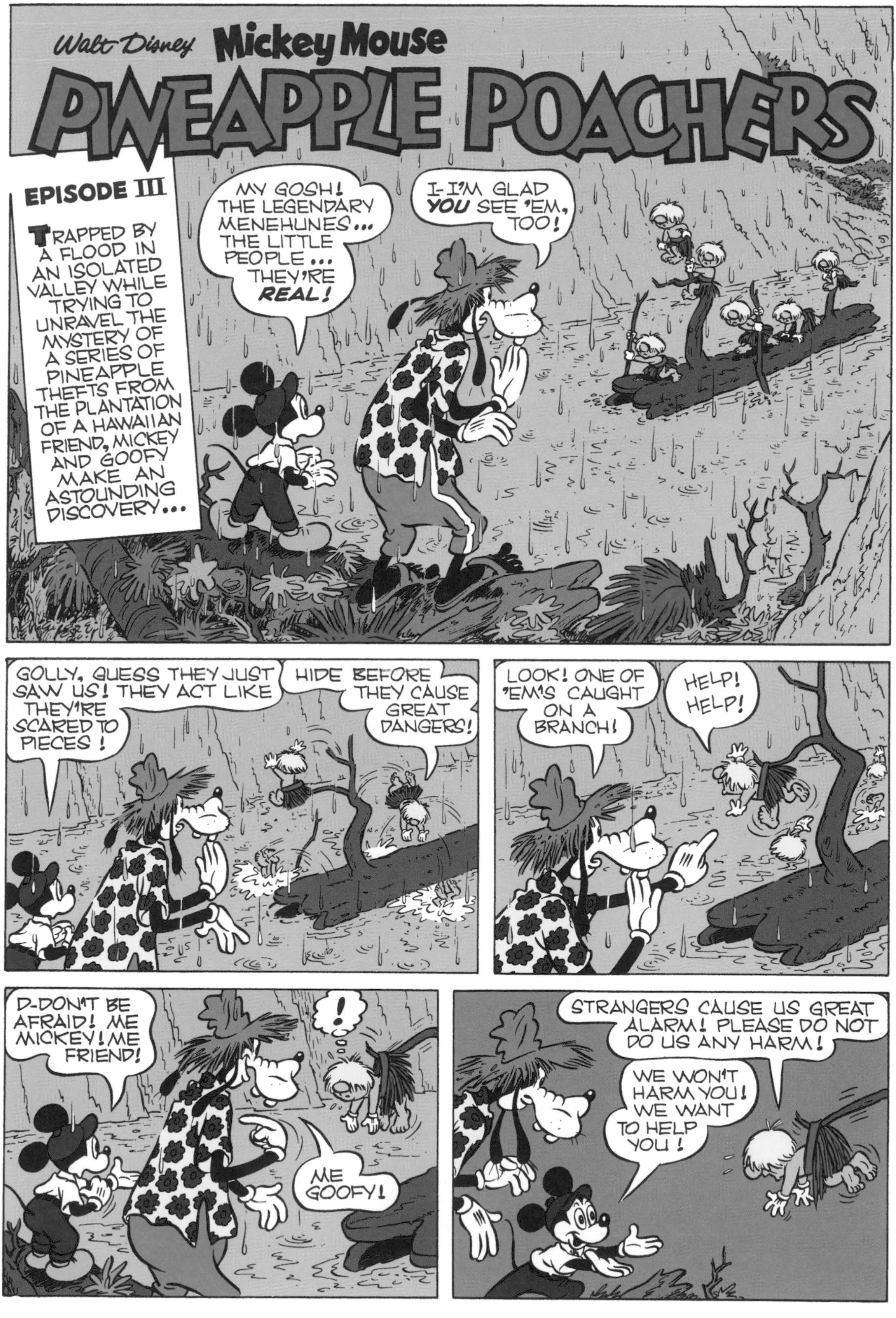
Walt Disney Mickey Mouse
PINEAPPLE POACHERS
EPISODE III
TRAPPED BY A FLOOD IN AN ISOLATED VALLEY WHILE TRYING TO UNRAVEL THE MYSTERY OF A SERIES OF PINEAPPLE THEFTS FROM THE PLANTATION OF A HAWAIIAN FRIEND, MICKEY AND GOOFY MAKE AN ASTOUNDING DISCOVERY...
MY GOSH! THE LEGENDARY MENEHUNES... THE LITTLE PEOPLE... THEY'RE REAL!
I-I'M GLAD YOU SEE 'EM, TOO!
GOLLY, GUESS THEY JUST SAW US! THEY ACT LIKE THEY'RE SCARED TO PIECES!
HIDE BEFORE THEY CAUSE GREAT DANGERS!
LOOK! ONE OF 'EM'S CAUGHT ON A BRANCH!
HELP! HELP!
D-DON'T BE AFRAID! ME MICKEY! ME FRIEND!
!
ME GOOFY!
STRANGERS CAUSE US GREAT ALARM! PLEASE DO NOT DO US ANY HARM!
WE WON'T HARM YOU! WE WANT TO HELP YOU!

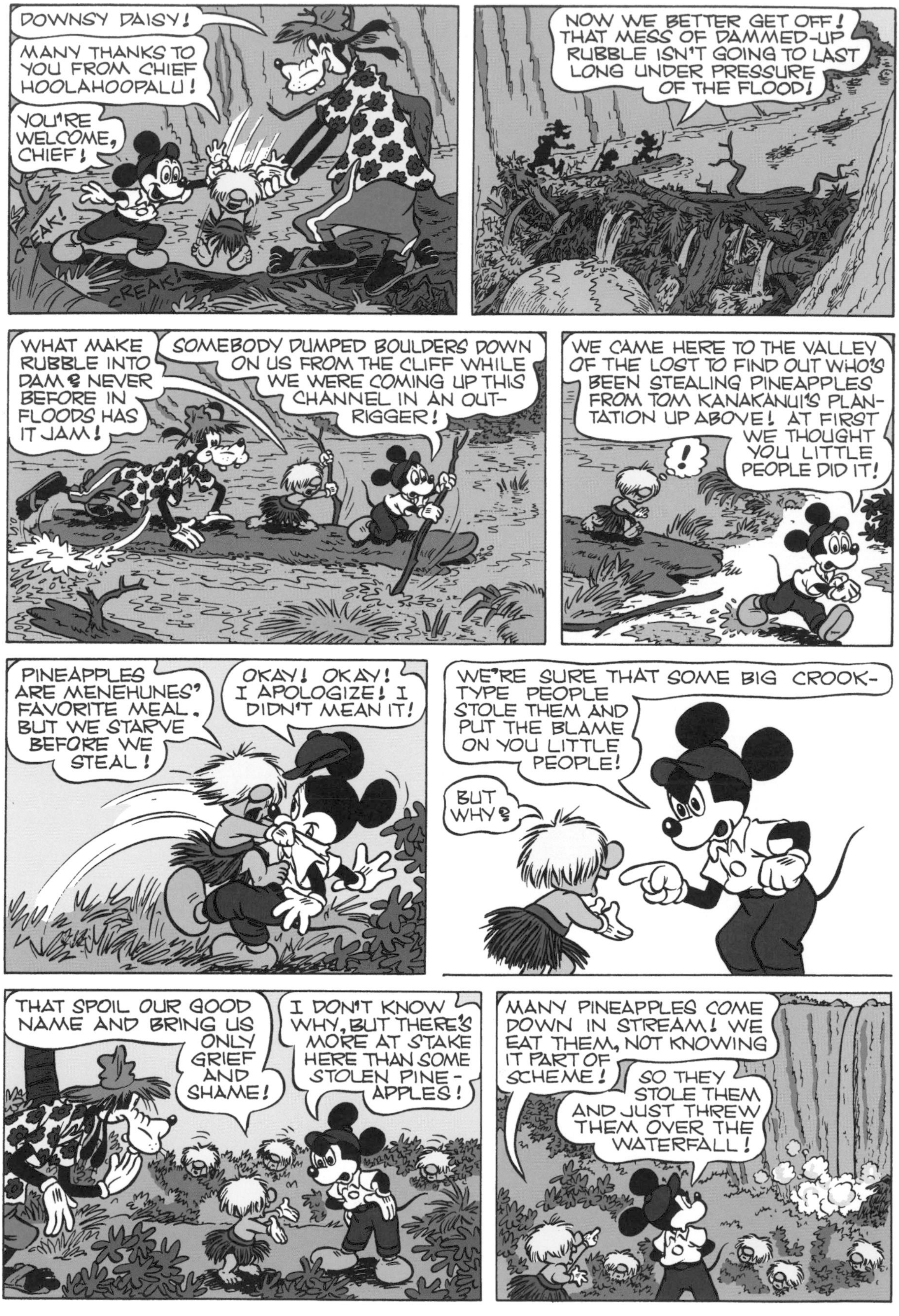

DOWNSY DAISY!
MANY THANKS TO YOU FROM CHIEF HOOLAHOOPALU!
YOU'RE WELCOME, CHIEF!
CREAK!
CREAK!
NOW WE BETTER GET OFF! THAT MESS OF DAMMED-UP RUBBLE ISN'T GOING TO LAST LONG UNDER PRESSURE OF THE FLOOD!
WHAT MAKE RUBBLE INTO DAM? NEVER BEFORE IN FLOODS HAS IT JAM!
SOMEBODY DUMPED BOULDERS DOWN ON US FROM THE CLIFF WHILE WE WERE COMING UP THIS CHANNEL IN AN OUT-RIGGER!
WE CAME HERE TO THE VALLEY OF THE LOST TO FIND OUT WHO'S BEEN STEALING PINEAPPLES FROM TOM KANAKANUI'S PLANTATION UP ABOVE! AT FIRST WE THOUGHT YOU LITTLE PEOPLE DID IT!
!
PINEAPPLES ARE MENEHUNES' FAVORITE MEAL. BUT WE STARVE BEFORE WE STEAL!
OKAY! OKAY! I APOLOGIZE! I DIDN'T MEAN IT!
WE'RE SURE THAT SOME BIG CROOK-TYPE PEOPLE STOLE THEM AND PUT THE BLAME ON YOU LITTLE PEOPLE!
BUT WHY?
THAT SPOIL OUR GOOD NAME AND BRING US ONLY GRIEF AND SHAME!
I DON'T KNOW WHY, BUT THERE'S MORE AT STAKE HERE THAN SOME STOLEN PINE-APPLES!
MANY PINEAPPLES COME DOWN IN STREAM! WE EAT THEM, NOT KNOWING IT PART OF SCHEME!
SO THEY STOLE THEM AND JUST THREW THEM OVER THE WATERFALL!

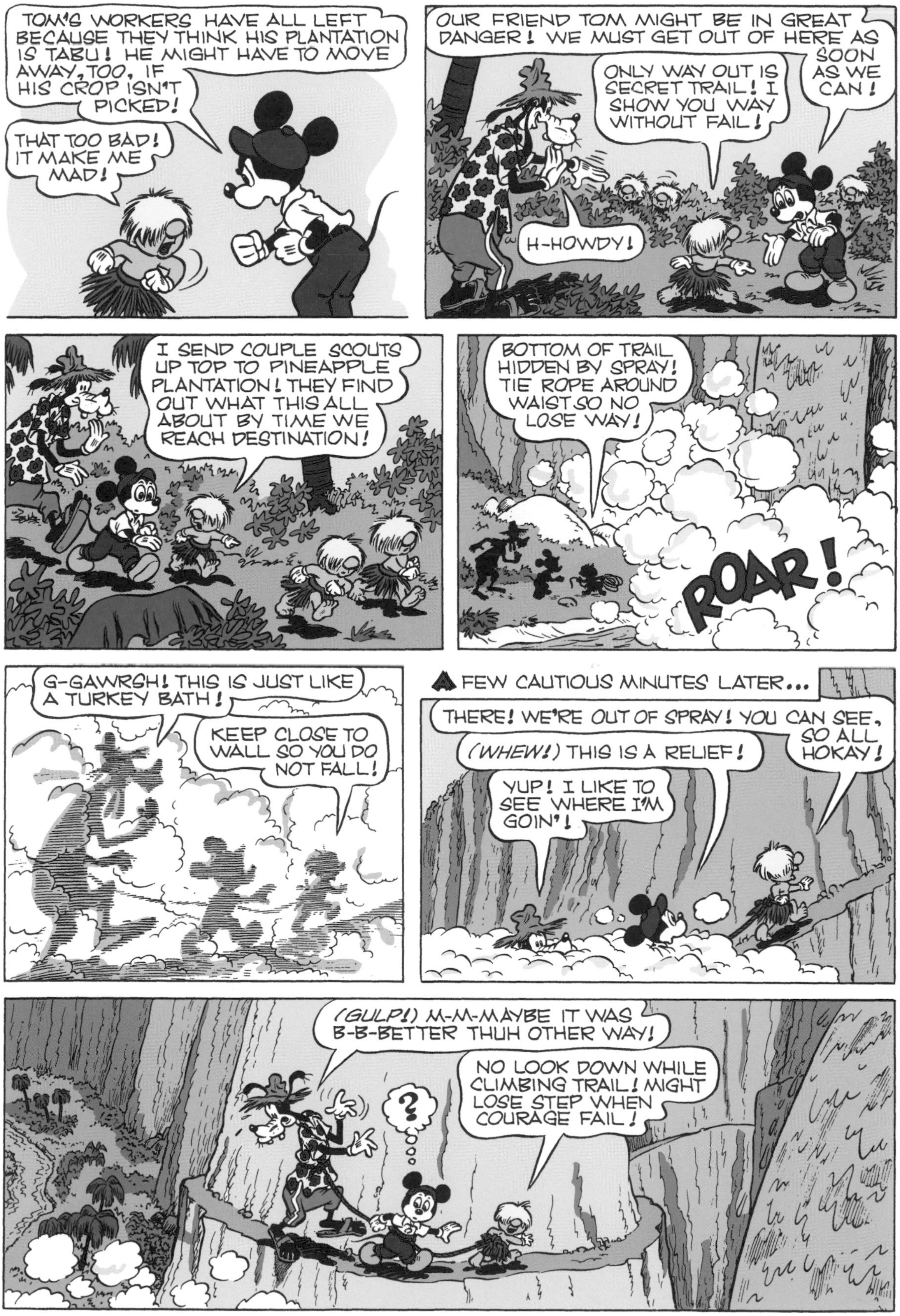
TOM'S WORKERS HAVE ALL LEFT BECAUSE THEY THINK HIS PLANTATION IS TABU! HE MIGHT HAVE TO MOVE AWAY, TOO, IF HIS CROP ISN'T PICKED!
THAT TOO BAD! IT MAKE ME MAD!
OUR FRIEND TOM MIGHT BE IN GREAT DANGER! WE MUST GET OUT OF HERE AS SOON AS WE CAN!
ONLY WAY OUT IS SECRET TRAIL! I SHOW YOU WAY WITHOUT FAIL!
H-HOWDY!
I SEND COUPLE SCOUTS UP TOP TO PINEAPPLE PLANTATION! THEY FIND OUT WHAT THIS ALL ABOUT BY TIME WE REACH DESTINATION!
BOTTOM OF TRAIL HIDDEN BY SPRAY! TIE ROPE AROUND WAIST SO NO LOSE WAY!
ROAR!
G-GAWRSH! THIS IS JUST LIKE A TURKEY BATH!
KEEP CLOSE TO WALL SO YOU DO NOT FALL!
A FEW CAUTIOUS MINUTES LATER...
THERE! WE'RE OUT OF SPRAY! YOU CAN SEE, SO ALL HOKAY!
(WHEW!) THIS IS A RELIEF!
YUP! I LIKE TO SEE WHERE I'M GOIN'!
(GULP!) M-M-MAYBE IT WAS B-B-BETTER THUH OTHER WAY!
NO LOOK DOWN WHILE CLIMBING TRAIL! MIGHT LOSE STEP WHEN COURAGE FAIL!
?

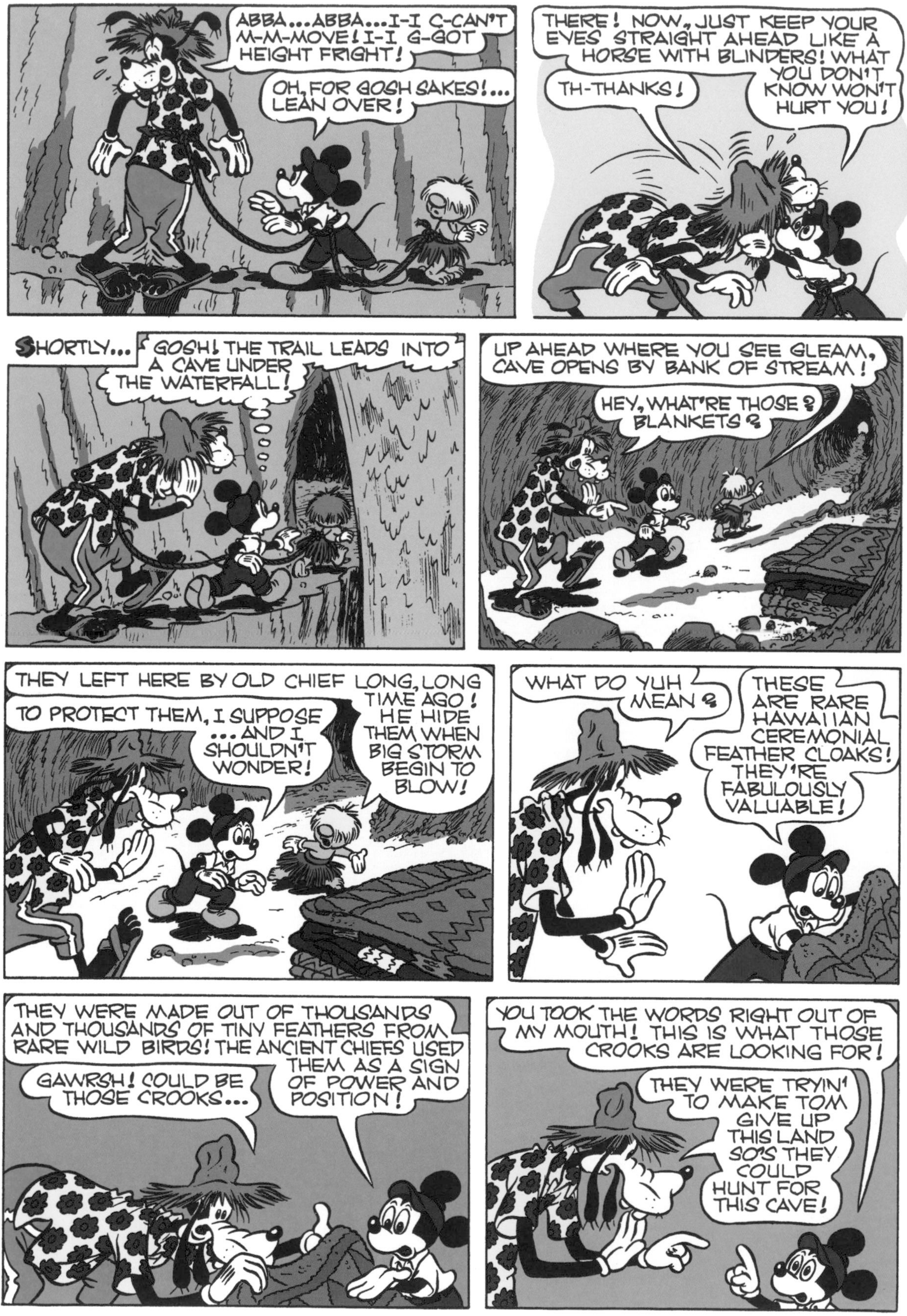
ABBA...ABBA...I-I C-CAN'T M-M-MOVE! I-I G-GOT HEIGHT FRIGHT!
OH, FOR GOSH SAKES!... LEAN OVER!
THERE! NOW, JUST KEEP YOUR EYES STRAIGHT AHEAD LIKE A HORSE WITH BLINDERS! WHAT YOU DON'T KNOW WON'T HURT YOU!
TH-THANKS!
SHORTLY...
GOSH! THE TRAIL LEADS INTO A CAVE UNDER THE WATERFALL!
UP AHEAD WHERE YOU SEE GLEAM, CAVE OPENS BY BANK OF STREAM!
HEY, WHAT'RE THOSE? BLANKETS?
THEY LEFT HERE BY OLD CHIEF LONG, LONG TIME AGO! HE HIDE THEM WHEN BIG STORM BEGIN TO BLOW!
TO PROTECT THEM, I SUPPOSE ...AND I SHOULDN'T WONDER!
WHAT DO YUH MEAN?
THESE ARE RARE HAWAIIAN CEREMONIAL FEATHER CLOAKS! THEY'RE FABULOUSLY VALUABLE!
THEY WERE MADE OUT OF THOUSANDS AND THOUSANDS OF TINY FEATHERS FROM RARE WILD BIRDS! THE ANCIENT CHIEFS USED THEM AS A SIGN OF POWER AND POSITION!
GAWRSH! COULD BE THOSE CROOKS...
YOU TOOK THE WORDS RIGHT OUT OF MY MOUTH! THIS IS WHAT THOSE CROOKS ARE LOOKING FOR!
THEY WERE TRYIN' TO MAKE TOM GIVE UP THIS LAND SO'S THEY COULD HUNT FOR THIS CAVE!

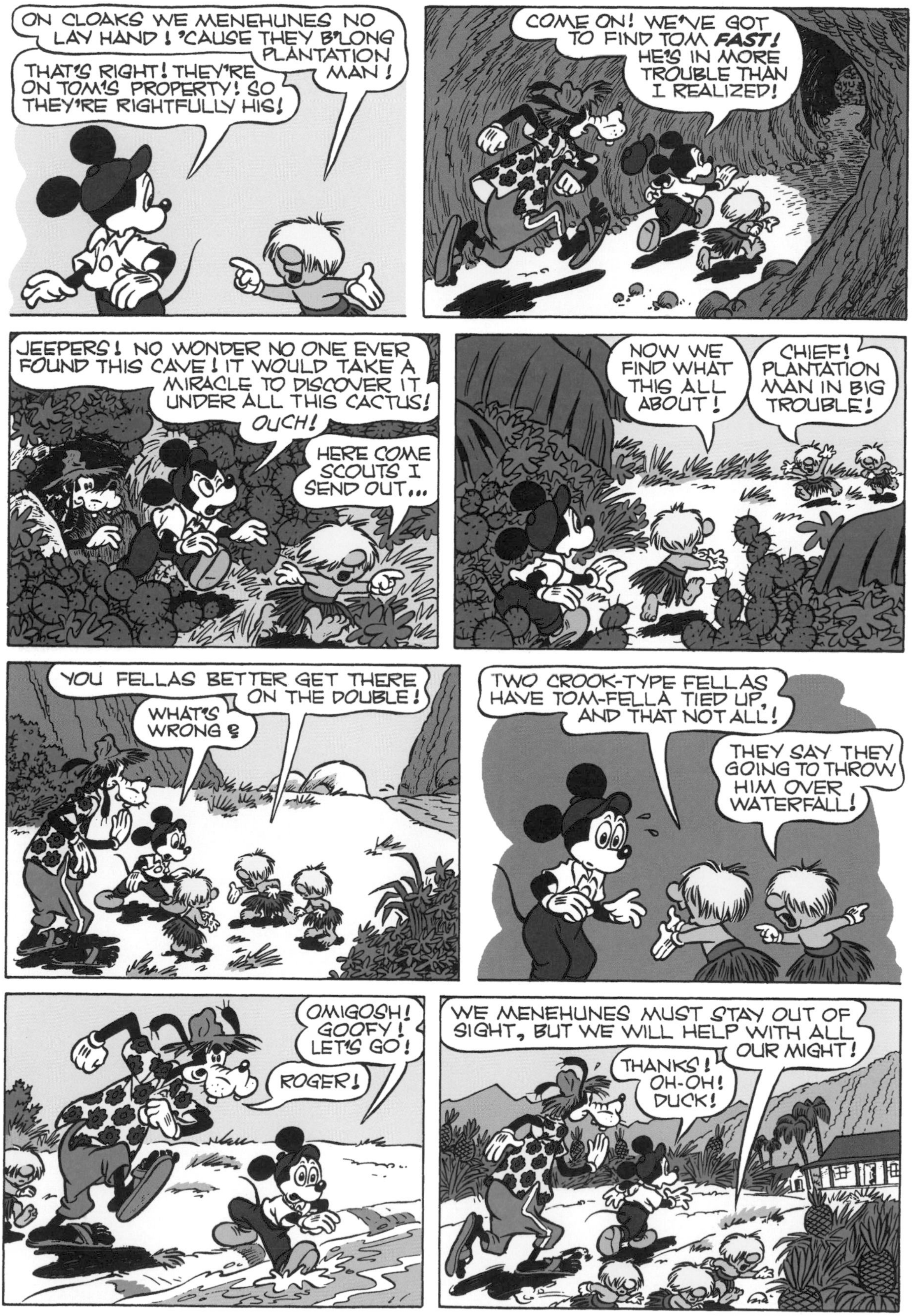
ON CLOAKS WE MENEHUNES NO LAY HAND! 'CAUSE THEY B'LONG PLANTATION MAN!
THAT'S RIGHT! THEY'RE ON TOM'S PROPERTY! SO THEY'RE RIGHTFULLY HIS!
COME ON! WE'VE GOT TO FIND TOM FAST! HE'S IN MORE TROUBLE THAN I REALIZED!
JEEPERS! NO WONDER NO ONE EVER FOUND THIS CAVE! IT WOULD TAKE A MIRACLE TO DISCOVER IT UNDER ALL THIS CACTUS! OUCH!
HERE COME SCOUTS I SEND OUT...
NOW WE FIND WHAT THIS ALL ABOUT!
CHIEF! PLANTATION MAN IN BIG TROUBLE!
YOU FELLAS BETTER GET THERE ON THE DOUBLE!
WHAT'S WRONG?
TWO CROOK-TYPE FELLAS HAVE TOM-FELLA TIED UP, AND THAT NOT ALL!
THEY SAY THEY GOING TO THROW HIM OVER WATERFALL!
OMIGOSH! GOOFY! LET'S GO!
ROGER!
WE MENEHUNES MUST STAY OUT OF SIGHT, BUT WE WILL HELP WITH ALL OUR MIGHT!
THANKS! OH-OH! DUCK!

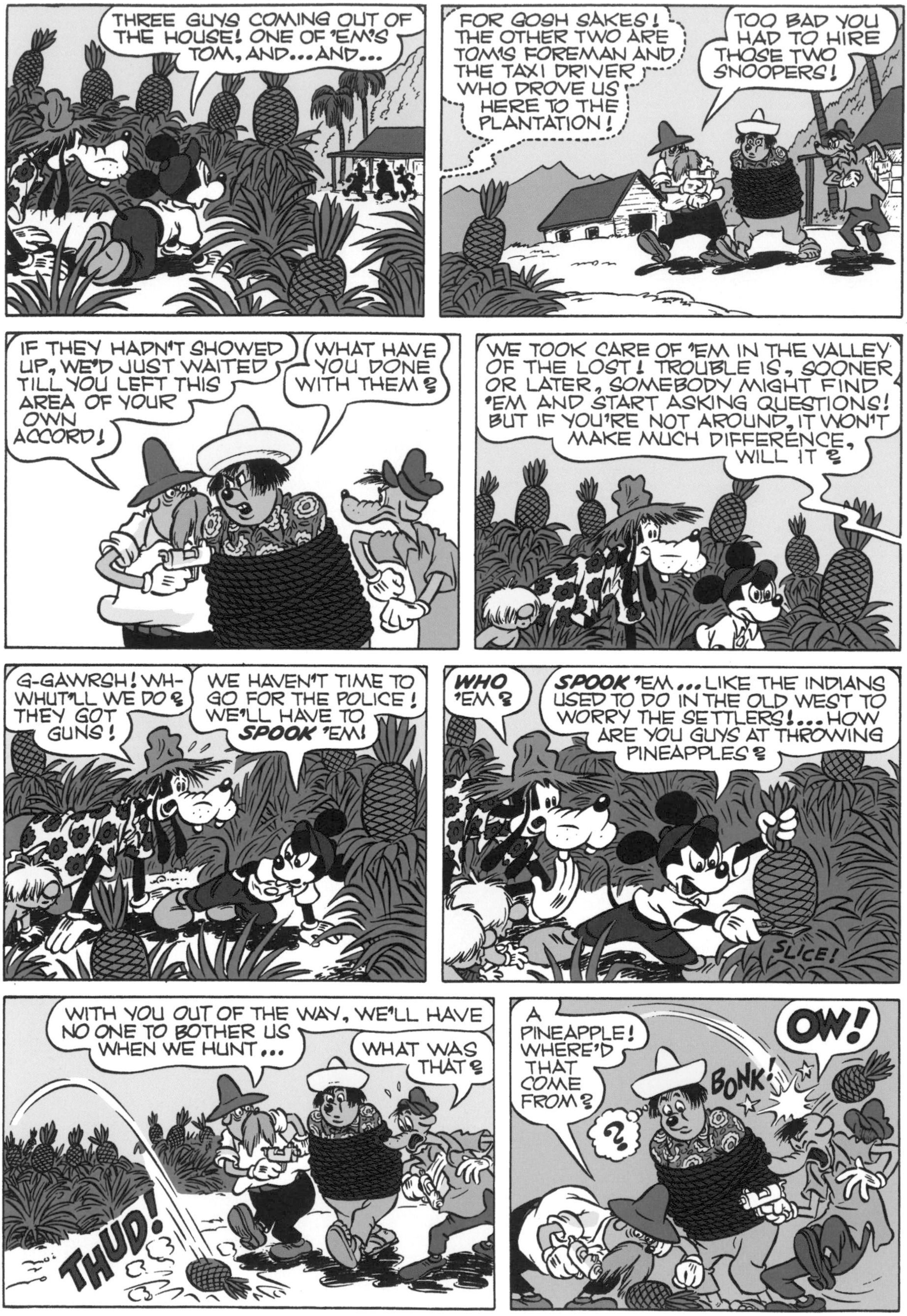
THREE GUYS COMING OUT OF THE HOUSE! ONE OF 'EM'S TOM, AND... AND...
FOR GOSH SAKES! THE OTHER TWO ARE TOM'S FOREMAN AND THE TAXI DRIVER WHO DROVE US HERE TO THE PLANTATION!
TOO BAD YOU HAD TO HIRE THOSE TWO SNOOPERS!
IF THEY HADN'T SHOWED UP, WE'D JUST WAITED TILL YOU LEFT THIS AREA OF YOUR OWN ACCORD!
WHAT HAVE YOU DONE WITH THEM?
WE TOOK CARE OF 'EM IN THE VALLEY OF THE LOST! TROUBLE IS, SOONER OR LATER, SOMEBODY MIGHT FIND 'EM AND START ASKING QUESTIONS! BUT IF YOU'RE NOT AROUND, IT WON'T MAKE MUCH DIFFERENCE, WILL IT?
G-GAWRSH! WH-WHUT'LL WE DO? THEY GOT GUNS!
WE HAVEN'T TIME TO GO FOR THE POLICE! WE'LL HAVE TO SPOOK 'EM!
WHO 'EM?
SPOOK 'EM... LIKE THE INDIANS USED TO DO IN THE OLD WEST TO WORRY THE SETTLERS!... HOW ARE YOU GUYS AT THROWING PINEAPPLES?
SLICE!
WITH YOU OUT OF THE WAY, WE'LL HAVE NO ONE TO BOTHER US WHEN WE HUNT...
WHAT WAS THAT?
THUD!
A PINEAPPLE! WHERE'D THAT COME FROM?
?
BONK!
OW!

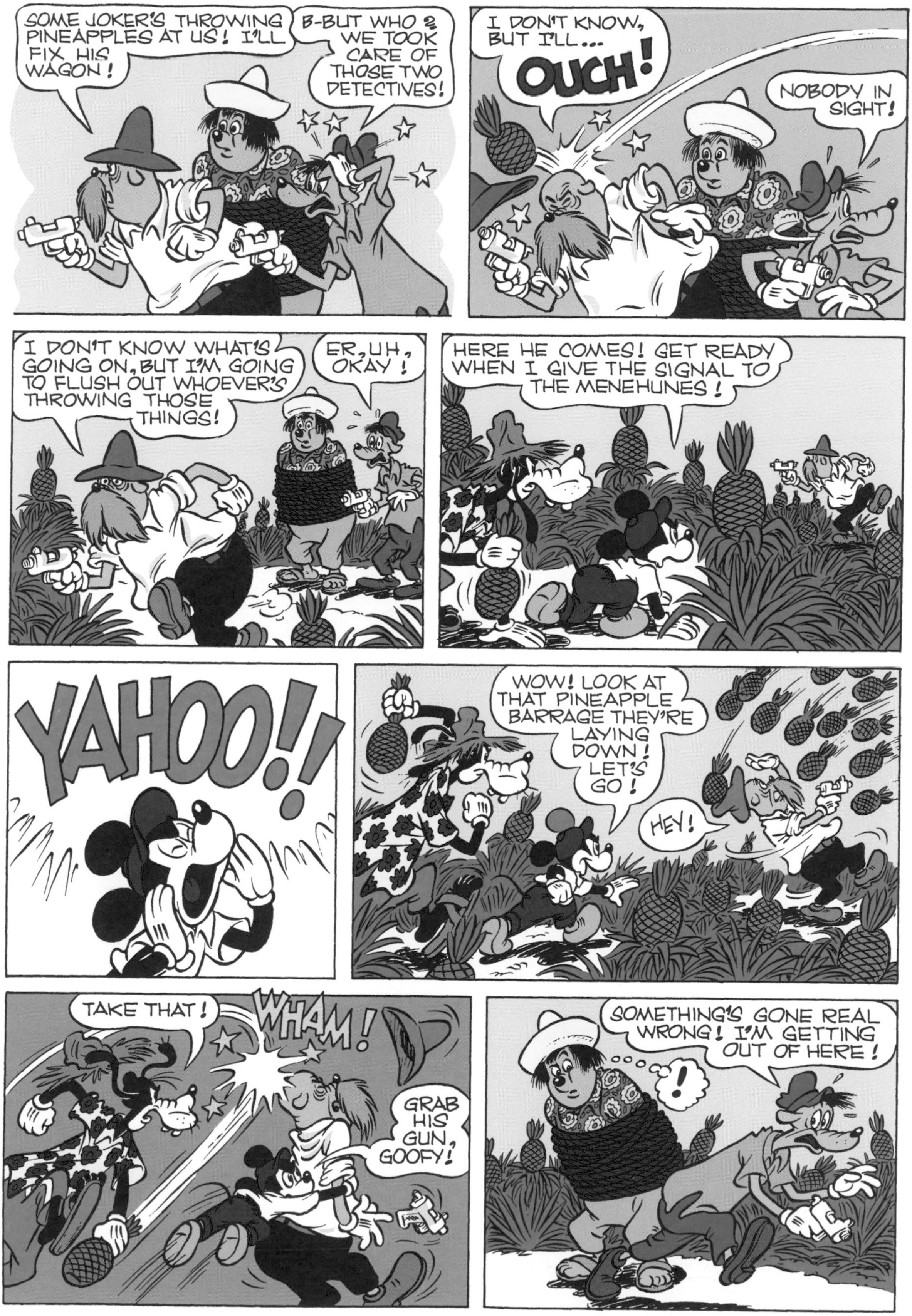
SOME JOKER'S THROWING PINEAPPLES AT US! I'LL FIX HIS WAGON!
B-BUT WHO? WE TOOK CARE OF THOSE TWO DETECTIVES!
I DON'T KNOW, BUT I'LL...
OUCH!
NOBODY IN SIGHT!
I DON'T KNOW WHAT'S GOING ON, BUT I'M GOING TO FLUSH OUT WHOEVER'S THROWING THOSE THINGS!
ER, UH, OKAY!
HERE HE COMES! GET READY WHEN I GIVE THE SIGNAL TO THE MENEHUNES!
YAHOO!!
WOW! LOOK AT THAT PINEAPPLE BARRAGE THEY'RE LAYING DOWN! LET'S GO!
HEY!
TAKE THAT!
WHAM!
GRAB HIS GUN, GOOFY!
SOMETHING'S GONE REAL WRONG! I'M GETTING OUT OF HERE!
!

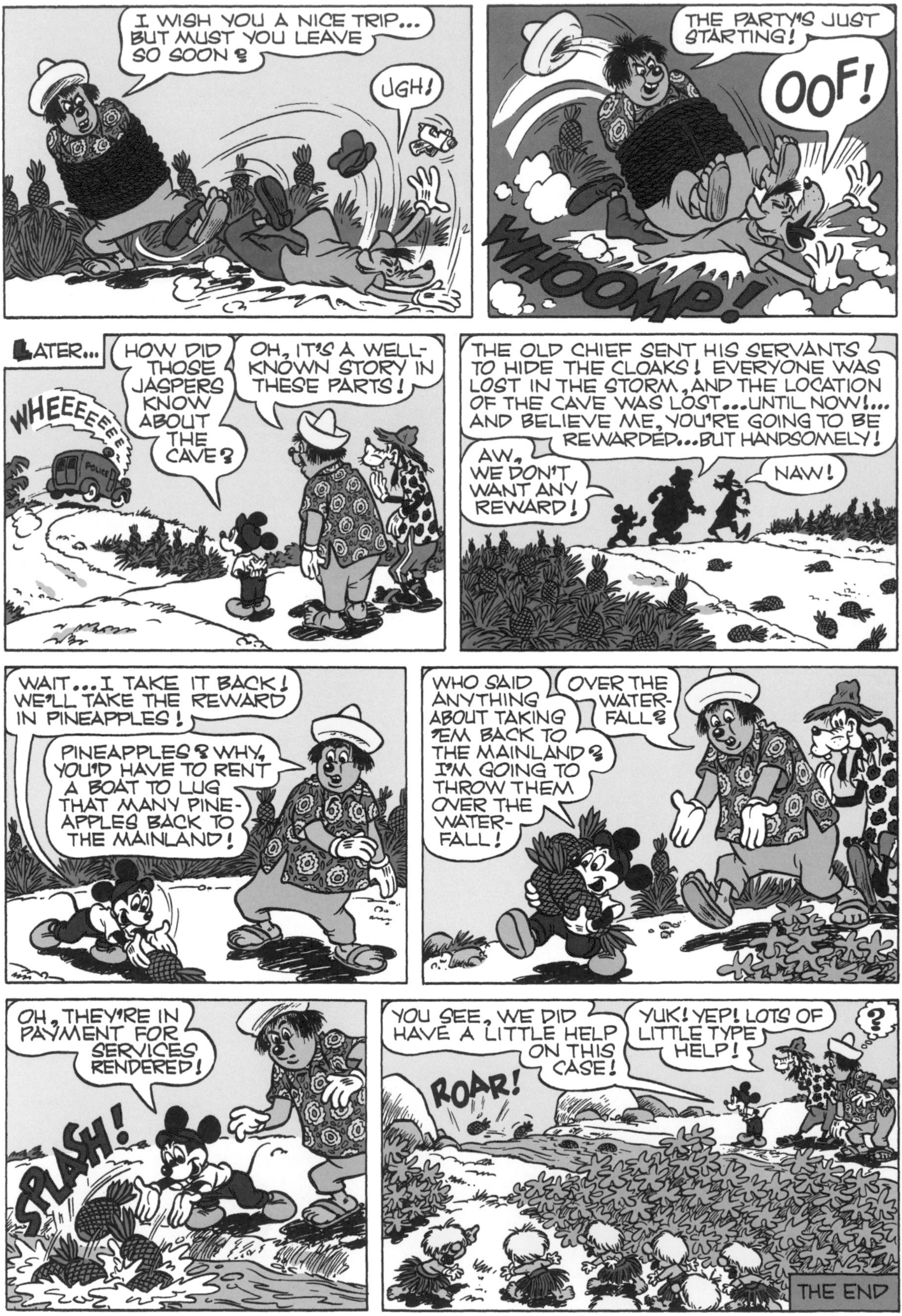
I WISH YOU A NICE TRIP... BUT MUST YOU LEAVE SO SOON?
UGH!
THE PARTY'S JUST STARTING!
OOF!
WHOOMP!
LATER...
HOW DID THOSE JASPERS KNOW ABOUT THE CAVE?
OH, IT'S A WELL-KNOWN STORY IN THESE PARTS!
WHEEEEEEE
POLICE
THE OLD CHIEF SENT HIS SERVANTS TO HIDE THE CLOAKS! EVERYONE WAS LOST IN THE STORM, AND THE LOCATION OF THE CAVE WAS LOST...UNTIL NOW!... AND BELIEVE ME, YOU'RE GOING TO BE REWARDED...BUT HANDSOMELY!
AW, WE DON'T WANT ANY REWARD!
NAW!
WAIT... I TAKE IT BACK! WE'LL TAKE THE REWARD IN PINEAPPLES!
PINEAPPLES? WHY, YOU'D HAVE TO RENT A BOAT TO LUG THAT MANY PINE-APPLES BACK TO THE MAINLAND!
WHO SAID ANYTHING ABOUT TAKING 'EM BACK TO THE MAINLAND? I'M GOING TO THROW THEM OVER THE WATER-FALL!
OVER THE WATER-FALL?
OH, THEY'RE IN PAYMENT FOR SERVICES RENDERED!
SPLASH!
YOU SEE, WE DID HAVE A LITTLE HELP ON THIS CASE!
YUK! YEP! LOTS OF LITTLE TYPE HELP!
?
ROAR!
THE END

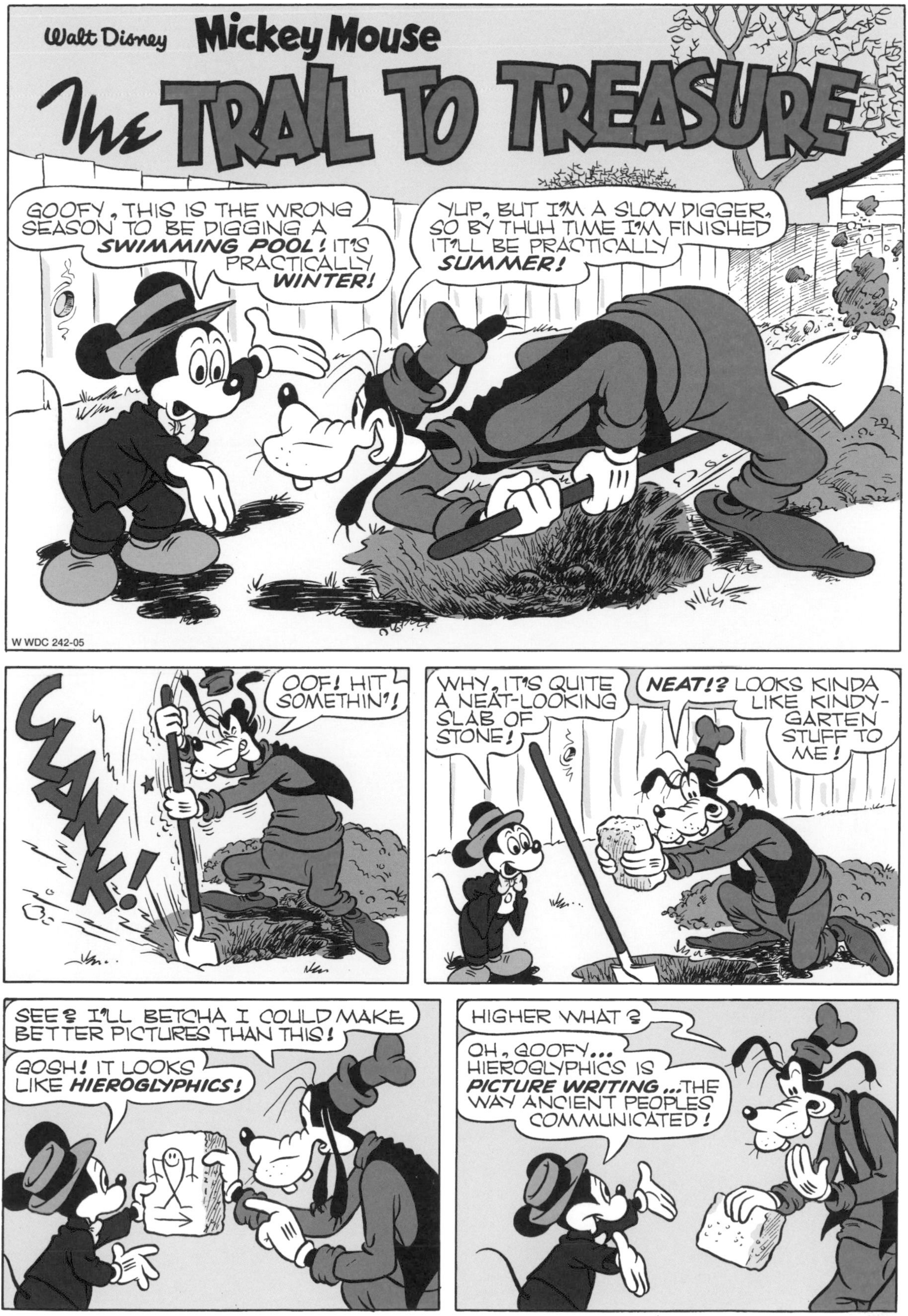

Walt Disney Mickey Mouse
The TRAIL TO TREASURE
GOOFY, THIS IS THE WRONG SEASON TO BE DIGGING A SWIMMING POOL! IT'S PRACTICALLY WINTER!
YUP, BUT I'M A SLOW DIGGER, SO BY THUH TIME I'M FINISHED IT'LL BE PRACTICALLY SUMMER!
W WDC 242-05
CLANK!
OOF! HIT SOMETHIN'!
WHY, IT'S QUITE A NEAT-LOOKING SLAB OF STONE!
NEAT!? LOOKS KINDA LIKE KINDY-GARTEN STUFF TO ME!
SEE? I'LL BETCHA I COULD MAKE BETTER PICTURES THAN THIS!
GOSH! IT LOOKS LIKE HIEROGLYPHICS!
HIGHER WHAT?
OH, GOOFY... HIEROGLYPHICS IS PICTURE WRITING... THE WAY ANCIENT PEOPLES COMMUNICATED!

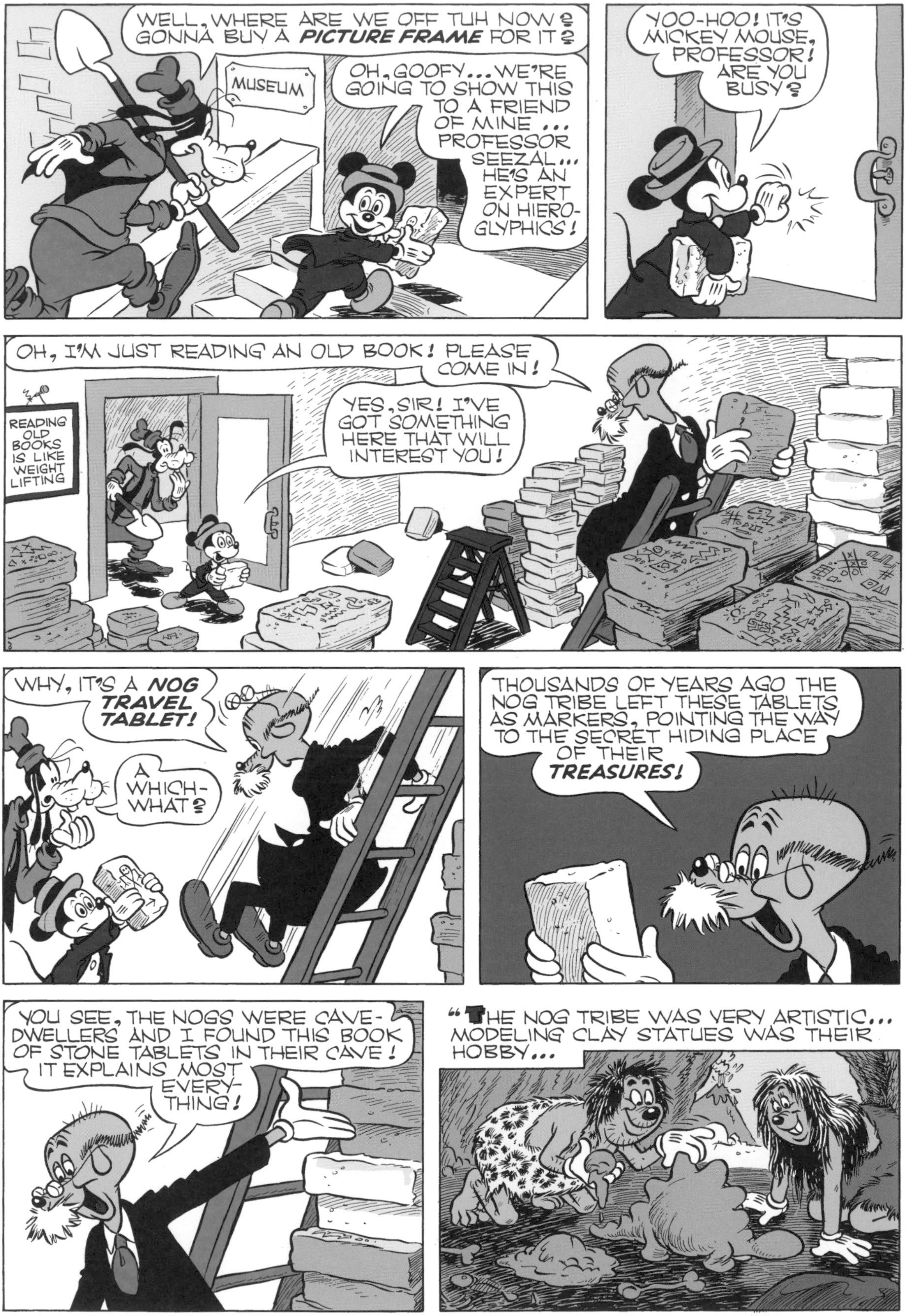
WELL, WHERE ARE WE OFF TUH NOW? GONNA BUY A PICTURE FRAME FOR IT?
MUSEUM
OH, GOOFY... WE'RE GOING TO SHOW THIS TO A FRIEND OF MINE ... PROFESSOR SEEZAL... HE'S AN EXPERT ON HIEROGLYPHICS!
YOO-HOO! IT'S MICKEY MOUSE, PROFESSOR! ARE YOU BUSY?
OH, I'M JUST READING AN OLD BOOK! PLEASE COME IN!
READING OLD BOOKS IS LIKE WEIGHT LIFTING
YES, SIR! I'VE GOT SOMETHING HERE THAT WILL INTEREST YOU!
WHY, IT'S A NOG TRAVEL TABLET!
A WHICH-WHAT?
THOUSANDS OF YEARS AGO THE NOG TRIBE LEFT THESE TABLETS AS MARKERS, POINTING THE WAY TO THE SECRET HIDING PLACE OF THEIR TREASURES!
YOU SEE, THE NOGS WERE CAVE-DWELLERS AND I FOUND THIS BOOK OF STONE TABLETS IN THEIR CAVE! IT EXPLAINS MOST EVERYTHING!
"THE NOG TRIBE WAS VERY ARTISTIC... MODELING CLAY STATUES WAS THEIR HOBBY...

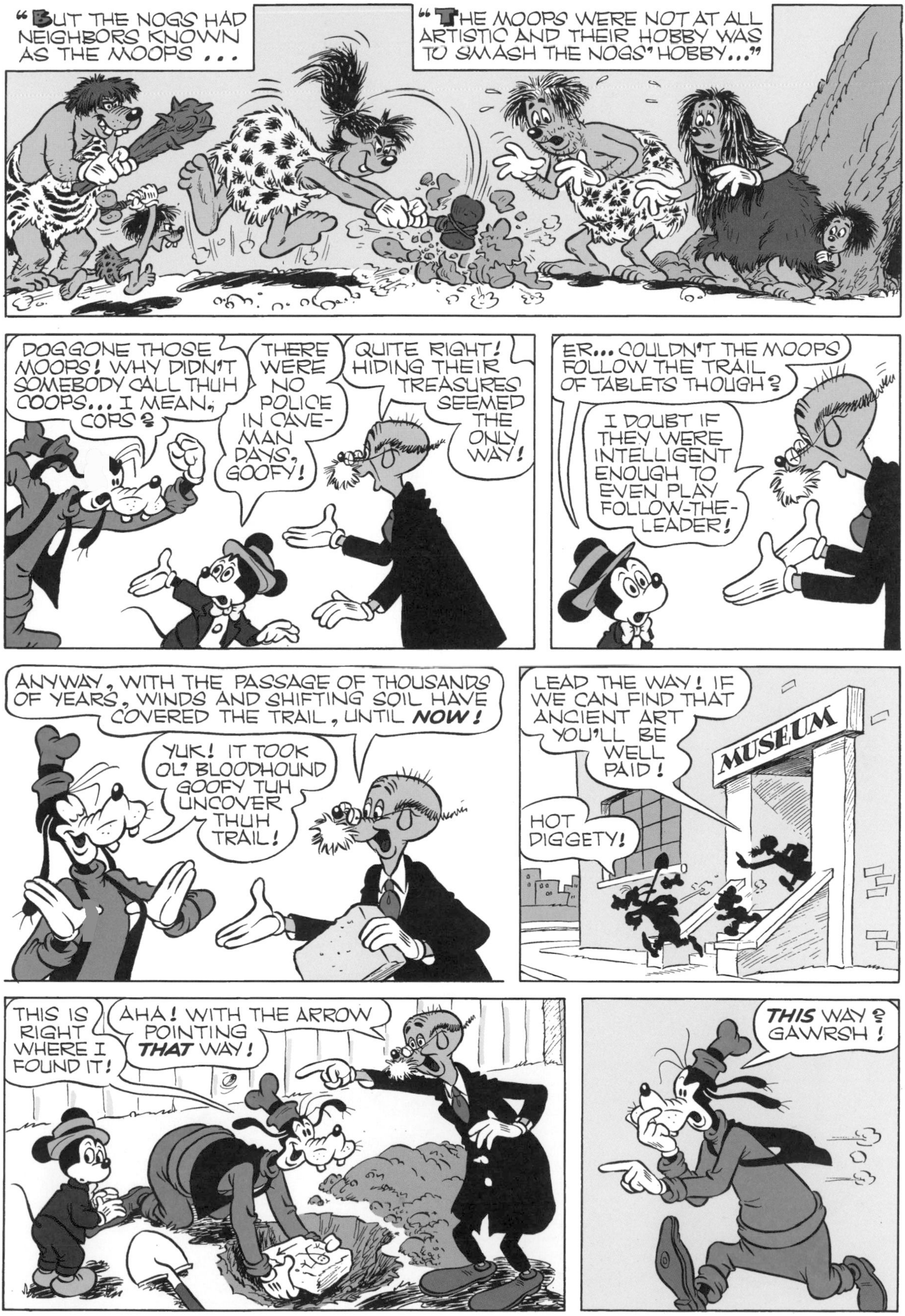
"BUT THE NOGS HAD NEIGHBORS KNOWN AS THE MOOPS . . .
"THE MOOPS WERE NOT AT ALL ARTISTIC AND THEIR HOBBY WAS TO SMASH THE NOGS' HOBBY..."
DOGGONE THOSE MOOPS! WHY DIDN'T SOMEBODY CALL THUH COOPS... I MEAN, COPS?
THERE WERE NO POLICE IN CAVE-MAN DAYS, GOOFY!
QUITE RIGHT! HIDING THEIR TREASURES SEEMED THE ONLY WAY!
ER... COULDN'T THE MOOPS FOLLOW THE TRAIL OF TABLETS THOUGH?
I DOUBT IF THEY WERE INTELLIGENT ENOUGH TO EVEN PLAY FOLLOW-THE-LEADER!
ANYWAY, WITH THE PASSAGE OF THOUSANDS OF YEARS, WINDS AND SHIFTING SOIL HAVE COVERED THE TRAIL, UNTIL NOW!
YUK! IT TOOK OL' BLOODHOUND GOOFY TUH UNCOVER THUH TRAIL!
LEAD THE WAY! IF WE CAN FIND THAT ANCIENT ART YOU'LL BE WELL PAID!
MUSEUM
HOT DIGGETY!
THIS IS RIGHT WHERE I FOUND IT!
AHA! WITH THE ARROW POINTING THAT WAY!
THIS WAY? GAWRSH!

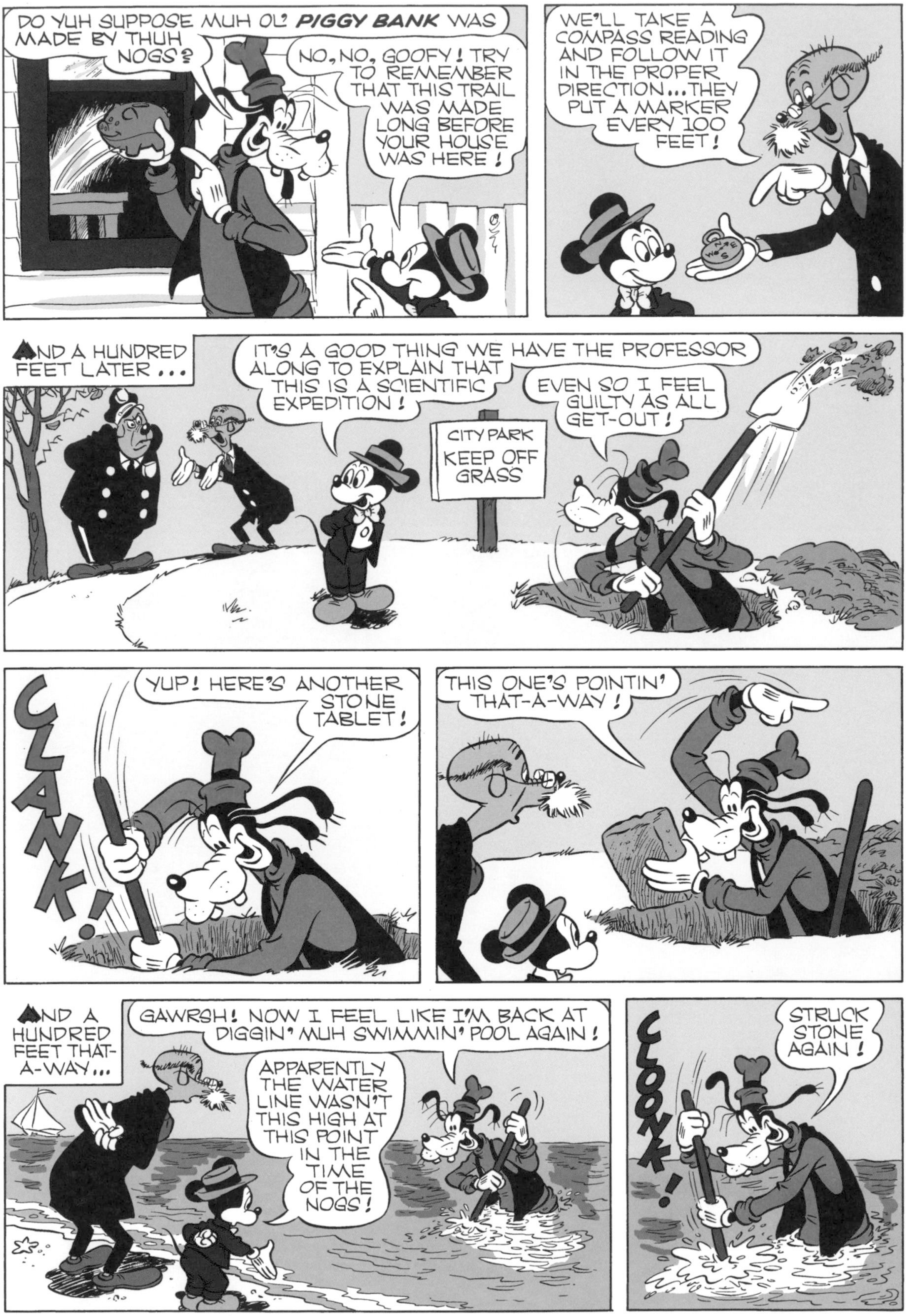
DO YUH SUPPOSE MUH OL' PIGGY BANK WAS MADE BY THUH NOGS?
NO, NO, GOOFY! TRY TO REMEMBER THAT THIS TRAIL WAS MADE LONG BEFORE YOUR HOUSE WAS HERE!
WE'LL TAKE A COMPASS READING AND FOLLOW IT IN THE PROPER DIRECTION... THEY PUT A MARKER EVERY 100 FEET!
AND A HUNDRED FEET LATER...
IT'S A GOOD THING WE HAVE THE PROFESSOR ALONG TO EXPLAIN THAT THIS IS A SCIENTIFIC EXPEDITION!
EVEN SO I FEEL GUILTY AS ALL GET-OUT!
CITY PARK
KEEP OFF GRASS
CLANK!
YUP! HERE'S ANOTHER STONE TABLET!
THIS ONE'S POINTIN' THAT-A-WAY!
AND A HUNDRED FEET THAT-A-WAY...
GAWRSH! NOW I FEEL LIKE I'M BACK AT DIGGIN' MUH SWIMMIN' POOL AGAIN!
APPARENTLY THE WATER LINE WASN'T THIS HIGH AT THIS POINT IN THE TIME OF THE NOGS!
CLOONK!
STRUCK STONE AGAIN!

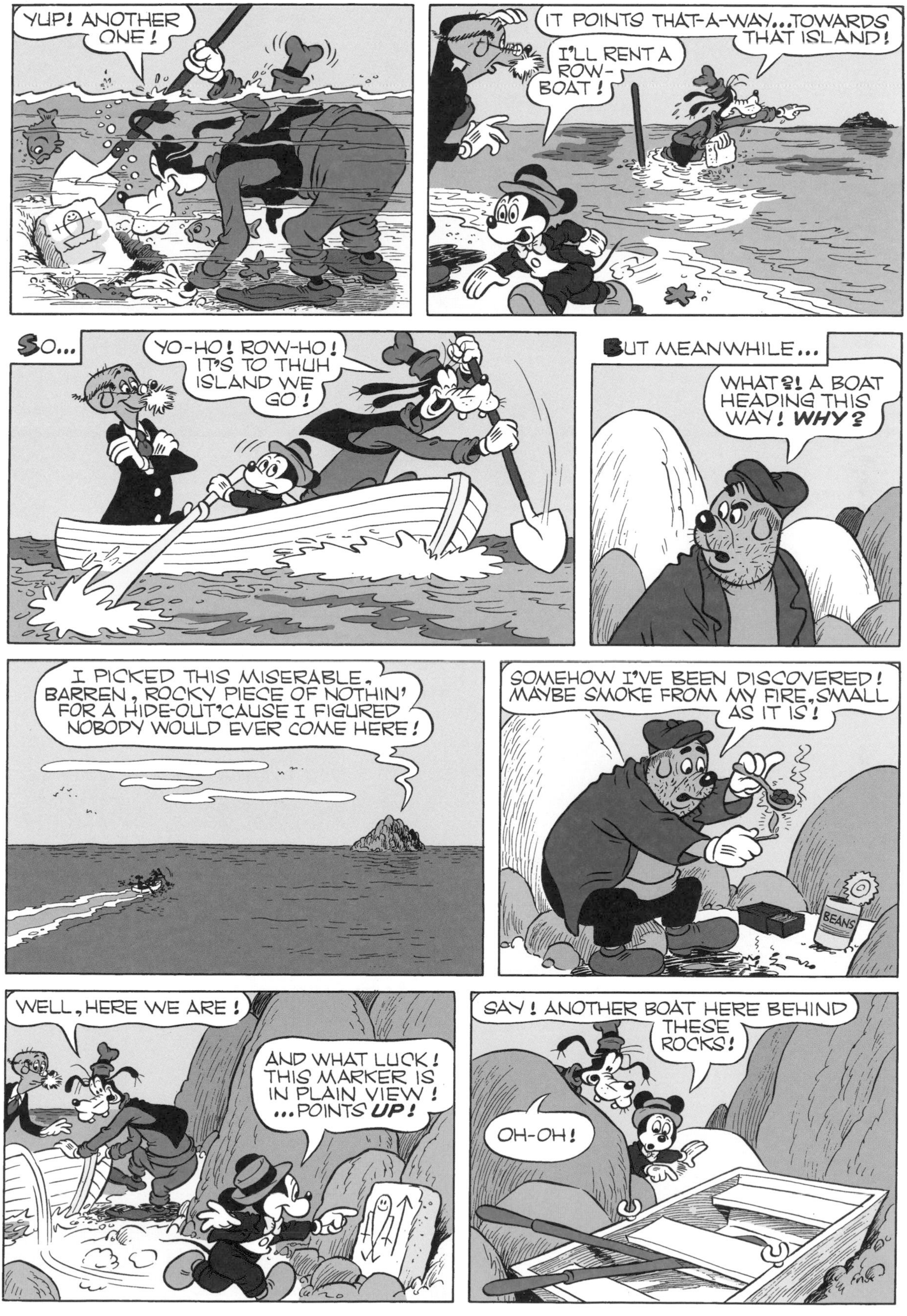
YUP! ANOTHER ONE!
IT POINTS THAT-A-WAY...TOWARDS THAT ISLAND!
I'LL RENT A ROW-BOAT!
SO...
YO-HO! ROW-HO! IT'S TO THUH ISLAND WE GO!
BUT MEANWHILE...
WHAT?! A BOAT HEADING THIS WAY! WHY?
I PICKED THIS MISERABLE, BARREN, ROCKY PIECE OF NOTHIN' FOR A HIDE-OUT 'CAUSE I FIGURED NOBODY WOULD EVER COME HERE!
SOMEHOW I'VE BEEN DISCOVERED! MAYBE SMOKE FROM MY FIRE, SMALL AS IT IS!
BEANS
WELL, HERE WE ARE!
AND WHAT LUCK! THIS MARKER IS IN PLAIN VIEW! ...POINTS UP!
SAY! ANOTHER BOAT HERE BEHIND THESE ROCKS!
OH-OH!

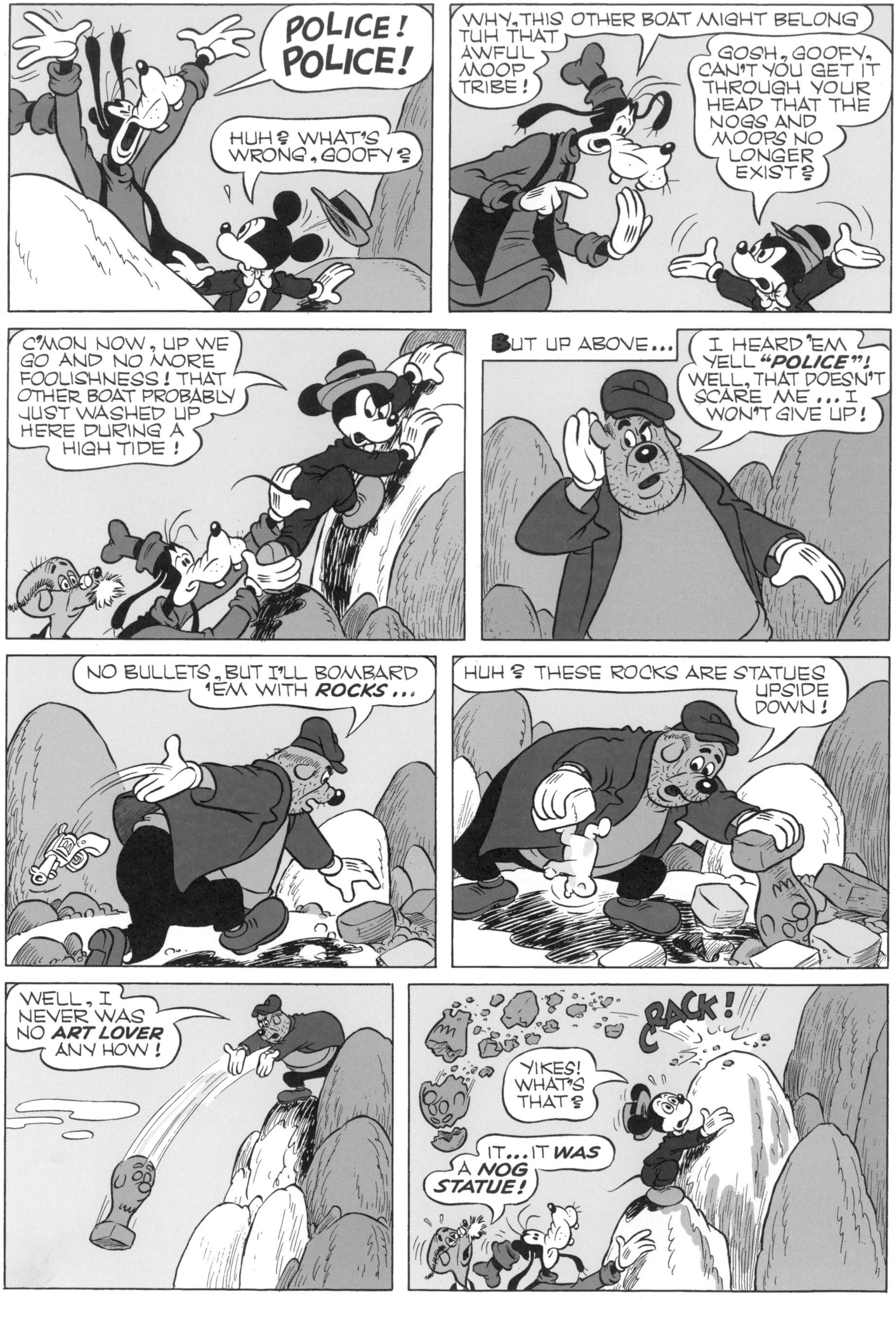
POLICE! POLICE!
HUH? WHAT'S WRONG, GOOFY?
WHY, THIS OTHER BOAT MIGHT BELONG TUH THAT AWFUL MOOP TRIBE!
GOSH, GOOFY, CAN'T YOU GET IT THROUGH YOUR HEAD THAT THE NOGS AND MOOPS NO LONGER EXIST?
C'MON NOW, UP WE GO AND NO MORE FOOLISHNESS! THAT OTHER BOAT PROBABLY JUST WASHED UP HERE DURING A HIGH TIDE!
BUT UP ABOVE...
I HEARD 'EM YELL "POLICE"! WELL, THAT DOESN'T SCARE ME ... I WON'T GIVE UP!
NO BULLETS, BUT I'LL BOMBARD 'EM WITH ROCKS...
HUH? THESE ROCKS ARE STATUES UPSIDE DOWN!
WELL, I NEVER WAS NO ART LOVER ANY HOW!
CRACK!
YIKES! WHAT'S THAT?
IT... IT WAS A NOG STATUE!

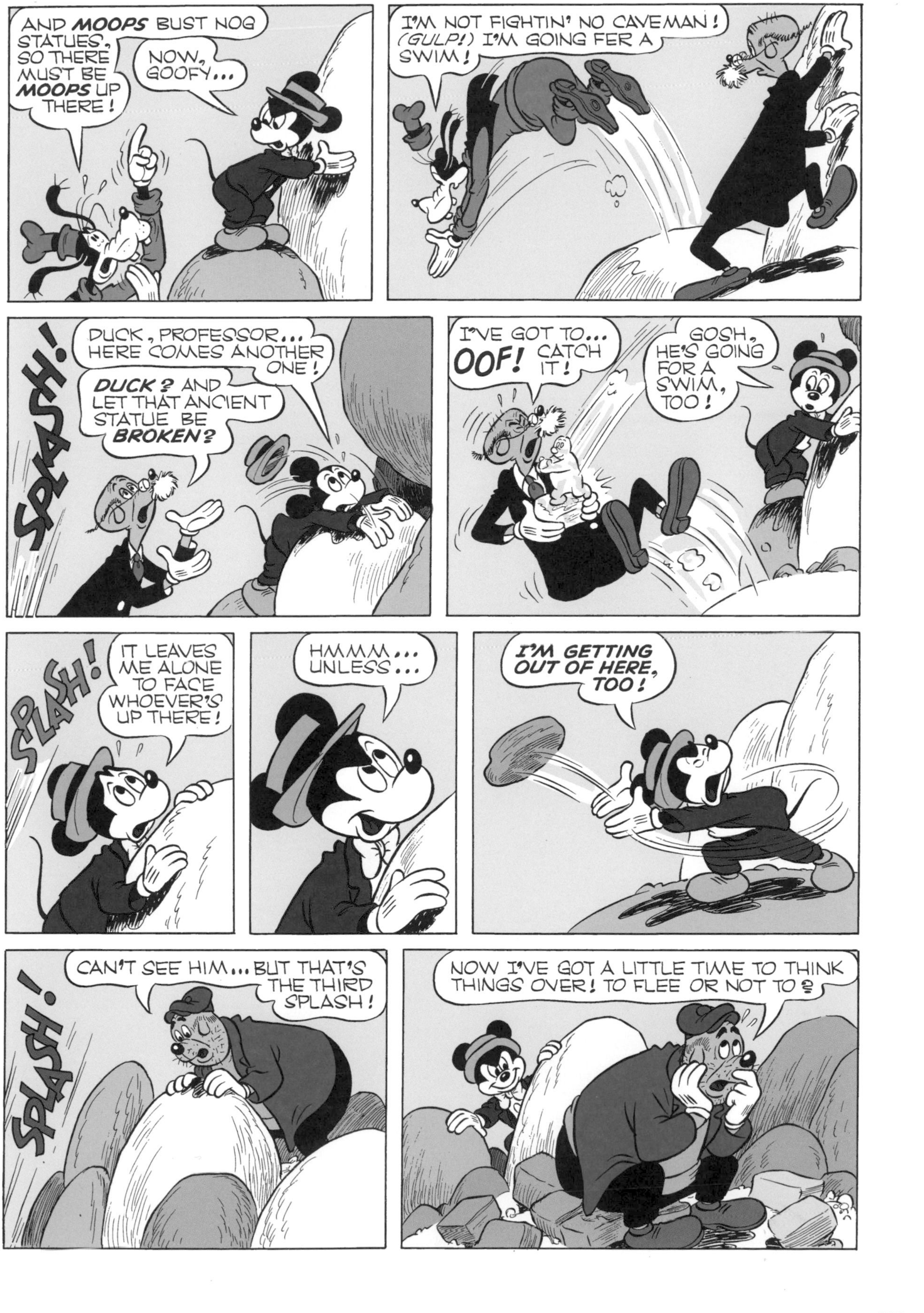
AND MOOPS BUST NOG STATUES, SO THERE MUST BE MOOPS UP THERE!
NOW, GOOFY...
I'M NOT FIGHTIN' NO CAVEMAN! (GULP!) I'M GOING FER A SWIM!
SPLASH!
DUCK, PROFESSOR... HERE COMES ANOTHER ONE!
DUCK? AND LET THAT ANCIENT STATUE BE BROKEN?
I'VE GOT TO... OOF! CATCH IT!
GOSH, HE'S GOING FOR A SWIM, TOO!
SPLASH!
IT LEAVES ME ALONE TO FACE WHOEVER'S UP THERE!
HMMM... UNLESS...
I'M GETTING OUT OF HERE, TOO!
SPLASH!
CAN'T SEE HIM... BUT THAT'S THE THIRD SPLASH!
NOW I'VE GOT A LITTLE TIME TO THINK THINGS OVER! TO FLEE OR NOT TO?

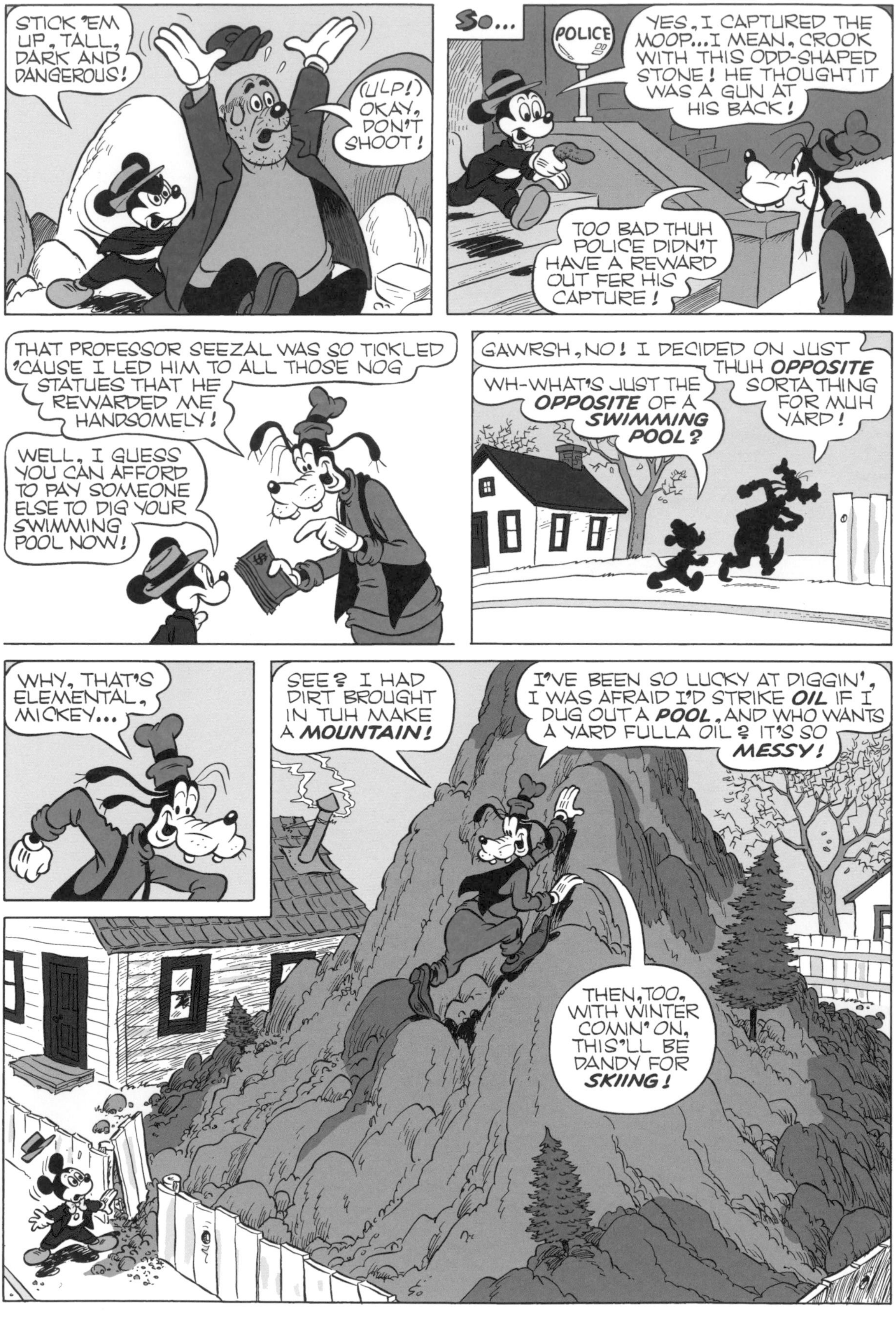

STICK 'EM UP, TALL, DARK AND DANGEROUS!
(ULP!) OKAY, DON'T SHOOT!
SO...
POLICE
YES, I CAPTURED THE MOOP... I MEAN, CROOK WITH THIS ODD-SHAPED STONE! HE THOUGHT IT WAS A GUN AT HIS BACK!
TOO BAD THUH POLICE DIDN'T HAVE A REWARD OUT FER HIS CAPTURE!
THAT PROFESSOR SEEZAL WAS SO TICKLED 'CAUSE I LED HIM TO ALL THOSE NOG STATUES THAT HE REWARDED ME HANDSOMELY!
WELL, I GUESS YOU CAN AFFORD TO PAY SOMEONE ELSE TO DIG YOUR SWIMMING POOL NOW!
GAWRSH, NO! I DECIDED ON JUST THUH OPPOSITE SORTA THING FOR MUH YARD!
WH-WHAT'S JUST THE OPPOSITE OF A SWIMMING POOL?
WHY, THAT'S ELEMENTAL, MICKEY...
SEE? I HAD DIRT BROUGHT IN TUH MAKE A MOUNTAIN!
I'VE BEEN SO LUCKY AT DIGGIN', I WAS AFRAID I'D STRIKE OIL IF I DUG OUT A POOL, AND WHO WANTS A YARD FULLA OIL? IT'S SO MESSY!
THEN, TOO, WITH WINTER COMIN' ON, THIS'LL BE DANDY FOR SKIING!

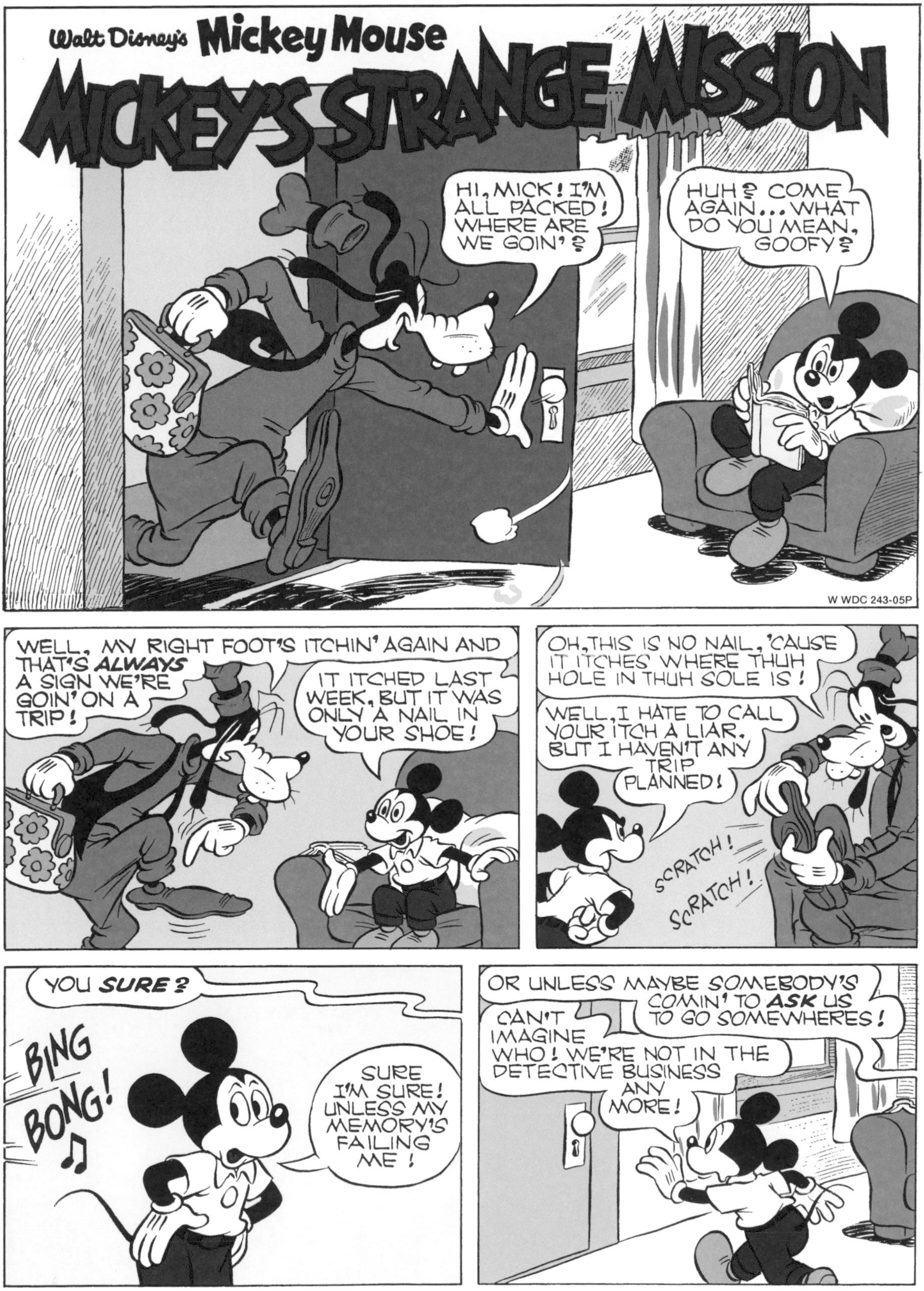

Walt Disney's Mickey Mouse
MICKEY'S STRANGE MISSION
HI, MICK! I'M ALL PACKED! WHERE ARE WE GOIN'?
HUH? COME AGAIN... WHAT DO YOU MEAN, GOOFY?
W WDC 243-05P
WELL, MY RIGHT FOOT'S ITCHIN' AGAIN AND THAT'S ALWAYS A SIGN WE'RE GOIN' ON A TRIP!
IT ITCHED LAST WEEK, BUT IT WAS ONLY A NAIL IN YOUR SHOE!
OH, THIS IS NO NAIL, 'CAUSE IT ITCHES WHERE THUH HOLE IN THUH SOLE IS!
WELL, I HATE TO CALL YOUR ITCH A LIAR, BUT I HAVEN'T ANY TRIP PLANNED!
SCRATCH! SCRATCH!
YOU SURE?
BING BONG!
SURE I'M SURE! UNLESS MY MEMORY'S FAILING ME!
OR UNLESS MAYBE SOMEBODY'S COMIN' TO ASK US TO GO SOMEWHERES!
CAN'T IMAGINE WHO! WE'RE NOT IN THE DETECTIVE BUSINESS ANY MORE!

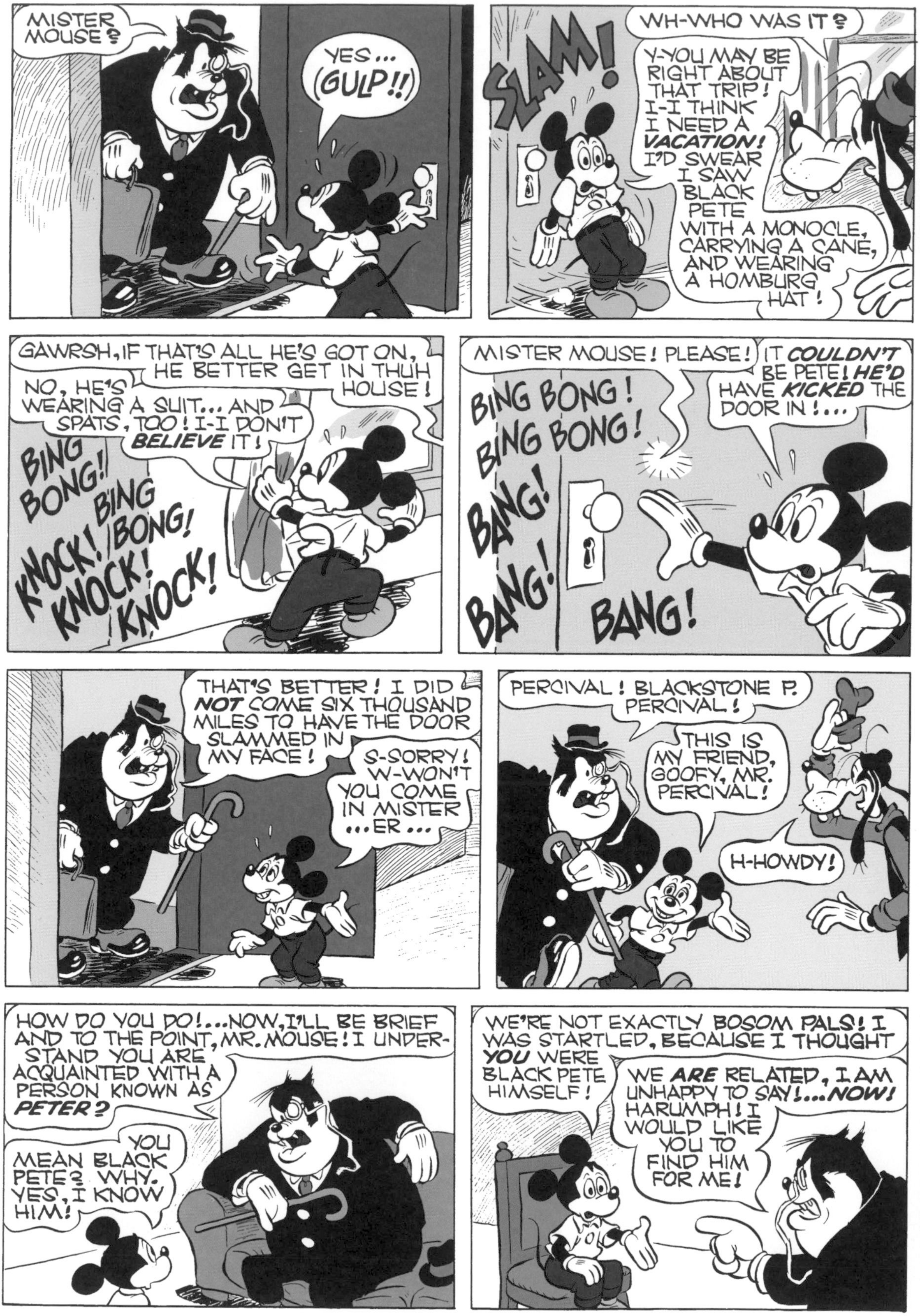
MISTER MOUSE?
YES... (GULP!!)
SLAM!
WH-WHO WAS IT?
Y-YOU MAY BE RIGHT ABOUT THAT TRIP! I-I THINK I NEED A VACATION! I'D SWEAR I SAW BLACK PETE WITH A MONOCLE, CARRYING A CANE, AND WEARING A HOMBURG HAT!
GAWRSH, IF THAT'S ALL HE'S GOT ON, HE BETTER GET IN THUH HOUSE!
NO, HE'S WEARING A SUIT... AND SPATS, TOO! I-I DON'T BELIEVE IT!
BING BONG!! BING BONG!
KNOCK! KNOCK! KNOCK!
MISTER MOUSE! PLEASE!
IT COULDN'T BE PETE! HE'D HAVE KICKED THE DOOR IN!...
BING BONG! BING BONG!
BANG! BANG! BANG!
THAT'S BETTER! I DID NOT COME SIX THOUSAND MILES TO HAVE THE DOOR SLAMMED IN MY FACE!
S-SORRY! W-WON'T YOU COME IN MISTER ...ER...
PERCIVAL! BLACKSTONE P. PERCIVAL!
THIS IS MY FRIEND, GOOFY, MR. PERCIVAL!
H-HOWDY!
HOW DO YOU DO!...NOW, I'LL BE BRIEF AND TO THE POINT, MR. MOUSE! I UNDERSTAND YOU ARE ACQUAINTED WITH A PERSON KNOWN AS PETER?
YOU MEAN BLACK PETE? WHY, YES, I KNOW HIM!
WE'RE NOT EXACTLY BOSOM PALS! I WAS STARTLED, BECAUSE I THOUGHT YOU WERE BLACK PETE HIMSELF!
WE ARE RELATED, I AM UNHAPPY TO SAY!...NOW! HARUMPH! I WOULD LIKE YOU TO FIND HIM FOR ME!

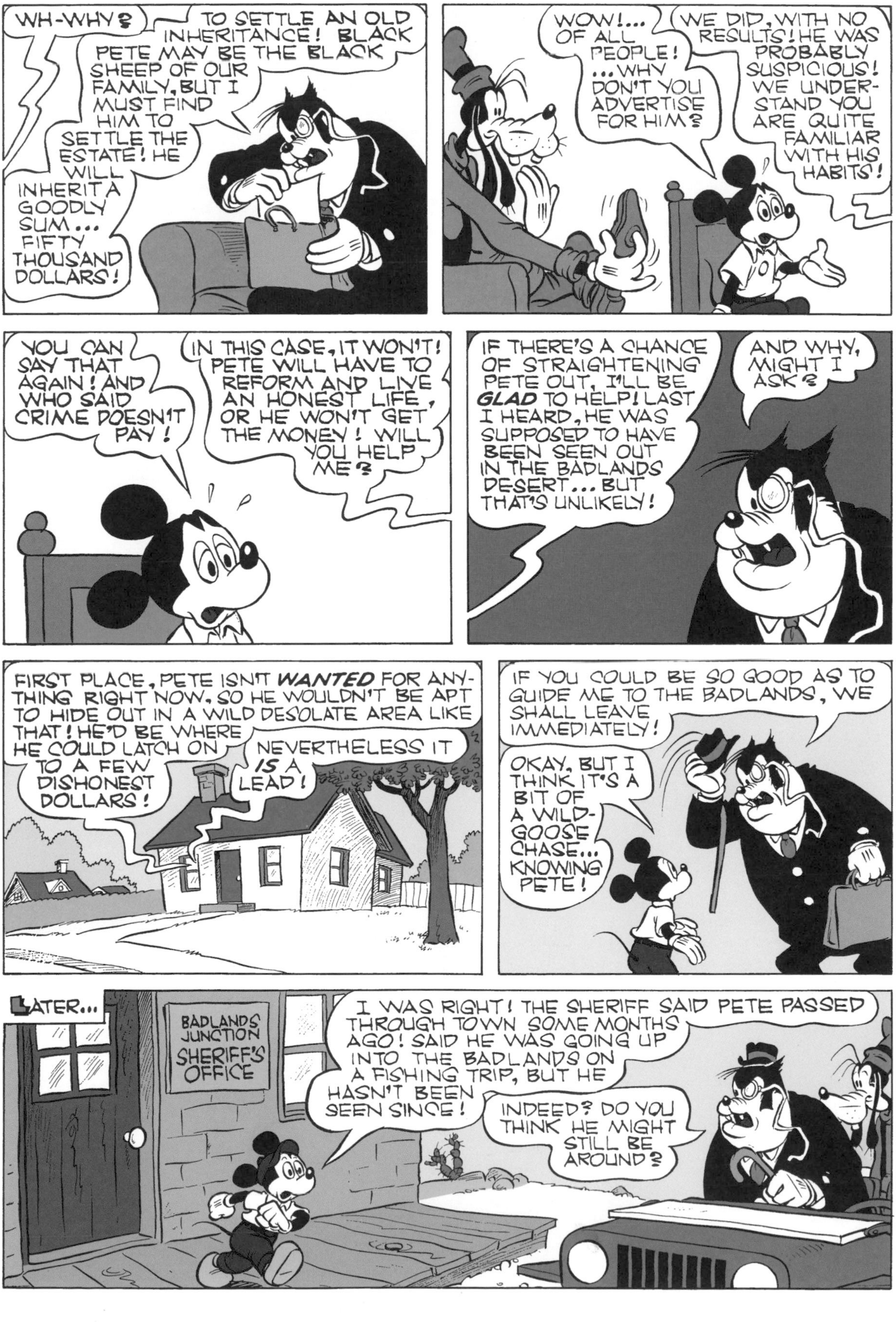

WH-WHY?
TO SETTLE AN OLD INHERITANCE! BLACK PETE MAY BE THE BLACK SHEEP OF OUR FAMILY, BUT I MUST FIND HIM TO SETTLE THE ESTATE! HE WILL INHERIT A GOODLY SUM... FIFTY THOUSAND DOLLARS!
WOW!... OF ALL PEOPLE! ...WHY DON'T YOU ADVERTISE FOR HIM?
WE DID, WITH NO RESULTS! HE WAS PROBABLY SUSPICIOUS! WE UNDERSTAND YOU ARE QUITE FAMILIAR WITH HIS HABITS!
YOU CAN SAY THAT AGAIN! AND WHO SAID CRIME DOESN'T PAY!
IN THIS CASE, IT WON'T! PETE WILL HAVE TO REFORM AND LIVE AN HONEST LIFE, OR HE WON'T GET THE MONEY! WILL YOU HELP ME?
IF THERE'S A CHANCE OF STRAIGHTENING PETE OUT, I'LL BE GLAD TO HELP! LAST I HEARD, HE WAS SUPPOSED TO HAVE BEEN SEEN OUT IN THE BADLANDS DESERT... BUT THAT'S UNLIKELY!
AND WHY, MIGHT I ASK?
FIRST PLACE, PETE ISN'T WANTED FOR ANYTHING RIGHT NOW, SO HE WOULDN'T BE APT TO HIDE OUT IN A WILD DESOLATE AREA LIKE THAT! HE'D BE WHERE HE COULD LATCH ON TO A FEW DISHONEST DOLLARS!
NEVERTHELESS IT IS A LEAD!
IF YOU COULD BE SO GOOD AS TO GUIDE ME TO THE BADLANDS, WE SHALL LEAVE IMMEDIATELY!
OKAY, BUT I THINK IT'S A BIT OF A WILD-GOOSE CHASE... KNOWING PETE!
LATER...
BADLANDS JUNCTION SHERIFF'S OFFICE
I WAS RIGHT! THE SHERIFF SAID PETE PASSED THROUGH TOWN SOME MONTHS AGO! SAID HE WAS GOING UP INTO THE BADLANDS ON A FISHING TRIP, BUT HE HASN'T BEEN SEEN SINCE!
INDEED? DO YOU THINK HE MIGHT STILL BE AROUND?

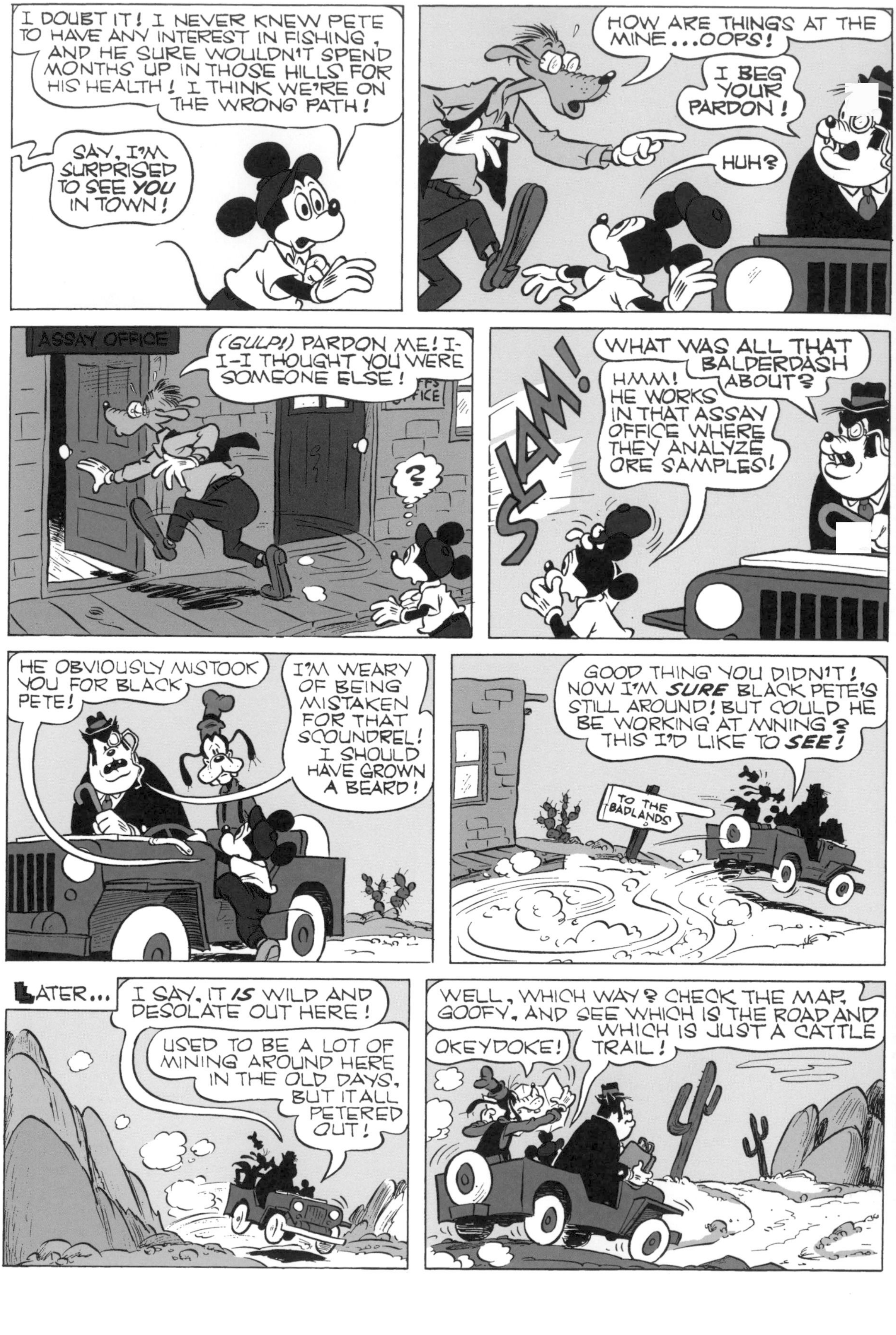
I DOUBT IT! I NEVER KNEW PETE TO HAVE ANY INTEREST IN FISHING, AND HE SURE WOULDN'T SPEND MONTHS UP IN THOSE HILLS FOR HIS HEALTH! I THINK WE'RE ON THE WRONG PATH!
SAY, I'M SURPRISED TO SEE YOU IN TOWN!
HOW ARE THINGS AT THE MINE...OOPS!
I BEG YOUR PARDON!
HUH?
ASSAY OFFICE
(GULP!) PARDON ME! I-I-I THOUGHT YOU WERE SOMEONE ELSE!
?
SLAM!
WHAT WAS ALL THAT BALDERDASH ABOUT?
HMM! HE WORKS IN THAT ASSAY OFFICE WHERE THEY ANALYZE ORE SAMPLES!
HE OBVIOUSLY MISTOOK YOU FOR BLACK PETE!
I'M WEARY OF BEING MISTAKEN FOR THAT SCOUNDREL! I SHOULD HAVE GROWN A BEARD!
GOOD THING YOU DIDN'T! NOW I'M SURE BLACK PETE'S STILL AROUND! BUT COULD HE BE WORKING AT MINING? THIS I'D LIKE TO SEE!
TO THE BADLANDS
LATER...
I SAY, IT IS WILD AND DESOLATE OUT HERE!
USED TO BE A LOT OF MINING AROUND HERE IN THE OLD DAYS, BUT IT ALL PETERED OUT!
WELL, WHICH WAY? CHECK THE MAP, GOOFY, AND SEE WHICH IS THE ROAD AND WHICH IS JUST A CATTLE TRAIL!
OKEYDOKE!

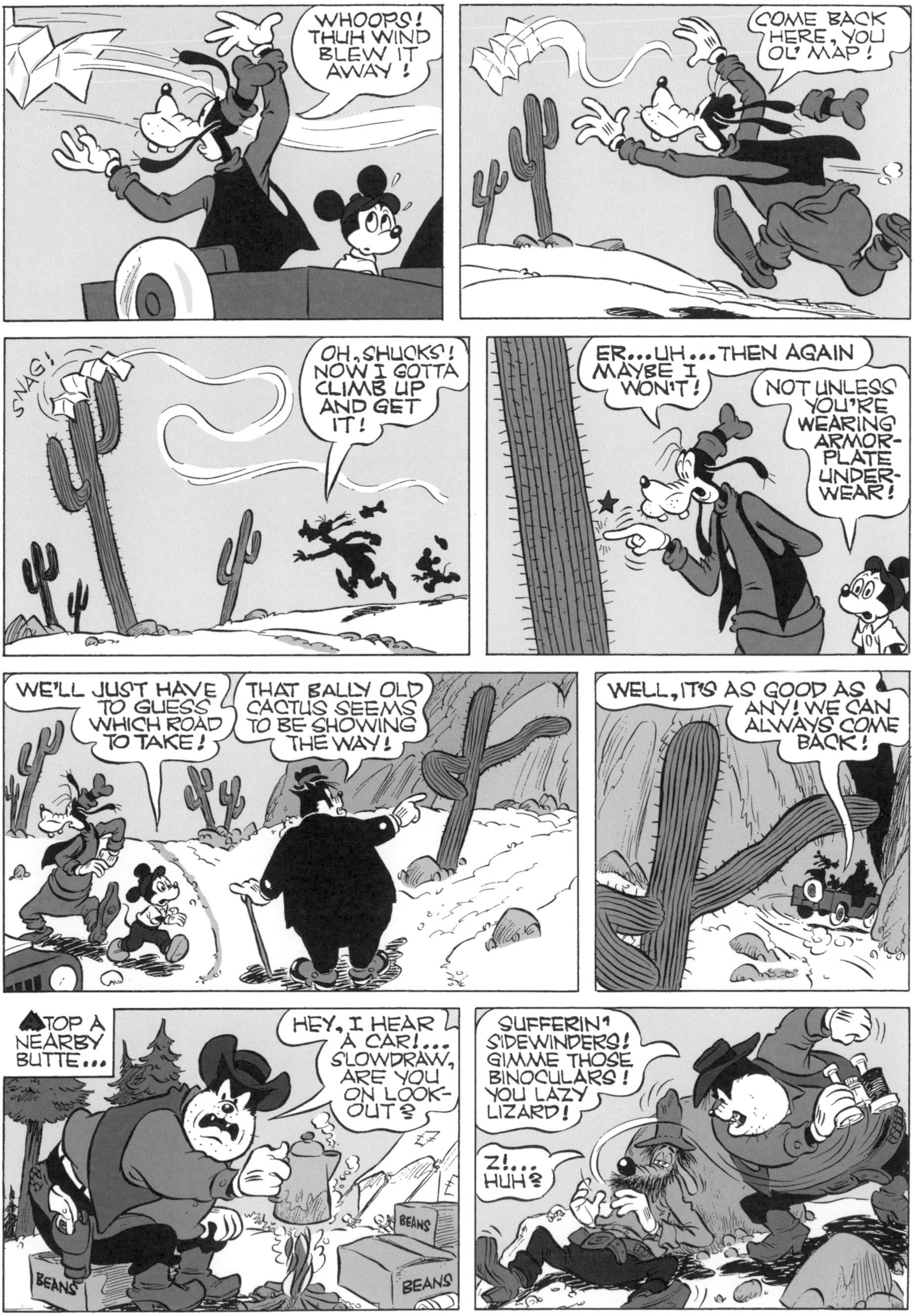
WHOOPS! THUH WIND BLEW IT AWAY!
COME BACK HERE, YOU OL' MAP!
SNAG!
OH, SHUCKS! NOW I GOTTA CLIMB UP AND GET IT!
ER...UH...THEN AGAIN MAYBE I WON'T!
NOT UNLESS YOU'RE WEARING ARMOR-PLATE UNDER-WEAR!
WE'LL JUST HAVE TO GUESS WHICH ROAD TO TAKE!
THAT BALLY OLD CACTUS SEEMS TO BE SHOWING THE WAY!
WELL, IT'S AS GOOD AS ANY! WE CAN ALWAYS COME BACK!
ATOP A NEARBY BUTTE...
HEY, I HEAR A CAR!... SLOWDRAW, ARE YOU ON LOOK-OUT?
BEANS
BEANS
BEANS
SUFFERIN' SIDEWINDERS! GIMME THOSE BINOCULARS! YOU LAZY LIZARD!
Z!... HUH?

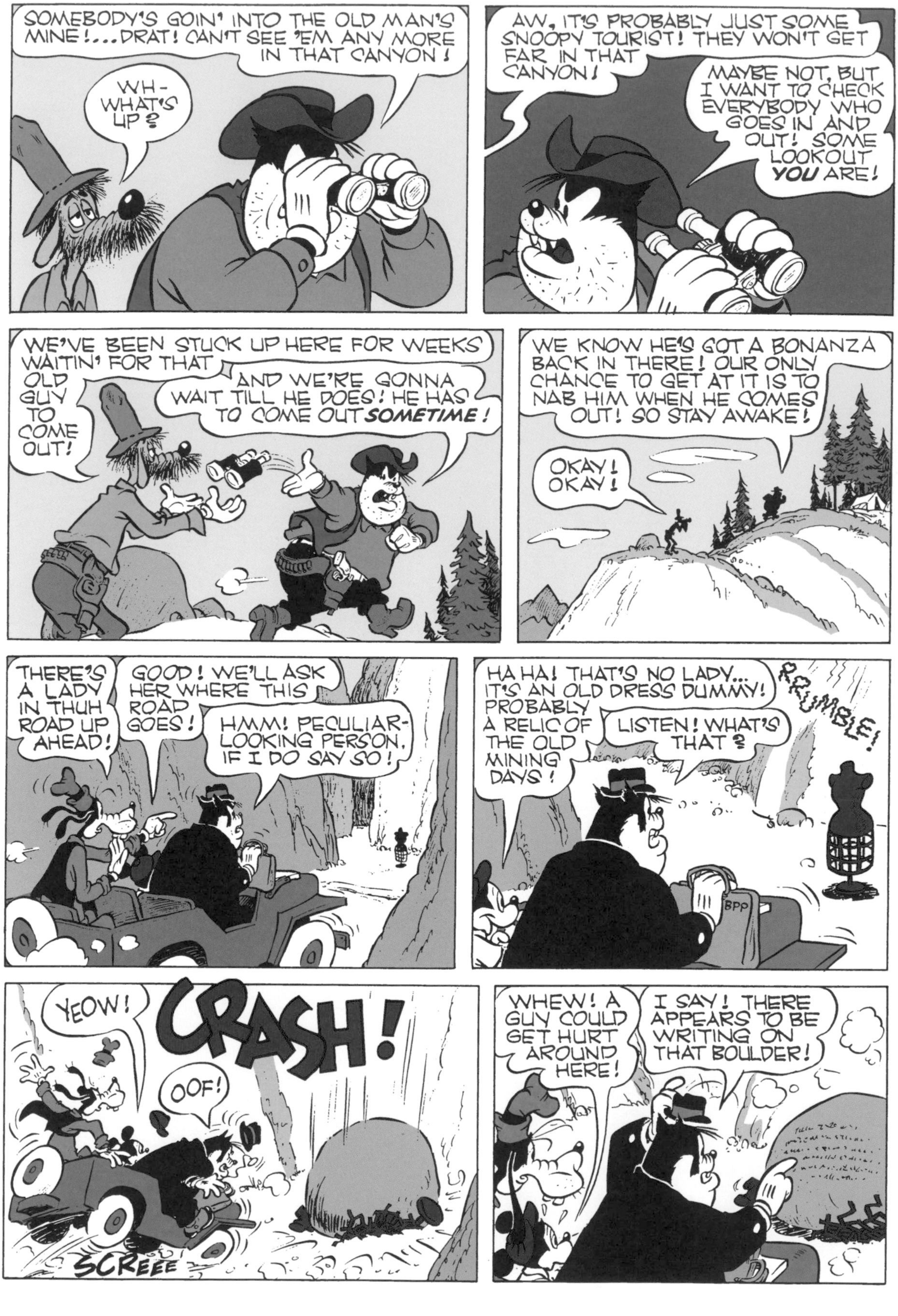
SOMEBODY'S GOIN' INTO THE OLD MAN'S MINE! ... DRAT! CAN'T SEE 'EM ANY MORE IN THAT CANYON!
WH-WHAT'S UP?
AW, IT'S PROBABLY JUST SOME SNOOPY TOURIST! THEY WON'T GET FAR IN THAT CANYON!
MAYBE NOT, BUT I WANT TO CHECK EVERYBODY WHO GOES IN AND OUT! SOME LOOKOUT YOU ARE!
WE'VE BEEN STUCK UP HERE FOR WEEKS WAITIN' FOR THAT OLD GUY TO COME OUT!
AND WE'RE GONNA WAIT TILL HE DOES! HE HAS TO COME OUT SOMETIME!
WE KNOW HE'S GOT A BONANZA BACK IN THERE! OUR ONLY CHANCE TO GET AT IT IS TO NAB HIM WHEN HE COMES OUT! SO STAY AWAKE!
OKAY! OKAY!
THERE'S A LADY IN THUH ROAD UP AHEAD!
GOOD! WE'LL ASK HER WHERE THIS ROAD GOES!
HMM! PECULIAR-LOOKING PERSON, IF I DO SAY SO!
HA HA! THAT'S NO LADY... IT'S AN OLD DRESS DUMMY! PROBABLY A RELIC OF THE OLD MINING DAYS!
RRUMBLE!
LISTEN! WHAT'S THAT?
BPP
YEOW!
CRASH!
OOF!
SCREEE
WHEW! A GUY COULD GET HURT AROUND HERE!
I SAY! THERE APPEARS TO BE WRITING ON THAT BOULDER!

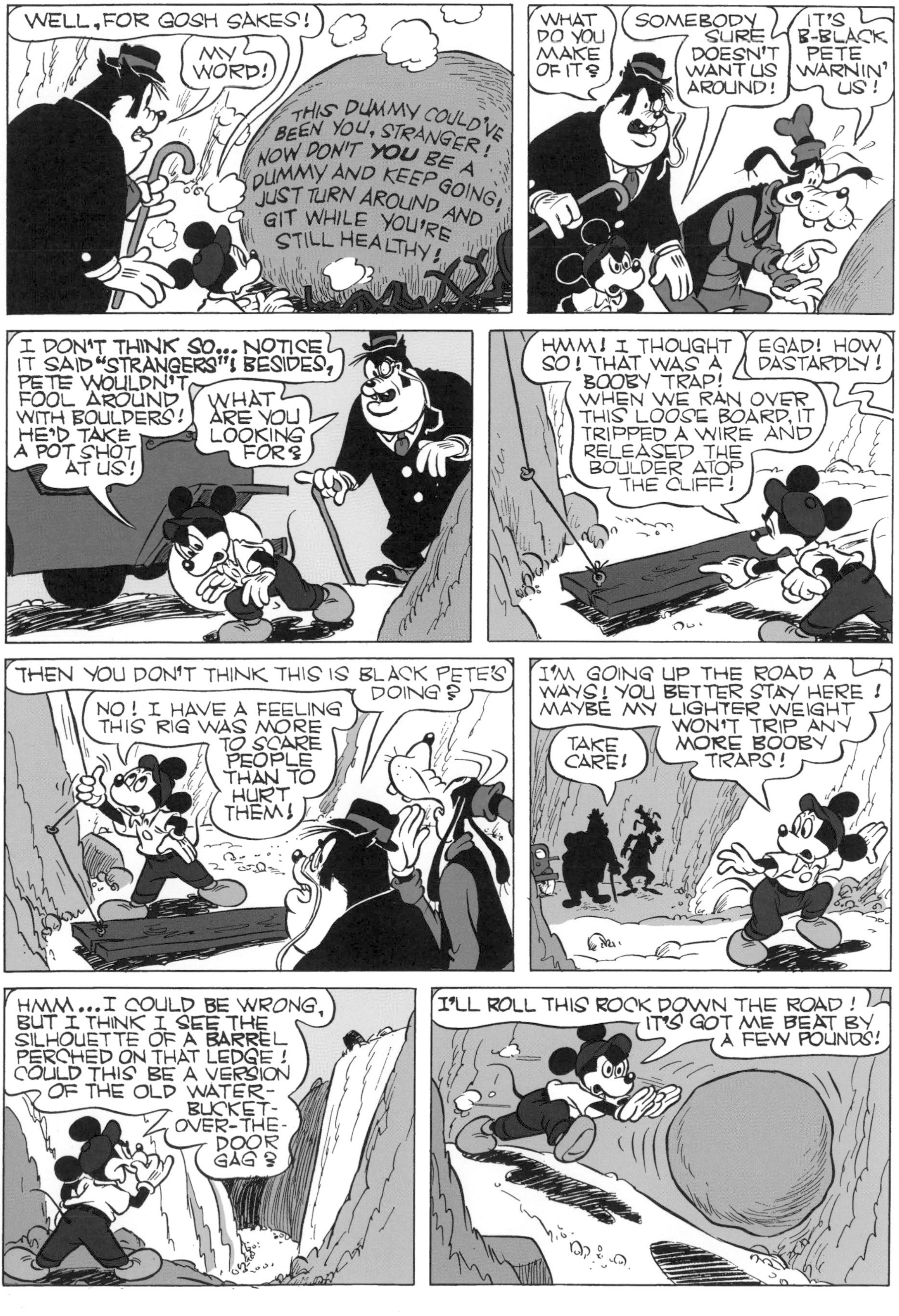
WELL, FOR GOSH SAKES!
MY WORD!
THIS DUMMY COULD'VE BEEN YOU, STRANGER! NOW DON'T YOU BE A DUMMY AND KEEP GOING! JUST TURN AROUND AND GIT WHILE YOU'RE STILL HEALTHY!
WHAT DO YOU MAKE OF IT?
SOMEBODY SURE DOESN'T WANT US AROUND!
IT'S B-BLACK PETE WARNIN' US!
I DON'T THINK SO... NOTICE IT SAID "STRANGERS"! BESIDES, PETE WOULDN'T FOOL AROUND WITH BOULDERS! HE'D TAKE A POT SHOT AT US!
WHAT ARE YOU LOOKING FOR?
HMM! I THOUGHT SO! THAT WAS A BOOBY TRAP! WHEN WE RAN OVER THIS LOOSE BOARD, IT TRIPPED A WIRE AND RELEASED THE BOULDER ATOP THE CLIFF!
EGAD! HOW DASTARDLY!
THEN YOU DON'T THINK THIS IS BLACK PETE'S DOING?
NO! I HAVE A FEELING THIS RIG WAS MORE TO SCARE PEOPLE THAN TO HURT THEM!
I'M GOING UP THE ROAD A WAYS! YOU BETTER STAY HERE! MAYBE MY LIGHTER WEIGHT WON'T TRIP ANY MORE BOOBY TRAPS!
TAKE CARE!
HMM... I COULD BE WRONG, BUT I THINK I SEE THE SILHOUETTE OF A BARREL PERCHED ON THAT LEDGE! COULD THIS BE A VERSION OF THE OLD WATER-BUCKET-OVER-THE-DOOR GAG?
I'LL ROLL THIS ROCK DOWN THE ROAD! IT'S GOT ME BEAT BY A FEW POUNDS!

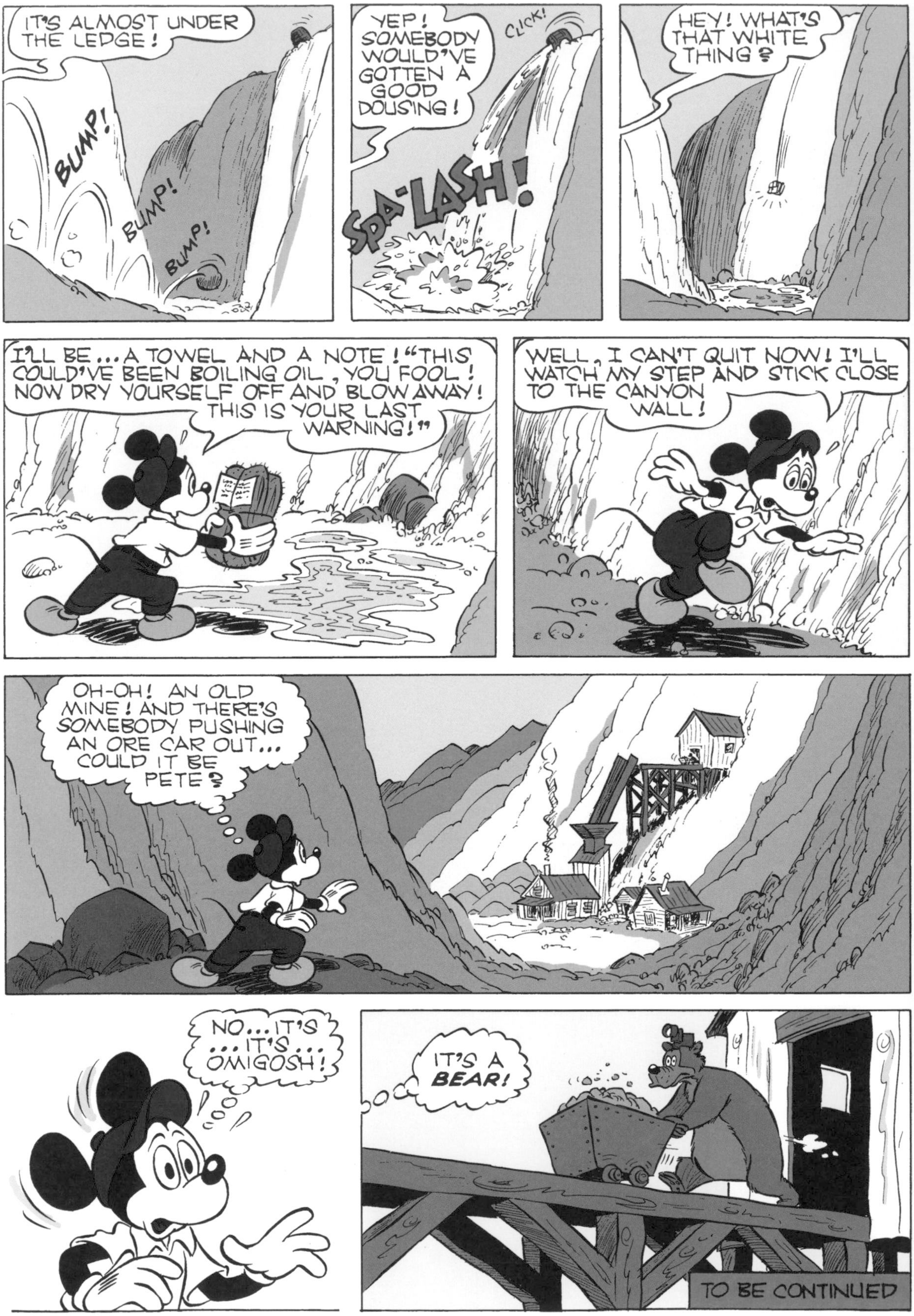
IT'S ALMOST UNDER THE LEDGE!
BUMP!
BUMP!
BUMP!
YEP! SOMEBODY WOULD'VE GOTTEN A GOOD DOUSING!
CLICK!
SPA-LASH!
HEY! WHAT'S THAT WHITE THING?
I'LL BE... A TOWEL AND A NOTE! "THIS COULD'VE BEEN BOILING OIL, YOU FOOL! NOW DRY YOURSELF OFF AND BLOW AWAY! THIS IS YOUR LAST WARNING!"
WELL, I CAN'T QUIT NOW! I'LL WATCH MY STEP AND STICK CLOSE TO THE CANYON WALL!
OH-OH! AN OLD MINE! AND THERE'S SOMEBODY PUSHING AN ORE CAR OUT... COULD IT BE PETE?
NO... IT'S ... IT'S ... OMIGOSH!
IT'S A BEAR!
TO BE CONTINUED

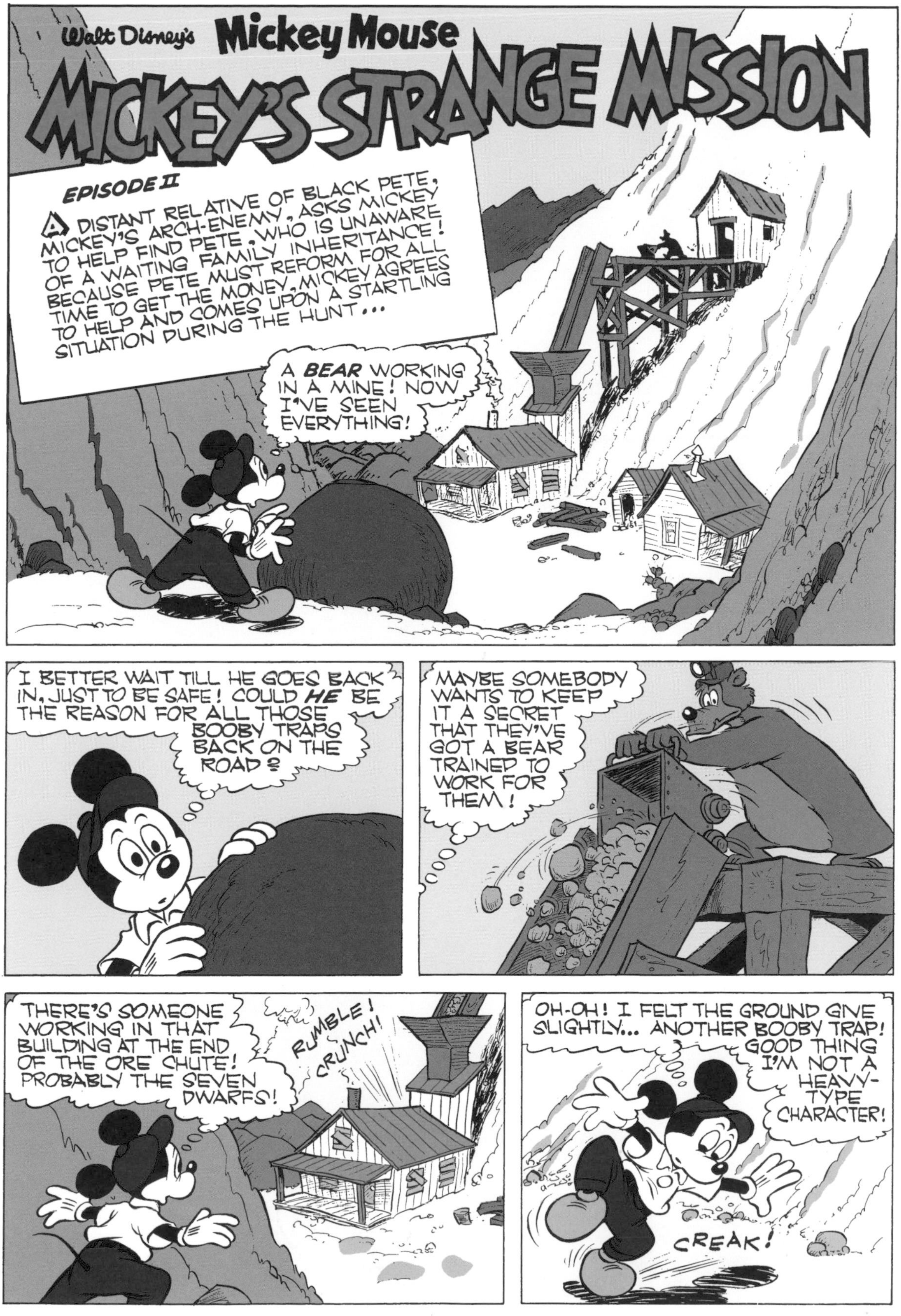
Walt Disney's Mickey Mouse
MICKEY'S STRANGE MISSION
EPISODE II
A DISTANT RELATIVE OF BLACK PETE, MICKEY'S ARCH-ENEMY, ASKS MICKEY TO HELP FIND PETE, WHO IS UNAWARE OF A WAITING FAMILY INHERITANCE! BECAUSE PETE MUST REFORM FOR ALL TIME TO GET THE MONEY, MICKEY AGREES TO HELP AND COMES UPON A STARTLING SITUATION DURING THE HUNT...
A BEAR WORKING IN A MINE! NOW I'VE SEEN EVERYTHING!
I BETTER WAIT TILL HE GOES BACK IN, JUST TO BE SAFE! COULD HE BE THE REASON FOR ALL THOSE BOOBY TRAPS BACK ON THE ROAD?
MAYBE SOMEBODY WANTS TO KEEP IT A SECRET THAT THEY'VE GOT A BEAR TRAINED TO WORK FOR THEM!
THERE'S SOMEONE WORKING IN THAT BUILDING AT THE END OF THE ORE CHUTE! PROBABLY THE SEVEN DWARFS!
RUMBLE!
CRUNCH!
OH-OH! I FELT THE GROUND GIVE SLIGHTLY... ANOTHER BOOBY TRAP! GOOD THING I'M NOT A HEAVY-TYPE CHARACTER!
CREAK!

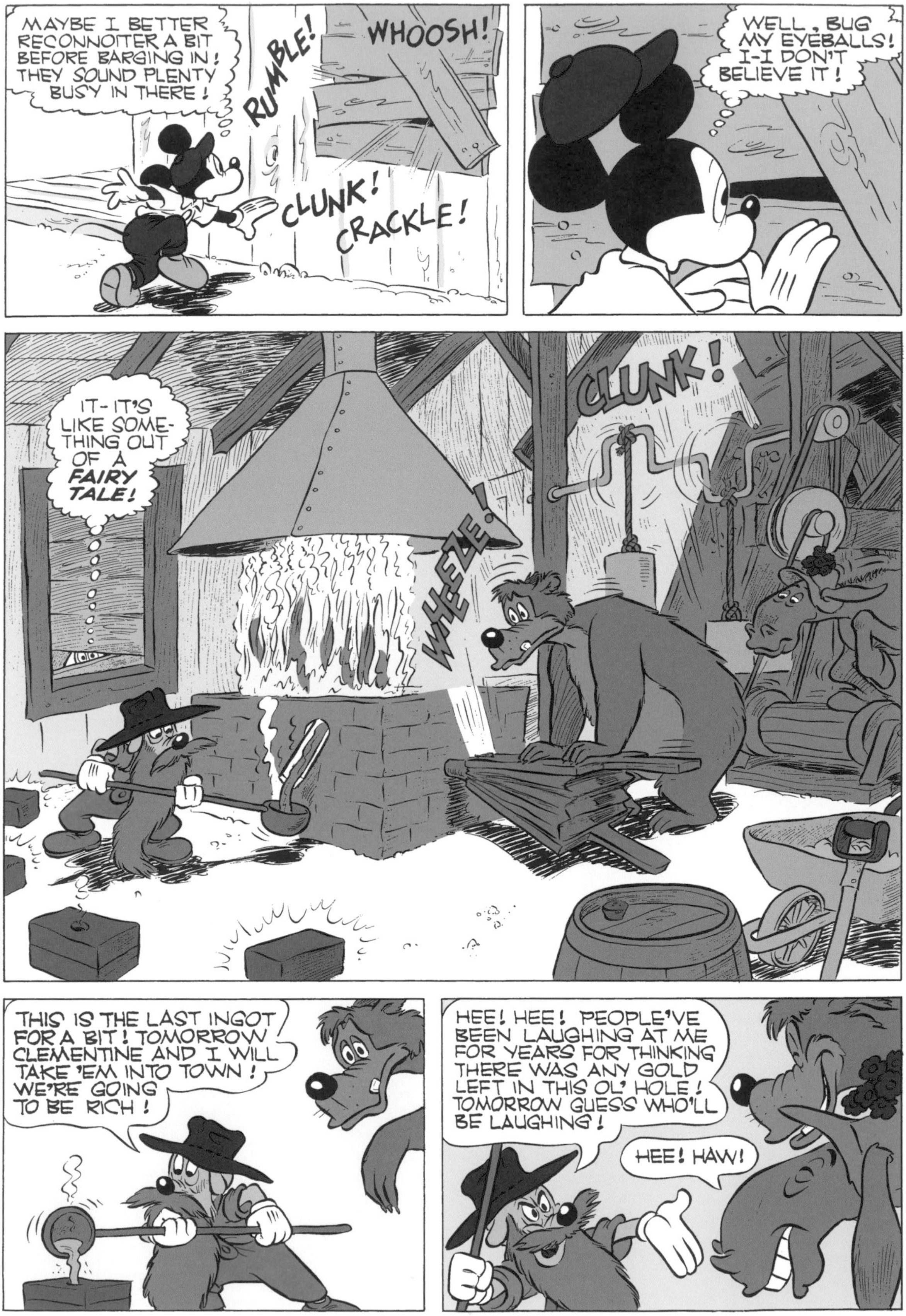
MAYBE I BETTER RECONNOITER A BIT BEFORE BARGING IN! THEY SOUND PLENTY BUSY IN THERE!
RUMBLE!
WHOOSH!
CLUNK!
CRACKLE!
WELL, BUG MY EYEBALLS! I-I DON'T BELIEVE IT!
IT-IT'S LIKE SOMETHING OUT OF A FAIRY TALE!
CLUNK!
WHEEZE!
THIS IS THE LAST INGOT FOR A BIT! TOMORROW CLEMENTINE AND I WILL TAKE 'EM INTO TOWN! WE'RE GOING TO BE RICH!
HEE! HEE! PEOPLE'VE BEEN LAUGHING AT ME FOR YEARS FOR THINKING THERE WAS ANY GOLD LEFT IN THIS OL' HOLE! TOMORROW GUESS WHO'LL BE LAUGHING!
HEE! HAW!

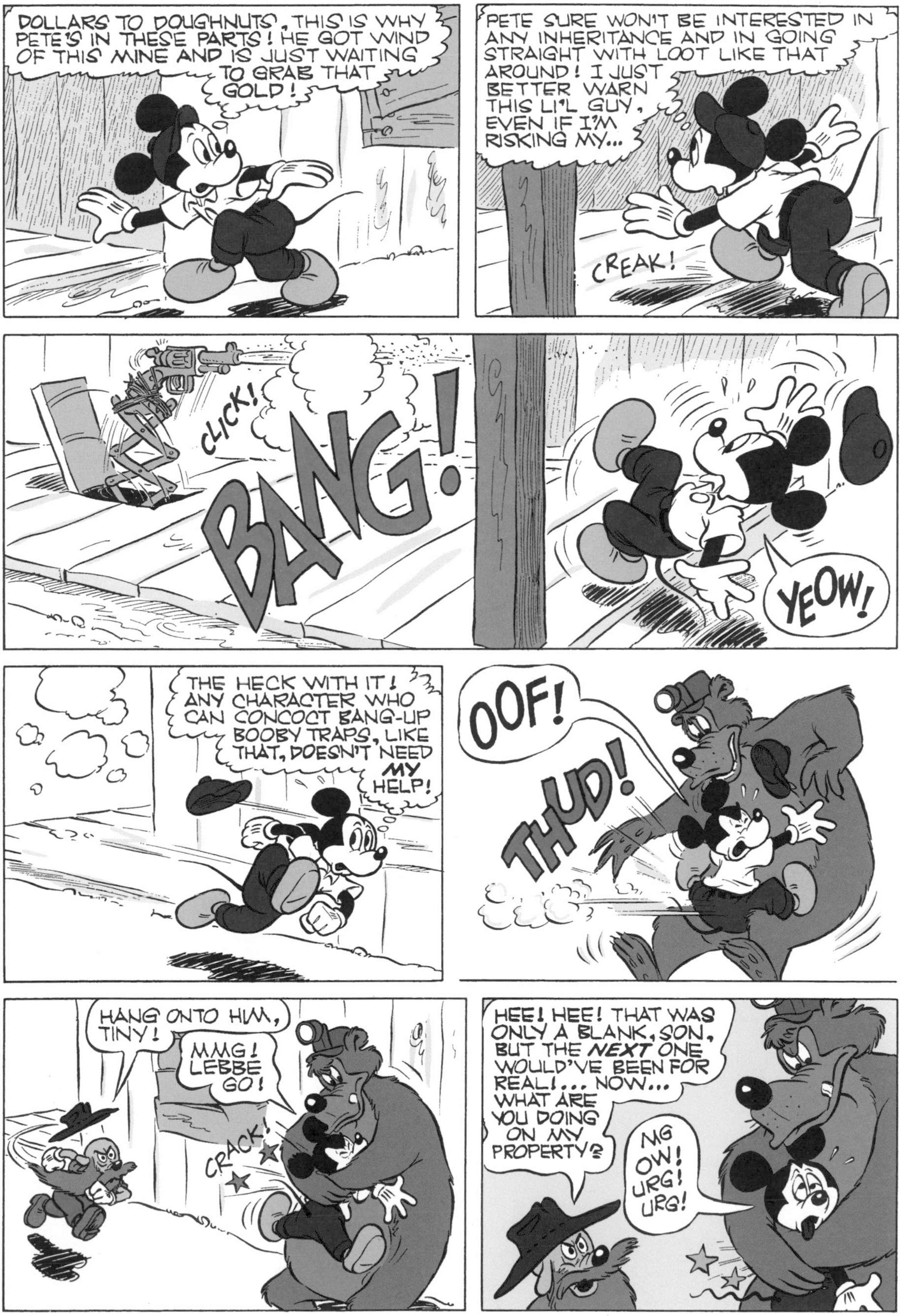
DOLLARS TO DOUGHNUTS, THIS IS WHY PETE'S IN THESE PARTS! HE GOT WIND OF THIS MINE AND IS JUST WAITING TO GRAB THAT GOLD!
PETE SURE WON'T BE INTERESTED IN ANY INHERITANCE AND IN GOING STRAIGHT WITH LOOT LIKE THAT AROUND! I JUST BETTER WARN THIS LI'L GUY, EVEN IF I'M RISKING MY...
CREAK!
CLICK!
BANG!
YEOW!
THE HECK WITH IT! ANY CHARACTER WHO CAN CONCOCT BANG-UP BOOBY TRAPS, LIKE THAT, DOESN'T NEED MY HELP!
OOF!
THUD!
HANG ONTO HIM, TINY!
MMG! LEBBE GO!
CRACK!
HEE! HEE! THAT WAS ONLY A BLANK, SON, BUT THE NEXT ONE WOULD'VE BEEN FOR REAL!... NOW... WHAT ARE YOU DOING ON MY PROPERTY?
MG OW! URG! URG!

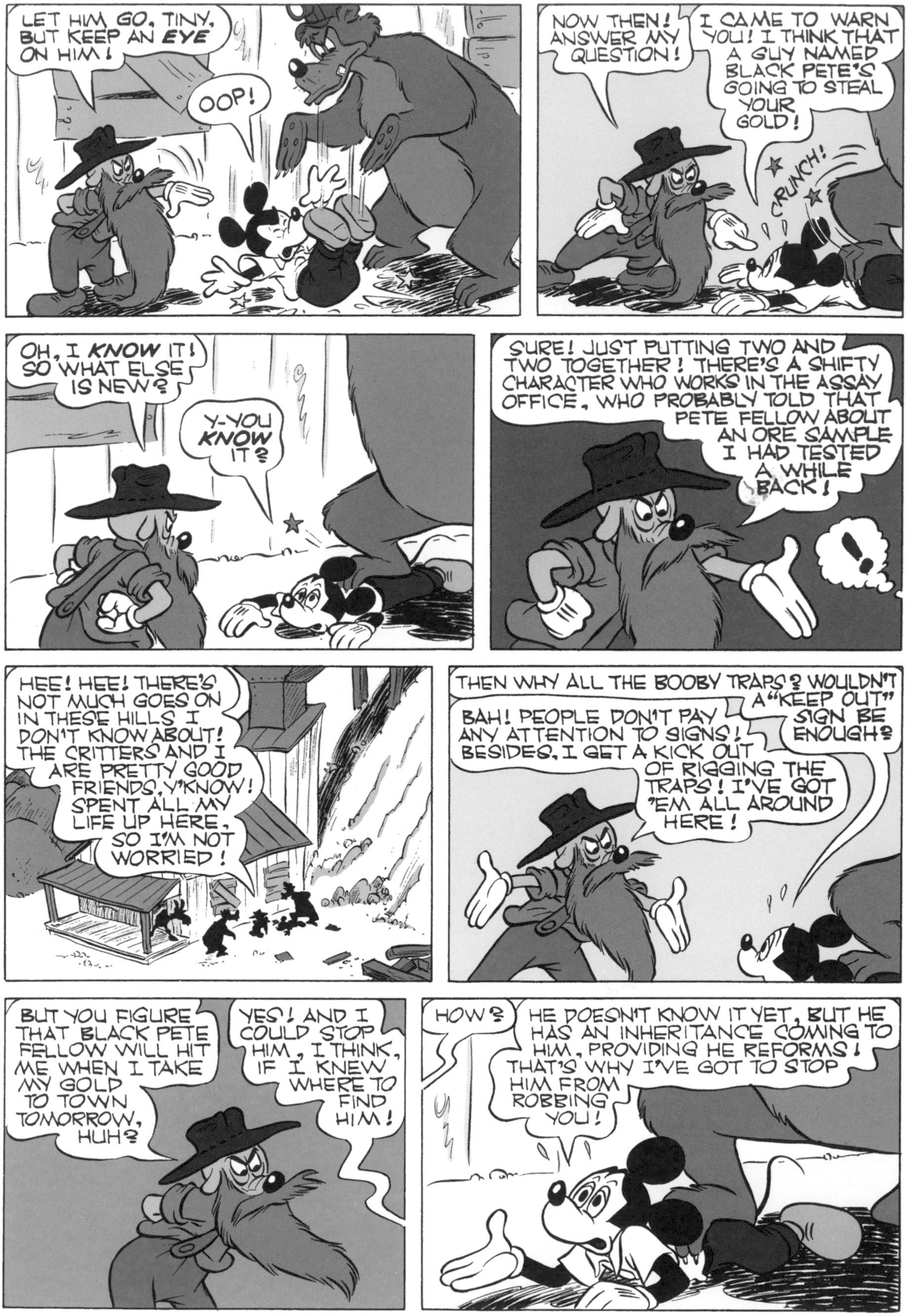
LET HIM GO, TINY, BUT KEEP AN *EYE* ON HIM!
OOP!
NOW THEN! ANSWER MY QUESTION!
I CAME TO WARN YOU! I THINK THAT A GUY NAMED BLACK PETE'S GOING TO STEAL YOUR GOLD!
CRUNCH!
OH, I *KNOW* IT! SO WHAT ELSE IS NEW?
Y-YOU *KNOW* IT?
SURE! JUST PUTTING TWO AND TWO TOGETHER! THERE'S A SHIFTY CHARACTER WHO WORKS IN THE ASSAY OFFICE, WHO PROBABLY TOLD THAT PETE FELLOW ABOUT AN ORE SAMPLE I HAD TESTED A WHILE BACK!
!
HEE! HEE! THERE'S NOT MUCH GOES ON IN THESE HILLS I DON'T KNOW ABOUT! THE CRITTERS AND I ARE PRETTY GOOD FRIENDS, Y'KNOW! SPENT ALL MY LIFE UP HERE, SO I'M NOT WORRIED!
THEN WHY ALL THE BOOBY TRAPS? WOULDN'T A "KEEP OUT" SIGN BE ENOUGH?
BAH! PEOPLE DON'T PAY ANY ATTENTION TO SIGNS! BESIDES, I GET A KICK OUT OF RIGGING THE TRAPS! I'VE GOT 'EM ALL AROUND HERE!
BUT YOU FIGURE THAT BLACK PETE FELLOW WILL HIT ME WHEN I TAKE MY GOLD TO TOWN TOMORROW, HUH?
YES! AND I COULD STOP HIM, I THINK, IF I KNEW WHERE TO FIND HIM!
HOW?
HE DOESN'T KNOW IT YET, BUT HE HAS AN INHERITANCE COMING TO HIM, PROVIDING HE REFORMS! THAT'S WHY I'VE GOT TO STOP HIM FROM ROBBING YOU!

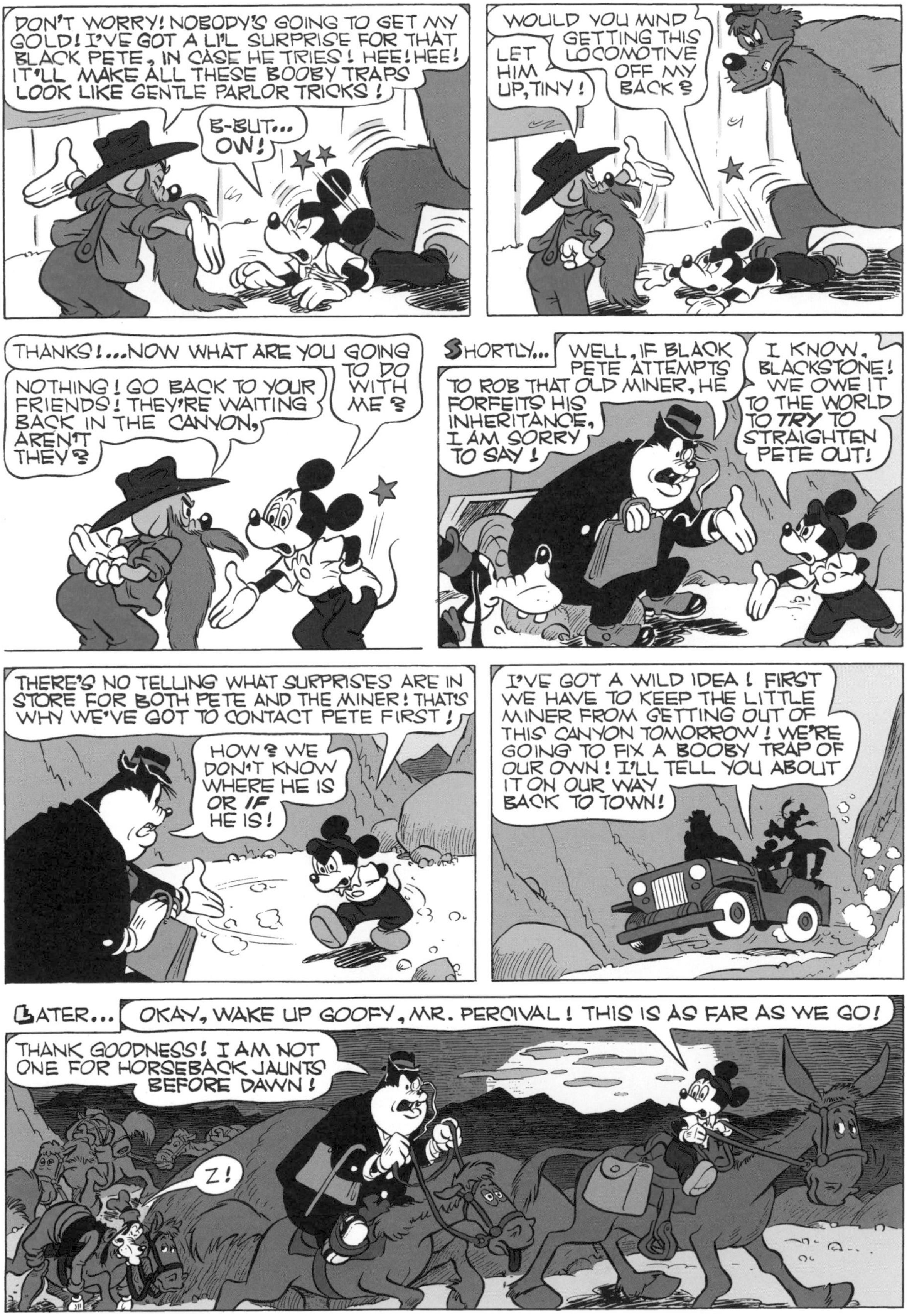
DON'T WORRY! NOBODY'S GOING TO GET MY GOLD! I'VE GOT A LI'L SURPRISE FOR THAT BLACK PETE, IN CASE HE TRIES! HEE! HEE! IT'LL MAKE ALL THESE BOOBY TRAPS LOOK LIKE GENTLE PARLOR TRICKS!
B-BUT... OW!
WOULD YOU MIND GETTING THIS LOCOMOTIVE OFF MY BACK?
LET HIM UP, TINY!
THANKS! ...NOW WHAT ARE YOU GOING TO DO WITH ME?
NOTHING! GO BACK TO YOUR FRIENDS! THEY'RE WAITING BACK IN THE CANYON, AREN'T THEY?
SHORTLY...
WELL, IF BLACK PETE ATTEMPTS TO ROB THAT OLD MINER, HE FORFEITS HIS INHERITANCE, I AM SORRY TO SAY!
I KNOW, BLACKSTONE! WE OWE IT TO THE WORLD TO TRY TO STRAIGHTEN PETE OUT!
THERE'S NO TELLING WHAT SURPRISES ARE IN STORE FOR BOTH PETE AND THE MINER! THAT'S WHY WE'VE GOT TO CONTACT PETE FIRST!
HOW? WE DON'T KNOW WHERE HE IS OR IF HE IS!
I'VE GOT A WILD IDEA! FIRST WE HAVE TO KEEP THE LITTLE MINER FROM GETTING OUT OF THIS CANYON TOMORROW! WE'RE GOING TO FIX A BOOBY TRAP OF OUR OWN! I'LL TELL YOU ABOUT IT ON OUR WAY BACK TO TOWN!
LATER...
OKAY, WAKE UP GOOFY, MR. PERCIVAL! THIS IS AS FAR AS WE GO!
THANK GOODNESS! I AM NOT ONE FOR HORSEBACK JAUNTS BEFORE DAWN!
Z!

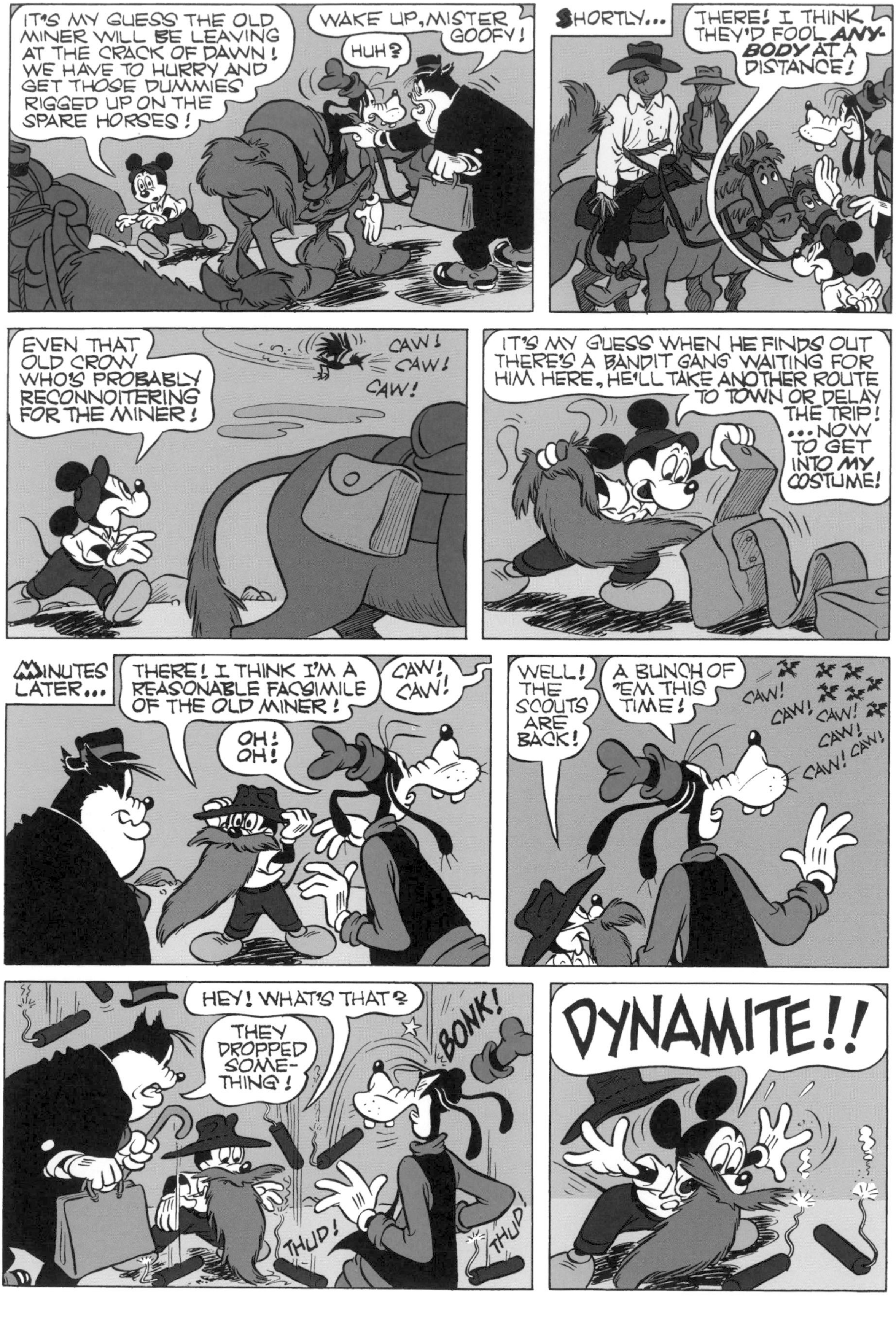
IT'S MY GUESS THE OLD MINER WILL BE LEAVING AT THE CRACK OF DAWN! WE HAVE TO HURRY AND GET THOSE DUMMIES RIGGED UP ON THE SPARE HORSES!
WAKE UP, MISTER GOOFY!
HUH?
SHORTLY...
THERE! I THINK THEY'D FOOL ANY-BODY AT A DISTANCE!
EVEN THAT OLD CROW WHO'S PROBABLY RECONNOITERING FOR THE MINER!
CAW! CAW! CAW!
IT'S MY GUESS WHEN HE FINDS OUT THERE'S A BANDIT GANG WAITING FOR HIM HERE, HE'LL TAKE ANOTHER ROUTE TO TOWN OR DELAY THE TRIP! ...NOW TO GET INTO MY COSTUME!
MINUTES LATER...
THERE! I THINK I'M A REASONABLE FACSIMILE OF THE OLD MINER!
CAW! CAW!
OH! OH!
WELL! THE SCOUTS ARE BACK!
A BUNCH OF 'EM THIS TIME!
CAW! CAW! CAW! CAW! CAW! CAW!
HEY! WHAT'S THAT?
THEY DROPPED SOME-THING!
BONK!
THUD!
THUD!
DYNAMITE!!

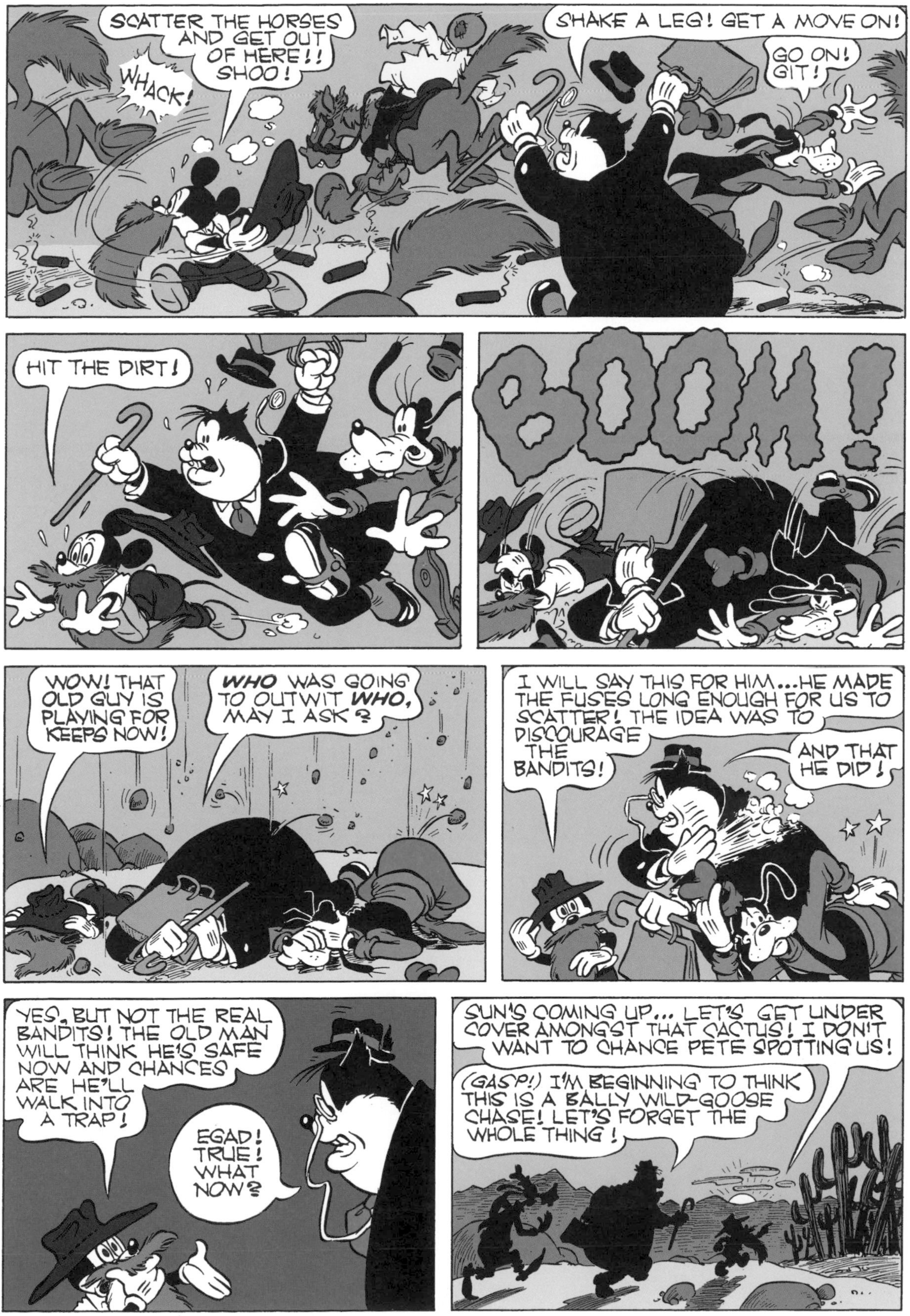

SCATTER THE HORSES AND GET OUT OF HERE!! SHOO!
WHACK!
SHAKE A LEG! GET A MOVE ON!
GO ON! GIT!
HIT THE DIRT!
BOOM!
WOW! THAT OLD GUY IS PLAYING FOR KEEPS NOW!
WHO WAS GOING TO OUTWIT WHO, MAY I ASK?
I WILL SAY THIS FOR HIM... HE MADE THE FUSES LONG ENOUGH FOR US TO SCATTER! THE IDEA WAS TO DISCOURAGE THE BANDITS!
AND THAT HE DID!
YES, BUT NOT THE REAL BANDITS! THE OLD MAN WILL THINK HE'S SAFE NOW AND CHANCES ARE HE'LL WALK INTO A TRAP!
EGAD! TRUE! WHAT NOW?
SUN'S COMING UP... LET'S GET UNDER COVER AMONGST THAT CACTUS! I DON'T WANT TO CHANCE PETE SPOTTING US!
(GASP!) I'M BEGINNING TO THINK THIS IS A BALLY WILD-GOOSE CHASE! LET'S FORGET THE WHOLE THING!

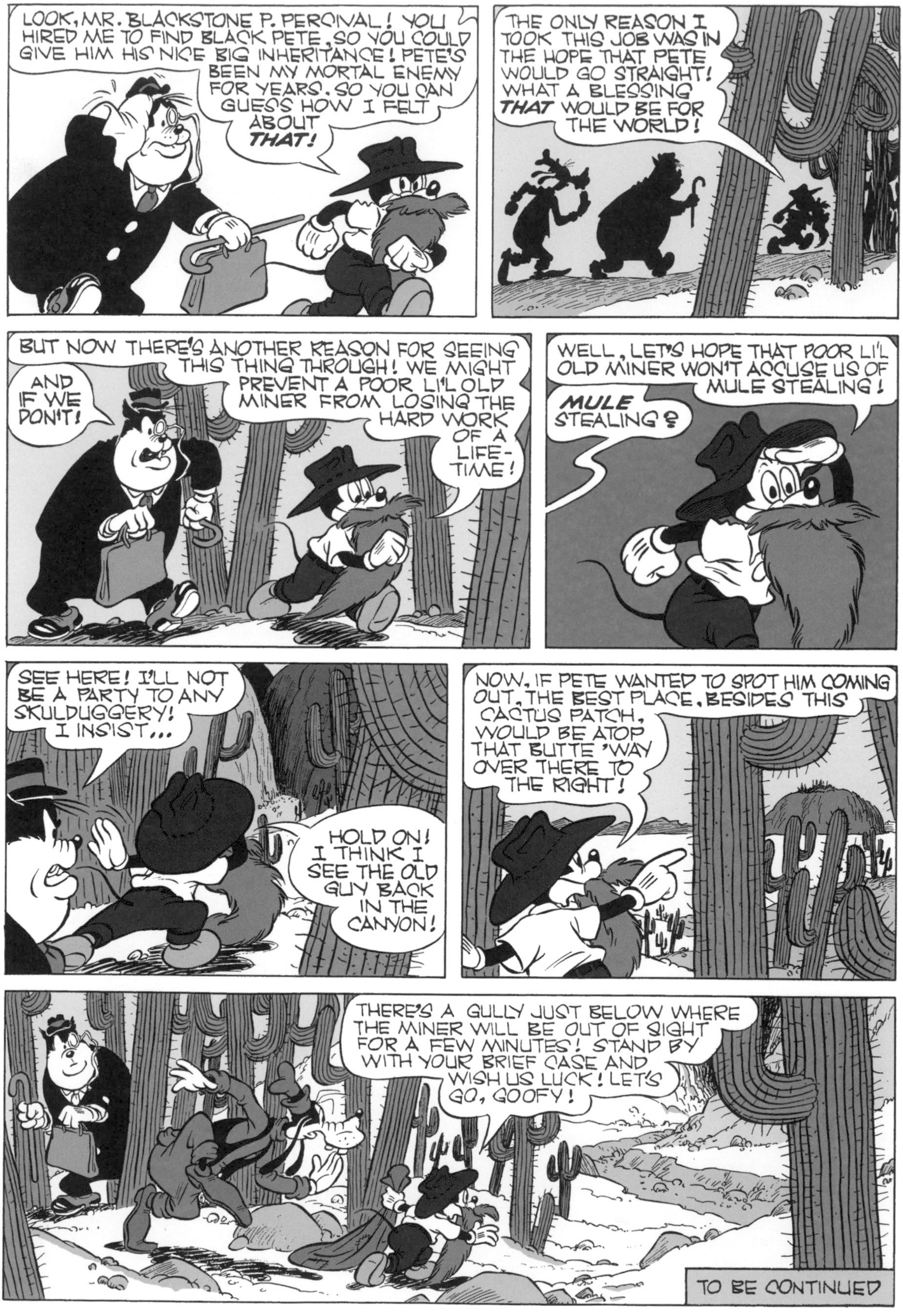
LOOK, MR. BLACKSTONE P. PERCIVAL! YOU HIRED ME TO FIND BLACK PETE, SO YOU COULD GIVE HIM HIS NICE BIG INHERITANCE! PETE'S BEEN MY MORTAL ENEMY FOR YEARS. SO YOU CAN GUESS HOW I FELT ABOUT THAT!
THE ONLY REASON I TOOK THIS JOB WAS IN THE HOPE THAT PETE WOULD GO STRAIGHT! WHAT A BLESSING THAT WOULD BE FOR THE WORLD!
BUT NOW THERE'S ANOTHER REASON FOR SEEING THIS THING THROUGH! WE MIGHT PREVENT A POOR LI'L OLD MINER FROM LOSING THE HARD WORK OF A LIFE-TIME!
AND IF WE DON'T!
WELL, LET'S HOPE THAT POOR LI'L OLD MINER WON'T ACCUSE US OF MULE STEALING!
MULE STEALING?
SEE HERE! I'LL NOT BE A PARTY TO ANY SKULDUGGERY! I INSIST...
HOLD ON! I THINK I SEE THE OLD GUY BACK IN THE CANYON!
NOW, IF PETE WANTED TO SPOT HIM COMING OUT, THE BEST PLACE, BESIDES THIS CACTUS PATCH, WOULD BE ATOP THAT BUTTE 'WAY OVER THERE TO THE RIGHT!
THERE'S A GULLY JUST BELOW WHERE THE MINER WILL BE OUT OF SIGHT FOR A FEW MINUTES! STAND BY WITH YOUR BRIEF CASE AND WISH US LUCK! LET'S GO, GOOFY!
TO BE CONTINUED

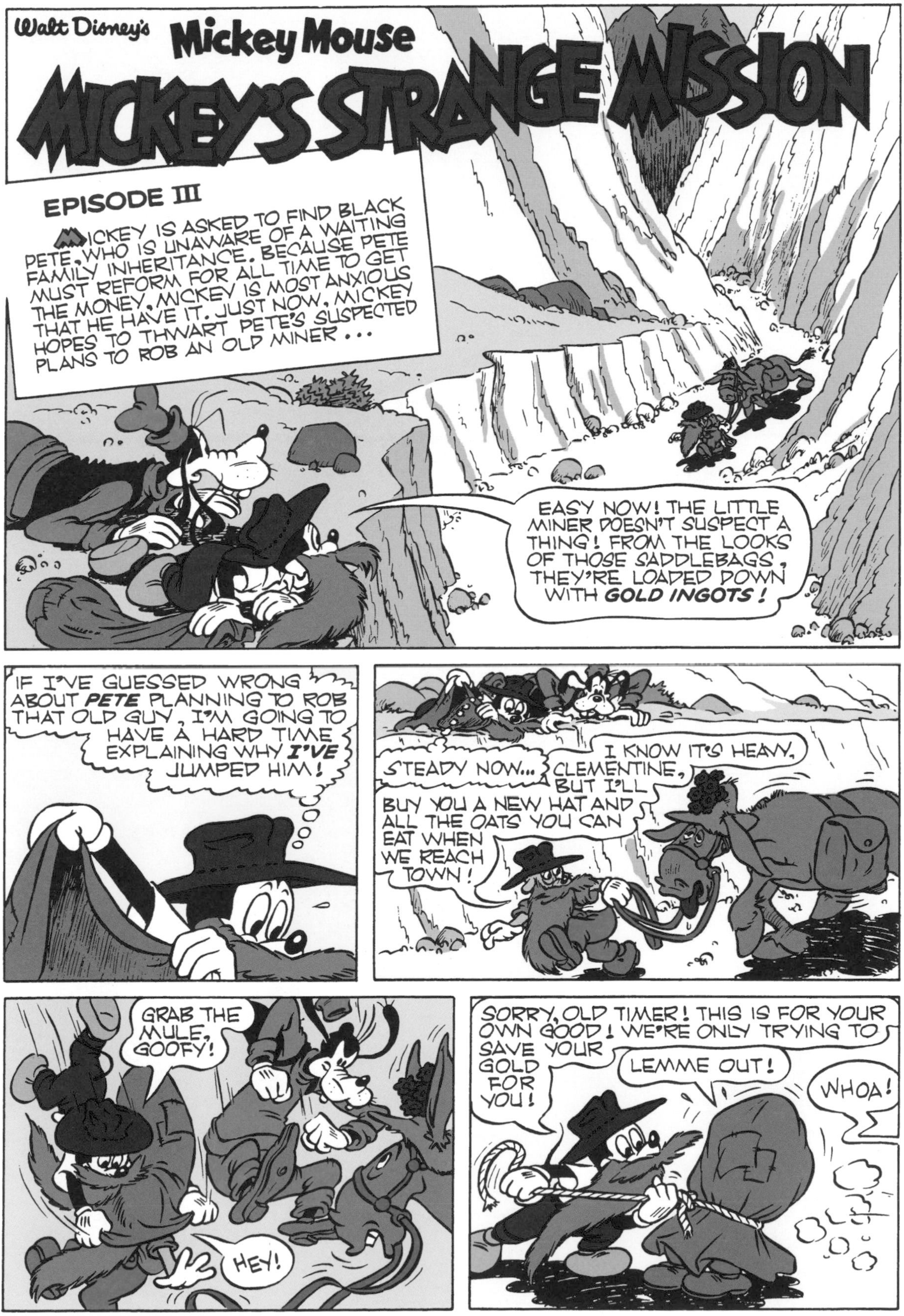

Walt Disney's Mickey Mouse
MICKEY'S STRANGE MISSION
EPISODE III
MICKEY IS ASKED TO FIND BLACK PETE, WHO IS UNAWARE OF A WAITING FAMILY INHERITANCE. BECAUSE PETE MUST REFORM FOR ALL TIME TO GET THE MONEY, MICKEY IS MOST ANXIOUS THAT HE HAVE IT. JUST NOW, MICKEY HOPES TO THWART PETE'S SUSPECTED PLANS TO ROB AN OLD MINER . . .
EASY NOW! THE LITTLE MINER DOESN'T SUSPECT A THING! FROM THE LOOKS OF THOSE SADDLEBAGS, THEY'RE LOADED DOWN WITH GOLD INGOTS!
IF I'VE GUESSED WRONG ABOUT PETE PLANNING TO ROB THAT OLD GUY, I'M GOING TO HAVE A HARD TIME EXPLAINING WHY I'VE JUMPED HIM!
STEADY NOW...
I KNOW IT'S HEAVY, CLEMENTINE, BUT I'LL BUY YOU A NEW HAT AND ALL THE OATS YOU CAN EAT WHEN WE REACH TOWN!
GRAB THE MULE, GOOFY!
HEY!
SORRY, OLD TIMER! THIS IS FOR YOUR OWN GOOD! WE'RE ONLY TRYING TO SAVE YOUR GOLD FOR YOU!
LEMME OUT!
WHOA!

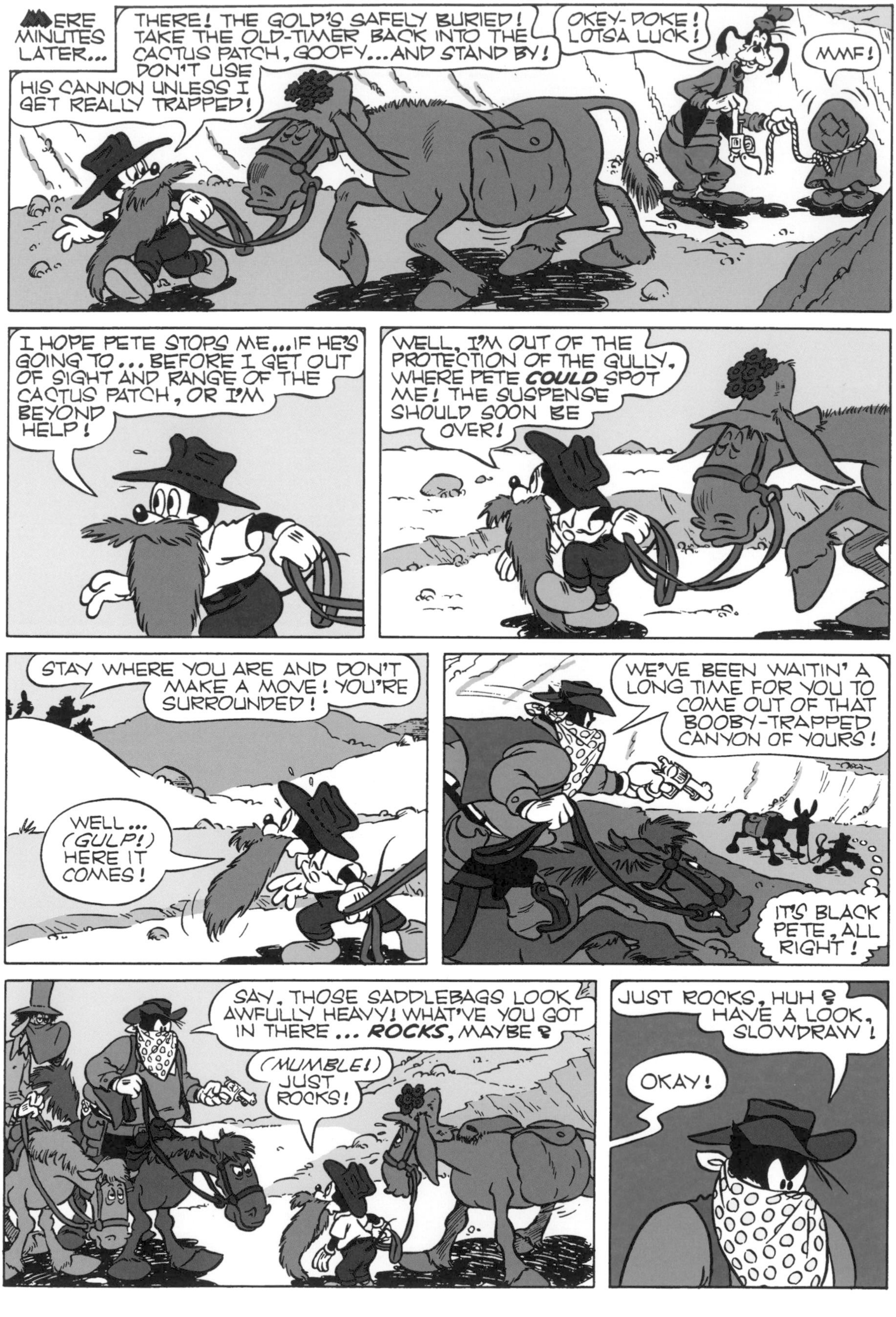
MERE MINUTES LATER...
THERE! THE GOLD'S SAFELY BURIED! TAKE THE OLD-TIMER BACK INTO THE CACTUS PATCH, GOOFY... AND STAND BY! DON'T USE HIS CANNON UNLESS I GET REALLY TRAPPED!
OKEY-DOKE! LOTSA LUCK!
MMF!
I HOPE PETE STOPS ME... IF HE'S GOING TO... BEFORE I GET OUT OF SIGHT AND RANGE OF THE CACTUS PATCH, OR I'M BEYOND HELP!
WELL, I'M OUT OF THE PROTECTION OF THE GULLY, WHERE PETE COULD SPOT ME! THE SUSPENSE SHOULD SOON BE OVER!
STAY WHERE YOU ARE AND DON'T MAKE A MOVE! YOU'RE SURROUNDED!
WELL... (GULP!) HERE IT COMES!
WE'VE BEEN WAITIN' A LONG TIME FOR YOU TO COME OUT OF THAT BOOBY-TRAPPED CANYON OF YOURS!
IT'S BLACK PETE, ALL RIGHT!
SAY, THOSE SADDLEBAGS LOOK AWFULLY HEAVY! WHAT'VE YOU GOT IN THERE... ROCKS, MAYBE?
(MUMBLE!) JUST ROCKS!
JUST ROCKS, HUH? HAVE A LOOK, SLOWDRAW!
OKAY!

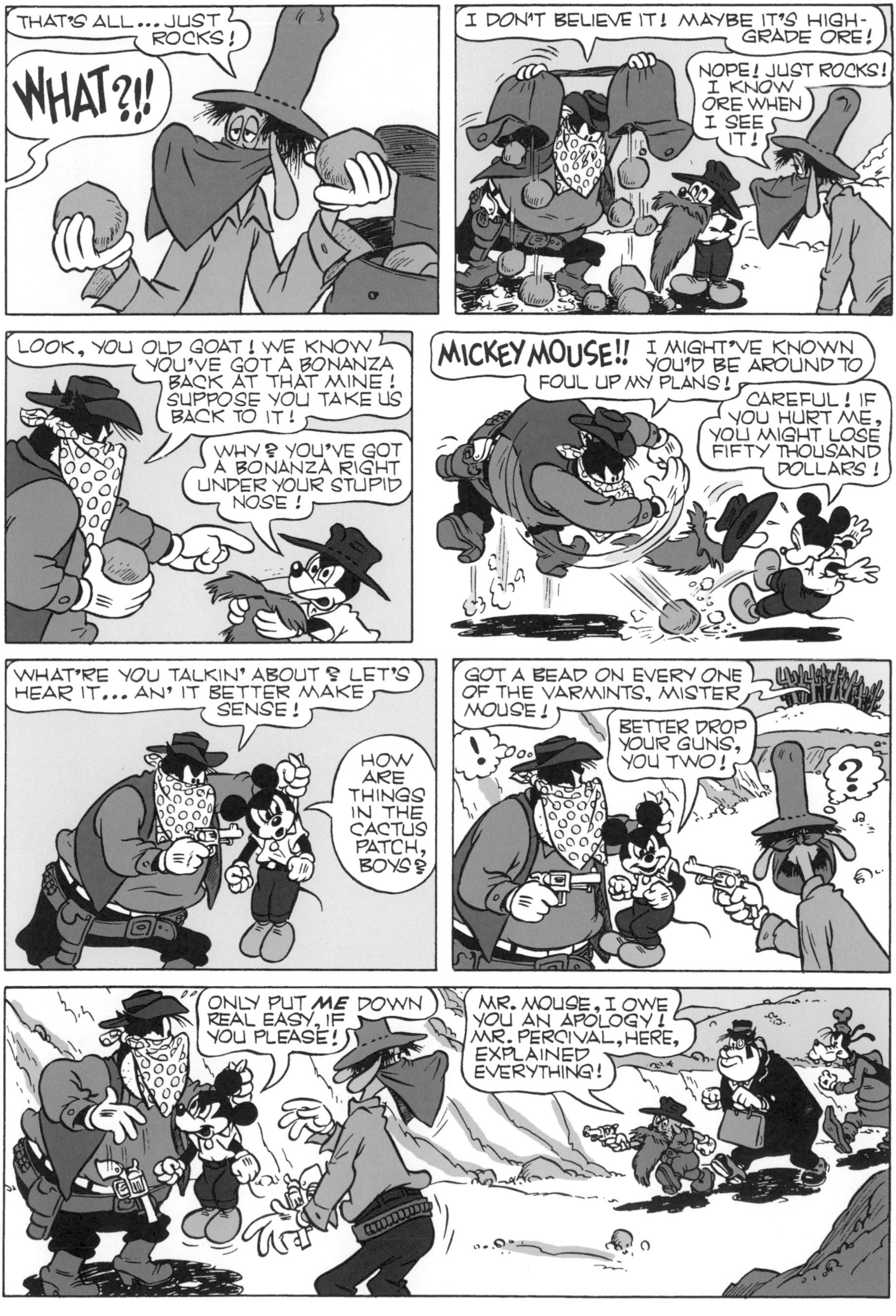
THAT'S ALL... JUST ROCKS!
WHAT?!!
I DON'T BELIEVE IT! MAYBE IT'S HIGH-GRADE ORE!
NOPE! JUST ROCKS! I KNOW ORE WHEN I SEE IT!
LOOK, YOU OLD GOAT! WE KNOW YOU'VE GOT A BONANZA BACK AT THAT MINE! SUPPOSE YOU TAKE US BACK TO IT!
WHY? YOU'VE GOT A BONANZA RIGHT UNDER YOUR STUPID NOSE!
MICKEY MOUSE!! I MIGHT'VE KNOWN YOU'D BE AROUND TO FOUL UP MY PLANS!
CAREFUL! IF YOU HURT ME, YOU MIGHT LOSE FIFTY THOUSAND DOLLARS!
WHAT'RE YOU TALKIN' ABOUT? LET'S HEAR IT... AN' IT BETTER MAKE SENSE!
HOW ARE THINGS IN THE CACTUS PATCH, BOYS?
GOT A BEAD ON EVERY ONE OF THE VARMINTS, MISTER MOUSE!
BETTER DROP YOUR GUNS, YOU TWO!
!
?
ONLY PUT ME DOWN REAL EASY, IF YOU PLEASE!
MR. MOUSE, I OWE YOU AN APOLOGY! MR. PERCIVAL, HERE, EXPLAINED EVERYTHING!

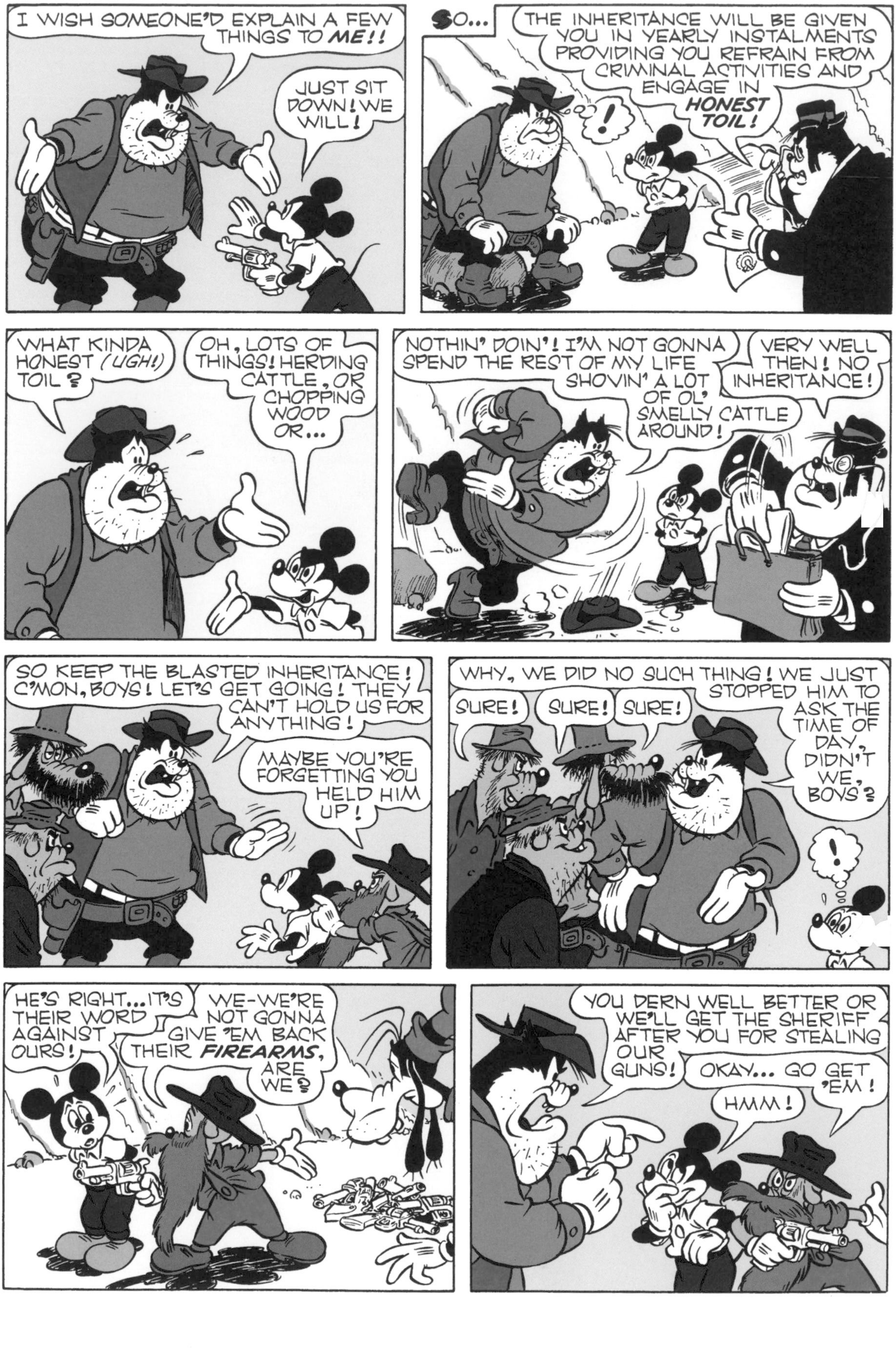
I WISH SOMEONE'D EXPLAIN A FEW THINGS TO ME!!
JUST SIT DOWN! WE WILL!
SO...
THE INHERITANCE WILL BE GIVEN YOU IN YEARLY INSTALMENTS PROVIDING YOU REFRAIN FROM CRIMINAL ACTIVITIES AND ENGAGE IN HONEST TOIL!
!
WHAT KINDA HONEST (UGH!) TOIL?
OH, LOTS OF THINGS! HERDING CATTLE, OR CHOPPING WOOD OR...
NOTHIN' DOIN'! I'M NOT GONNA SPEND THE REST OF MY LIFE SHOVIN' A LOT OF OL' SMELLY CATTLE AROUND!
VERY WELL THEN! NO INHERITANCE!
SO KEEP THE BLASTED INHERITANCE! C'MON, BOYS! LET'S GET GOING! THEY CAN'T HOLD US FOR ANYTHING!
MAYBE YOU'RE FORGETTING YOU HELD HIM UP!
WHY, WE DID NO SUCH THING! WE JUST STOPPED HIM TO ASK THE TIME OF DAY, DIDN'T WE, BOYS?
SURE!
SURE!
SURE!
!
HE'S RIGHT... IT'S THEIR WORD AGAINST OURS!
WE-WE'RE NOT GONNA GIVE 'EM BACK THEIR FIREARMS, ARE WE?
YOU DERN WELL BETTER OR WE'LL GET THE SHERIFF AFTER YOU FOR STEALING OUR GUNS!
HMM!
OKAY... GO GET 'EM!

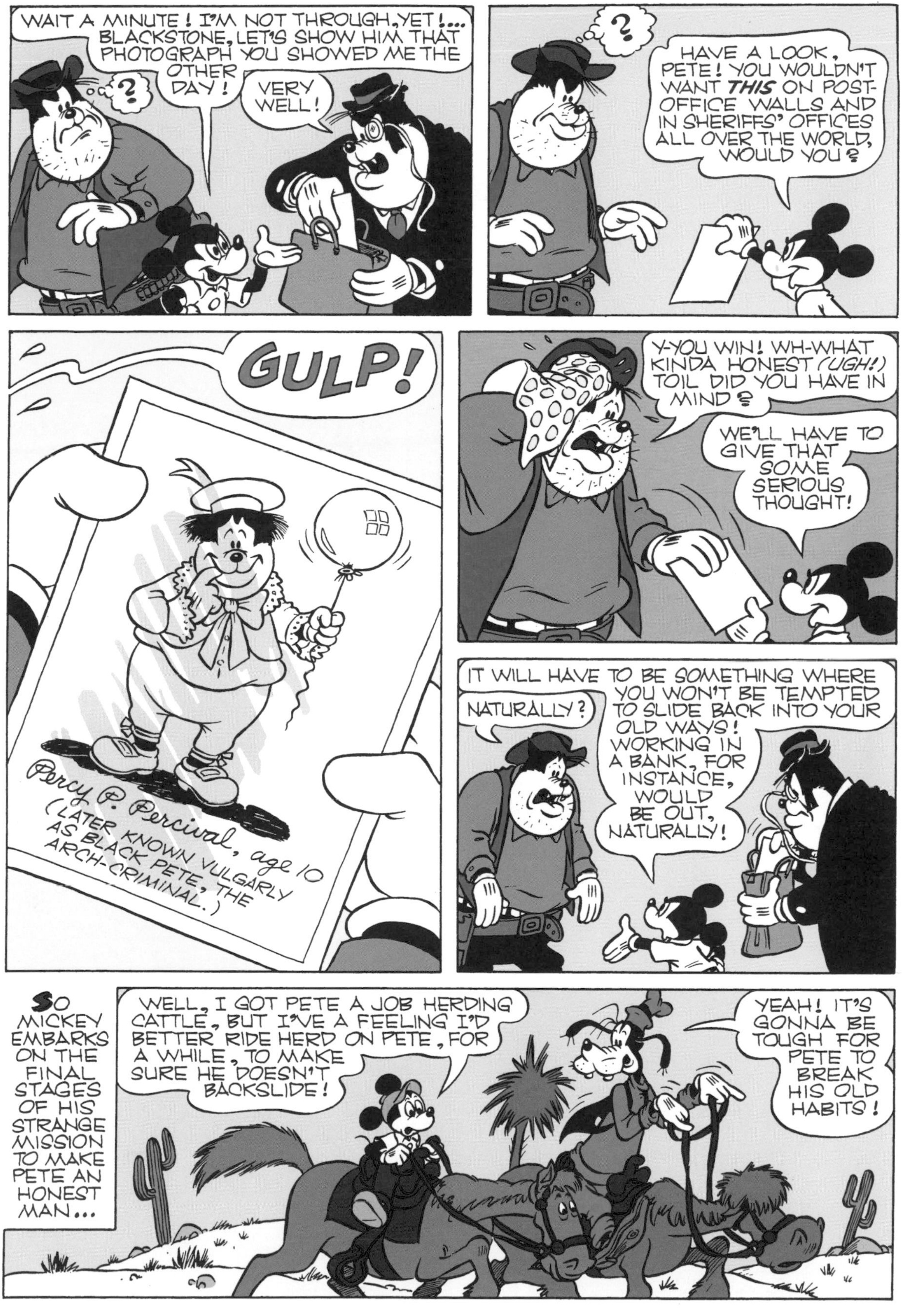
WAIT A MINUTE! I'M NOT THROUGH, YET!... BLACKSTONE, LET'S SHOW HIM THAT PHOTOGRAPH YOU SHOWED ME THE OTHER DAY!
?
VERY WELL!
?
HAVE A LOOK, PETE! YOU WOULDN'T WANT THIS ON POST-OFFICE WALLS AND IN SHERIFFS' OFFICES ALL OVER THE WORLD, WOULD YOU?
GULP!
Percy P. Percival, age 10
(LATER KNOWN VULGARLY AS BLACK PETE, THE ARCH-CRIMINAL.)
Y-YOU WIN! WH-WHAT KINDA HONEST (UGH!) TOIL DID YOU HAVE IN MIND?
WE'LL HAVE TO GIVE THAT SOME SERIOUS THOUGHT!
IT WILL HAVE TO BE SOMETHING WHERE YOU WON'T BE TEMPTED TO SLIDE BACK INTO YOUR OLD WAYS! WORKING IN A BANK, FOR INSTANCE, WOULD BE OUT, NATURALLY!
NATURALLY?
SO MICKEY EMBARKS ON THE FINAL STAGES OF HIS STRANGE MISSION TO MAKE PETE AN HONEST MAN...
WELL, I GOT PETE A JOB HERDING CATTLE, BUT I'VE A FEELING I'D BETTER RIDE HERD ON PETE, FOR A WHILE, TO MAKE SURE HE DOESN'T BACKSLIDE!
YEAH! IT'S GONNA BE TOUGH FOR PETE TO BREAK HIS OLD HABITS!

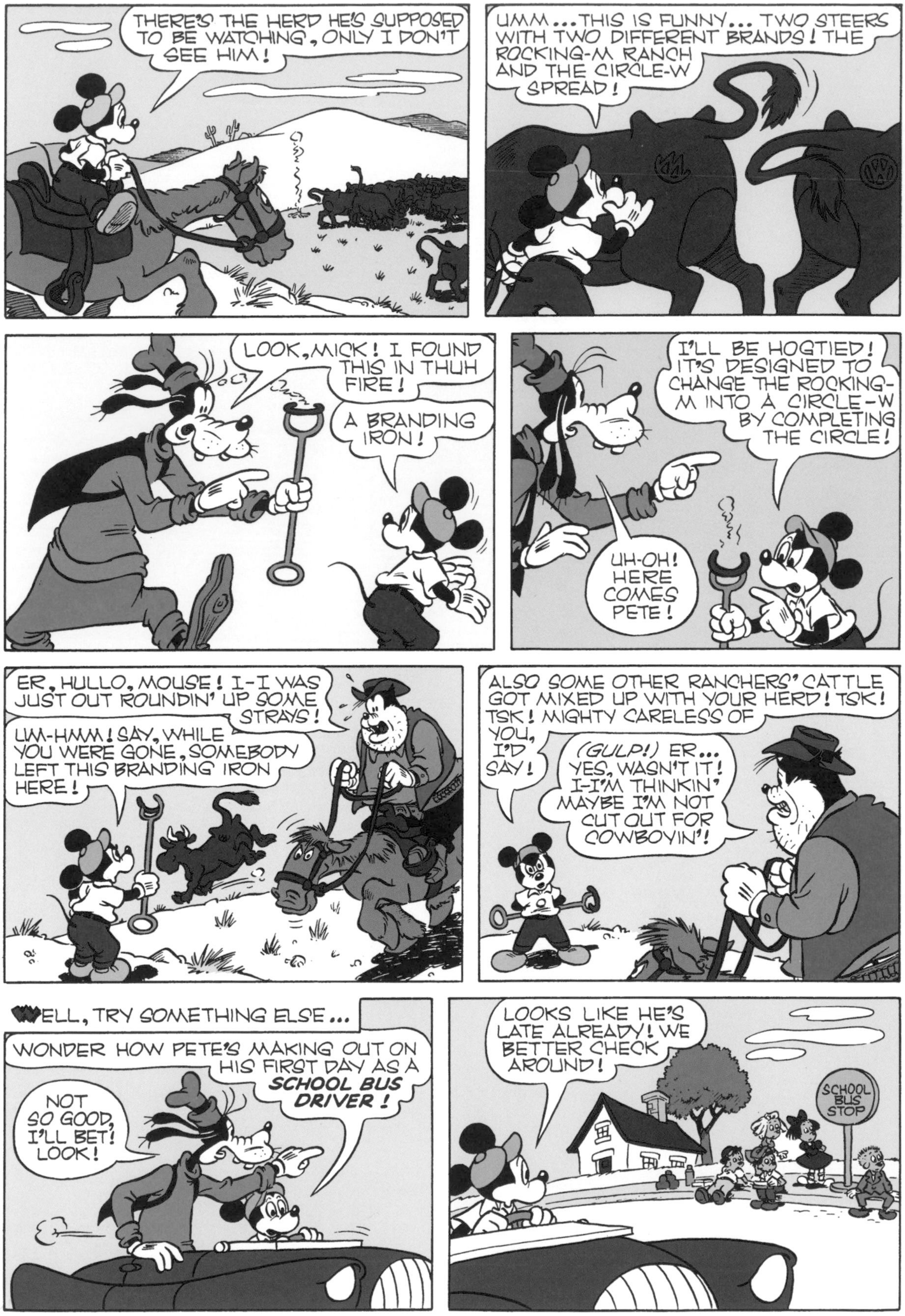

THERE'S THE HERD HE'S SUPPOSED TO BE WATCHING, ONLY I DON'T SEE HIM!
UMM... THIS IS FUNNY... TWO STEERS WITH TWO DIFFERENT BRANDS! THE ROCKING-M RANCH AND THE CIRCLE-W SPREAD!
LOOK, MICK! I FOUND THIS IN THUH FIRE!
A BRANDING IRON!
I'LL BE HOGTIED! IT'S DESIGNED TO CHANGE THE ROCKING-M INTO A CIRCLE-W BY COMPLETING THE CIRCLE!
UH-OH! HERE COMES PETE!
ER, HULLO, MOUSE! I-I WAS JUST OUT ROUNDIN' UP SOME STRAYS!
UM-HMM! SAY, WHILE YOU WERE GONE, SOMEBODY LEFT THIS BRANDING IRON HERE!
ALSO SOME OTHER RANCHERS' CATTLE GOT MIXED UP WITH YOUR HERD! TSK! TSK! MIGHTY CARELESS OF YOU, I'D SAY!
(GULP!) ER... YES, WASN'T IT! I-I'M THINKIN' MAYBE I'M NOT CUT OUT FOR COWBOYIN'!
WELL, TRY SOMETHING ELSE...
WONDER HOW PETE'S MAKING OUT ON HIS FIRST DAY AS A SCHOOL BUS DRIVER!
NOT SO GOOD, I'LL BET! LOOK!
LOOKS LIKE HE'S LATE ALREADY! WE BETTER CHECK AROUND!
SCHOOL BUS STOP

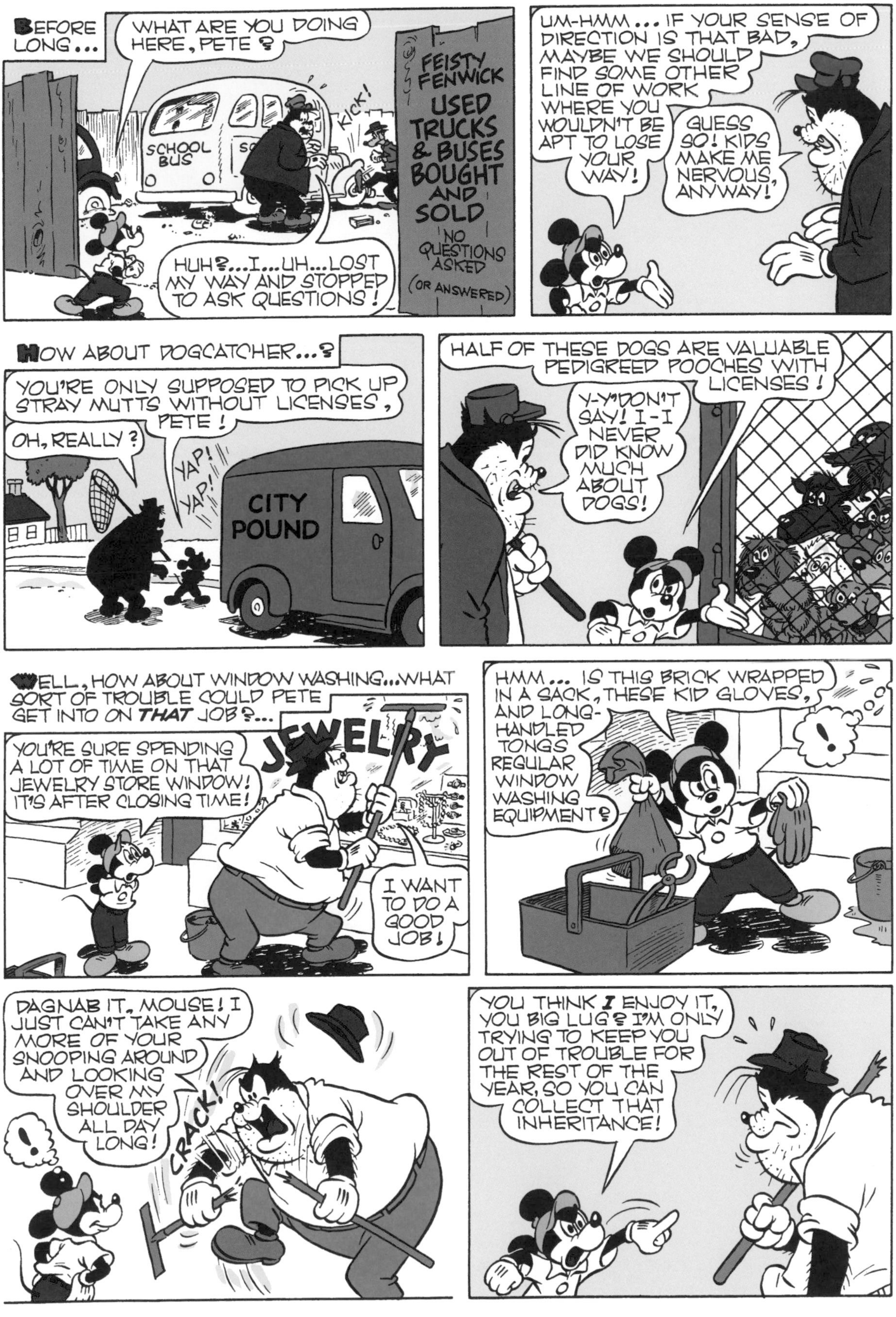
BEFORE LONG...
WHAT ARE YOU DOING HERE, PETE?
KICK!
SCHOOL BUS
FEISTY FENWICK USED TRUCKS & BUSES BOUGHT AND SOLD NO QUESTIONS ASKED (OR ANSWERED)
HUH?...I...UH...LOST MY WAY AND STOPPED TO ASK QUESTIONS!
UM-HMM... IF YOUR SENSE OF DIRECTION IS THAT BAD, MAYBE WE SHOULD FIND SOME OTHER LINE OF WORK WHERE YOU WOULDN'T BE APT TO LOSE YOUR WAY!
GUESS SO! KIDS MAKE ME NERVOUS, ANYWAY!
HOW ABOUT DOGCATCHER...?
YOU'RE ONLY SUPPOSED TO PICK UP STRAY MUTTS WITHOUT LICENSES, PETE!
OH, REALLY?
YAP! YAP!
CITY POUND
HALF OF THESE DOGS ARE VALUABLE PEDIGREED POOCHES WITH LICENSES!
Y-Y'DON'T SAY! I-I NEVER DID KNOW MUCH ABOUT DOGS!
WELL, HOW ABOUT WINDOW WASHING...WHAT SORT OF TROUBLE COULD PETE GET INTO ON THAT JOB?...
JEWELRY
YOU'RE SURE SPENDING A LOT OF TIME ON THAT JEWELRY STORE WINDOW! IT'S AFTER CLOSING TIME!
I WANT TO DO A GOOD JOB!
HMM... IS THIS BRICK WRAPPED IN A SACK, THESE KID GLOVES, AND LONG-HANDLED TONGS REGULAR WINDOW WASHING EQUIPMENT?
!
DAGNAB IT, MOUSE! I JUST CAN'T TAKE ANY MORE OF YOUR SNOOPING AROUND AND LOOKING OVER MY SHOULDER ALL DAY LONG!
CRACK!
!
YOU THINK I ENJOY IT, YOU BIG LUG? I'M ONLY TRYING TO KEEP YOU OUT OF TROUBLE FOR THE REST OF THE YEAR, SO YOU CAN COLLECT THAT INHERITANCE!

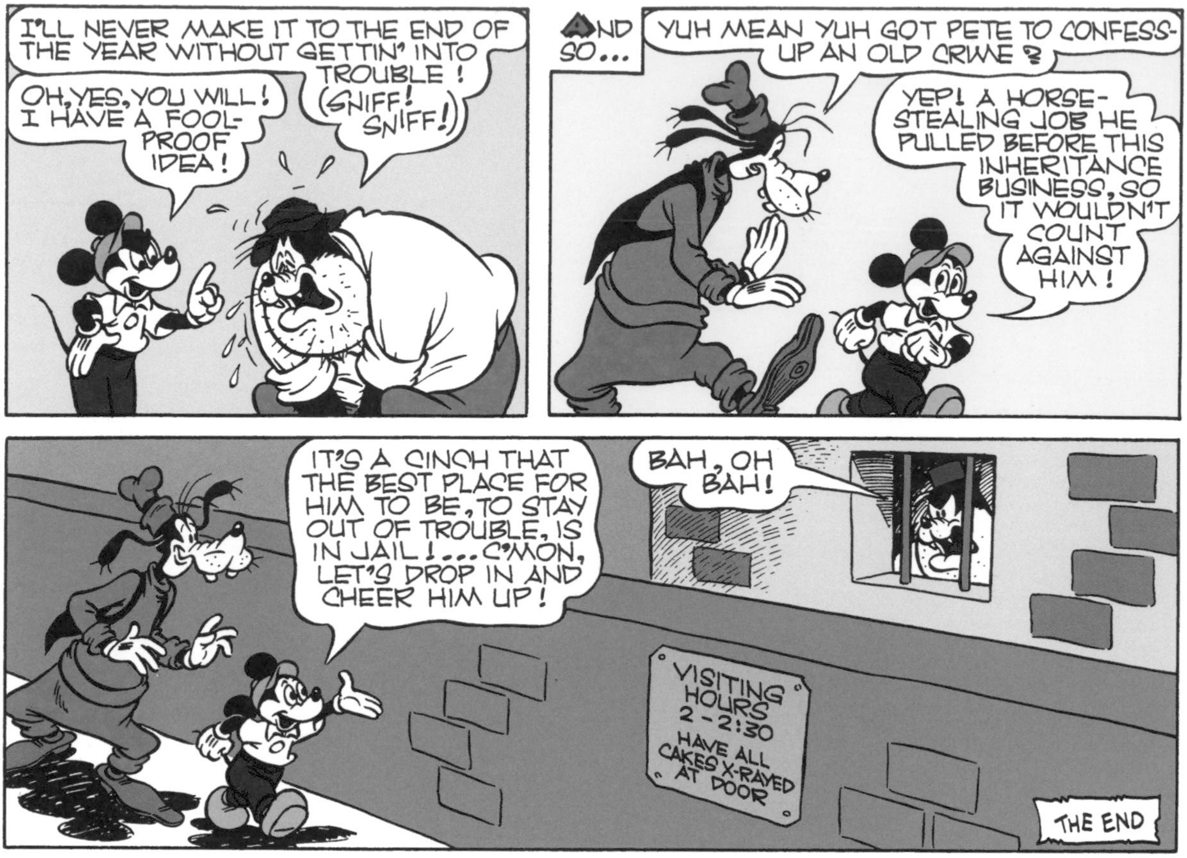
I'LL NEVER MAKE IT TO THE END OF THE YEAR WITHOUT GETTIN' INTO TROUBLE !
(SNIFF! SNIFF!)
OH, YES, YOU WILL! I HAVE A FOOL-PROOF IDEA!
AND SO...
YUH MEAN YUH GOT PETE TO CONFESS-UP AN OLD CRIME ?
YEP! A HORSE-STEALING JOB HE PULLED BEFORE THIS INHERITANCE BUSINESS, SO IT WOULDN'T COUNT AGAINST HIM!
IT'S A CINCH THAT THE BEST PLACE FOR HIM TO BE, TO STAY OUT OF TROUBLE, IS IN JAIL! ... C'MON, LET'S DROP IN AND CHEER HIM UP!
BAH, OH BAH!
VISITING HOURS 2 - 2:30
HAVE ALL CAKES X-RAYED AT DOOR
THE END

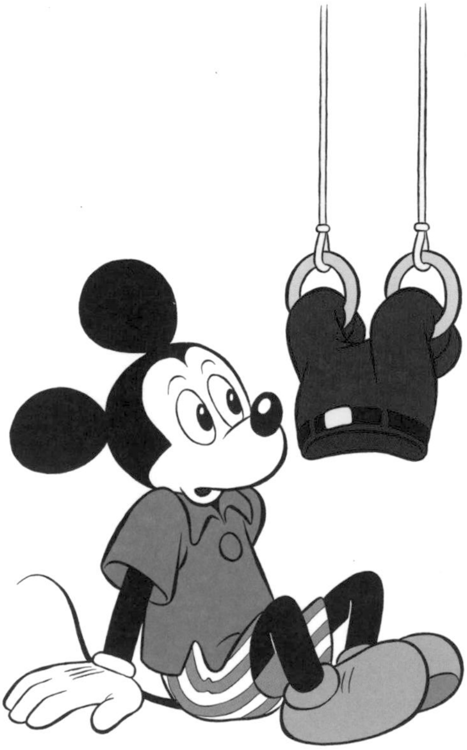

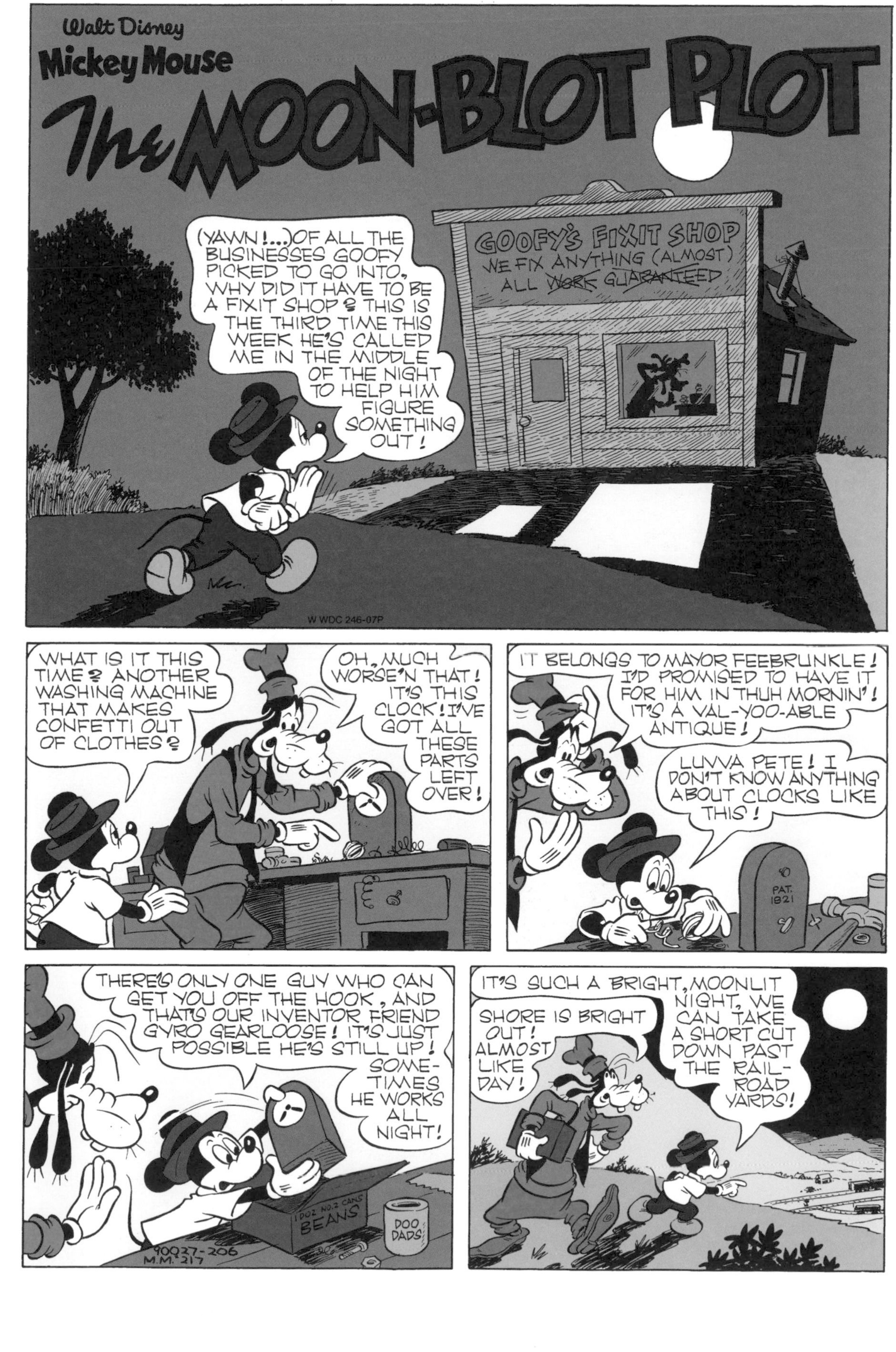
Walt Disney
Mickey Mouse
The MOON-BLOT PLOT
GOOFY'S FIXIT SHOP
WE FIX ANYTHING (ALMOST)
ALL WORK GUARANTEED
(YAWN!...)OF ALL THE BUSINESSES GOOFY PICKED TO GO INTO, WHY DID IT HAVE TO BE A FIXIT SHOP? THIS IS THE THIRD TIME THIS WEEK HE'S CALLED ME IN THE MIDDLE OF THE NIGHT TO HELP HIM FIGURE SOMETHING OUT!
W WDC 246-07P
WHAT IS IT THIS TIME? ANOTHER WASHING MACHINE THAT MAKES CONFETTI OUT OF CLOTHES?
OH, MUCH WORSE'N THAT! IT'S THIS CLOCK! I'VE GOT ALL THESE PARTS LEFT OVER!
IT BELONGS TO MAYOR FEEBRUNKLE! I'D PROMISED TO HAVE IT FOR HIM IN THUH MORNIN'! IT'S A VAL-YOO-ABLE ANTIQUE!
LUVVA PETE! I DON'T KNOW ANYTHING ABOUT CLOCKS LIKE THIS!
PAT. 1821
THERE'S ONLY ONE GUY WHO CAN GET YOU OFF THE HOOK, AND THAT'S OUR INVENTOR FRIEND GYRO GEARLOOSE! IT'S JUST POSSIBLE HE'S STILL UP! SOMETIMES HE WORKS ALL NIGHT!
1 DOZ NO. 2 CANS BEANS
DOO DADS
90027-206
M.M. 217
IT'S SUCH A BRIGHT, MOONLIT NIGHT, WE CAN TAKE A SHORT CUT DOWN PAST THE RAILROAD YARDS!
SHORE IS BRIGHT OUT! ALMOST LIKE DAY!

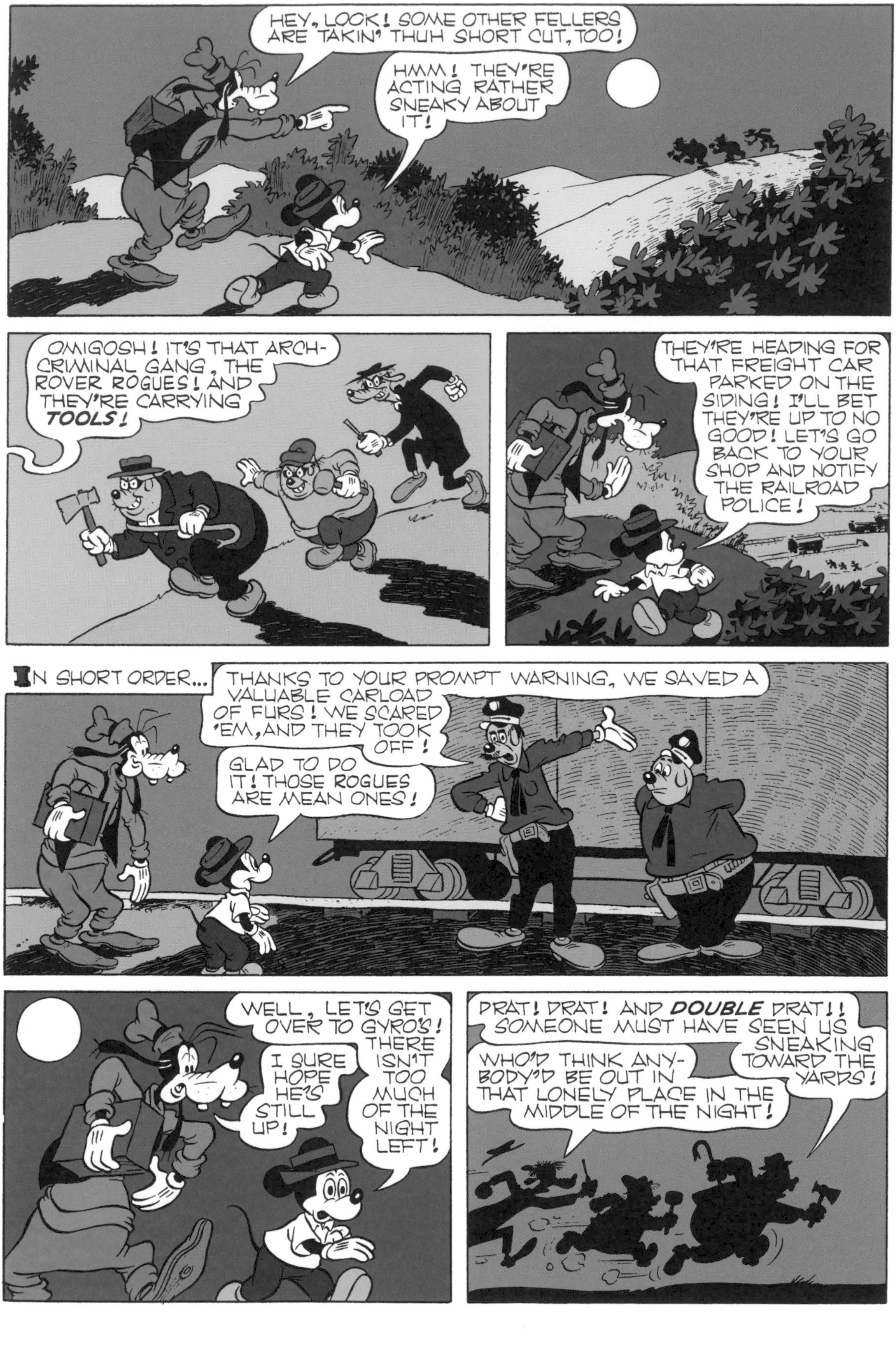
HEY, LOOK! SOME OTHER FELLERS ARE TAKIN' THUH SHORT CUT, TOO!
HMM! THEY'RE ACTING RATHER SNEAKY ABOUT IT!
OMIGOSH! IT'S THAT ARCH-CRIMINAL GANG, THE ROVER ROGUES! AND THEY'RE CARRYING TOOLS!
THEY'RE HEADING FOR THAT FREIGHT CAR PARKED ON THE SIDING! I'LL BET THEY'RE UP TO NO GOOD! LET'S GO BACK TO YOUR SHOP AND NOTIFY THE RAILROAD POLICE!
IN SHORT ORDER...
THANKS TO YOUR PROMPT WARNING, WE SAVED A VALUABLE CARLOAD OF FURS! WE SCARED 'EM, AND THEY TOOK OFF!
GLAD TO DO IT! THOSE ROGUES ARE MEAN ONES!
WELL, LET'S GET OVER TO GYRO'S! THERE ISN'T TOO MUCH OF THE NIGHT LEFT!
I SURE HOPE HE'S STILL UP!
DRAT! DRAT! AND DOUBLE DRAT!! SOMEONE MUST HAVE SEEN US SNEAKING TOWARD THE YARDS!
WHO'D THINK ANYBODY'D BE OUT IN THAT LONELY PLACE IN THE MIDDLE OF THE NIGHT!

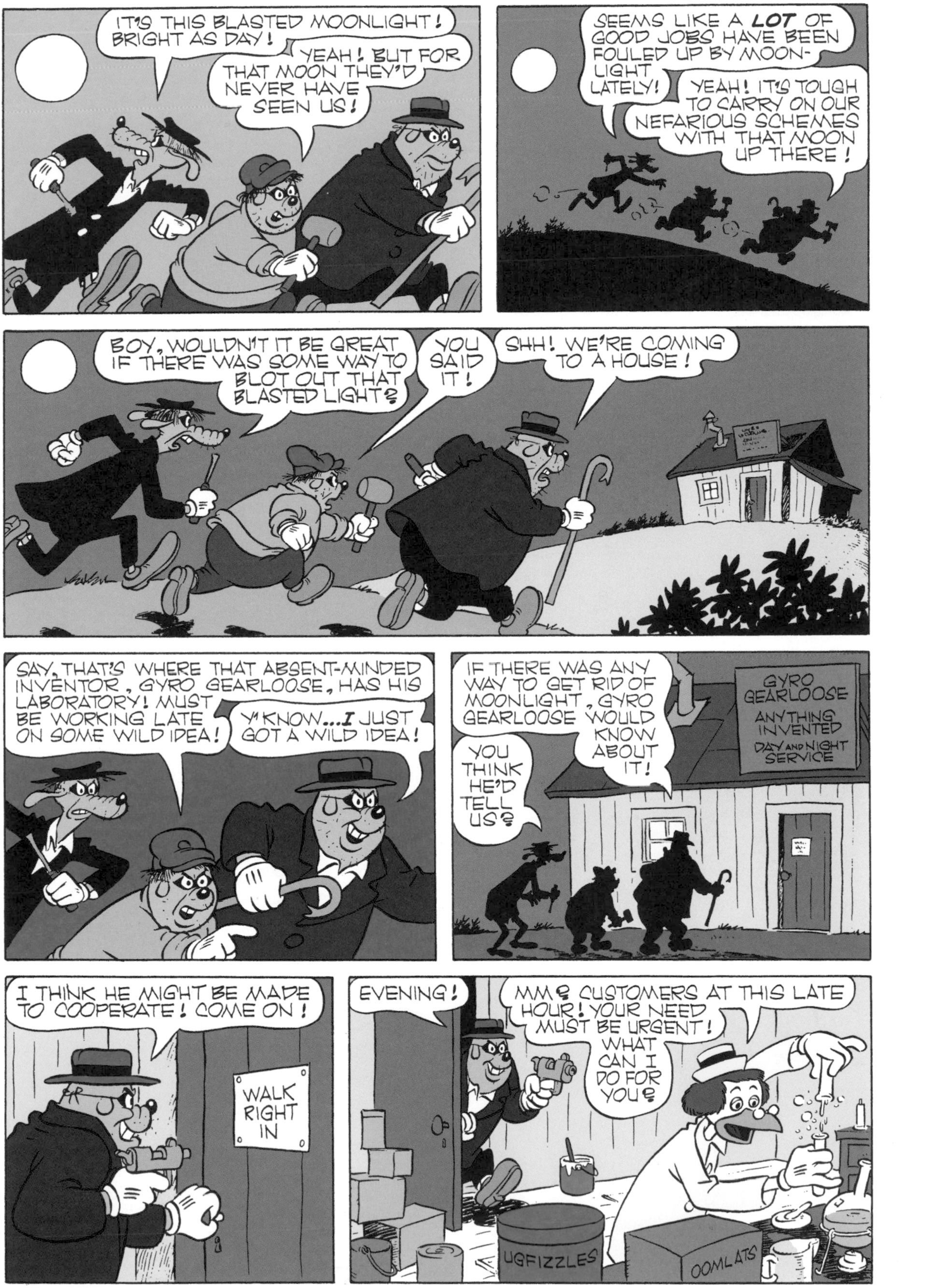
IT'S THIS BLASTED MOONLIGHT! BRIGHT AS DAY!
YEAH! BUT FOR THAT MOON THEY'D NEVER HAVE SEEN US!
SEEMS LIKE A LOT OF GOOD JOBS HAVE BEEN FOULED UP BY MOONLIGHT LATELY!
YEAH! IT'S TOUGH TO CARRY ON OUR NEFARIOUS SCHEMES WITH THAT MOON UP THERE!
BOY, WOULDN'T IT BE GREAT IF THERE WAS SOME WAY TO BLOT OUT THAT BLASTED LIGHT?
YOU SAID IT!
SHH! WE'RE COMING TO A HOUSE!
SAY, THAT'S WHERE THAT ABSENT-MINDED INVENTOR, GYRO GEARLOOSE, HAS HIS LABORATORY! MUST BE WORKING LATE ON SOME WILD IDEA!
Y'KNOW... I JUST GOT A WILD IDEA!
IF THERE WAS ANY WAY TO GET RID OF MOONLIGHT, GYRO GEARLOOSE WOULD KNOW ABOUT IT!
YOU THINK HE'D TELL US?
GYRO GEARLOOSE
ANYTHING INVENTED
DAY AND NIGHT SERVICE
I THINK HE MIGHT BE MADE TO COOPERATE! COME ON!
WALK RIGHT IN
EVENING!
MM? CUSTOMERS AT THIS LATE HOUR! YOUR NEED MUST BE URGENT! WHAT CAN I DO FOR YOU?
UGFIZZLES
OOMLATS

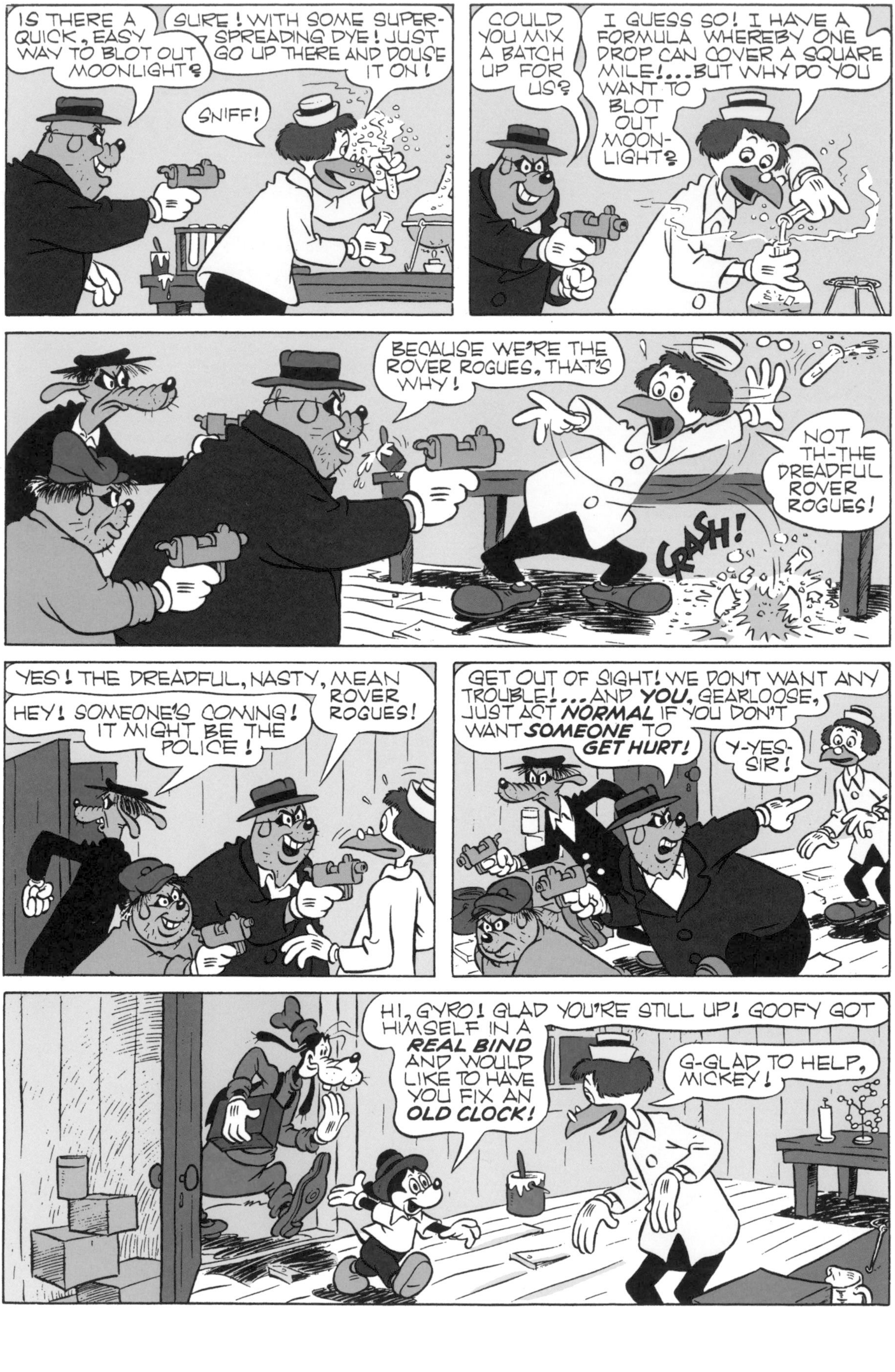
IS THERE A QUICK, EASY WAY TO BLOT OUT MOONLIGHT?
SURE! WITH SOME SUPER-SPREADING DYE! JUST GO UP THERE AND DOUSE IT ON!
SNIFF!
COULD YOU MIX A BATCH UP FOR US?
I GUESS SO! I HAVE A FORMULA WHEREBY ONE DROP CAN COVER A SQUARE MILE!...BUT WHY DO YOU WANT TO BLOT OUT MOONLIGHT?
BECAUSE WE'RE THE ROVER ROGUES, THAT'S WHY!
NOT TH-THE DREADFUL ROVER ROGUES!
CRASH!
YES! THE DREADFUL, NASTY, MEAN ROVER ROGUES!
HEY! SOMEONE'S COMING! IT MIGHT BE THE POLICE!
GET OUT OF SIGHT! WE DON'T WANT ANY TROUBLE!...AND YOU, GEARLOOSE, JUST ACT NORMAL IF YOU DON'T WANT SOMEONE TO GET HURT!
Y-YES-SIR!
HI, GYRO! GLAD YOU'RE STILL UP! GOOFY GOT HIMSELF IN A REAL BIND AND WOULD LIKE TO HAVE YOU FIX AN OLD CLOCK!
G-GLAD TO HELP, MICKEY!

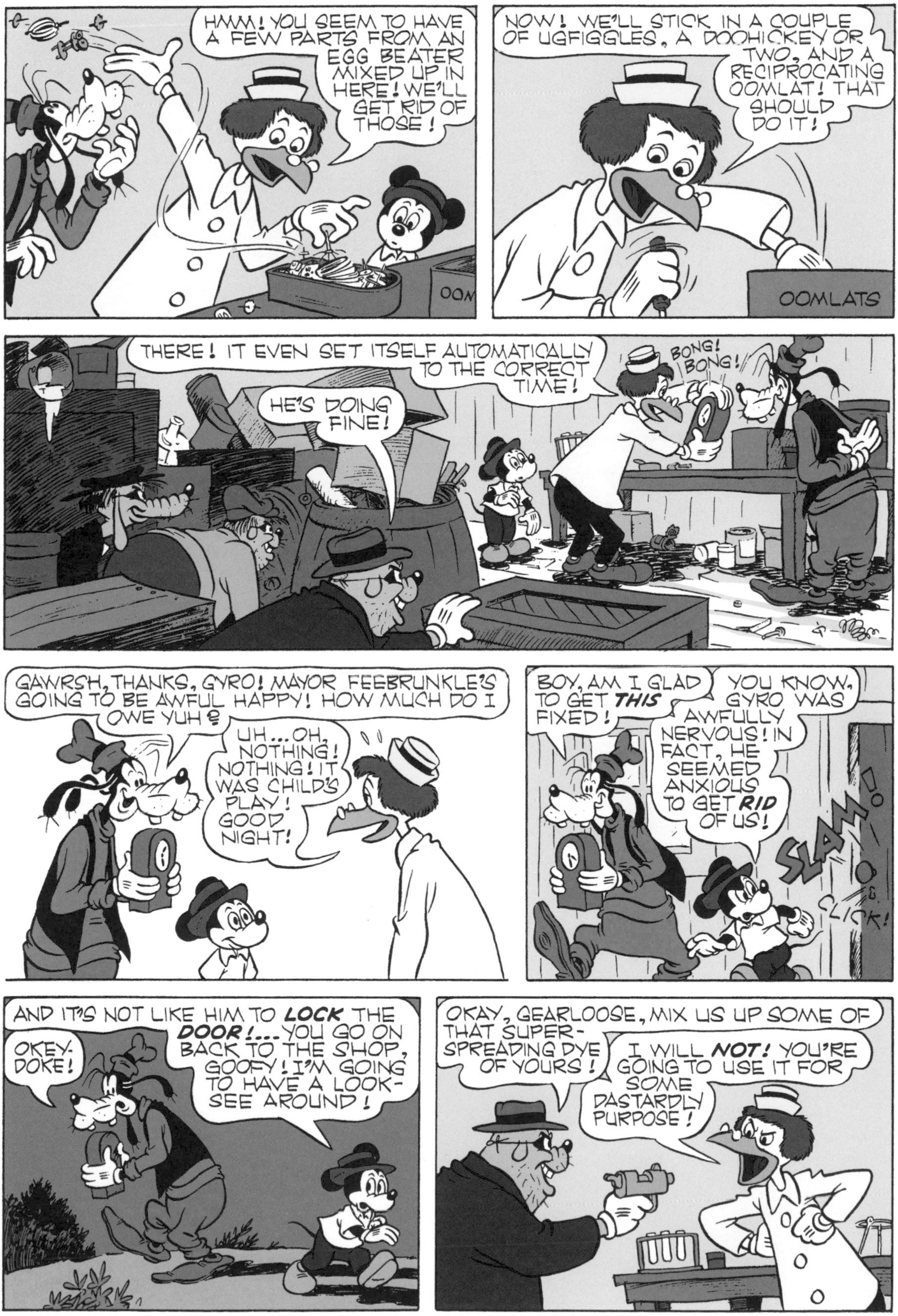
HMM! YOU SEEM TO HAVE A FEW PARTS FROM AN EGG BEATER MIXED UP IN HERE! WE'LL GET RID OF THOSE!
OOM
NOW! WE'LL STICK IN A COUPLE OF UGFIGGLES, A DOOHICKEY OR TWO, AND A RECIPROCATING OOMLAT! THAT SHOULD DO IT!
OOMLATS
THERE! IT EVEN SET ITSELF AUTOMATICALLY TO THE CORRECT TIME!
BONG! BONG!
HE'S DOING FINE!
GAWRSH, THANKS, GYRO! MAYOR FEEBRUNKLE'S GOING TO BE AWFUL HAPPY! HOW MUCH DO I OWE YUH?
UH...OH, NOTHING! NOTHING! IT WAS CHILD'S PLAY! GOOD NIGHT!
BOY, AM I GLAD TO GET THIS FIXED!
YOU KNOW, GYRO WAS AWFULLY NERVOUS! IN FACT, HE SEEMED ANXIOUS TO GET RID OF US!
SLAM!
CLICK!
AND IT'S NOT LIKE HIM TO LOCK THE DOOR!... YOU GO ON BACK TO THE SHOP, GOOFY! I'M GOING TO HAVE A LOOK-SEE AROUND!
OKEY-DOKE!
OKAY, GEARLOOSE, MIX US UP SOME OF THAT SUPER-SPREADING DYE OF YOURS!
I WILL NOT! YOU'RE GOING TO USE IT FOR SOME DASTARDLY PURPOSE!

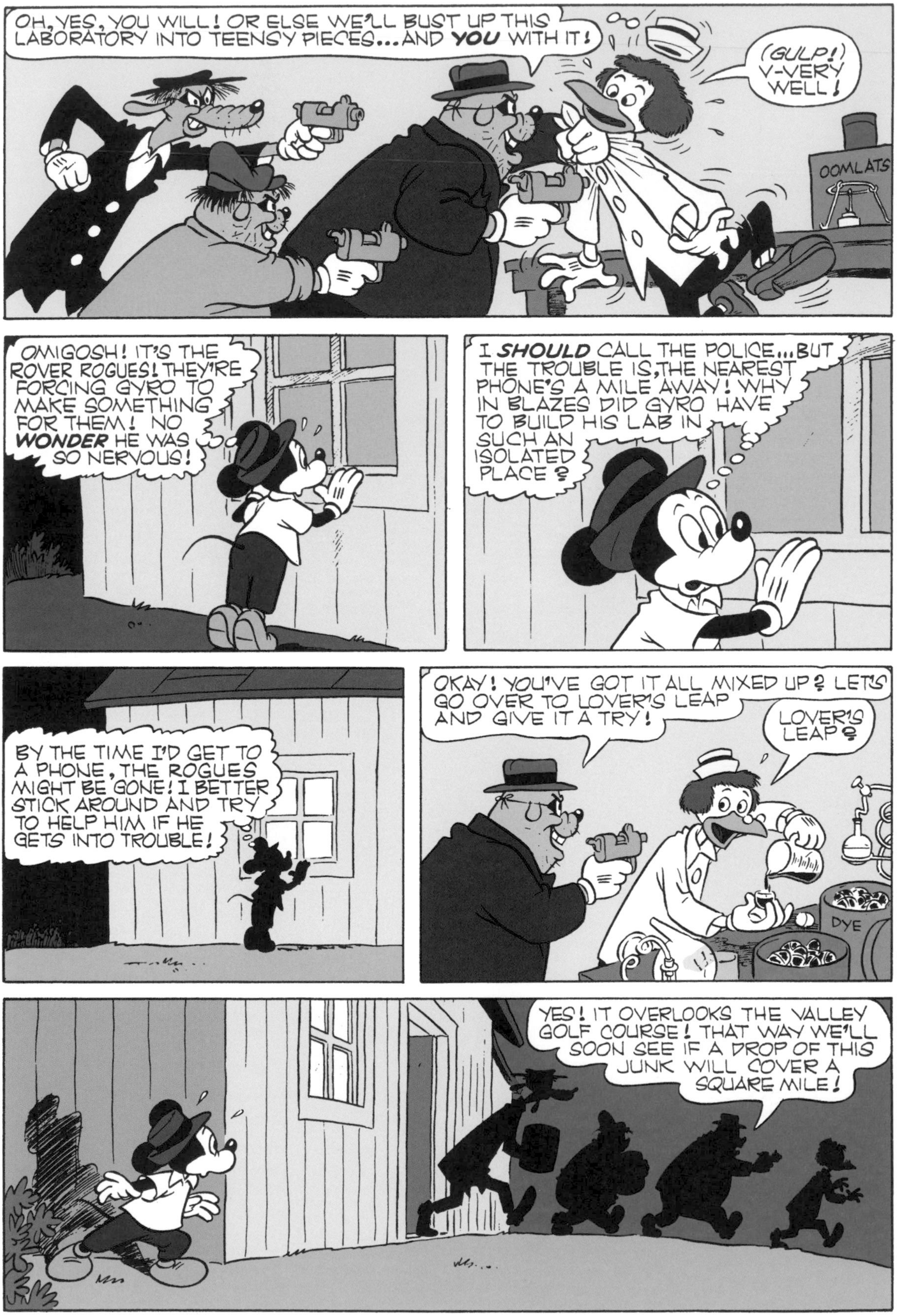

OH, YES, YOU WILL! OR ELSE WE'LL BUST UP THIS LABORATORY INTO TEENSY PIECES...AND YOU WITH IT!
(GULP!) V-VERY WELL!
OOMLATS
OMIGOSH! IT'S THE ROVER ROGUES! THEY'RE FORCING GYRO TO MAKE SOMETHING FOR THEM! NO WONDER HE WAS SO NERVOUS!
I SHOULD CALL THE POLICE...BUT THE TROUBLE IS, THE NEAREST PHONE'S A MILE AWAY! WHY IN BLAZES DID GYRO HAVE TO BUILD HIS LAB IN SUCH AN ISOLATED PLACE?
BY THE TIME I'D GET TO A PHONE, THE ROGUES MIGHT BE GONE! I BETTER STICK AROUND AND TRY TO HELP HIM IF HE GETS INTO TROUBLE!
OKAY! YOU'VE GOT IT ALL MIXED UP? LET'S GO OVER TO LOVER'S LEAP AND GIVE IT A TRY!
LOVER'S LEAP?
DYE
YES! IT OVERLOOKS THE VALLEY GOLF COURSE! THAT WAY WE'LL SOON SEE IF A DROP OF THIS JUNK WILL COVER A SQUARE MILE!

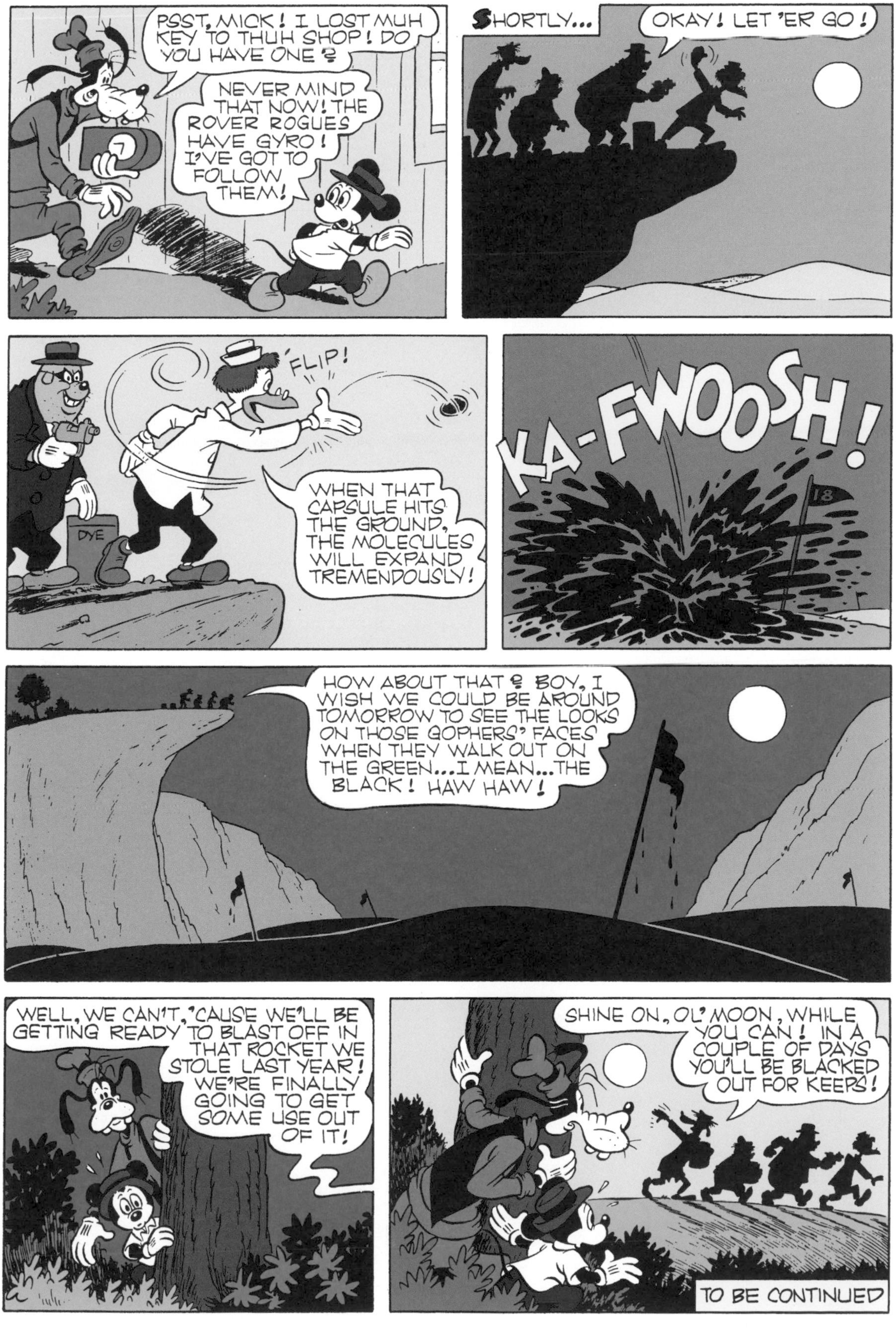
PSST, MICK! I LOST MUH KEY TO THUH SHOP! DO YOU HAVE ONE?
NEVER MIND THAT NOW! THE ROVER ROGUES HAVE GYRO! I'VE GOT TO FOLLOW THEM!
SHORTLY...
OKAY! LET 'ER GO!
FLIP!
WHEN THAT CAPSULE HITS THE GROUND, THE MOLECULES WILL EXPAND TREMENDOUSLY!
DYE
KA-FWOOSH!
18
HOW ABOUT THAT? BOY, I WISH WE COULD BE AROUND TOMORROW TO SEE THE LOOKS ON THOSE GOPHERS' FACES WHEN THEY WALK OUT ON THE GREEN...I MEAN...THE BLACK! HAW HAW!
WELL, WE CAN'T, 'CAUSE WE'LL BE GETTING READY TO BLAST OFF IN THAT ROCKET WE STOLE LAST YEAR! WE'RE FINALLY GOING TO GET SOME USE OUT OF IT!
SHINE ON, OL' MOON, WHILE YOU CAN! IN A COUPLE OF DAYS YOU'LL BE BLACKED OUT FOR KEEPS!
TO BE CONTINUED

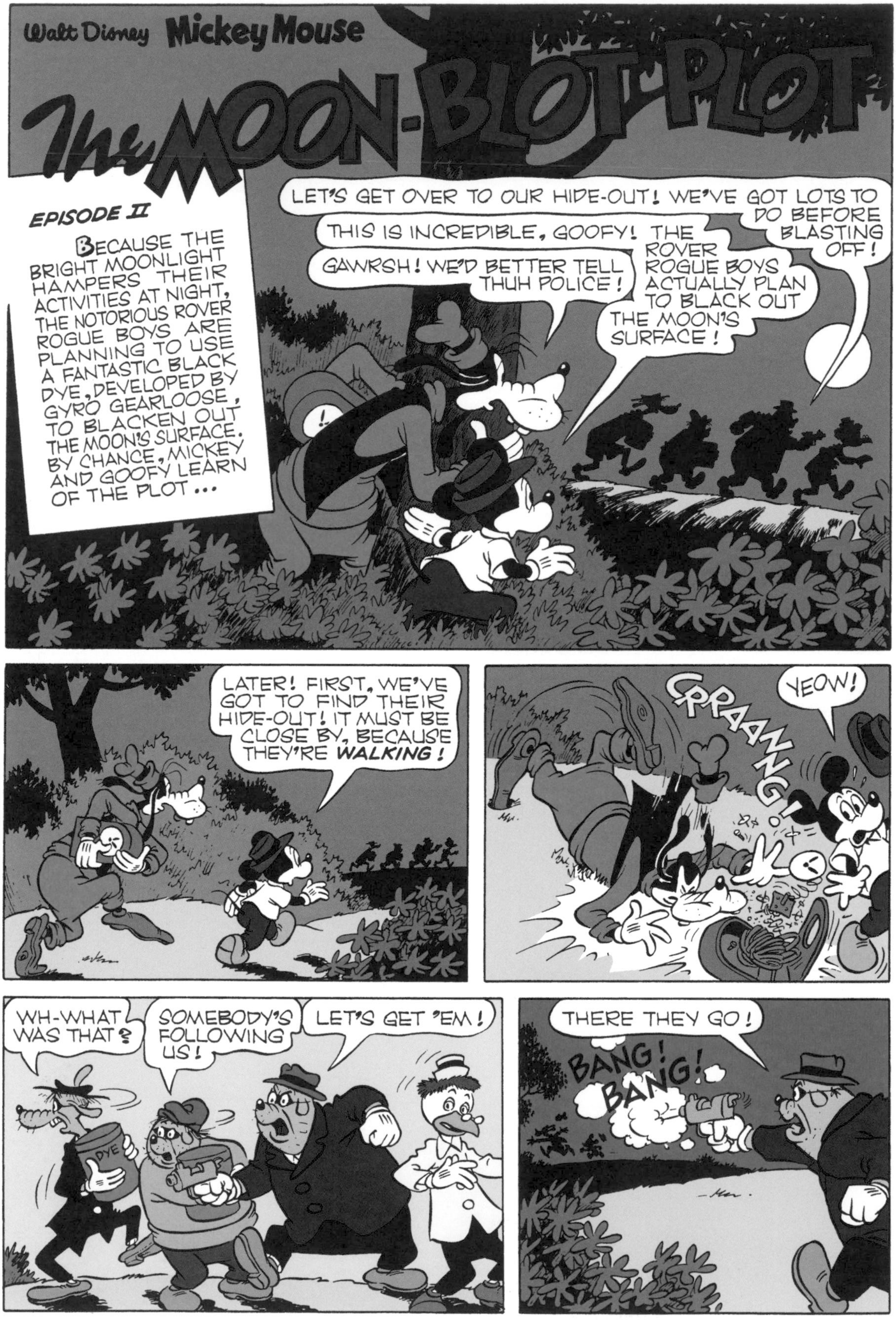
Walt Disney Mickey Mouse
The MOON-BLOT-PLOT
EPISODE II
BECAUSE THE BRIGHT MOONLIGHT HAMPERS THEIR ACTIVITIES AT NIGHT, THE NOTORIOUS ROVER ROGUE BOYS ARE PLANNING TO USE A FANTASTIC BLACK DYE, DEVELOPED BY GYRO GEARLOOSE, TO BLACKEN OUT THE MOON'S SURFACE. BY CHANCE, MICKEY AND GOOFY LEARN OF THE PLOT...
LET'S GET OVER TO OUR HIDE-OUT! WE'VE GOT LOTS TO DO BEFORE BLASTING OFF!
THIS IS INCREDIBLE, GOOFY! THE ROVER ROGUE BOYS ACTUALLY PLAN TO BLACK OUT THE MOON'S SURFACE!
GAWRSH! WE'D BETTER TELL THUH POLICE!
LATER! FIRST, WE'VE GOT TO FIND THEIR HIDE-OUT! IT MUST BE CLOSE BY, BECAUSE THEY'RE WALKING!
CRRAANNG!
YEOW!
WH-WHAT WAS THAT?
SOMEBODY'S FOLLOWING US!
LET'S GET 'EM!
DYE
THERE THEY GO!
BANG! BANG!

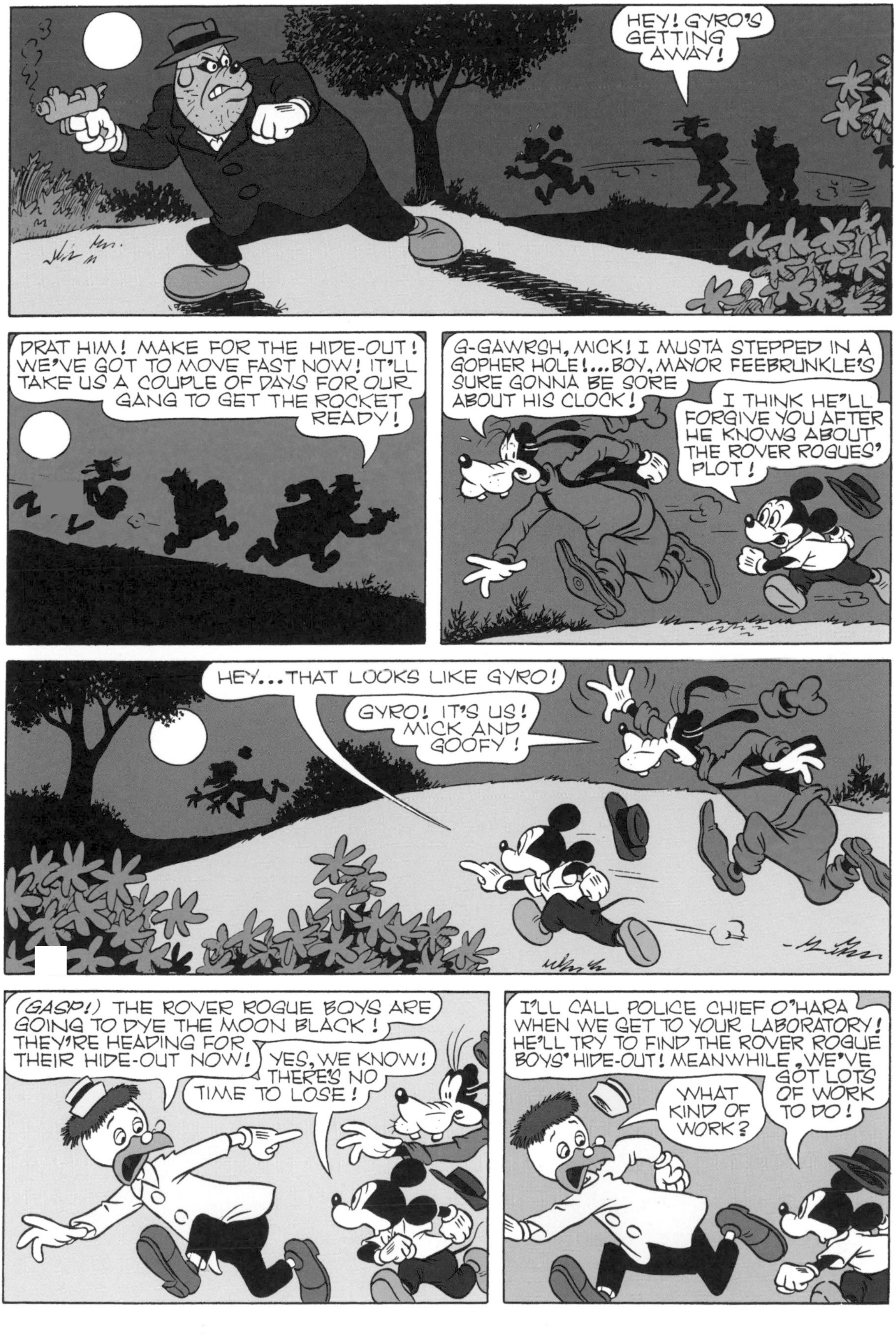
HEY! GYRO'S GETTING AWAY!
DRAT HIM! MAKE FOR THE HIDE-OUT! WE'VE GOT TO MOVE FAST NOW! IT'LL TAKE US A COUPLE OF DAYS FOR OUR GANG TO GET THE ROCKET READY!
G-GAWRSH, MICK! I MUSTA STEPPED IN A GOPHER HOLE!...BOY, MAYOR FEEBRUNKLE'S SURE GONNA BE SORE ABOUT HIS CLOCK!
I THINK HE'LL FORGIVE YOU AFTER HE KNOWS ABOUT THE ROVER ROGUES' PLOT!
HEY...THAT LOOKS LIKE GYRO!
GYRO! IT'S US! MICK AND GOOFY!
(GASP!) THE ROVER ROGUE BOYS ARE GOING TO DYE THE MOON BLACK! THEY'RE HEADING FOR THEIR HIDE-OUT NOW!
YES, WE KNOW! THERE'S NO TIME TO LOSE!
I'LL CALL POLICE CHIEF O'HARA WHEN WE GET TO YOUR LABORATORY! HE'LL TRY TO FIND THE ROVER ROGUE BOYS' HIDE-OUT! MEANWHILE, WE'VE GOT LOTS OF WORK TO DO!
WHAT KIND OF WORK?

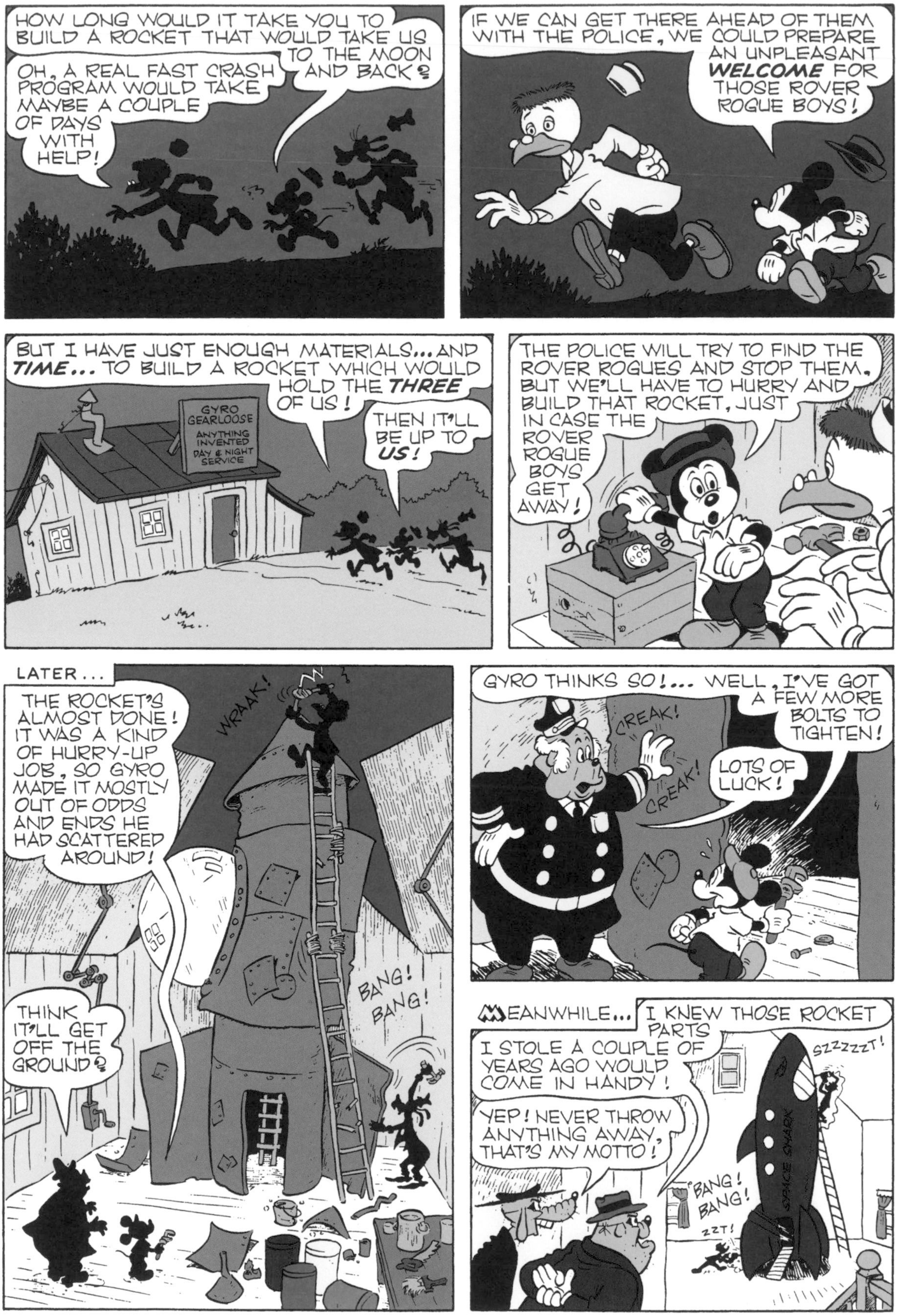
HOW LONG WOULD IT TAKE YOU TO BUILD A ROCKET THAT WOULD TAKE US TO THE MOON AND BACK?
OH, A REAL FAST CRASH PROGRAM WOULD TAKE MAYBE A COUPLE OF DAYS WITH HELP!
IF WE CAN GET THERE AHEAD OF THEM WITH THE POLICE, WE COULD PREPARE AN UNPLEASANT WELCOME FOR THOSE ROVER ROGUE BOYS!
BUT I HAVE JUST ENOUGH MATERIALS... AND TIME... TO BUILD A ROCKET WHICH WOULD HOLD THE THREE OF US!
GYRO GEARLOOSE
ANYTHING INVENTED
DAY & NIGHT SERVICE
THEN IT'LL BE UP TO US!
THE POLICE WILL TRY TO FIND THE ROVER ROGUES AND STOP THEM, BUT WE'LL HAVE TO HURRY AND BUILD THAT ROCKET, JUST IN CASE THE ROVER ROGUE BOYS GET AWAY!
LATER...
THE ROCKET'S ALMOST DONE! IT WAS A KIND OF HURRY-UP JOB, SO GYRO MADE IT MOSTLY OUT OF ODDS AND ENDS HE HAD SCATTERED AROUND!
WRAAK!
BANG! BANG!
THINK IT'LL GET OFF THE GROUND?
GYRO THINKS SO!... WELL, I'VE GOT A FEW MORE BOLTS TO TIGHTEN!
CREAK!
CREAK!
LOTS OF LUCK!
MEANWHILE...
I KNEW THOSE ROCKET PARTS I STOLE A COUPLE OF YEARS AGO WOULD COME IN HANDY!
YEP! NEVER THROW ANYTHING AWAY, THAT'S MY MOTTO!
SZZZZZT!
SPACE SHARK
BANG! BANG!
ZZT!

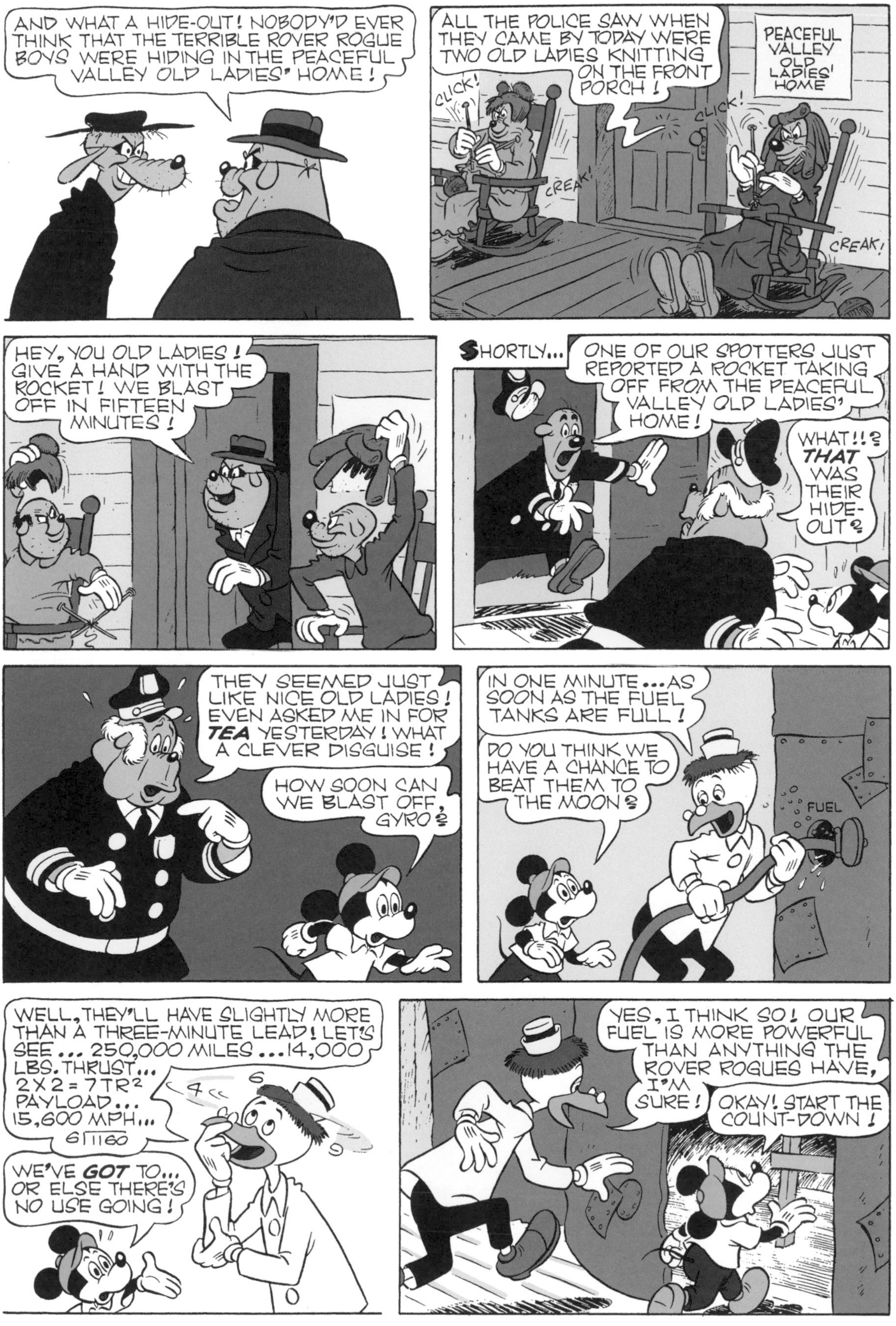
AND WHAT A HIDE-OUT! NOBODY'D EVER THINK THAT THE TERRIBLE ROVER ROGUE BOYS WERE HIDING IN THE PEACEFUL VALLEY OLD LADIES' HOME!
ALL THE POLICE SAW WHEN THEY CAME BY TODAY WERE TWO OLD LADIES KNITTING ON THE FRONT PORCH!
PEACEFUL VALLEY OLD LADIES' HOME
CLICK!
CLICK!
CREAK!
CREAK!
HEY, YOU OLD LADIES! GIVE A HAND WITH THE ROCKET! WE BLAST OFF IN FIFTEEN MINUTES!
SHORTLY...
ONE OF OUR SPOTTERS JUST REPORTED A ROCKET TAKING OFF FROM THE PEACEFUL VALLEY OLD LADIES' HOME!
WHAT!!? THAT WAS THEIR HIDE-OUT?
THEY SEEMED JUST LIKE NICE OLD LADIES! EVEN ASKED ME IN FOR TEA YESTERDAY! WHAT A CLEVER DISGUISE!
HOW SOON CAN WE BLAST OFF, GYRO?
IN ONE MINUTE... AS SOON AS THE FUEL TANKS ARE FULL!
DO YOU THINK WE HAVE A CHANCE TO BEAT THEM TO THE MOON?
FUEL
WELL, THEY'LL HAVE SLIGHTLY MORE THAN A THREE-MINUTE LEAD! LET'S SEE... 250,000 MILES... 14,000 LBS. THRUST... $2 X 2 = 7TR^2$ PAYLOAD... 15,600 MPH...
WE'VE GOT TO... OR ELSE THERE'S NO USE GOING!
YES, I THINK SO! OUR FUEL IS MORE POWERFUL THAN ANYTHING THE ROVER ROGUES HAVE, I'M SURE!
OKAY! START THE COUNT-DOWN!

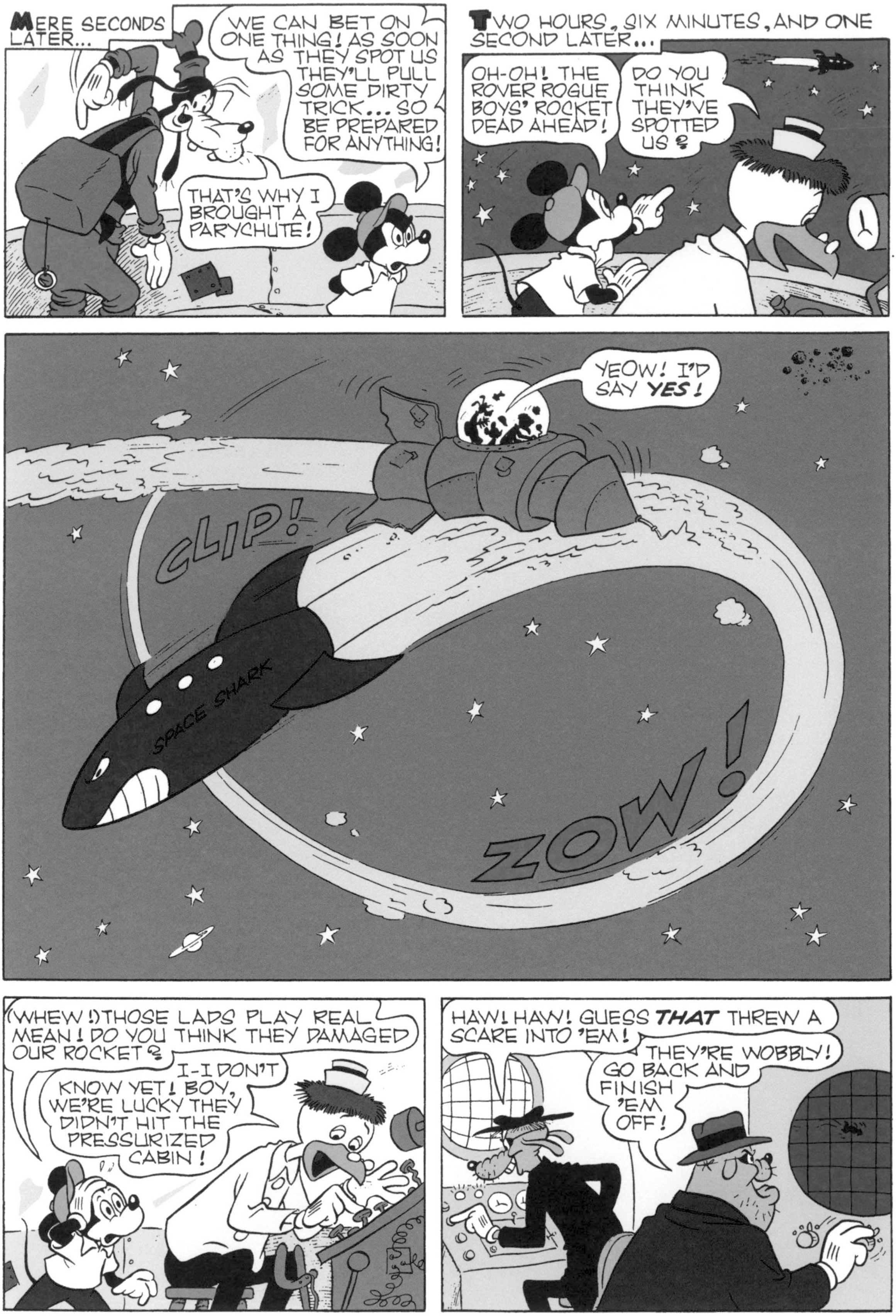
MERE SECONDS LATER...
WE CAN BET ON ONE THING! AS SOON AS THEY SPOT US THEY'LL PULL SOME DIRTY TRICK... SO BE PREPARED FOR ANYTHING!
THAT'S WHY I BROUGHT A PARYCHUTE!
TWO HOURS, SIX MINUTES, AND ONE SECOND LATER...
OH-OH! THE ROVER ROGUE BOYS' ROCKET DEAD AHEAD!
DO YOU THINK THEY'VE SPOTTED US?
YEOW! I'D SAY **YES**!
CLIP!
SPACE SHARK
ZOW!
(WHEW!) THOSE LADS PLAY REAL MEAN! DO YOU THINK THEY DAMAGED OUR ROCKET?
I-I DON'T KNOW YET! BOY, WE'RE LUCKY THEY DIDN'T HIT THE PRESSURIZED CABIN!
HAW! HAW! GUESS **THAT** THREW A SCARE INTO 'EM!
THEY'RE WOBBLY! GO BACK AND FINISH 'EM OFF!

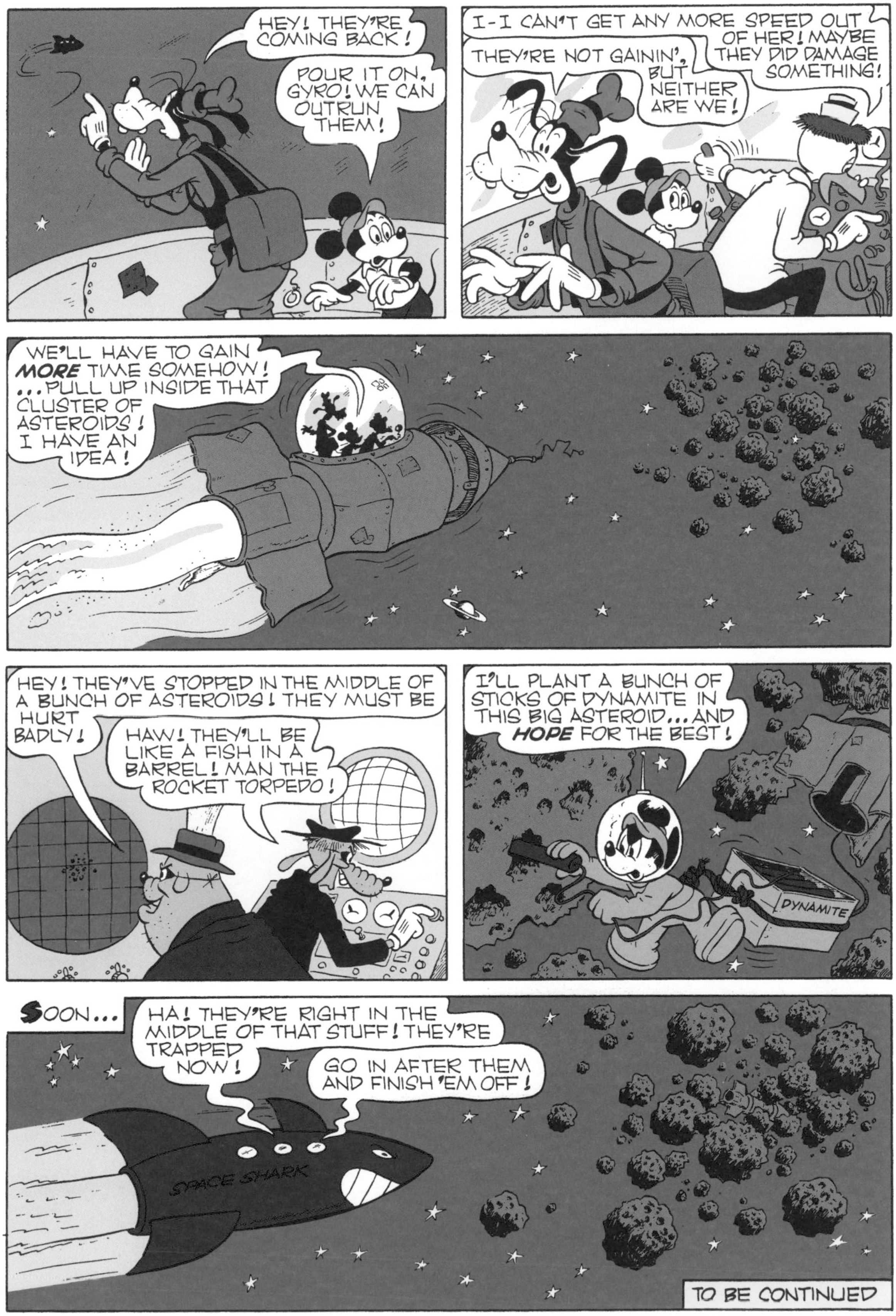
HEY! THEY'RE COMING BACK!
POUR IT ON, GYRO! WE CAN OUTRUN THEM!
I-I CAN'T GET ANY MORE SPEED OUT OF HER! MAYBE THEY DID DAMAGE SOMETHING!
THEY'RE NOT GAININ', BUT NEITHER ARE WE!
WE'LL HAVE TO GAIN MORE TIME SOMEHOW! ...PULL UP INSIDE THAT CLUSTER OF ASTEROIDS! I HAVE AN IDEA!
HEY! THEY'VE STOPPED IN THE MIDDLE OF A BUNCH OF ASTEROIDS! THEY MUST BE HURT BADLY!
HAW! THEY'LL BE LIKE A FISH IN A BARREL! MAN THE ROCKET TORPEDO!
I'LL PLANT A BUNCH OF STICKS OF DYNAMITE IN THIS BIG ASTEROID...AND HOPE FOR THE BEST!
DYNAMITE
SOON...
HA! THEY'RE RIGHT IN THE MIDDLE OF THAT STUFF! THEY'RE TRAPPED NOW!
GO IN AFTER THEM AND FINISH 'EM OFF!
SPACE SHARK
TO BE CONTINUED

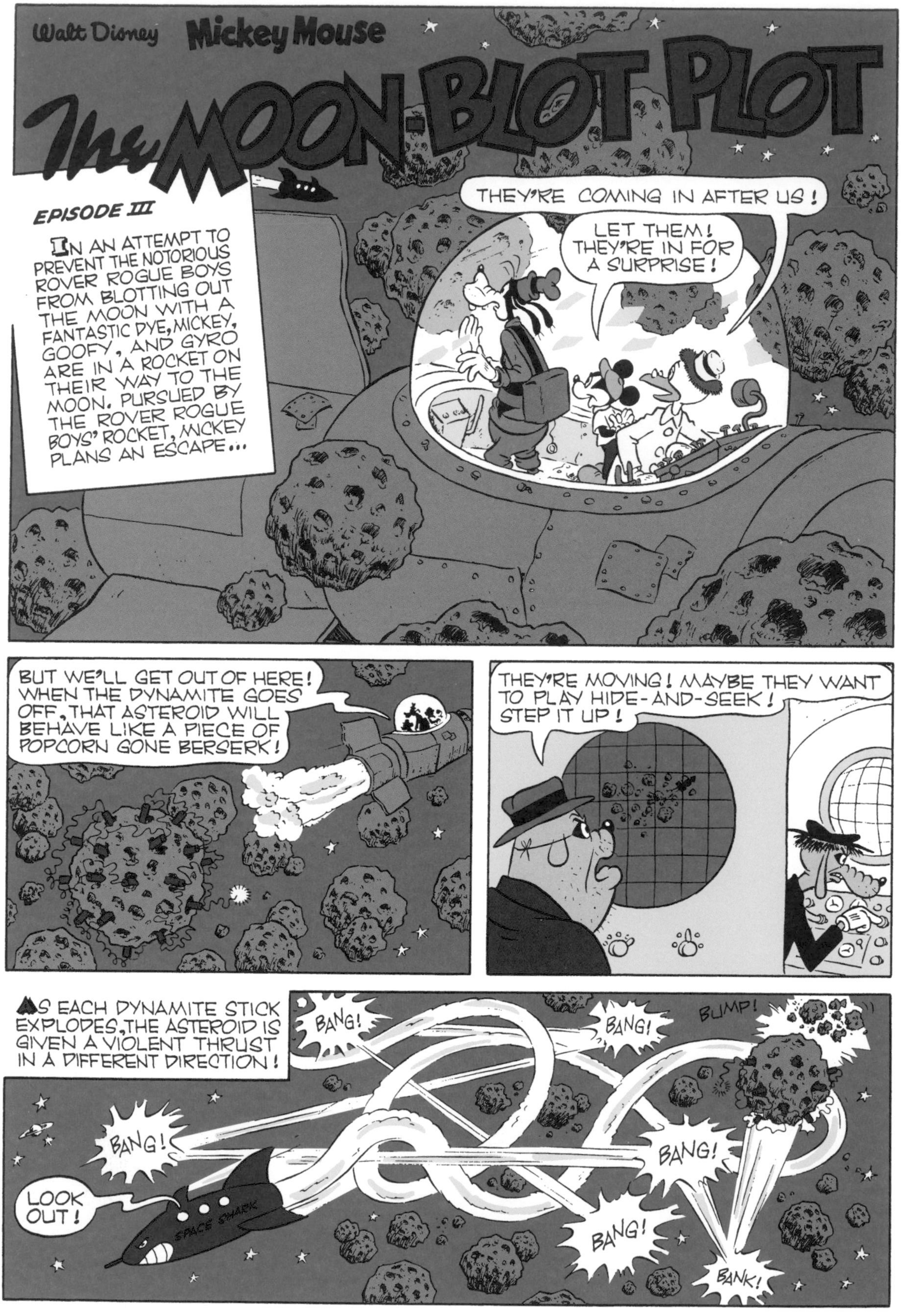

Walt Disney Mickey Mouse
The MOON-BLOT PLOT
EPISODE III
IN AN ATTEMPT TO PREVENT THE NOTORIOUS ROVER ROGUE BOYS FROM BLOTTING OUT THE MOON WITH A FANTASTIC DYE, MICKEY, GOOFY, AND GYRO ARE IN A ROCKET ON THEIR WAY TO THE MOON. PURSUED BY THE ROVER ROGUE BOYS' ROCKET, MICKEY PLANS AN ESCAPE...
THEY'RE COMING IN AFTER US!
LET THEM! THEY'RE IN FOR A SURPRISE!
BUT WE'LL GET OUT OF HERE! WHEN THE DYNAMITE GOES OFF, THAT ASTEROID WILL BEHAVE LIKE A PIECE OF POPCORN GONE BERSERK!
THEY'RE MOVING! MAYBE THEY WANT TO PLAY HIDE-AND-SEEK! STEP IT UP!
AS EACH DYNAMITE STICK EXPLODES, THE ASTEROID IS GIVEN A VIOLENT THRUST IN A DIFFERENT DIRECTION!
BANG!
BANG!
BUMP!
BANG!
BANG!
LOOK OUT!
SPACE SHARK
BANG!
BANK!

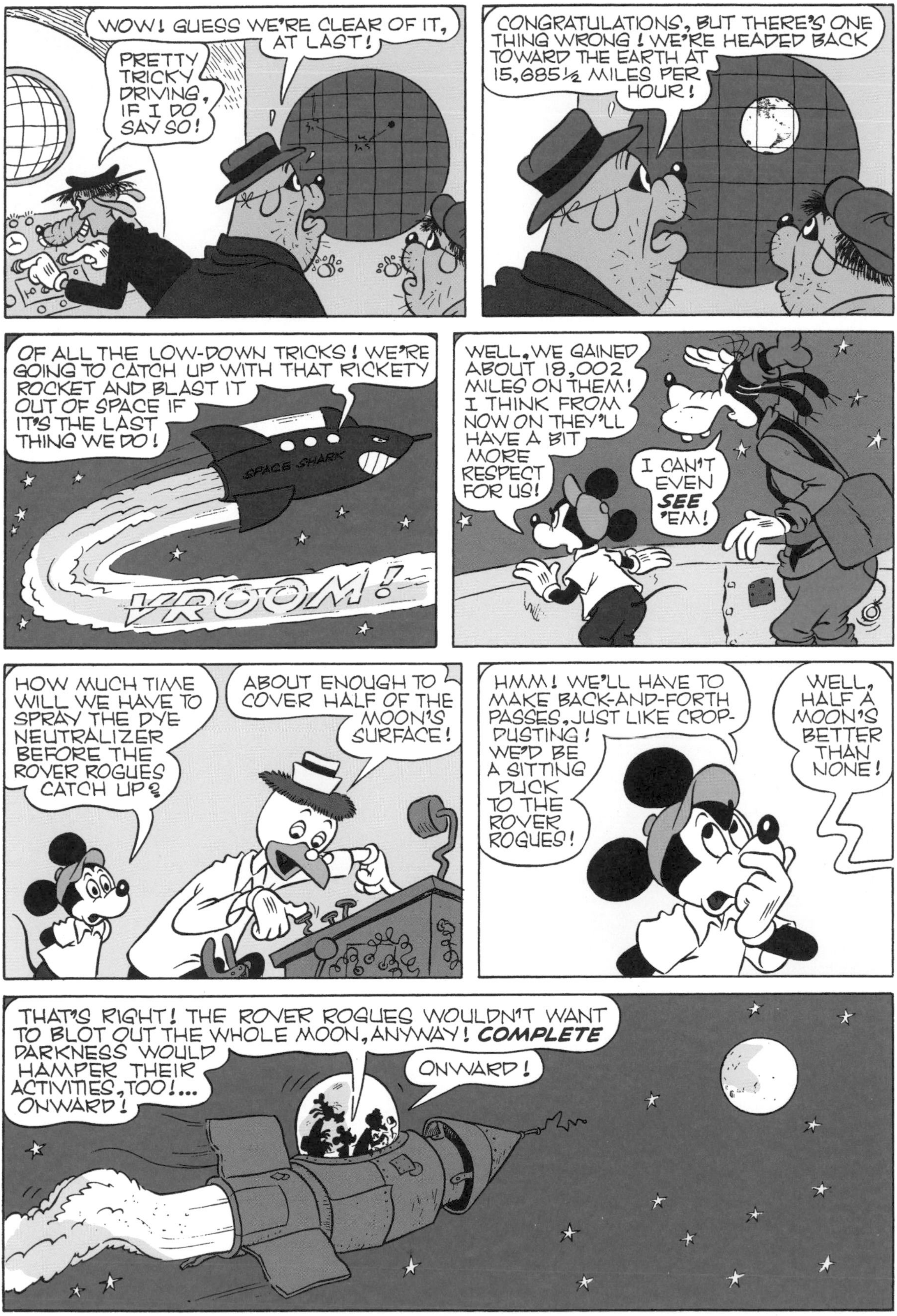
WOW! GUESS WE'RE CLEAR OF IT, AT LAST!
PRETTY TRICKY DRIVING, IF I DO SAY SO!
CONGRATULATIONS, BUT THERE'S ONE THING WRONG! WE'RE HEADED BACK TOWARD THE EARTH AT 15,685½ MILES PER HOUR!
OF ALL THE LOW-DOWN TRICKS! WE'RE GOING TO CATCH UP WITH THAT RICKETY ROCKET AND BLAST IT OUT OF SPACE IF IT'S THE LAST THING WE DO!
SPACE SHARK
VROOM!
WELL, WE GAINED ABOUT 18,002 MILES ON THEM! I THINK FROM NOW ON THEY'LL HAVE A BIT MORE RESPECT FOR US!
I CAN'T EVEN **SEE** 'EM!
HOW MUCH TIME WILL WE HAVE TO SPRAY THE DYE NEUTRALIZER BEFORE THE ROVER ROGUES CATCH UP?
ABOUT ENOUGH TO COVER HALF OF THE MOON'S SURFACE!
HMM! WE'LL HAVE TO MAKE BACK-AND-FORTH PASSES, JUST LIKE CROP-DUSTING! WE'D BE A SITTING DUCK TO THE ROVER ROGUES!
WELL, HALF A MOON'S BETTER THAN NONE!
THAT'S RIGHT! THE ROVER ROGUES WOULDN'T WANT TO BLOT OUT THE WHOLE MOON, ANYWAY! **COMPLETE** DARKNESS WOULD HAMPER THEIR ACTIVITIES, TOO!... ONWARD!
ONWARD!

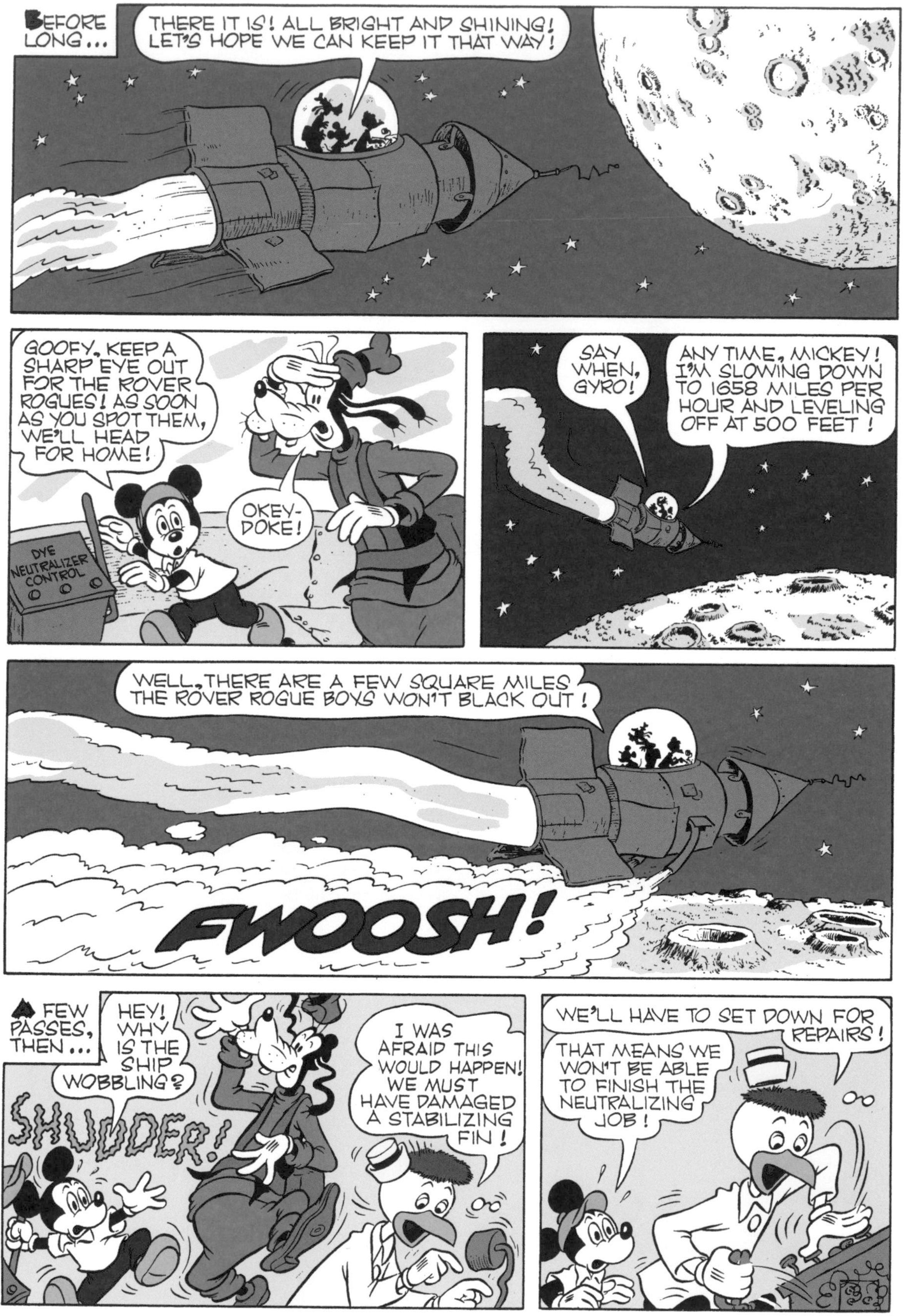
BEFORE LONG...
THERE IT IS! ALL BRIGHT AND SHINING! LET'S HOPE WE CAN KEEP IT THAT WAY!
GOOFY, KEEP A SHARP EYE OUT FOR THE ROVER ROGUES! AS SOON AS YOU SPOT THEM, WE'LL HEAD FOR HOME!
OKEY-DOKE!
DYE NEUTRALIZER CONTROL
SAY WHEN, GYRO!
ANY TIME, MICKEY! I'M SLOWING DOWN TO 1658 MILES PER HOUR AND LEVELING OFF AT 500 FEET!
WELL, THERE ARE A FEW SQUARE MILES THE ROVER ROGUE BOYS WON'T BLACK OUT!
FWOOSH!
A FEW PASSES, THEN...
HEY! WHY IS THE SHIP WOBBLING?
SHUDDER!
I WAS AFRAID THIS WOULD HAPPEN! WE MUST HAVE DAMAGED A STABILIZING FIN!
WE'LL HAVE TO SET DOWN FOR REPAIRS!
THAT MEANS WE WON'T BE ABLE TO FINISH THE NEUTRALIZING JOB!

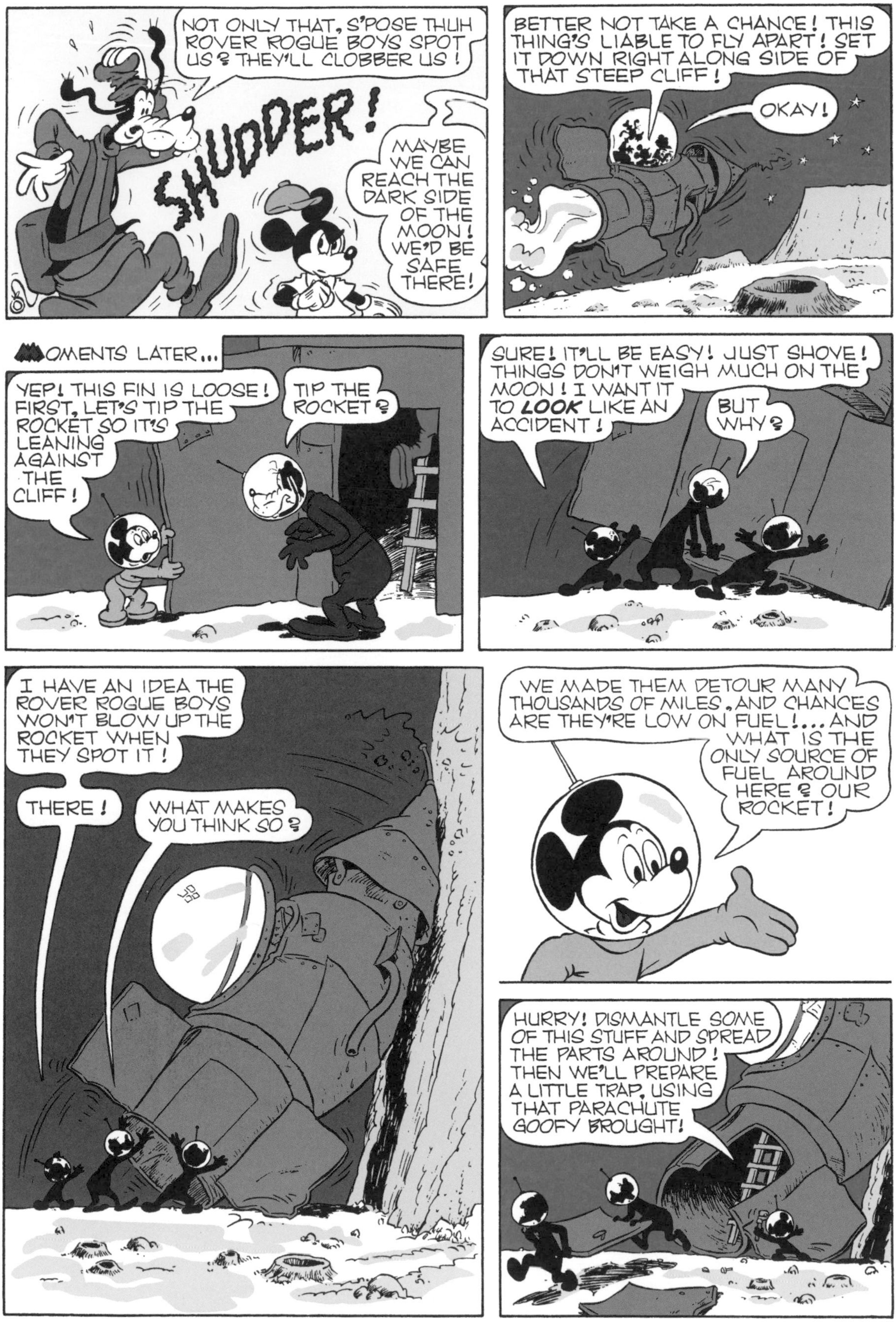
NOT ONLY THAT, S'POSE THUH ROVER ROGUE BOYS SPOT US? THEY'LL CLOBBER US!
SHUDDER!
MAYBE WE CAN REACH THE DARK SIDE OF THE MOON! WE'D BE SAFE THERE!
BETTER NOT TAKE A CHANCE! THIS THING'S LIABLE TO FLY APART! SET IT DOWN RIGHT ALONG SIDE OF THAT STEEP CLIFF!
OKAY!
MOMENTS LATER...
YEP! THIS FIN IS LOOSE! FIRST, LET'S TIP THE ROCKET SO IT'S LEANING AGAINST THE CLIFF!
TIP THE ROCKET?
SURE! IT'LL BE EASY! JUST SHOVE! THINGS DON'T WEIGH MUCH ON THE MOON! I WANT IT TO LOOK LIKE AN ACCIDENT!
BUT WHY?
I HAVE AN IDEA THE ROVER ROGUE BOYS WON'T BLOW UP THE ROCKET WHEN THEY SPOT IT!
THERE!
WHAT MAKES YOU THINK SO?
WE MADE THEM DETOUR MANY THOUSANDS OF MILES, AND CHANCES ARE THEY'RE LOW ON FUEL!... AND WHAT IS THE ONLY SOURCE OF FUEL AROUND HERE? OUR ROCKET!
HURRY! DISMANTLE SOME OF THIS STUFF AND SPREAD THE PARTS AROUND! THEN WE'LL PREPARE A LITTLE TRAP, USING THAT PARACHUTE GOOFY BROUGHT!

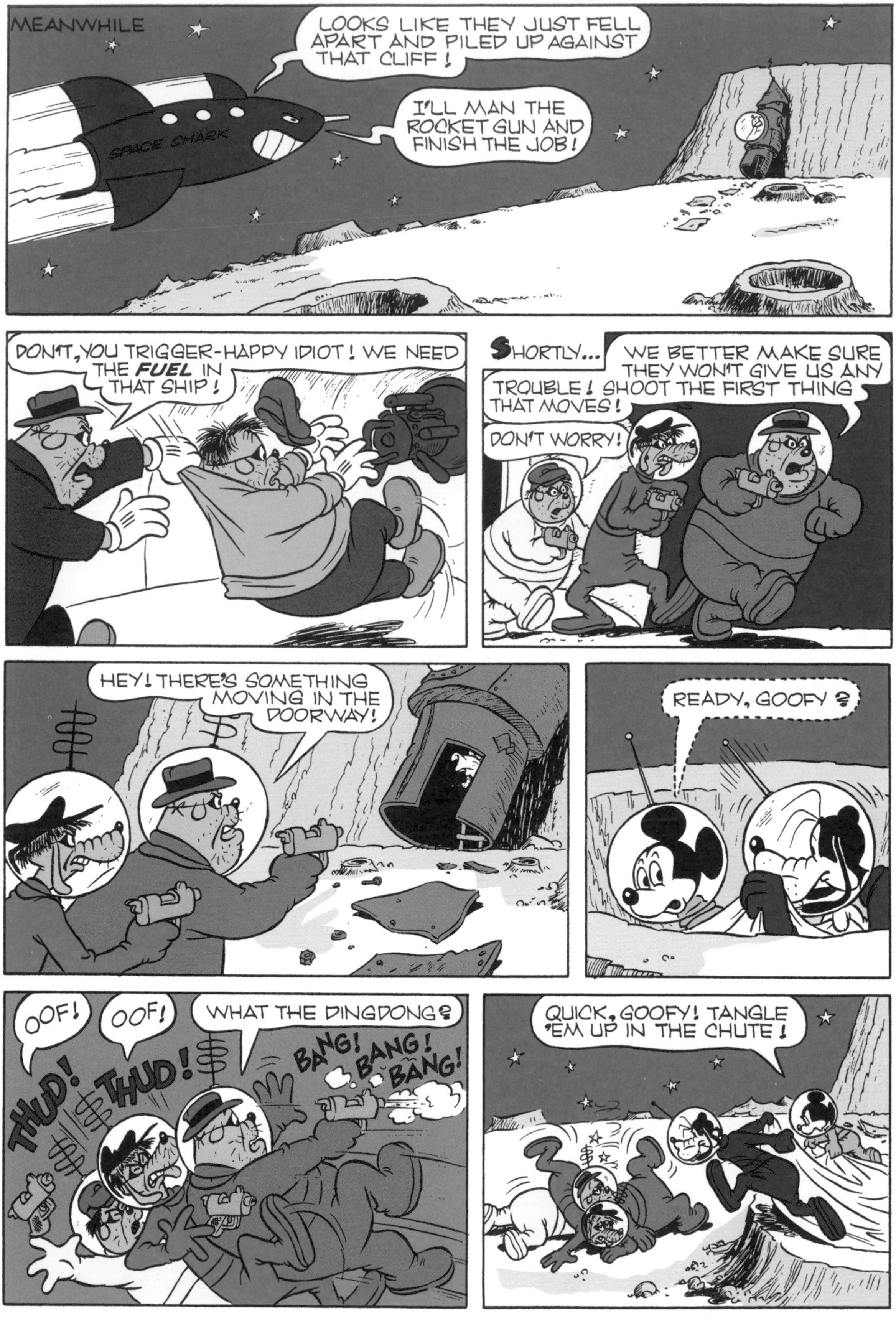
MEANWHILE
LOOKS LIKE THEY JUST FELL APART AND PILED UP AGAINST THAT CLIFF!
I'LL MAN THE ROCKET GUN AND FINISH THE JOB!
SPACE SHARK
DON'T, YOU TRIGGER-HAPPY IDIOT! WE NEED THE FUEL IN THAT SHIP!
SHORTLY...
WE BETTER MAKE SURE THEY WON'T GIVE US ANY TROUBLE! SHOOT THE FIRST THING THAT MOVES!
DON'T WORRY!
HEY! THERE'S SOMETHING MOVING IN THE DOORWAY!
READY, GOOFY?
OOF!
OOF!
WHAT THE DINGDONG?
THUD!
THUD!
BANG! BANG! BANG!
QUICK, GOOFY! TANGLE 'EM UP IN THE CHUTE!

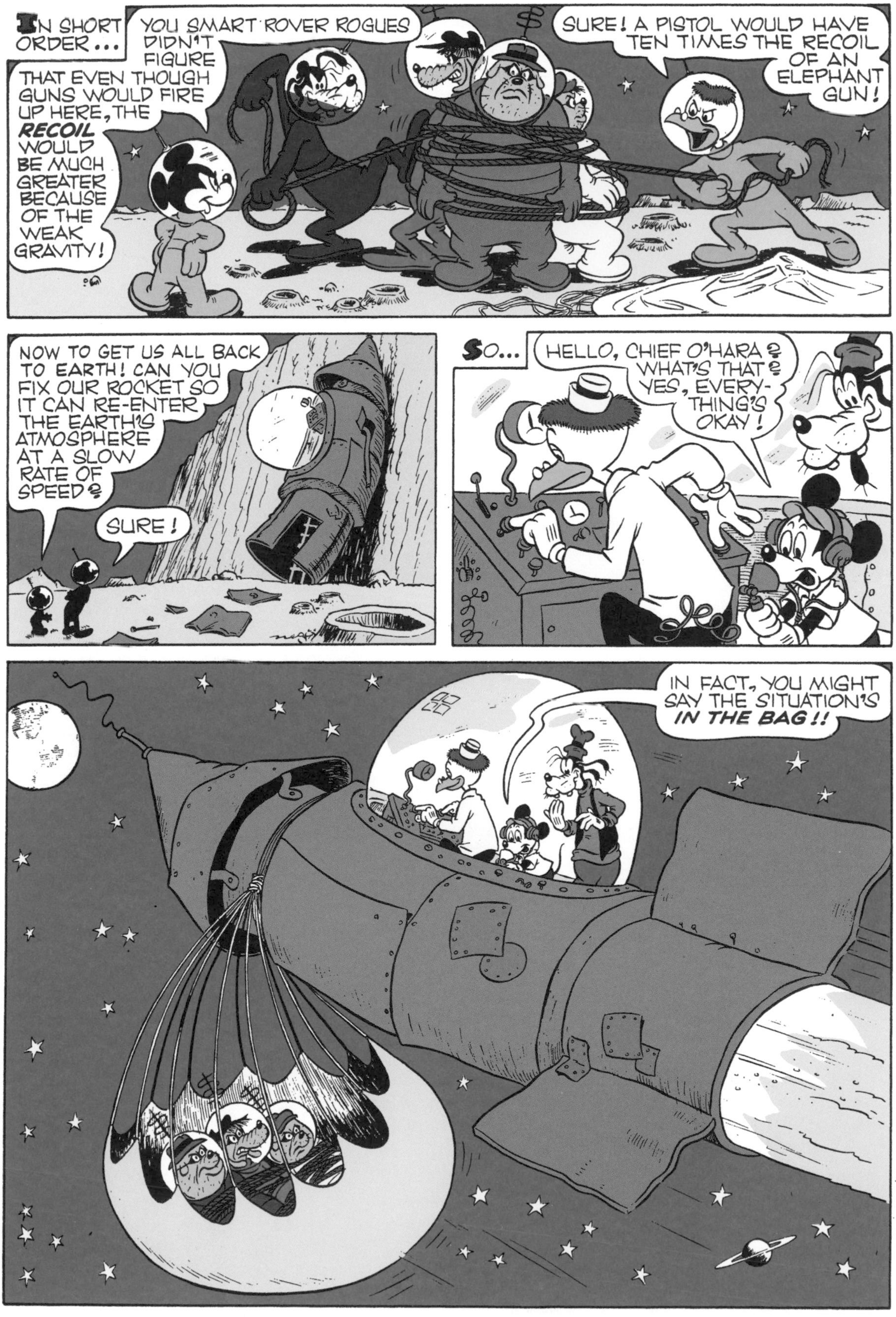
IN SHORT ORDER...
YOU SMART ROVER ROGUES DIDN'T FIGURE THAT EVEN THOUGH GUNS WOULD FIRE UP HERE, THE ***RECOIL*** WOULD BE MUCH GREATER BECAUSE OF THE WEAK GRAVITY!
SURE! A PISTOL WOULD HAVE TEN TIMES THE RECOIL OF AN ELEPHANT GUN!
NOW TO GET US ALL BACK TO EARTH! CAN YOU FIX OUR ROCKET SO IT CAN RE-ENTER THE EARTH'S ATMOSPHERE AT A SLOW RATE OF SPEED?
SURE!
SO...
HELLO, CHIEF O'HARA? WHAT'S THAT? YES, EVERYTHING'S OKAY!
IN FACT, YOU MIGHT SAY THE SITUATION'S ***IN THE BAG!!***

Paul Murry

by GERMUND VON WOWERN

IT WAS A cold winter's evening in the new year of 1938. Heavy snow covered northwest Missouri and the city of St. Joseph. Paul Murry, a 26-year-old artist and employee of the Artcrafts Engraving Co., suddenly found himself stranded in the city when his bus home was cancelled.

Unaware that he was making a life-changing decision, Murry walked over to the old Missouri Theater to see a new animated feature film, *Snow White and the Seven Dwarfs*. In an interview three decades later with comics scholar Donald Ault, Murry briefly recalled that long-ago evening: "I didn't realize when I was looking at [*Snow White and the Seven Dwarfs*], that five months later I would be in Hollywood."

At the time of Ault's interview, Murry could look back at thousands of penciled and inked comic book pages—his Mickey Mouse stories had been printed in hundreds of millions of newsstand comic books, and his Disney artwork had captivated children around the globe.

That snowy evening in 1938, little in Paul Murry's life foretold such a successful career. Born November 25, 1911, he was raised in Stanberry, 45 miles north of St. Joseph, and spent his young years on a farm, living with his grandparents and devoting himself to farm chores. His mother's fate is unknown; she disappears from records not long after his birth. His father remarried in 1917, just days after Paul's sixth birthday. Murry's unpretentious countryside childhood shaped him for life. The image of Murry that emerges from interviews, family members, and acquaintances is that of a highly pragmatic person. His granddaughter Shannon Murry captured his spirit perhaps better than anyone: "Paul liked things simple. He seemed to be a lonely man, yet preferred it that way. He always poked fun at everything,

Paul Murry in 1951. Photo © and courtesy Richard Huemer.

almost as if he saw life in a cartoon manner."

Yet he did not interact much with other professional artists, with whom he felt he had little in common. He loved the outdoors and playing the harmonica, and he often rose early to play before sitting down at his drawing table.

It was likely Murry's unyielding nature—combined with his interest in drawing—that landed him his employment at the engraving company, despite his lack of formal art education. According to Murry's own account, he entered a puzzle contest in 1937 and decorated his entry with drawings, which caught the eye of the organizers. Not only did he win first prize—a piano—but he was offered a position at the engraving company doing what he later described as "commercial advertising" art. With that work experience—and *Snow White* fresh in mind—he answered an ad from the Disney studio and was given a trainee position. His grandmother then sold the piano, which paid for his trip across the country.

Thus, on June 6, 1938, Murry walked through the doors of the Disney Studio for the first time. Less than four months later, on September 26, he was officially hired and placed in the training department. Murry's employment as in-betweener and assistant animator at the studio taught him a lot. He soon found himself assisting Fred Moore, the studio's principal Mickey man, whose animation work Murry admired immensely. Murry's years with Moore, which included work on *Fantasia* (1940), formed his view of what "Disney art" should look like. Moore's major lesson for Murry—which Murry carried with him to the comics—was that any Disney character drawn correctly had to lend itself to animation. Murry never mimicked popular artists whose styles relied on improvising from panel to panel, imprecise ink lines, stiff poses, tweaking of perspectives, or breaking of the fourth wall. Instead, Murry's fairly thick ink lines, drawn with a seemingly determined and steady hand, gave his comics artwork a distinct and easily recognizable quality.

Murry was a fast learner in the Disney animation department. After *Fantasia*, he went on to work on *Dumbo* (1941) and *Saludos Amigos* (1942). Gradually, however, he got more involved with the comic strip department—and with its manager, *Mickey Mouse* daily strip artist Floyd Gottfredson, who assigned Murry an increasing number of important jobs. His first comic art task was to pencil the José Carioca *Silly Symphonies* Sunday strips in early 1943, replacing artist Bob Grant, who had been drafted. The work suited Murry well. José was supplanted as the lead character in *Silly Symphonies* by Panchito, from the film *The Three Caballeros*, in 1944; then the *Symphonies* strip itself was replaced by *Brer Rabbit* beginning October 14, 1945.

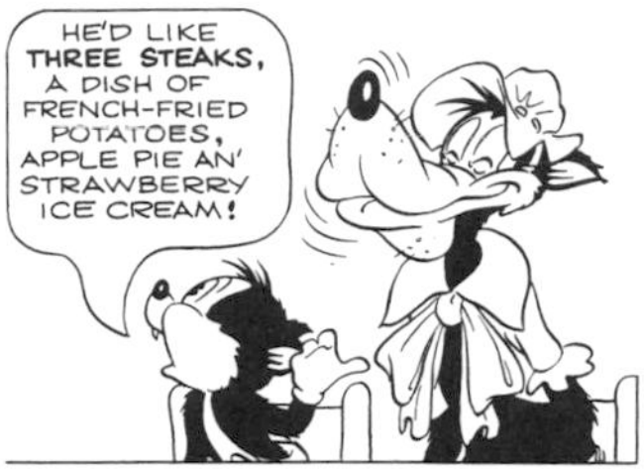
HE'D LIKE THREE STEAKS, A DISH OF FRENCH-FRIED POTATOES, APPLE PIE AN' STRAWBERRY ICE CREAM!

The Big Bad Wolf disguises himself as a foundling baby (!) to score free food from an orphanage in Murry's story for *Walt Disney's Comics and Stories* #83 (1947).

In a glimpse of what the future held for him, Murry also occasionally ghosted the *Mickey Mouse* daily strip between 1944 and 1946, when Gottfredson needed help to catch up on his deadlines. Seen from today's vantage point, these strips showcase Murry's eventual *Mickey Mouse* comic book style. But always the critic—not least of his own work—Murry did not hold his early *Mickey* newspaper strips in high regard when later asked about them.

Upon Murry's arrival in California, he had initially rented a studio apartment within walking distance of the Disney studio. But in 1939, he married and moved in with Gladys Bennett, already the mother of seven children. Their son together, John, was born in 1941, followed by their daughter Peggy in 1944. In 1946, with a total of nine children to support, they decided that Murry should leave his job with Disney and pursue a freelance career.

In the summer of 1946 they bought a piece of land in Wendling, Oregon, a lumber town in which the sawmill had closed a few months earlier and property was cheap. Murry got a job picking ferns, but he also produced a large number of gag cartoons. Murry had sold such gags to various magazines as early as 1943, while still working at Disney, but he seems to have ramped up to at least one inked cartoon per day from 1947 to 1949. Most of his cartoon work was published in the risqué magazines of the time. For some, he teamed with gag writer George A. Posner, resulting in numerous cartoons signed "Posner Murry."

It was the Brer Rabbit characters that pulled Murry back to the Disney properties and the resumption of his comics career. His first stories for comic books were drawn for Western Publishing and appeared in Dell Publishing's *Four Color* #129, December 1946, a Brer Rabbit issue. (Western, which held the license to create Disney comic books, arranged financing and distribution through Dell for many years. In 1962, Western ended that deal and continued on its own as Gold Key Comics.)

In between work on gag cartoons, Murry also drew several Brer Rabbit and Li'l Bad Wolf stories in 1947 for Western's flagship title, *Walt Disney's Comics and Stories*, thus keeping his hand in the comic book business.

In 1949, the Murrys returned to California. After another brief stint as a Disney in-betweener, Murry partnered with former Disney and Max Fleischer talent Dick Huemer to draw a humorous cowboy newspaper comic strip called *Buck O'Rue*. Huemer had created the character as early as 1948, but two years later the project was still in a holding pattern. With Murry's bouncy graphic characterization added to the mix, however, the strip was picked up for syndication and debuted in January 1951. Set in Mesa Trubil—a Wild West town "so rotten it got booted out of the U.S. of A."—*Buck O'Rue* combined its Western landscapes with a wild and cartoony rogues' gallery.

Unfortunately, while it is obvious from the artwork that Murry enjoyed *Buck O'Rue*, the strip ran for less than two years in a very limited number of newspapers. On the upside, its demise coincided with an early 1950s sales boom in Western/Dell/Disney comics, and Murry was in the right place at the right time. Murry's first three Mickey Mouse stories were long ones: "The Monster Whale" (*Walt Disney's Vacation Parade* #1, 1950), "The Mystery of the

Double-Cross Ranch" (Mickey Mouse *Four Color* #313, 1951), and "The Ruby Eye of Homar Guy-Am" (*Four Color* #343, 1951). But it was only the start.

Mickey serials had been a regular feature in *Walt Disney's Comics and Stories* from the beginning, but they were just reformatted newspaper strip adventures, drawn primarily by Gottfredson. Now Western wanted to produce original Mickey comic book stories, so in 1949, it began inviting artists to illustrate new adventures. Having already drawn the three *Four Color* stories, Murry fit the bill, and his chance came in 1953. Magic occurred instantly when Murry's artwork was paired with the skills of writer Carl Fallberg, who was also a cartoonist and a devoted railroad enthusiast. "The Last Resort," featured in Volume 3 of this series, was the first of their *Walt Disney's Comics and Stories* Mickey Mouse serials.

The comic book Mickey Mouse, as he had graphically evolved by that time, was a serious-minded and relatively inexpressive figure, so Murry instead relied on Goofy to bring graphic comedy and humor to the panels—sometimes he featured the Goof in action sequences that seem almost animated. It was Murry who introduced the classic comics pose of Goofy holding his hand in front of his mouth, all the better to make him look dumbfounded.

Another integral part of the Fallberg/Murry stories' appeal was their settings: wild woods, rugged mountains, mysterious swamps, or deep underwater. Murry excelled in his intricate renderings of weather elements such as rain, fog, snow, wind, and storms, and Fallberg soon began supplying him with scripts designed specifically to capture that aspect of his imagination.

Thus, like his Disney comics contemporary, Carl Barks, Murry found a stable income—and began his work on the stories he is most associated with—shortly after turning 40 years old. Like Barks, Murry had already experienced years of hard work and struggle to support himself and his family. Like Barks, Murry used his life experience to create compelling stories well worth reading. The background elements of the Mickey stories inspired Murry to create graphically spectacular pages, while the use of the Disney characters allowed him to show off the storytelling skills he had learned during his years in animation.

Carl Fallberg left the Mickey Mouse serials in 1962, and, with only a few exceptions, Murry continued to draw them until 1973. But they were not his sole output. With the exception of occasional gag pages, Murry never wrote his own stories—Western frequently called on him to draw scripts with a wide variety of other characters, including Donald Duck and Pluto, and he was even assigned a handful of non-Disney Woody Woodpecker stories. That versatility made Murry a prominent artist in the mid-1960s transformation of American Disney comics. Declining sales and competition for readers drove the editors at Western to target the Disney stories at a younger audience. They also introduced new characters and combined heroes from previously separate universes within single stories: Goofy could team up with Mowgli, or Donald Duck with Captain Hook. The mix suited Murry well, and he became the main artist of novel comic book titles—such as *Super Goof* and *The Phantom Blot*—which featured those crossover stories.

That peak in productivity was short-lived. In the 1970s, Murry's assignments turned him almost exclusively into a Mickey Mouse artist again, including, in 1971, a pivotal series of Mouse model sheets for Walt Disney Publications. As time wore on, Murry became less than enthusiastic about the comic books to which he contributed, gradually drawing fewer pages. His last regular Mickey Mouse story appeared in 1984 in *Walt Disney's Comics and Stories* #510, the final Western Publishing issue. Four more were later published posthumously.

Paul Murry spent his retirement years with his wife in their desert home just outside of Palmdale, California, taking wildlife and nature photographs, gardening their five acres, and playing his beloved harmonica. Comics became a very distant part of his life, and he likely preferred it that way. He died August 4, 1989, at age 77. But his delightful work lives on, and fans around the world continue to enjoy it. ♣

Numerous scholars have generously shared information with me about Paul Murry's life and work. There is not room here to thank each one, but I would like to acknowledge three of them for their contributions: Donald Ault, for his devoted work preserving the history of many Disney comics artists, including taping a long interview with Paul Murry; Klaus Spillman, who interviewed Murry in letter form in the early 1980s; and last — but certainly not least — Murry's granddaughter Shannon Murry, who shared her insightful thoughts and knowledge about Murry's life and career.